MARRIED TO THE BRATVA BOSS

A BWWM Dark Mafia Romance

Jolie Damman

CONTENTS

CHAPTER 1

Dark clouds hovered in the sky, hiding the twinkle of the stars. I couldn't see much of my surroundings, of what was happening in front of me. I took a deep breath and tried to calm myself down, eager to hear the noise of the train as it slowed down.

It was my only escape. The only way to get away from his hands and begin a new life, where he would never be able to find me.

A Russian mob boss. I'd thought he was a good man, but it turned out he was nothing more than a worthless asshole. In the end, I came to learn that he only wanted me for his own benefit, and I couldn't allow that to become a part of my life.

I wasn't going to be his trophy for him to show off to the people he truly cared about. If he wanted a wife, then he'd better look somewhere else.

The train track stood not too far from me. I was on this short hill overlooking it. If the train slowed down enough – and it should, since I was right at the border with Canada – then I should have enough time to jump onto it.

Once I was safe and sound inside one of its containers, I'd cross the border without anyone ever noticing me. I knew my plan had a good chance of not working, but the information I'd gathered told me this was one of the entries to Canada least patrolled by national authorities.

Though I guess I should point out Artem had probably already ordered some of his men to come hunting for me at about this part of the state, too. He was doing everything in his power to capture me.

My father was behind the whole thing, too. For him, striking a deal with Artem was what was going to keep his mafia family afloat. Everything for the family, right? Yeah, right. Except that he didn't care about me enough.

Didn't give a damn about my feelings, what I thought of the whole thing, of Artem, and I was pretty sure that just because he married a woman my grandfather chose for him, he thought I should follow in his footsteps.

Well, that wasn't going to happen anymore.

I had everything I needed to leave the country for good. All things considered, Artem's men shouldn't have a clue about my current whereabouts. They were all too busy putting out the fire I'd started in their hideout.

Artem was an idiot. He thought I didn't have it in me.

I loved someone else, but now he was dead. He was a good man. Not rich, not influential, and he didn't have a battalion of men working for him, but he loved me for the woman I was.

They shot him in front of me. Artem and his men. I still remembered holding his corpse in my arms, crying as tears fell on his face. I was never going to forgive him for what he did. Everything he put me through…

They were things I was going to remember forever, and if Artem did manage to catch me, I'd rather kill myself.

That's not to say he wasn't a good-looking man. He was tall, with broad shoulders, wide chest, narrow waist, and with a deep voice that echoed his dominance over his man. He had everything to make any woman in the world drool over him, but those aspects of his looks didn't mean shit to me if he couldn't have a good heart.

His heart was made of steel. It was cold and uninviting. He spent most of his time inside his office, plotting strikes against his enemies and developing plans to corrupt the national congress.

I wished I'd come out of his hiding place with documents detailing his plans, but that was easier said than done. When shit hit the fan, I bolted out of there as fast as my legs could take me, stole one of his men's black cars, and came here.

I didn't know where I was going. Not really, anyway. I knew about this place, the 'hole' in the border with Canada, and that my chances of getting there through here were better than most, but that still didn't mean I'd come here knowing what all of my steps should be like.

I took in a deep breath, pulling down the right strap of my backpack. I did have some help before coming here. Some men from my father's mafia family that took pity on me and decided they'd rather help me than see me married to such a worthless piece of shit.

There was also something else they couldn't stand, too. Artem shooting Ethan in cold blood, just because he was the man I truly loved. He was their best friend. They shared my hatred for the Russian Boss and they could never forgive him.

Did they manage to come out of it in one piece? I didn't know, but when I was escaping that prison, it was utter chaos. Men desperately snagging fire extinguishers to put out the fire, guys grabbing their M4's to make sure there were no infiltrators, and gunshots and more gunshots echoing in the dead of the night.

I was lucky, I guess. I had to bust open the main gate while guards had not left the premises yet, but I still got lucky they didn't have enough men to chase me. The roads of the district their building was in were sinuous and dangerous, after all.

One needed to be careful when driving through them. Despite my thumping heart, I was able to make it here, and this was my chance to change my whole life. I was going to make it over there, too.

Reach Canada and give Artem the middle finger. His eyes and

hands would never be able to find me there. After reaching my final destination, I was going to have a couple of friends willing to keep me safe from him. They were part of another mafia family, but they were more palatable.

My ears picked up the distinct noise of the train going down the track, making my heart thump with excitement. I turned my head from side to side, unable to find any of Artem's men in the vicinity.

They weren't here and they weren't going to find me here. I should have more than enough time to cross the border.

Chances were I was going to find some illegal immigrants in some of the boxcars. They were likely to keep their mouths shut regarding my presence, so I didn't have anything to worry about in that regard.

Turning my head to the left, I couldn't help but worry if my information was right or not. Did they really not check all the boxcars that came in and out of the country in the trains? Did they really know which boxcars had illegal aliens or not?

So many questions, and so little time to answer them now. I guessed they didn't matter. I couldn't flee to another part of the country. While I wished I could continue living here in America, there was no more chance I could have a normal life in this nation. Artem would most likely sniff me out if I remained here for much longer.

Leaving America was my only choice. After reaching Canada and getting my bearings there, I was going to buy myself a fake ID, change my hairstyle, hair color, and even go through some plastic surgeries.

Artem had a lot less power over there, but that still didn't mean he wouldn't be able to find me. He was more than capable of doing that, which meant I was still going to have to be extra careful in my new life in Canada.

The deadness of the night was the only thing keeping me company now. Well, that and the twigs and bushes that surrounded the train tracks. The bushes were tall and bulky enough to keep me hidden.

Not that it mattered much anyway. The guy driving the train was likely not paying much attention to what was around the tracks, his eyes focused on what was in front of the tracks themselves. His only worry was that he didn't want to run over someone attempting to commit suicide.

He wouldn't even hear me climbing the train and proceeding to one of the boxcars. Despite the chaotic nature of my escape, I had almost everything planned out. I was going to have to face some challenges, but I was sure I could beat them.

I took in another deep breath when my eyes spotted the floodlight of the train illuminating the tracks in front of it, the engine slowing down. Other than the noise of the machine itself, the night was dead silent, like I was the only person in the vicinity.

I crouched and hid behind some bushes when the train's first cabin passed in front of me, the man driving it a guy in his 50's that was devouring a greasy burger. My stomach churned at the sight of that. I couldn't imagine myself ever eating anything as nasty this late, way past the time for dinner.

I hadn't eaten a burger in a pretty long time, and I was planning on extending that for a lot longer. I wasn't fat or anything like that, but I still had some fat I wished to burn. I didn't like the curves of my body much. They were too big and wide.

Standing up, I walked down the hill and climbed up the train, hoisting myself up. I was on one of its many sections without anything in it. No container, no boxcar – nothing. It was nothing more than a flat surface, the hinges trembling as the train continued going down the track.

Not too far from here, my eyes spotted the fence that sealed off this area from the one that was right across it. After crossing it, I was going to be in Canada. A guard post and a collection of military vehicles patrolled both sides of the border and while they did frighten me a little, they didn't make me consider the option of not going on with this.

I was going to. I was going to cross the border and make it over there. It was my only option.

I turned to the other side and tried the door of the boxcar. It opened, just as a friend of mine had said it was going to. My eyes couldn't make out what was hiding in the darkness the first few seconds, but soon they were able to.

Men, women, kids, and families. All not just from America, but also from other countries. All traveling to a new nation to hide themselves from the terror inflicted by the federal government on its own people.

Their eyes glanced at me for a fraction of a second before dropping to the floor. They weren't surprised at all I was here and going with them to the other side of the border. Chances were more people joined in during the train's long route. Its origin was on the other side of the country, so that wasn't a far-fetched assumption.

I looked for a dark, solitary spot in one of the corners of the boxcar after closing the door behind me. Snow wasn't falling yet, but I knew that soon it was going to. That's what the weather news had told me before I put my escape plan into practice anyway.

I had my backpack with me, which I pulled off and tucked between my thighs. I bent my legs in front of me and pushed myself up against the corner I'd secured for the trip. The guards at the border should turn a blind eye to this boxcar, though we were still going to hear them checking out the rest of the train.

I'd paid them more than enough to allow the train to cross the border. It should all work as according to plan, despite the high chances of something or someone fucking it up.

I inhaled and exhaled. It was the only thing I could keep doing to calm down my racing heart.

CHAPTER 2

It took me more time than I thought I was going to, but eventually I finished crossing the border. Now, standing in another country, I couldn't help but breathe in the fresh air of the alpine trees and impending snow. I could smell it coming. I was like an animal now, so much more aware of my surroundings and signs that were given off by nature.

I took off to the other side of the road moments before a black car pulled over by me. I couldn't but smile, though. Everything was still working as planned. There was a moment when I thought one of the guards at the border was going to open the boxcar with me and all the other illegal aliens in it, but someone stopped him before he could have.

He'd told his friend that boxcar had already been checked and was supposed to be left alone. The worried guard, assuming his friend was speaking the truth, gave up and went on to check something else in the train.

I'd exhaled loudly out of relief then. That had been a close one – too close for comfort.

The side window of the car rolled down, a man sitting behind the steering wheel smiling as he looked at me.

"Almost thought you weren't going to make it, Faye."

"I thought the same, but it all worked out in the end, didn't it?" I said, opening the door of his car and plopping down on one of the backseats, my eyes spotting his guards. There were one riding shotgun and another sitting by me, all of them wearing dark jackets with lime green ties.

They were from an Irish mafia gang. It was one of the most influential in the country, and under their dominion, I should be safe.

Dad never liked me befriending them over the multiple times I visited Canada, but he never could do much about it. He was a terrible father, but he couldn't control everything I did. He was always far too busy with his business stuff and striking deals with politicians over in Washington DC.

Inside the car, I felt safe. My eyes admired my surroundings, the vehicles, the houses, and the buildings while they drove toward their hideout. Like any other famous gang in these parts, they owned not a house but an estate in one of the richest neighborhoods in Toronto.

Upon reaching it, the main car gate slid open, allowing us through. The car rounded a large roundabout with perfect grass and palm trees in it, one of the guards coming out and opening the door for me.

He didn't need to have done that, but I could tell why he did it. They were looking at this as their next opportunity to solidify their dominance here in Toronto. With me living here, dad and the rest of his mafia family were going to have to eat out of their hands, and even though that made me feel a little bad, it didn't deter me from going on with this.

I needed my independence, and I didn't want to marry that asshole that went as far as killing my boyfriend. I was never going to forgive him for that.

A maid and a butler opened the double to the entry hall and one of them took me to my bedroom. When he finished showing me the room, with Ethan accompanying him, I collapsed onto the bed.

I needed a fresh shower, a change of clothes, and a good reason to not cry. I knew I shouldn't cry. I didn't want to show those men I was weak. I needed their help, but as far as they were concerned,

I was still a woman they couldn't touch.

If they tried that, they were sure I would find a way to flee their estate too and find someone else willing to keep me hidden. In such a scenario, they wouldn't have the leverage they needed to claim my father's territory in Lost Hope.

And Lost Hope was one of the many cities they were trying to extend their tentacles to, claiming it and making it theirs. It was one of the few prime regions for illegal drug transportation, thanks to the many rivers that crossed through to Toronto.

I covered my face with my hands, holding the tears that were threatening to come out. I forced my hands to drop and then pushed myself off the bed, surveying the room with my eyes before taking off my clothes.

Prior to doing that, I also checked for cameras or any listening devices hidden behind the furniture or under the bed. While I was sure they thought of me as their friend, I was far too paranoid to not think they were listening in on me.

They could also have put micro-cameras here too, but as far as I could tell, they were nowhere to be seen.

I headed to the bathroom, threw some shampoo in my hair, washed my body with liquid soap, and then toweled myself dry after turning off the showerhead. I considered heading out to eat something, but even though my stomach was rumbling like a WW1 tank, it wasn't worth the hassle that would be having to talk to one of them.

I knew them well and I knew they liked to talk a lot. This branch of the Irish mafia liked to converse quite a bit with other people when they didn't have anything better to do.

Soon they were going to announce I was under their protection and begin negotiations with my dad. A pang of guilt surged in my heart again, but I kept it contained. I wasn't going to allow such a thing to make me think I was doing the wrong thing.

I was following my heart.

After a change of clothes, I looked out the window, contemplating a life for me that could have been. I could have married Ethan and we could have become one of the happiest couples in the whole world.

He was always so funny, cracking jokes and what not. His curious eyes reminded me of how much I was going to miss him, and I already missed him quite a lot. Contrary to what most people would say, I was sure that was only going to get worse as time went on.

I whirled around when a knock sounded on the door to my room. Who could it be at this time of the night? Was there something of grave importance that needed to be dealt with now? Couldn't it wait until tomorrow morning?

Regardless of the answer to those questions, I headed to the closet, slid the door open, grabbed a pair of flimsy light blue shorts, and headed to the door. They should be appropriate enough for the short exchange of words I was going to have with the man or woman in the hallway.

It could be a man or a woman. She could even be the same woman I'd seen before, the one that was one of their maids and had opened the door to the entry hall for me. She had her hair tied to a bun and looked as professional as she needed to be for someone working for these criminals.

I opened the door as my eyes bulged. It was Sean. Sean O'Sullivan from the O'Sullivan Irish mafia, with his shirt unbuttoned, eyes steely as they dawned on me. I drew in a short breath, my flimsy shirt and shorts making me feel too exposed.

The last thing I expected was to find him standing before me like this, arm put on the doorway, winking when he noticed the reaction I was trying to keep hidden from him. I didn't think it would be appropriate if he found out I harbored feelings for him better left unmentioned.

"Hey there, Faye. Just thought you needed someone to talk to tonight, after everything that happened."

His tone was playful, sexy even. Sean was the kind of man that was used to getting what he wanted. He'd already set his eyes on me and was going to do everything in his power to make me fall head over heels for him.

And yet, I didn't have any pretensions of the sort. Not tonight, not when I had so many things to make peace with. One of them was, of course, convincing myself I wouldn't feel guilty in the future, when father held no more power in his hands.

When he didn't have any more control in my life, anguishing until he died. There was only one outcome this was going to follow, and it was going to be that one, no doubt about it.

"No," I confronted him as I held back a chuckle, pushing the door a little. "I'm fine, really. I don't need to talk to anyone now."

He dropped the arm he'd put on the doorway, stepping into the room as the smirk he was sporting before faded away. He didn't even ask for permission as he strolled right in, pushing me away with the strength and intensity of his presence.

An air of authority surrounded him and I didn't know how I was supposed to deal with him now. He came here with his shirt exposing his chest, showing off his chiseled and perfect muscles.

I wasn't stupid. I knew what was going on in his mind. I just hadn't thought he couldn't contain his temptations long enough until what he was doing felt more natural. I wasn't going to fuck anyone tonight – not after the shit I was still going through.

Chances were dad was going to send some of his soldiers to sneak in. He wouldn't send enough men to storm the place. That would be a waste of resources for him, but he was going to cook up a plan to get me out of their estate.

And Sean and his men needed to be ready for that. If they weren't, they were going to be swallowed by the strength of my dad's mafia family.

His eyes scanned the room, a question popping out of his mouth. "So, are you liking the place?"

"Yes, it has everything I need. Thank you," I responded moments before he launched himself in my direction, kicking the door closed with his right foot.

"Faye, there's no need to keep pretending otherwise. When you landed your eyes on me before… Well, I'm not going to force anything out of you. I need you to tell me I'm not mistaken here and don't try to hide anything. I'm going to know if you do."

"I don't know what you mean," I argued, pushing him off me.

It'd been hours since my escape from Artem's hideout and they should have already figured out what had happened. And if they didn't know I'd already come here, they were soon going to. Artem's mafia family wasn't at the top of their game for no reason, after all. They were some of the deadliest, and some of the best in the underworld.

I used all of my strength when pushing him off of me, but he wasn't bulging. He kept his body pinned in place, his muscles working as he launched an arm around my waist as the other kept the path to the right blocked.

He was pinning me against the wall, and I couldn't do anything to stop him.

Even though I didn't think it was likely to happen, I was hoping something ground-breaking was going to shake everything up. Maybe Artem's men would show up, realizing I was about to get raped and that I couldn't be returned to him as 'damaged goods.'

But that was when everything was turned upside down, even more than it already was.

CHAPTER 3

He was doing everything in his power to make me hate him, even though he was one of the men in his mafia family I liked the most. I couldn't believe he was doing this to me, his lips getting so close to touching mine.

His hand that was settled on my waist kneaded my skin, his resolve clear. He was going to do everything he could to claim my heart and change my mind about him. If only he wasn't doing it this way, forcing himself on me, I'd be waiting until it was the right time to reveal my true feelings for him.

But now that he was trying to take advantage of me like this, coercing my heart to be thumping hard in my chest, all I knew was that I needed to flee their estate too.

They wouldn't stop chasing me, even if he came to his senses now.

"Sean, let me go."

"Or what? You're going to run off to your dad or something like that?"

"I just might, or I might look for somebody else's help."

"Huh? Really? Do you really know someone else that can keep you safe, that wants you? I don't think so, princess."

"Sean… I thought you were better than this."

He chuckled.

"Since the first time you came here, I've been thinking about this moment. I've been obsessing over it, and now that it's finally happening, I just can't contain myself."

"Are you really willing to go through with this? You know that you are committing a crime that not even the mob would swallow."

He shook his head slowly, closing his eyes.

"You're making this more difficult for me, and in turn, for me as well. Just submit yourself willingly, and then I'll make you mine. You will be my Irish queen. This chocolate-skin of yours... It's exotic, and I love it."

Just as he finished saying that, he tried to kiss me, but I snapped my head to the right. His lips landed on my cheek and a grumble escaped his plump, rosy lips.

"But I do love myself a difficult girl," he joked, the hand that was blocking the exit to the right skipping to the side of my face. I tried turning my head, but his hold was true and resolute. I felt that if I tried that again too hard, he wouldn't hesitate to rough me up.

Dad's anger and temperament would be beyond the roof if that happened, forcing him to make mistakes he otherwise wouldn't. And maybe, just maybe, Sean here was trying to concoct that.

How stupid he was. Did he think dad hadn't been through much worse before in his life, when he was trying to better establish his hold of the city?

His fingers massaged the skin of my lower back, his hand traveling down when a moan escaped my lips. I criticized myself for that as soon as it happened, for I knew it only served to ascertain his assumption that I had a huge crush on him I couldn't control.

"Ahhh, there it is," he teased, his hand beginning to pull down my shorts when a shot echoed in the air. It came from the outside, his head snapping to the left.

"What in the world?" He asked, but he wasn't going to get any answer from me. If anything, I was going to keep my lips sealed.

Something was going down, and it could be devastating enough to get me out of here. After all the hurdles I went through,

I was still going to have to flee another mafia gang.

"Stay right here," he ordered, but I wasn't going to obey his command. I hurried out of the room with him, his eyes bulging as he turned to me when he noticed my footsteps echoing from behind him.

"I asked you to stay there in your fucking room," he added, his tone coated with venom and hatred.

I wished I could obey him, but I wasn't going to. And maybe I should have done the smarter thing and stayed in the room while he hurried out to check what was going on in his mansion.

He stopped in the middle of the hallway when a group of his men came rushing in, their hands holding assault rifles, shotguns and pistols.

They were ready for war, and I couldn't help but wonder if that was what was going down here.

"What is going on?" Sean asked.

"I don't know, boss, but I don't like it one bit. I think we're being attacked."

"Fuck!" He cussed, spitting onto the floor. "I don't have a good feeling about this as well. I heard a gunshot and if it's someone thinking he might get the drop on us, then he's soon going to learn we are not the type that dick around."

Sean turned to one of his soldiers, ordering, "Get her back into her room. I don't want anyone to hurt her, and they just might have come here to do that."

One of his men grabbed me by my right arm and dragged me over back to my bedroom, closing the door.

One of Sean's remaining soldiers strolled to the door and leaned on the wall next to the other side of the door.

The one that had taken me into the room closed it as he said, "I'm going to keep you company until the situation is resolved. Shouldn't take too long for the boss to figure out what is going on here."

I couldn't help but worry. If father or Artem had sent their men to snag me from their estate, then this promised to be a dangerous shootout. I wasn't sure if I was ready to face that now.

I heard their echoing footsteps as they hurried out of the mansion. I couldn't quite understand what seemed to be happening here.

If they were being attacked, then some kind of shootout should already be going on here, and in that case it would be loud enough for me to hear everything, including every gunshot fired.

"Who the hell are these people?" I heard Sean asking when gunshots filled the void of the night, turning the silence into a deafening shootout.

My hand flew to my chest as I tried to look outside, but the soldier in the bedroom yanked me back with his strong hand as he grumbled, "You stay right there. Your life is too precious for us."

Too precious for them? He was kind of making me wonder now if I shouldn't be considering the option of killing myself.

I wouldn't do that, though. I loved life far too much now, and I still had my dreams. I wished to make them true, and I knew I was going to be able to do that. Just needed to flee this shitty estate first, though.

A shot echoed in the air, the soldier that was peering out of the window toppling over. His body landed on the floor, the assault rifle he was holding skidding on the floor. I considered skipping over to it when the door was thrown open.

I expected to be my dad the one rushing over to me, but it was none other than that same man I'd seen before – the one keeping guard of me, the bedroom, and the hallway. He chewed a cigarette as he strolled into the room.

"Seems that things are heating up here. Don't worry. I'm going to get you out of this mess before they get their hands on you."

"You're nothing more than Sean's dog," I criticized him, wishing he was going to bite the bait.

"Sure I am, but only after I fuck that little dandy ass of yours," he joked, smirking.

He took me out of the room and as he marched down the hallway with me, I asked, "What's happening? Who's attacking you?"

"Seems that the guy that was supposed to marry you knows you're here. I thought you managed to cover your tracks. You're nothing more than a worthless fool."

Fuck. Was it real? Did Artem truly send his men over here to recapture me? I'd thought he wouldn't dare. I'd thought he was going to wait until things were settled with the O'Sullivan family, but it seemed I was wrong.

I couldn't help but feel a rush of relief flooding my heart. While I was sure that nothing would change if he managed to snag me from the Irish's hands, the fact I'd managed to escape his hideout meant something.

It meant I could make it happen again. I could escape his hideout one more time if it came to that.

I breathed in, trying to calm myself down. I needed to focus on what was important here, and that was finding a way to fool both of them. They were in disarray. They were all focused on the ensuing shootout, gunshots echoing in the silence of the night, some bullets shattering fancy plates in cupboards.

I shrieked when a bullet whizzed past my ear. That was too close. Too close for comfort.

The seriousness of this situation dawned on me all of sudden. Here I was, in another country, with no documentation, running away from two mafia gangs while the other was keeping me in captivity.

I felt betrayed. I'd assumed Sean and his men were going to be friendly enough to keep me in their estate while they groomed me to become one of their most important members. I'd be down with marrying him had he made the offer some months after living here.

But it seemed… No, I was certain that all of that was in the past now. I was their prisoner now and I should consider myself lucky if I managed to escape their prison.

The soldier whose name I doubted I was ever going to learn kicked open the main double door that led to the back of their property. Men in dark suits with red ties opened fire on him. He tossed me over to behind one of the pillars that supported the roof of the porch, his hands pulling the trigger of his assault rifle.

He opened fire on his assailants, screaming at the top of his lungs. He was packing, his waist holder even containing a couple of grenades he could throw.

He ducked behind the pillar as he opened fire on his attackers one more time. More of Artem's men showed up, shooting at him. They were pinning him down, and it seemed there was nothing he could do to change the tide of the momentum he now found himself in.

I considered helping him out, but then thought better about it. What would that help me with? They were shooting at each other, but I wasn't their target. I was their prize, the one they were fighting for.

As soon as that remembrance crossed my mind, I hurried out of my hiding spot and bolted to the other side of the property, the one with the complex garden and tall trees. I could hide in there. They would all get confused and I could have enough time to cook up a strategy to better establish my life here in Canada.

I could then even move to the countryside, where they would have a tougher time finding me. They all knew how much I liked living in the bustle and the hustle of the big cities. They would look for me there first.

Shouts and cries with my name echoed through the air as they bolted in my direction, but despite how tired I was – and hungry too – they were unable to catch up to me before I reached the garden. From the inside, it felt and looked more like a maze.

I could still hear their footsteps and gunshots as they killed themselves and chased me, but for now, I was safe.

Safe, but not for too long, for an unexpected visitor had just made himself known to me…

CHAPTER 4

It was Artem. I'd have recognized his snout, those lips, and steely eyes anywhere. He stood in the middle of the maze, his hand holding nothing. He didn't have a gun with him. Not one that I could see anyway.

His eyes looked resolute as they dawned on me, his confidence overflowing.

He didn't think I was going to manage to escape him again, and I'd say he was right. I felt a little lost now, dazed even.

I'd never thought he was going to come here himself. He was putting himself in danger. One of Sean's men and maybe even Sean himself could show up here out of the blue, killing him inside this maze.

"What are you doing here?" I asked. Despite his sudden apparition, I wasn't going to become a chicken afraid of him. Oh no, no chance that was going to happen here. I'd always been a hardass to him, and that wasn't going to change.

"What do you think?" He questioned, proceeding to me.

But just as he finished taking another step, I shouted, "Stay away from me, or I'm going to use the gun I have with me!"

He smirked. "You don't have any gun with you. Not a single pistol. You're just bluffing, and that is more than obvious."

My lips trembled when I argued back, "You're wrong. I know how to defend myself now. I wouldn't have come here without a gun."

"If that's the case, then pull it out, and let's test your aim.

I'd like to see if you've learned something worthwhile during the time you've spent away from me, my dear future wife."

"I'm not going to become your wife, ever!"

"I respect your choice, I really do," he argued, his voice adopting a soothing tone. But I wasn't going to fall for it. All he was achieving was making me hate him more and more, and I'd thought that wasn't possible.

I scoffed. "If you did, you wouldn't be trying to marry me."

"I'm only doing that because it's your best choice of survival. You see, your dad and his family aren't doing well financially, so he needs me now."

I bit my bottom lip. He was right. Dad wasn't doing well. The other mafia gangs were ganging up on him and bullying his soldiers and operations. This was all about the survival of his family and everything he deemed valuable.

Could I fault him for feeling that way about his current situation? No, but I could blame him for trying to marry me to such a despicable man. There were so many better choices, other men willing to help him out with keeping his family afloat...

I guessed it was his friendship with him and the fact that he took Artem under his wing when he lived in Russia so many years ago that were speaking louder than anything in his mind and were also driving him to be making this choice.

Still, that didn't mean I had to put up with it.

"That might be true, but I still don't like you. You killed Ethan right before my eyes. I still feel the weight of his dying body in my hands."

He waved his hand, the side of his neck twitching.

"I only did that because I had no other choice. He was planning on killing me, all because he thought he could marry you. Since you were born, I've been keeping my eyes on you, Faye, and I'm going to be your husband. You can't change fate."

"No, but at least I can fight it for as long as I can," I retorted when he stepped to me some more, gunshots echoing the distance. The men looking for me were still traversing in the maze and if I didn't get out of here soon enough, they were going to find me.

I still couldn't help but admire the sharpness of his looks, his trimmed beard, and even the chicken feet at the corners of his eye sockets. It was like he'd built himself to look like that. The dream man for every woman in the world – In terms of looks, at least.

"Fight for as long as you wish, Faye, but it's not going to change anything. I'm going to be the catalyst of change here. I'm going to make you see that I have reason, that you can't help but fall in love with me."

Footsteps echoed from behind me, and I couldn't help but get frightened of them. That O'Sullivan soldier and his men were getting close. I didn't need to tell Artem anything about that. His hearing and sense of space and what was happening around him were probably better than mine.

If anything, he should be the one urging me to get out of here.

He took a deep breath, saying, "So, what is it going to be? Are you going to come with me or not? I'm not going to make the same offer twice."

"Offer?"

"I'm going to force you to come with me if it comes to that. I don't want you feeling like a prisoner under my care again, but if I need to... I guess that would be it.

"What?" I asked when that soldier from before and his men rushed into the center of the maze from behind me, their hands holding their frightening assault rifles.

He bulged his eyes as soon as they landed on Artem.

"Artem? Hot damn. I didn't think I was going to find the boss of the most important and influential Russian gang in Lost Hope hiding in our estate. It's like Christmas has come earlier for me."

Artem only chuckled, his eyes blinking slowly, as if he couldn't care less about this turn of events. If these men had come here, and there were more than five of them, then they should be enough to take him down.

Scratch that, actually. Just one of them and his gun would be enough to end his chances of coming out of this alive.

And that was so true that, in turn, it made me wonder what was going on in his mind now. He had to be cooking up a plan to kill all of them. Perhaps he even had a button hidden underneath one of the pockets of his pants he was going to use to call his men to his exact location now.

With Artem, everything was possible.

I drew in a short breath when Artem duck behind a pillar in the center of the maze, his hand pulling a small gun from underneath the waistband of his pants. What the hell? I couldn't believe he had a gun with him this whole time.

I thought he was defenseless. I guessed I should have been more careful with my assertion regarding his plans. Now that I was thinking about it, it would have been too stupid of him to have come here without something he could make use of to defend himself.

I hid behind a pillar of marble too when another shootout ensued.

The O'Sullivan member that was supposed to keep an eye on me screamed at the top of his lungs when a shot from the other side roared in the air. It was Artem, and he'd managed to kill him.

The thug's body laid flat on the grass, his eyes so lifeless I had to cover my mouth to not scream. This was happening the exact way I was wishing it wasn't going to. I was hoping I was going to be able to run out of their estate without anyone noticing me, and now it felt like all eyes were focused on me.

It wouldn't be long until Sean arrived here too, I presumed.

The skirmish lasted a long while until all the thugs hiding behind pillars on my side of the center of the maze fell over on the ground, their eyes devoid of any signs of life. Just like that, as if they were never alive to begin with, they were not with us anymore.

My heart thumped in my chest, but the aforementioned realization was enough to soothe my racing heart. I had only Artem to deal with now, and various assault rifles I could make use of. The O'Sullivan gang wasn't going to the way of the dodo, but they sure as hell were taking a massive blow now.

I guessed I kind of underestimated the strength of the Yurevs. They were not just demolishing this Irish family, but also doing everything possible to make sure they could never come out of this the same.

At least that meant Sean was going to have to remain in hiding for now. Doing what, I didn't know, but I sure as hell didn't care.

Now was my chance.

I launched myself to one of the guns a thug was still holding in his hand. His fingers curled freely when I snagged it off of them, hiding behind another pillar when an important choice became clear to me.

I was going to have to kill Artem and find a way to climb over the tall wall of their estate. It was the only way to make my dream come true. I didn't have it all planned out, but I did already have a sketch of a plan to live the rest of my life in Canada.

I just needed to find someone willing enough to forge my new identification. With that, I'd be able to buy a house or a flat, marry and have kids. It would be so frigging good.

I drew in a short breath when a voice sounded from behind me. I snapped my head to him when he wrapped his arms around my neck and torso with force. His strength was enough to make me drop the assault rifle I was holding in my hand.

I didn't know the name of it, just that by pulling its trigger, I'd be able to end this torment and plan a new life for me.

One without any Mafia, these men trying to make me marry him, and Artem holding me against my will.

"Hmmm, always knew you have some fight in you, but I didn't think you were going to try to kill me. I'm quite disappointed, really. We're not starting off on the right foot, are we?"

"We never could. You're nothing more than an asshole that thinks you can make everyone abide to your will."

"There's a big difference between thinking and making it happen, and I've been making it happen since my birth, Faye. You can't deny I'm the biggest agent of change not only in Lost Hope, but also in the whole country."

"Oh yeah? You think that is going to remain unchanged for the rest of your life, that there aren't people out there looking to destroy your family too?"

He sighed, showing his disappointment.

"I thought you were better than that, but now I see you're nothing more than a fool. You're naïve, Faye, and soon you're going to learn that is not a good thing."

I squirmed, trying to break free, but his hold of me was true and relentless. Seconds after, I felt the pressure of something sharp stinging my skin. My eyes snapped to it when I found a needle as he added some kind of obscure substance into my body.

My eyes felt heavy all of sudden, darkness encroaching my vision. The last thing I remembered seeing was his face as he said something. It got in through one ear and then flew out through the other.

I couldn't make sense of it. The bastard drugged me and was now ending all my chances of living in Canada.

He was bringing me to live in the USA again.

CHAPTER 5

I found myself inside a bedroom, the morning's light coming through the windows gentle and inviting. It was like I could forget everything that happened and pretend that nothing of that had ever been real.

Like I was living my new life in Canada's countryside, playing in the snow and making countless snow men.

I grunted when I sat up on the bed, blinking while I wondered what the hell was going on now. I had a terrible dream, one that involved my dad marrying me off to another man – a man that went as far as killing my boyfriend in cold blood, all because he assumed the latter was planning to kill him.

How stupid was he? Ethan was so sweet he would never be able to hurt a fly. Courageous, but also so sweet. Under the influence of that thought, I couldn't help but pull my phone out of the pocket of my flimsy shorts. I craved talking to him now, hearing his voice.

I'd put on this short in my dream. Well, I guessed that was just the Zolpidem doing its thing still. Fuck. Next time I needed to take less of it. I was having some insomnia problems, so I guessed I got a little desperate and took more than the prescribed dosage.

When I pulled my phone out of the pocket of my shorts, a thought surged through my mind. Ethan dead in my arms, his last breaths as he slowly but surely slipped away into the world of the dead.

I shook my head, attempting to clear it. It couldn't be. That couldn't have happened. He should be alive and kicking still, about to finish his Master's degree and then make my dream of living in Canada real.

I looked out the window and was a little surprised when I didn't find myself inside the estate my dad owned. Such a realization didn't worry me, though. Maybe Ethan had taken me to a different kind of hotel, one that looked more like a mansion.

I dialed his number and waited until he picked up the call, but that didn't happen. My phone kept ringing his, time passing. I still didn't feel worried there was something odd going on here.

There could be so many explanations for his 'sudden' disappearance. Maybe he was busy in the laboratory of Lost Hope College. He was studying to become an Environmental Engineer too, on top of the Civil Engineering degree he liked to show off to everyone he met.

I tossed my phone behind my head when I came to the conclusion that he was too busy for me. Fucking hell. And here I was thinking he truly loved me. Guy was married to his research and thesis.

It was ridiculous, but I didn't hold it against him too. At least one of us was focused on making it in life and to not have to depend on our parents.

I walked to the balcony and closed my eyes, taking in the smell of the trees, grass, and the plants of the garden. There was something so refreshing about starting the day with a calm and peaceful mind I could never hope to emulate in another manner.

That's when it all hit me, the fact that I wasn't in my home or some random ass apartment building in the middle of nowhere in Lost Hope. I was still in that disgusting city – Artem's mansion.

His estate and everything that came with it.

I was lying my forearms on the wall of the balcony before I pushed myself off of it, stumbling back into the bedroom while flashes of previous occurrences assaulted my mind. Artem and his gun, a shot that pierced through the air, Ethan dying in my arms, his blood soaking through the fabric of my clothes.

Rage bubbled up in my heart as one objective took root in my mind – killing Artem and making him regret that he killed Ethan. I wasn't going to marry that good-for-nothing asshole, who was so obsessed with me he'd been following me since my birth.

How fucked up was that?

The door opened all of sudden. In his mansion, I was nothing. I didn't have any control over who could open the door, when, and what they were going to be bringing with them. This time, it was Artem, smiling from ear to ear like he knew I was going to become his obedient wife now.

His hand held a bouquet. It was beautiful and it made me feel like scooting over to sniff the smell of it, but I wasn't going to do it. The red and yellow roses weren't going to make me betray my true self.

I wished to see this man dead and if everything went as according to plan again, I was going to make that real. His blood coming out of the hole I was going to make in his chest, his mouth opening as he tried to breathe but couldn't make his lungs work again, with life sniffing out of his eyes…

I wished to make that happen soon, and I was more than willing to become his killer.

"I've brought this bouquet for you. Hope you're going to like it," he said, offering it to me.

Artem was tall. A head taller than me, and his chest and shoulders were so broad they made me feel small. He made me wish I was a man so that I didn't have to be feeling so vulnerable before him.

Most of all, I didn't want to be feeling like he could snap my neck now with ease if I didn't do everything he was dreaming about.

"I don't like it, and I don't want anything from you. You drugged me!"

"I only did that because I thought you were going to need it, and wouldn't you know it? You very well did. You kept squirming and trying to shoot me with a gun, and I also couldn't have allowed you to spend another day as an illegal alien in Canada. You're American and this is your only home."

"Liar! I'm not going to be American for much longer. I'm going to ruin your life. Just you wait for that."

A moment of silence ensued.

"Are you going to accept the bouquet or not?"

"Do I have a choice or is it like with everything else in your life when it comes to dealing with other people?"

"With a bouquet? Of course you have a choice, though I wouldn't like it if you refused it. I like this bouquet and I think it's pretty. Don't you share the same opinion, my dear future wife?"

"I'm not going to marry you."

"I think we've been through that already," he said, stepping to me, being so close now I could smell his perfume. Strong with a hint of gentleness, almost like the man that hid behind his mask.

I wouldn't say he could ever be gentle with me, though. Even if he was attempting to do that now, with him holding the bouquet in his right hand and trying to make up for the fact he drugged me, he was still the same asshole I knew a bit too well.

To truly make up for something like that, he was going to have to let me leave this mansion and never come back.

"I still don't get why you want me so much…" I said.

"It's simple. I'm in love with you," he said, quirking up a corner of his lips.

"Oh, right. The man that controls one of the most important crime families in the whole world needs me. I'm no one. Dad's family is dying and you know that."

"Well, there's that and also the fact I really like him," he commented, offering the bouquet again. "Look, I'm not going to get out of the room if you don't at least smell the bouquet once and allow me to keep it in here."

"Why? Does it have some kind of hidden camera in it that

you're going to use to spy on me?"

"No, nothing of the sort," he said, his voice assuming a gentler tone. "They're nothing more than some flowers, though they do reflect my love for you, my dear. You might think it's not real, but it is here, right within my heart. It's the only reason I bothered with finding you when you were in Canada."

I opened my mouth, but realized there wasn't much more that I could say to change his mind. He was obsessed with me and he wasn't going to leave the room unless I did what he was asking of me.

I didn't want to smell the roses. I knew they smelled well and looked beautiful like nothing else, but I still didn't want to do anything that was going to make him feel like he owned me now.

And dad… Was he going to come here now and give me a harsh sermon for having burned down their hideout while they were having one of their most important meetings of their lives? I heard that even the head of the House of Representatives had been there, discussing with them how they were going to make more money through corruption.

Politicians like them craved just one thing – to keep the population dependent on them for the rest of their lives…

I took the bouquet in my hand and tossed it through the window, dusting off my hands.

Just like that, I showed him that it didn't matter if he were to buy me expensive gifts or not. I wasn't going to change who I was. I was going to continue being the independent and strong woman that allowed me to put up with men like him.

I was going to find a way out of this place, and it didn't matter how I was going to do that. I was willing to do everything in my power to make it happen.

There was a twitch under his left eye, but he didn't say anything else for some seconds. If he was really thinking that the bouquet was going to slightly make me change my opinion of him, then he was just naïve.

I'd just finished establishing what our lives together were going to be like.

"What a pity. Such a waste of flowers."

"Well, I didn't really like them."

"Is there a particular kind you like then, my dear?"

"Stop calling me 'your dear.' I'm not that and I'm never going to be."

"You see," he said, stepping toward me as he forced me to bump my backside against one of the walls of the bedroom. "I'm not going to give up on changing your mind about me. Soon enough, you're going to be calling me your 'dear' too."

I swallowed all of my spit and tried to spit on his face, but his hand latched on my face as soon as he heard the noise coming from within my throat. "And that is not going to happen as well. I'm much smarter than you take me to be."

"If you were, you would have done something before I burned down your hideout."

He smiled, his head coming so close to mine I could smell his breath of mint and expensive whiskey.

"Ahhh, you see. I kind of allowed that to happen."

"What?" I questioned. His hand was making it difficult for me to speak, but I was still doing my best to pronounce the words. It didn't matter how strong his grip on my mouth was, I was still going to argue with him until he had nothing else to say.

"Sean... I had to find him eventually and end his family. Your arrival to his estate was part of the plan. I was able to pick them out, one by one, while they were all gathered at the same place. One of the O'Sullivan family's strengths was that they moved from place to place all the time, never allowing too many of them to remain in the same location for too long. But thanks to you, they made their first and last mistake. They are never coming back, and their inexistence now allows me to better control politics in Toronto too. And after branching out of there, I'm going to control their country too."

Asshole.

I couldn't believe it. He played me like I was a ventriloquist's doll.

CHAPTER 6

I found myself in the same situation as with Sean. He was abusing his position of power over me, making me think I couldn't come out of this unless I obeyed every single thing he had planned out for this occasion. He was aware he owned this estate and he was going to use that as the stepping stone to get between my legs.

For him, it was all about that, wasn't it? Getting between them because he thought of me as a difficult woman, the one not willing to budge, no matter what happened.

I attempted to kick him in his crotch, but he just launched his body with force against me, making me not only feel his bulge pressing against my belly, but also force the air out of my lungs.

His hand was still making it difficult for me to speak. His head getting so close to mine, I couldn't help but fear if he was going to kiss me without my okay, without winning my heart over first.

He didn't have to. He was the owner of this estate and he could do pretty much anything, including that.

"You think I'm just going to kiss you like this, Faye?"

"I wouldn't put it past you. You're nothing more than a spoiled kid. You grew up rich and powerful, with everyone around you claiming that you were some kind of special kid that was going to rule the whole world one day."

"Well, I just might make that happen," he taunted, settling his hand on my leg, sliding it up. "I love the feel of your skin against mine. It's like touching silk."

"You're an asshole. If my dad finds out about this-"

"Shhh, no need to get him involved. He's not going to find out about anything, and even if he does, he won't be able to do much."

"You think you're some sort of special mafia boss that is going to kill all of your competitors."

"Yeah, I think I might make that happen. I killed Sean, after all, and he was one of the many that stood in my way. His family is no more and they are all rotting on the grounds of their estate. Not even the police are going to bother getting them out of there until their bodies are rotting so much the neighbors will complain."

"Jesus, you're a sick psycho," I said, my chin and jaw in pain. His grip around them was tough and decisive. He didn't like me talking. He liked me obedient, doing everything he could ever ask of me.

His fingers kneaded the skin of my thigh, pushing up my flimsy shorts. I wished so much to put on a pair of jeans. I wished I could kill him right at this instant and end this madness. If only dad wasn't so desperate to save his own skin and that of his mafia family, all of this would be so different now.

"That's a new one," he said, his lips brushing mine. "You're loving this, aren't you? Deep down there, you want to fuck me too."

"Never," I argued as I tried to spit on his face but found it impossible to do so. "I'm not going to allow you to bend me to your will."

His hand sneaking further up, he found the edge of my pair of panties. With his overwhelming presence keeping me pinned to the wall like this, his perfume overflowing my lungs, his hand dominating a part of me I didn't have much control over, I couldn't help but wonder for how much longer I was going to be able to resist him.

Until he made me moan and assured his mind of what he was assuming I felt for him – that he could be the biggest jerk in all of Lost Hope, I was still going to fall head over heels for him – he wasn't going to stop this.

Never was I going to allow that to happen. Never.

"It's pointless fighting against it," he taunted, his fingers now pulling my panties to the side, offering him the spot that he sought. "You're going to be mine. That smell… Hmmm, I know that smell. You're aroused, aren't you?"

"No!" I shouted, but he was having none of it. His predatory smile was enough to make me feel like he wasn't going to pay attention to any of my words anyway. He knew what he wanted and nothing and no one was going to change his opinion.

He knew he had me under his full control and if anything now, he was going to make me obey his wishes.

Just when I thought his finger was going to touch my clit, he pulled himself off of me, retreating to the balcony.

"You're not quite ready yet. A pity, but that's normal. You don't know me. Not like I do you, but I'm going to change that. I'll make sure of it. In here, in my home, you're going to live a life like no other."

"What?"

"I'm going to make sure you're treated like the Queen you are, Faye. You're mistaken about me."

"I'm not. You killed Ethan."

He shook his head, his hand sneaking into the front pocket of his coat before he pulled out of it a cigarette pack. He took one from within it, lit it up with his lighter, and then dropped the latter back into the left pocket of his dark pants.

"You're so mistaken about it all it's kind of funny, really."

"You think I find his death funny, that it's some sort of sick joke?" I asked, holding back tears.

"No, I'm saying you never really knew the true him, and I can prove I'm right."

I opened my mouth, but didn't say anything. Artem had to be bluffing. It was the only explanation to this that made sense to me.

"And if you think I'm bluffing, then come with me to my room. I'm going to show you I'm right."

I guess I had no choice but to bite his bait. I was curious. Being too curious about certain things was one of the many things about myself I wished to change. Curiosity killed the cat, right?

Well, in my case it seemed that now I was the cat.

He smoked his cigarette until there was nothing more of it other than the butt. He dropped it on the cigarette ashtray that was on top of one of the nightstands by the double bed. My mind was in such a disarray that I hadn't even noticed it was there. Maybe he'd put it there for whenever he felt like 'visiting' me in 'my' bedroom.

If he was indeed serious about treating me like a Queen, then at least the room he got right. It was huge, enormous, and I had all the space I could ever need. It was even bigger and more glamorous than the bedroom I'd been in Sean's estate.

There was a closet to one side, a piano to the other, the king-sized bed, lamps and more fancy lamps, a small candelabrum hanging from the roof, and that view of his garden that made me feel like pulling a chair and sitting in the balcony for hours on end.

He padded to the door, opening it.

"So, are you going to come with me or not?"

"Care to tell me where you're going to take me? Because I don't like going to random places with thugs."

He smirked.

"To my bedroom, and don't worry, I'm not going to take advantage of you over there. We still need to talk about the marriage, don't you think?"

Ah, of course. That bloody marriage. The thing that was keeping him so focused on me, on making me beg for his care and love.

"I'm not going to talk about any marriage with you. I just want to see what you have on Ethan."

"And that I'm going to do," he said, stepping outside. "I'm going to show you I didn't lie. He was trying to kill me, with the help of another gang. Did you really think he was innocent?"

I swallowed the lump in my throat, finding it difficult to believe he was saying the truth about Ethan. He was so sweet all the time. He could never have been making plans to kill another person, right?

Never. Artem was bluffing, and I could... kind... of see that in his eyes.

I sighed. I had no choice but to follow him now.

I proceeded to his bedroom, going through many hallways, with all of them showing different facets of his life. His parents, his extended family, his sister, him playing golf, him meeting up with the country's president, and the like.

Talk about someone that never knew poverty in his life, not that I could say I knew differently too.

He opened the door of his bedroom and proceeded to his desk. One of his drawers had a padlock that he opened with a small key and a combination of numbers. I wasn't able to make out all of them, but I did notice that he pressed the number one and then then the nine in succession.

If he kept some secrets of his in there, then that could be what I needed to ruin his life. All the FBI and the CIA would need was some proof that his family was knee-deep in crimes that would put them behind bars for decades.

As soon as he pulled the drawer open and plucked out of it several paper sheets, he pushed it close with his hand before he turned around.

"These are some photos taken of him, and I'm sure you're going to want to see them."

He unfolded his arm, offering me the photos he'd printed. I didn't know if I could believe him or not. For all I knew, he might as well have used someone else that looked like Ethan to prove to me he was doing something he shouldn't.

I still plucked the paper sheets out of his hand, turning around until my back was facing his. I didn't know if I could trust what my eyes were seeing, but I still didn't want him to see my reaction.

I felt that, if he did, he wouldn't hesitate to use it against me, too.

The first printed photo showed Ethan talking to someone I knew a bit too well. Sean. They stood in front of the cinema by 5th avenue in downtown Lost Hope. The photo was of high quality, showing to me that, indeed, they couldn't have used someone else to fake his claim that Ethan was planning his murder.

That photo still didn't mean much, but it did tell me this – Ethan had been hiding things from me he should have told me about. If he'd been talking with Sean, then with who else had been conversing with before his death?

And that's without mentioning their subject of conversation. Artem could indeed be right about his assertion that the latter was knee-deep in plans to off him.

I would still have preferred that he killed Artem. I loved Ethan, but there was also no denying that he'd been lying to me – and lying was one of the many things I could never tolerate.

A pang of pain hit my heart. I felt the tears trying to come out, but I was still not going to cry now. Not in front of Artem, who could look at that as another reason to take pity on me and have sex with me when I wasn't mentally ready for it.

Artem was a predator. He was going to strike when I was at my worst, when I was vulnerable, and perhaps these photos were all part of said plan.

I wouldn't put it past him.

CHAPTER 7

I took the photo I was looking at and put it behind all the others, shifting my weight. The new photo that my eyes were looking at this time showed Ethan holding a gun, surveying Artem's estate.

He was caught by their security cameras. I couldn't help but wonder again if he'd been recording me with them, too.

With his gun tucked in his waist, his eyes assessing the mansion, this photo was indeed confirming to me that Artem was right. The sweet man I'd come to love could have been planning out his assassination after all.

I looked at another photo and I gasped when I saw Ethan confronting Artem as they stood on a sidewalk, in a neighborhood I couldn't identify from the photo alone. Whatever it was they had been talking about them, it looked serious.

So serious that Ethan's face was an expression of anger mixed with disgust. The fact that Artem had been keeping tabs on him did raise a lot of questions in my mind that needed to be answered, but they didn't worry me. The guy had always been an asshole, and that was something I'd already grown used to.

But Ethan meeting up with him on a sidewalk in the middle of nowhere? That raised so many questions I didn't know for how much longer I could keep ignoring all this evidence. Ethan had been trying to kill him.

Well, that was good and bad at the same time. It did mean that Ethan was lying to me, but it also meant that he loved me so much he was willing to risk his life to make sure I was going to be only his.

Artem stepped forward and stood right behind me, his eyes checking out the photo I was holding.

"He was not himself that day. Or rather, maybe I should say that he was his normal self."

"What do you mean?"

"He thought I was all alone then. I was taking care of some business ventures I'd struck some months before that and he just pulled over his car and confronted me. Just like that. The balls he had. Ethan was stupid and smart at the same time."

"And… you weren't alone that time, right?"

"No, I'm never alone. Not even when I'm with you. Guards patrol this estate 24/7. Should something happen, they will know."

I gulped. He was right. Offing Artem meant a lot more than just ridding him of the face of the world. It meant planning everything, including every detail in my calculations, and I wasn't sure I could pull that off.

"And what else did Ethan say?"

He took a deep breath, saying, "That's when he promised he was going to kill me, and I couldn't ignore his threat. I said I was going to kill him the next time I saw him. A week or two later, he showed up with you here."

"You still had no right-"

"Oh, c'mon. You're not going to tell me I wasn't in the right, right? I saved myself and he was a loose cannon. He would have harmed you too. That I'm sure of."

I whirled around, meeting his steely eyes. It didn't seem to matter to him. Nothing of this seemed to be mattering that much to him, other than proving to me that Ethan was wrong, that he'd never been the right man for me.

But I wasn't going to allow him to change my opinion of him like that. I still thought of Ethan as the only choice I had at marrying and having a happy life in Canada.

"You're wrong! He was a good man. All you're proving with this, with these shitty photos," I said, throwing them up in the air, "is that he loved me too much. I hate you. I fucking hate you!"

I was punching his chest as he allowed me to do that, his body still as he looked more like a giant tower now than a normal man made of flesh and bones.

His hands grabbed my arms, stopping them. I thought he was going to hit me, but when I pulled my arms back, he opened his fingers and allowed me to distance myself away from him, stumbling.

"There's something else about him you need to know, and I don't think you're going to like it."

I scoffed. "There's nothing else of Ethan that you can show that is going to change my opinion about him."

He crouched, his hand picking up one of the photos on the floor.

"You're going to want to see this. Actually, when I gave you the photos, this is the one I most wanted you to see."

I was hugging myself when I spoke again.

"Why? To believe in your lies? I'm not going to look at any other photo. I know they are all lies."

"They are not lies, and I think you know that. You shouldn't be trying to lie to yourself. Now that's something that is only going to make you feel miserable."

His tone was professional and soothing, as if he knew this meeting with him had just one possible outcome – him destroying everything I knew about Ethan.

I shook my head, refusing to look at his photo. Minutes passed and I wondered if he was going to insist on the subject when he picked up the other photos off the floor, putting them all together in his hands.

"Alright. If you don't want to see them, then I'm just wasting my time here. We should move on to talk about the marriage. I want it to be something you're going to remember for years on end."

I knew he was taunting me and yet I couldn't ignore his words. I should just turn around and leave this room like it meant nothing to me. And yet, I did the opposite. I made a beeline to him and plucked the photo out of his hands.

He contained a smile as I checked out the photo. For a moment I couldn't quite believe what my eyes were seeing. It was Ethan and he wasn't alone. He was with someone else. A woman about his age that looked too beautiful to be anything other than his other girlfriend.

This had to be some sort of sick joke. Nothing more than a Photoshop manipulation trying to convince me of something that never happened.

And yet, Ethan was almost hugging her. He was keeping his arm looped around her waist, holding her to him as if she meant something to him that I could never have been.

My hands were shaking when I spoke.

"You're lying. This is a lie. Ethan couldn't have had someone else. I was his only love."

He shook his head. "Look, Faye. If you are not going to want to see the truth, there's nothing else I can do. There's a good reason why I want to marry you. I think pretty much everyone has been lying to you, other than me."

I was still holding the photo in my hand, refusing to believe in his lie. After all, it couldn't be anything other than more of his bullshit, right?

He was using this to bend me to his will. I was growing so sure of that I was starting to think this was nothing more than a ploy to destroy my mind.

He knew I was a strong person. The only way to make me weak enough was by making me think that everyone I knew, all of my friends, were lying to me.

And yet, I couldn't help but keep stealing looks at the photo I was holding. If this was some kind of Photoshop prank, then it was a damn good one.

"Here, I also have a video recording of it," he said before pulling open the lid of his laptop.

After some button pressings and sliding his finger on the touchpad, he loaded up the video he was looking for. When he pressed the play button, I knew I was going to watch something that was going to terrify me and open my eyes at the same time.

"Faye, I know this is difficult, but you have to see reason. Ethan was nothing more than another guy that thought you didn't really deserve him. Now, you might hate me and everything, but I'm still the only man that really cares about you. I'm the one showing you the truth, am I might not?"

The video that was playing was showing Ethan and that same woman from before. I had no idea what her name was, and I couldn't quite care about that. It didn't matter to me who she was and what she did for a living, only that she had been trying to steal my beloved.

I could never, ever forgive her for what she was doing, even if I didn't know if she was doing what she had been doing knowing that I was his girlfriend or not.

The video depicted the two of them in a nightclub, dancing, and kissing. It was like they'd been doing that for the sole purpose of pissing me off, and wouldn't you know it? It was working.

I'd fallen in love with Ethan, but now I was feeling that he'd deserved to die. I balled my hands and shut his laptop with force. I didn't want to have to continue watching the two of them kissing, and I sure as hell wasn't going to continue putting up with this.

"You've made your point, Artem. He's an asshole. You're an asshole. What's the difference between you two? It seems I'm destined to marry a man that is going to make me feel like a cockroach."

"That's not why I'm showing you this, and you know it. I only needed you to know that you need to look past your initial assumptions of other people."

"What?"

"Look," he argued, putting his photos back into the drawer of his desk, "I know this is all difficult for you, but I want you to remember who showed you the truth when you most needed it."

I scoffed.

"I need to get out of here, of this. I don't want to talk about Ethan ever again with you."

"It's okay," he said, his voice soothing and comforting again. I hated how he kept making me feel as if I was in the wrong. "It's okay to feel this way. I'm going to make sure nobody is going to bother you until you come out of your room. You can find the schedule for dinner, lunch, and other meals in your bedroom. It should have been pinned to one of the walls."

"You mean that I'm free to ignore you and pretty much everyone else living here?"

"You're free, though that doesn't mean you can walk out of the premises. The estate should be big enough for you. We even have a chapel in here for our marriage."

"I still haven't said I'm going to marry you."

"Well, don't worry about that," he said, smirking. "I have more than enough time to convince you. It won't be long until you'll be asking to marry me instead."

I scoffed, shutting the door behind me. He was crazy. He was imagining things that could never happen. Me asking to marry him? Not here, not ever, and not even if my life depended on it.

I would never.

CHAPTER 8

It wasn't the same morning or night when he invited me to his bedroom and showed me those things about Ethan. No, this was a different day. I didn't even know what day it was, if it was Sunday, the Monday, or the Tuesday. I did know the month, though. July, and soon there were going to be fireworks being set off in the distance.

They were all going to commemorate the fourth of July, and even though there had once been a moment in my life when I cared about it as much as they did, my opinion of it now changed.

I couldn't find much reason to love any of this, of my current life. And the worst thing to me was that dad didn't care enough about me. Not to show up here anyway, with him doing whatever he was doing to keep his mafia family afloat.

What Artem showed me about Ethan changed what I thought of him. I cried when he died in my arms, and now I couldn't help but feel disgusted that I had such a reaction for someone that had been loving someone else.

That woman... That bitch. I hadn't seen the signs and now I was feeling like everything in my life changed, for the worse. I felt that everyone had been lying to me. Everyone but the asshole who was keeping me locked up in here.

He was right. He was the only one that hadn't lied to me, though I imagined that soon he was going to.

He couldn't be much different from everyone else in my life. College and high school friends? I forgot they existed. They hadn't bothered with talking to me this whole time, and I doubted any of that was going to change soon, or any time in the future for that matter.

I cried that morning and the rest of the day, when I was in my bedroom thinking that nothing in my life was ever going to return to normal. I still remembered what my life had once been like without meeting this asshole.

He watched me grow up and now he was going to reap what he thought belonged to him.

I'd thought I'd put the whole Ethan thing behind me when I opened one of my suitcases and found a photo of him and me. My hand flew to my mouth, covering it before a gasp could escape through my lips.

Despite everyone living and working in his estate, it felt silent, like I was the only one living here.

I broke down crying then and there, still hiding in my room. I didn't have anyone here to make me company. I was pretty much all by myself, and such a realization was weighing down on my shoulders.

My whole body felt heavy like never before.

Tears were rolling down my cheeks when someone knocked on the door. I'd thought that Artem had ordered his maids and other workers to stay away from here and live me alone, but it seemed he'd lied.

Well, he'd said he was the only one that couldn't and wouldn't lie to me, and now it seemed he was going to become another member of the asshole team. The 'team' of people that didn't care about me at all, focusing only on their lives and making me feel like the worst human being in the world.

I didn't feel like going to open the door. If it was Artem, he would just have opened the door without knocking – just like all the many times he did that. He was like everyone else. He didn't care about me.

And I doubted he would ever change that side of his life, too.

Whoever was on the other side of the door kept knocking on it, though, driving me to cry even more. The thing was, with how heavy these walls were, the man or woman on the other side couldn't hear me crying.

They thought that everything was alright with me and that I was either just sleeping or watching a movie on the large TV in front of the comfy couch. It was a luxurious suite and I had everything I needed in it, including a large dumbwaiter for when I didn't feel like going to the dining room for food.

"Leave me alone! I'm not in the mood to talk to anyone."

His voice startled me when he spoke.

"Faye, I know you're crying, and I think you need someone to talk to now. I'm not going to try anything you don't want – trust me. I'm being your friend now."

Weeks had already passed since my coming here and he'd been doing good on his word to keep his distance. Most of the time, he was busy with his work stuff. Working behind the scenes and fueling political campaigns.

I was still working on getting enough proof on that and ratting him out to the FBI and CIA. The biggest impediment to me doing that was that I couldn't have access to his room with ease. He kept it locked with many padlocks and other techier locking mechanisms.

And I didn't want to talk to him either. He was an asshole. He killed Ethan, who was an asshole too, but at the time I was in love with him and that memory I had was never going to change.

If anything, it was only going to reinforce the fact that I fell in love with the wrong guy, again.

"Faye, it's okay. You need someone to talk to, and there's nobody in here that is going to come here and pretend to be your friend. You're going to explode if you keep all those feelings hidden in your mind."

"It's my mind and I do anything I want with it!"

"That's true, but you still need a friend, a person that is going to hear you and understand you."

"And you think you're going to be that person for me?" I asked, scoffing. It wasn't really a question, though. More like me just shouting for him to get the fuck away from the door and leave me alone with my mind-devouring thoughts.

I wasn't going to take any more of this. I was going to kick him away from here and finally have the peace I was seeking. I didn't want to talk to anyone and he wasn't going to change my mind about that.

I stood up in a wink and threw the door open. I kept it locked most of the time with my key, but this time I'd forgotten to do that. I was just too busy with my life, trying to make peace with everything that happened and the like to remember doing such a frivolous thing.

He wasn't smirking like I thought he was going to be when my eyes landed on him. In fact, I could almost tell that deep within his heart he cared about my feelings.

Artem, despite all the horrible things he made me feel, was now being kind. Since my coming here, he'd always been kind enough to heed my words, fulfill my wishes, make his employees go out in town to buy me whatever I needed, and overall make it so everyone was kind to me.

I was still not about to make any friends here, but still… My stay at his estate was better than I thought it was going to be, and in large part it was due to this tall and imposing man standing in front of me.

He wasn't wearing one of his expensive and jaw-dropping suits now, opting for a more stylish style without it. As 'stylish' as it was going to be for someone like him, I should point out. He wasn't the kind of man that enjoyed following trends.

He preferred walking his own path and now was no different, with his office suit and the lack of a tie. His office pants still showed that he was ready to work if need be, though I guessed that wasn't going to happen any time soon.

He came here because he knew he was going to have all the free time he needed to talk to me.

"Faye, it's good that you've opened the door. Your face looks horrible. I want to know what it is that is making you cry."

I scoffed again, marching back into the bedroom while keeping the door open. Just as I'd thought, he took the bait. He closed it behind him and turned the knob, making sure that he was going to be the only one with me here.

I sat down on the bed, sinking my face in my hands.

"You're never going to understand me."

He kept his distance, shifting his weight.

"Maybe not. We're never going to find that out if you don't give me enough time."

"What does it matter to you? What does any of this matter? Marrying me isn't going to solve your problems. Even if you're trying to be nice to me..."

"Ahhh, there it is. What I came here looking for. You can't ignore what's happening, right? That despite everything you thought, I'm the only one that is looking out for you."

I bit my bottom lip. I wasn't going to say that he was right. I wasn't crazy enough to say something like that with everything that was going on here.

He sat down on the bed but didn't do anything else, opting to let the time pass and leave me to my own thoughts.

I just... couldn't stop thinking about Ethan, about how much he meant to me, his eyes, his nose, his lips kissing mine. I felt like I could feel him hugging me, telling me how much I meant to him.

And it all turned out to be nothing more than a lie. A lie in which he made me think I was someone important to him, that he cared about me.

The man sitting right beside me now... I couldn't deny that he felt genuine and different.

Tears were still rolling down my cheeks and despite everything that happened between us, I felt compelled to open up to him. I knew that it didn't make much sense, that chances were he was going to laugh at me, but I still needed someone to talk to about all the things that tormented my mind.

"Thank you… for showing me the truth. It finished ruining my mind, but I'm thankful for it."

"Well, it wasn't my intention to ruin your life or anything of the sort. I just thought you deserved to know it."

I turned my head to him, meeting his steely grey eyes. I didn't know what it was with his words, but they rang true to me. They turned something on in my heart that I thought I couldn't feel for him.

I suppressed it as soon as it bubbled up, though. I didn't want to admit that I felt anything for this asshole that wasn't absolute hatred.

Even if calling him an asshole now didn't appear to make much sense.

Other than him keeping me locked up here, he was doing everything in his power to make me feel at home. I had everything I could have asked for. The best food, the best clothes, safety, and a man that hadn't hidden the truth when he could have done it.

It worked in his favor, but I still wouldn't have thought that he would share it with me. The fact that he did spoke volumes about the man that defined his being.

"You look beautiful now, even when crying."

"I'm not in the mood for that sort of talk," I said, standing up and rubbing at my eyes. I didn't want to admit that he was being nice and telling me sweet things. Goddamnit, why was I having such thoughts now?

Why were they tormenting me like this?

CHAPTER 9

I knew what he was going to say before he said it. "Look, Faye, I know that we didn't start off on the right foot, and I'm willing to change that. It would be difficult, but if you give me a chance, I know that we can make it work."

I scoffed. "You gotta be kidding me. After everything that you did, you want to make peace with me?" I paced around until I was running my fingers through my hair. "I don't think it works like that. Not in the way you're hoping it's going to, at least."

I couldn't deny that day by day, he was changing. He was becoming a better man and he had been showing that he cared about me, in his own way. It was still so difficult for me to look past everything that happened.

However, his presence here was pretty much what I was hoping someone would do for me. I just couldn't believe that of all the people I knew he was the only one showing some sweetness to me.

"I still can't believe that he was lying to me," I said, refusing to turn my face to meet him.

He walked until he was standing right behind me, putting one of his hands on my right shoulder.

"I know it's difficult. I was through something similar in my life before."

I scoffed, whirling around until I was meeting his eyes. They were steely, as they always were. It didn't matter what happened, what came to pass in his life, Artem was always going to be the same cold Russian boss that could steal the hearts of so many women.

And yet, he couldn't do the same with mine.

"You've never been through something like this one before. I know you're lying. You are telling me all these things just to get between my legs."

A moment of silence ensued as he weighed his words. His eyes kept the same coldness from before, always looking at me as if I was the most important person in the world for him. I kind of wished I could say the same about him, but the more time passed, the surer I grew that I was always going to hate him with my guts.

"I did," he stated. "There was a moment in my life when I thought that everything was going to come crumbling down on my head. When my whole family was killed and I was the only one spared in Russia."

I knew about that, or I thought I knew about it. His family was killed by the KGB and the authorities over there turned a blind eye to it. It all happened so fast that he was almost not able to recover from it.

The fact that he stood before me now was shocking, to say the least. This was a man that knew hardship, that had been through much worse before. I didn't want to admit this, but his sudden assertion about his past was now making me think that maybe I might give him the chance that he was seeking so much.

His hand moved to settle underneath my chin, tilting it up. I let him do that. I didn't know what was coming over me, but I was letting this Russian boss dictate how this moment should be paced. It was like his words were finally having the magical effect that he was seeking.

"You're a real thing of beauty. You don't deserve to be crying over any man. Not over that asshole that was cheating on you."

I didn't know what my mind was feeling at this moment, but his words were ringing true, as if Artem was reading my mind. I knew that didn't make any sense and that I was just thinking gibberish. I knew I shouldn't be letting him have this kind of effect on me, but I was also growing sure that I didn't have much control over my body and mind anymore.

His finger was now brushing my right cheek and his lips were looking too tempting for me. This tall and imposing Russian boss, his pepper and salt hair, the deepness of his voice, and how he seemed to command authority wherever he went – it was almost everything I could ever ask for in a man.

I was still not going to kiss him, though. Not after everything that happened. I had better self-respect than that. I wasn't going to do any of the things he was cooking up in his mind.

I walked away from him quickly and stood on the balcony. Even if Artem wasn't the brightest man in the world, he was going to understand that I didn't want to talk to him. Not at this moment. Not when I was still grieving Ethan's death and the fact that my father didn't care about me at all.

Chances were he had gotten the news that I was here again and was now focusing on his job. I blamed him and felt like punching his face until my knuckles were sore.

"I see," said Artem, turning around and padding to the door. "You need some time alone to think things through, but I can see that you already feel better. I'm going to be in my bedroom if you need me."

He opened the door and then closed it behind him. As soon as I couldn't hear his footsteps anymore, I began to miss him. I didn't know what was going on in my mind, but I was missing that asshole.

I was missing his presence and care. The more time passed, the more he was showing me that he was a different man.

Even if he was still trying to marry me.

CHAPTER 10

I was picking up flowers in the main garden when footsteps racing from behind me caught my attention. I'd been living in this mansion for a good while now and I was already kind of getting used to the routine.

There wasn't much to do here. I woke up in the mornings, with my waking up time getting more and more late. It didn't bother me since I didn't plan on beginning to work anytime soon. What's more, it wasn't like Artem had been reprimanding me for being like that. If anything, he was being supportive of me.

The woman that was racing to me was one of the few friends I'd already made here. She was the only one I felt connected to, even if only a little. She talked to me every time I cried, always supporting me in my decisions.

I would have opened a smile if this was a different circumstance, but I could already tell that it was anything but. Worry clouded her face and I could tell that whatever she had to tell me, it was serious.

So serious that it was making me purse my lips.

She halted a couple of feet from me, saying, "Oh, Mrs. Garza. I'm so sorry to be the bringer of bad news. I didn't believe it when they said it to me. I thought it was a bad joke."

"What? What are you going on about? I don't understand you."

She cleared her throat and pursed her lips. Whatever it was she had to tell me, it was affecting her mind beyond measure, as if of all the things that she thought could happen today, this was the last on her list.

"It's your father, miss."

"My father? Is he here? Please tell me you are not mistaken about this. If he is here, then I need to go see him. You know how much I hate him for not having shown up since I was taken back here."

"I know, but I don't think- Oh my God, I feel so bad about it."

I was already getting a little annoyed by how she was circling around the subject instead of telling me straight up what she'd heard. My heart rate was beginning to race a little as well, the palms of my hands sweating.

Part of me wasn't sure if I was ready to meet my father again. After he promised to Artem that I was to marry him, I couldn't even remember his face without hatred bubbling up in my heart. I was still not over that and I didn't think I was ever going to be.

"Just tell me what happened. I think I deserve to know every-thing."

Breathing, she recomposed herself. I felt a little bad that she was feeling this way, but at the moment my biggest worry was finding out what was happening to my father.

"I believe, miss, that he died in a terrible accident. I don't know the details, but it seems-"

Just as she finished saying that, my heart sank. It was like my whole world was crumbling down all around me. First it was get-ting kidnapped and then taken back here, with the promise of marrying Artem becoming more and more certain by the day, and now there was this to add to the pile of feces that was my life.

She wasn't lying to me. She was the only person in this whole estate that I trusted not to ever lie to me. And the sadness that clouded her face, and that wrinkled her skin - it made it all too clear to me.

My father was indeed dead.

I fought the tears trying to come out. The last thing I wanted was to cry in front of her again. I cried so many times when she was around that I'd already lost account. And I didn't want to add to the sadness that was already tormenting her.

Footsteps approached us again, and I ignored them. I didn't know who it was that was coming in my direction, but I didn't have time for him. And I knew it was a man because those footsteps were too heavy to be from a woman.

Whoever was coming here, though, most likely was going to ignore me. Other than Donna, there was nobody that cared about me enough to ask what was making me cry and whimper in this manner.

He stopped a couple of feet away, and his voice startled me when he spoke.

"Faye… I'm really sorry for what happened. I didn't think this day would come, much less that it was going to be today."

I opened my eyes in a heartbeat, finding it unbelievable that of all the people that could be standing in front of me now, he was the one. Artem. The man that despite all the sweet things he'd been doing for me, was still hellbent on forcing me to marry him.

He said it was non-negotiable.

And yet, when he offered me his arms, I couldn't help but stand up in a wink and launch myself toward him. I didn't punch him, though part of me was wishing I could do that. No, I hugged him and buried my head on his strong chest. It was the only thing I could to feel less bad about everything that was happening.

"I'm sorry for his death. I just heard about it too, and I'm going to look at it. I'll kill the asshole that murdered him," he promised, a tear rolling down his cheek when I opened my eyes again and looked at his face.

I thought it impossible, but sadness and hatred wrinkled his expression. He couldn't hide them. The redness around his eyes was telling of his feelings, of what this whole thing was making him feel.

He didn't think such a day would ever come, and his words…

His assertion. Someone killed my father. I guessed that would explain why he hadn't come to visit me this whole time.

"Why? Why would someone ever kill him?"

"Faye..." He said, his thumb brushing one of my cheeks. "You don't need to care about the reason it happened. Just know that I'm going to find the asshole that did it, and I'm going to put an end to his life."

I looked at his face, finding it unbelievable that he was willing to do so much for me. Father had been a good friend of his, and also a mentor, but I still didn't think he cared so much. The more time passed, the more Artem showed me he was a different man.

Maybe I made a hasty and wrong assertion about his intentions and the goodness of his heart when the whole marriage thing was announced.

Time and time again he proved that he was the only man for me, the only one truly seeking my love...

I didn't have time to be thinking about those things now anyway, so I ignored them and said, "Just make sure it's going to hurt. And I wish to see my father now, too."

He looked to the side, exhaling. "I'm not sure anything good can come out of that. They didn't just murder Damien – they butchered him."

"I don't care. I need to see him now and I'm not going to take a no for an answer."

He settled his hands on my shoulders when I retreated.

"For you, Faye, I'd do anything. I just want you to know beforehand that whoever murdered him is a monster. Your father's face-"

"I've seen worse. I just want to make sure I'm going to see him one more time before he's buried. And I don't want to have to speak with any family members we might still have. I'm sure they'll all be here looking to steal his money."

"We've found his will, and he's leaving everything he has for you, but there's a condition."

I knew what it was before he even said it.

"You're going to have to marry me."

I didn't like father that much. Or I thought I didn't like him a lot, but now… Now I could feel how much I was already missing him. The touch of his hand as it held mine when I was a kid, his comforting words when mom died, and everything that he bought for me when I thought I didn't have anyone willing to pamper me that much.

I was going to miss his laughs, his smile, his voice, and his commanding presence every time he met someone important in his estate that I wasn't supposed to talk to for my own safety. Suffice to say that despite the forced marriage, he looked out for me.

I was way too pampered. Had I not been, I would have managed to escape to Canada without the O'Sullivan's help. I would have avoided their attempts at raping me too, and now I'd be living a life like no other in a better country.

I let him hold my hand as he took me to where the murder happened. Donna stayed behind. I'd invited her to come too, but I could see why she refused. This was a family matter. Artem was involved because my father had been a good friend of his.

They were never going on those hunting expeditions that they loved so much, nor were they going to do anything together from now on.

Looking at Artem's face again, I could tell that he thought of just one thing now – ending the life of the person or group that murdered my father. And I was there, right behind him on that.

If I could help him with anything, I would.

They didn't take father to a normal hospital. Members of the mafia had their public birth records erased, so to the eyes of the government and all the hospitals in the country, they didn't exist. Sending him to a normal hospital would have drawn undesired attention, and at this moment that was one of the many things Artem didn't want to let happen.

I was with him on that, too. I didn't want the police asking questions about his death. We were going to solve it on our own, without their or anyone's help.

Father had been laid down on a single bed. We were in this old building almost outside of town, where nobody would dare search for anything or get suspicious about. It was the kind of place most people ignored, and in here, despite the cracks in the walls and the flaking of their paint, I felt safe.

It was silent, like a cemetery. I was sure to attend his burial ceremony, but I couldn't help but admit that this already kind of looked like the beginning of that.

As doctors and nurses hurried out of the room, leaving me alone with Artem and my dead father, I sank to my knees. Tears rolled down my cheeks while I whimpered, my hand touching his body while I wished I could make everything different.

I wished I could have gotten to know him better before this happened. We'd never spent too much time together, with him leaving me to my babysitter while he headed off to make sure his mafia family was going to keep growing.

After everything that happened and he did, his family was still going down the drain now. His accomplishments thus far didn't matter anymore. He was dead and he didn't have anyone who he thought could run the family in his absence.

Not that I knew much about that as well, considering how often he kept me out of the loop.

All I knew now was that the killer needed to be found, and he needed to face the full force of my hatred for my father.

Despite the forced marriage, he was still family.

CHAPTER 11

I was kneeling by the bed. I knew that I couldn't remain here for much longer. The doctors and nurses hired for this – for the last preparations until his burial – already looked impatient, standing behind the doorway and pacing around in the other room.

A siren echoed in the distance, Artem kneeling behind me as he put a hand on a shoulder of mine.

"He meant a lot to me too," he said, his voice showing how much he cared and that he wished to make the asshole that killed him pay for it.

"I thought I didn't like him at all. He didn't come to visit me after you took me back to your estate."

"I know, but I'm sure it wasn't his fault. He didn't tell me this, but I think he was trying to run away from whoever had put a bounty in his head. He should have informed me about it, though. I don't know what I would have done, but I would have planned something to prevent it."

I exhaled, still feeling tears rolling down my cheeks.

"Thank you, Artem, for being here and comforting me," I said, breathing in again. "Do you think you could give me some time alone, to think?"

"Sure," he responded, standing up and proceeding to the doorway. "I'm going to close the door. Call me if you need anything, okay?"

I nodded, not saying anything.

Father did look terrible, like a leopard had been gnawing his face before they found him. I didn't know the details, but they'd told me he was hidden somewhere in the woods around the town and had been left to rot there.

I couldn't believe whoever had killed him did that. Who had so little heart as to do something so despicable and condemnable?

Father had his guards and everything he'd thought he was going to need to keep him safe, but even that didn't turn out to be enough. Whoever hit him, did so with full force, with the intention of not letting him escape.

Despite the pure gore that was his face, one of his eyes missing, half of his mouth not present, the side of his face being a hole now, I couldn't stop looking at him and wondering if I could have done something different…

I could have come up with a plan, anything. I could have been useful.

If only I hadn't fled Artem's hideout and headed off to Canada, perhaps all of this wouldn't be happening now.

I didn't want to admit this, but I was leaning closer and closer to the option of marrying Artem. He said that the wedding was going to happen and that I didn't have much in terms of options, but also that he was going to keep giving me enough time until my mind was okay with it.

It was all he could do, and now, with the death of my father, he was going to be even more hellbent on making me marry him.

And I was becoming more and more okay with making that happen. After all, he was the only man in this whole world that seemed to care about me. The only downside was the wedding that meant so much to him.

I was still going to be thinking about that for some time, though.

"I'm going to do the right thing, dad, and I'm going to avenge you," I said before standing up and proceeding to the door.

I glanced at the body of my father one last time before opening the door, nodding to the doctors, nurses, and other workers so that they could finish the last preparations for the burial, and then made a beeline to Artem.

He was smoking a cigarette when he turned around, eyes meeting mine.

"Oh, Faye. I'm so sorry for everything that happened, but I think some of my men already have some clues-"

I didn't let him finish his sentence, hugging him as I sank my head on his wide chest, feeling the smell of his cologne sneaking into my lungs. He didn't say anything for a while and didn't move his body, tossing his cigarette as soon as he understood the weight of everything that was happening here.

Time passed as he thought I wasn't going to say anything until I tilted my head up, meeting his grey and steely eyes.

"I want to marry you. I want to kill the son of a bitch that killed my father."

It took his mind some time to process my words, finally speaking them when he let a smile paint his chiseled face.

"I knew you were going to come around, Faye. I love you. I've loved you since you became a real woman, and your words now… They mean so much to me."

His hands settled on my cheeks as he leaned down, kissing me. I felt his plump and soft lips touching mine, comforting me in such a way that it washed away all the pain that my heart was feeling.

The kiss lasted for a good while until he broke it. I was still hugging him when he said, "They are going to bury him in his house. We're going to make sure nobody is going to show there and ruin it, so don't worry. He will get the ceremony he deserves."

"Thank you, Artem, for everything," I said before grabbing his hand and holding it in mine as we proceeded out of the old building. The burial was going to happen tomorrow only, and until then I was going to have more than enough time to think things through.

His hand provided me with warmth and a sense of safety I didn't think possible. He opened the door of the black limousine and then sat down with me in it, his soft smile showing that he was more than content with my decision to marry him.

He was overjoyed by it.

CHAPTER 12

rtem was in the burial, standing right beside me. He wore a suit with a black tie, showing how much this ceremony meant to him. To fulfill his promise, he'd ordered enough of his men to keep the place safe, and it was working. I couldn't even hear any sound of cars driving on the road in front of the estate, and there were so many of his men patrolling the perimeter that I couldn't look anywhere without noticing at least a couple of them.

His hand was still holding mine and he didn't intend to let go of it anytime soon. Despite being among his men, I could tell that he was tense, and that was one of the many things about him I wished to change.

Artem was the kind of man that exhaled confidence and safety to other people, but deep in his mind, he couldn't help but worry that something – anything was going to explode on his face. That's why his face looked taut now, tainted with the worry that a shootout was going to ensue soon.

They lowered father's body in the hole as I cried and whimpered. This was it. Artem was going to have to absorb his mafia family, which meant that the Garza was going to be no more. My last name was going to be replaced by his too as soon as the marriage took place.

His other hand held a crucifix. Despite all the killings and crimes he committed, Artem believed in God and thought that he'd been doing the right thing. To his eyes, he was destined for greatness and couldn't let anyone or anything stand in his way.

And now, I was hoping I was going to be a part of that.

Men dressed in dark garments grabbed their shovels and started to cover the casket with the same soil that was in his estate. His mansion was meant to be mine, but I didn't want it. His real family – not the one that he called his mafia – was here and they were all displeased with his choice of having gifted it to me, and even more annoyed that I was giving it to my future husband.

My future husband… These words rang right in my mind now, but I still remembered all the pain they were tormenting me with not too long ago.

As they finished throwing dirt on the casket, Artem took me away from there and back into the mansion, where he couldn't help but kiss me. I kissed him back too, even though I knew this moment wasn't appropriate.

I was trying not to think of what the rest of my family would think if they found me kissing my fiancé before we married. They were pretty religious, so they wouldn't have a good opinion of that.

It took some trying, but I ignored that worry too. What was the point of letting them ruin this moment I was sharing with him?

We'd said our last words to my now-dead father. It didn't matter how much I tried it, they all sounded so fake and terrible to my ears. I still said them, though, and now that I was out of there, I was kind of hoping I could go back and say them again, with better enthusiasm and more emotion.

"You want to head back home now?" He asked, brushing my cheek with his thumb.

"Yes, I'm tired of putting up with my family and pretending that we're still happy with each other and united. I don't like having to fake my feelings."

"You don't need to fake them to me," he said before pecking my lips.

He took me out of the estate, without bothering to inform my extended family I was leaving. They came here hungry, but there wasn't anything for them to predate. They were all going to have to leave empty-handed, with their tails tucked between their legs.

He opened the door of the limousine for me and sat down with me in the back of it, signaling for the driver to take us home with a quick movement of his fingers. After he pulled over by the front of his mansion, he held my hand as he took me to our bedroom.

It was like he could read my mind, sitting down with me on his bed as he looped an arm of his around my shoulders and allowed me to rest my head on his chest again. I broke down one more time, crying not just because of the death of my father, but also because of everything happening in my life.

I couldn't believe how much it changed in so little time. The wedding was going to happen soon, he was going to become my husband, turning me into the Queen of his mafia family.

Officially, that couldn't be made real, but he'd promised he would heed my words and listen to my advice. As time passed, I couldn't wait until the wedding was behind me, even though my heart ached for it now.

My father wasn't going to be in it, but there was no denying he would be proud to know that, in the end, I decided to marry the husband he'd chosen for me.

Artem offered me some tissues, and I dried off my tears. He stood up and said, "I'm going to give you some time to think things through. I think you deserve that, after everything that happened today."

I didn't say anything. Artem read my mind once more. He provided me with all the warmth and comfort I was seeking, and now he was giving me the quiet I needed to mold all the events that transpired so far in my life.

Time passed and now more than ever I felt ready for the marriage. And so, when I came out of the room that day, I said to him that we needed to start making the necessary preparations for it and the party that would come afterward.

He opened a wide smile that day and embraced me, spinning with me while everyone that worked for him watched us.

They also couldn't wrap their heads around the fact that so much changed between us.

CHAPTER 13

Artem opened the door, stepping into the room. He looked nothing short of incredible, the light of the moon sneaking into the room and showing off his muscles, allowing me to delight myself in them.

Gosh, what a man he was, and to think that now he was mine…

I drew in a short breath when he approached me and closed the door behind him with a kick. I wanted to say something but couldn't. My lips were sealed shut, my heart hammering in my chest and making me wonder how much longer it was going to take him to claim me, on his bed.

It was enormous, allowing me to feel so safe as I lied on it. The prospect of his hands studying the curves of my body, his fingers kneading my skin, and his lips saying sweet things to me made me distance myself from him a little.

Most of all, I was feeling afraid now. I had some experience with sex, but he was a different beast altogether. He was going to claim me now and there wasn't much if anything I could do to stop him, and I wasn't wishing to do that anyway.

I wasn't naked, but it wasn't going to take him too long to take off my clothes. I wore just a nightie and a pair of panties and a bra. He'd demanded that I wore the last two for tonight. I'd been thinking about letting him claim me the whole week and when I felt it was the right time, I said to him I wanted it.

He opened a smile, his teeth shining against the moonlight. The lack of noise in his estate was one of the many reasons that made me feel scared of what might happen here. He was on a whole different level and wasn't going to be gentle with me when he got things going here.

When it came the right time, he was going to claim me with all of his strength and might, showing that despite that initial attempt of mine to run away from here, he'd always been in control of my fate.

The heat of his body bathed me as soon as he climbed up on the bed, putting himself on top of me as I whimpered. His hand closed around my mouth as he asked me to remain quiet. Being quiet here was going to be difficult, though, considering how huge he was, both in terms of his body and what he was packing down there.

I didn't stare to steal a look at it. I didn't want to ruin the surprise.

Artem also didn't wear much. Or maybe I should be saying that he wore too much for this singular moment. My hands groped his body as I couldn't help but need more of him, letting out a moan when his arms closed around mine.

I affirmed that remaining quiet here was going to be difficult, and I meant it.

My lack of silence didn't bother him as he kissed me from my lips to my neck, stopping when his lips met the fabric of my nightie.

"Hmmm, can't have this in the way," he grumbled, biting it with his teeth and ripping it off me. I felt exposed and I couldn't believe that he just did that, right in front of my eyes, without showing a trace of care.

He didn't mind that and neither did I. The nightie was of the expensive kind for a middle-class family, but for him it cost almost nothing. He bought it for me, but I was the one that chose it.

His hands caressed the underside of my thighs, feeling the skin as if it was his own. It pretty much was, considering that soon the marriage was going to happen and my name was going to be replaced by his.

He pulled me to him, bending his body as he looked for my groin region. "This thing is annoying too," he complained, ripping off my pair of lacy panties with his teeth. If there was a proper way for men like him to display their strength to their targets, then that was the one.

I felt exposed to him and I didn't know for how much longer I was going to last. I wished to extend this moment forever or until it was the right time to come, but with the way he was pushing me over the edge now, I didn't think I was going to last much longer.

His smile was predatory as he realized that too.

His tongue slithered out, rubbing my clit with it. His hands groped every inch of mine, making me bend my back like it was made of rubber. I moaned when his lips parted and words came out of his mouth.

"You're the love of my life."

I couldn't retribute his kind words with words of my own, opting to allow his hands to massage me and then pinch one of my nipples. His fingers were so caring I doubted there was another man out there that was like him.

Artem was the only man in the whole world that could show a woman this much love in one night.

His breath was hot when he kissed me again. When I thought that he was going to give me some time to recompose myself and retribute some of the kindness he was overflowing me with, he peppered my lips with more and more of his delicious kisses.

"You're the love of my life, and I can't live without you," he murmured into my ear.

I gasped when his finger found my little clit. He rubbed it with vigor, not giving me a second to think about what was happening here. His cock was hard and I was wishing he would give me enough time to whip it out for him, but once again, he fueled his assault, going as far as kissing my folds.

He kissed them for what appeared to have been an eternity before sitting on the bed. Finally, he was going to give me some time to retribute all the kindness he was peppering me with. His gentleness was beyond measure, which was nothing short of impressive for a man like him.

Artem was used to being rough to men. I guessed that when he was in bed with a woman, he always showed a side of his that was different.

I bit my bottom lip when he licked my folds one more time. I wished to please him now and there was no way in hell that I was going to allow him to keep doing everything here.

I pushed him against the headboard, finally getting him in the position that I sought. I licked my lips before pulling his boxers down his legs. His dick bounced up and down as soon as I was rid of it.

His smile penetrated my mind when I sniffed his manliness. His perfume, the smell in the air hinted at his coldness when dealing with his enemies and his warmth when he needed to show his care to the people he loved the most, and I couldn't stop smelling it as it kept mesmerizing me.

I took hold of his dick, looping my fingers around it, feeling the pulsing of his veins. Artem froze for a little bit, as if in a trance as he thought that I shouldn't be allowed to be doing this to him. But little did he know that I was doing the thing that his mind was asking for the most, and soon he was going to mold his resolve to accommodate that.

I kissed the tip of his dick, teasing him for a little while. He closed his eyes and threw his head back, drops of sweat trickling down his warm and gleaming skin. He wondered for a moment if he should be controlling this moment too but he soon pushed the thought to the depths of his mind.

There was no controlling me now, and he knew that like he knew his vast-reaching connections in Washington DC. And remembering that now, I couldn't help but think it was kind of disappointing that I ended up not following through with my plans to use that information to ruin his life.

I guessed I wasn't going to need to do that after all…

I took the plunge, wrapping my lips around his cockhead. There was something entrancing and lovable about the way he wasn't moving now, giving me all the power and control I needed to dictate the pace of this.

I added more of his inches down my throat, my eyes still closed. There was nothing quite like the feeling of his dick in my mouth, and the longer this went on, the longer I wondered when he was going to pepper my mouth with his load.

I needed that so much, his sticky load traveling down my mouth and throat, gracing me with his taste. Just the thought of him doing that was enough to make me feel like pushing him over the edge right at this moment, coercing him to orgasm without him wanting to do that.

I knew he was thinking about doing that, about showing me what he was hiding in his balls.

He was religious, but not that much, and this moment meant so much to him. He knew he could have waited until after the marriage, but he couldn't resist the temptation of claiming me before.

I kept bobbing up and down on his length for a good while until I felt his dick twitching. I couldn't let him shoot his load quite yet, so I bit the tip of his cockhead gently. It wasn't enough to hurt him, but it was sufficient to make him stop what he was doing.

And just when I was going to straddle him and lower myself on his shaft, he took hold of my hips, positioning me on top of him as if he was reading my mind. I groaned when I felt the tip of his dick coming in, and then cried out in pleasure when the rest invaded me with his thickness.

I was giving myself fully to him, and there was no better proof of that than allowing him to impale me with his might without first asking him if he was going to put a condom or not, if he was clean, or even if he was going to want to know if I was on the pill or not.

I guessed that nothing of that mattered at this moment, his hands pushing me up and then allowing me to travel down on his nine-inches meaty rod.

I bobbed up and down on him for a good while, until I felt his load coming out. He pumped it inside me in hot, creamy jets, with some of it escaping through my connection with him.

I couldn't lose any other drop of his milk. My walls squeezed tight around his hardness, and I wasn't letting go of it until he was finished stuffing me with his sperm. And even after that, I didn't know if I would feel good letting go of him.

Time passed, his breathing meeting the pace of mine. When I felt his shaft losing its strength and softening up, I nestled up under his arm, bathing myself in the comfort that only he could present me with.

"I can't live without you, Faye, and I'm going to make the marriage so special you'll never forget it."

Once again, I didn't say anything, just letting his words feel me with joy, love, and the proof of his care for me.

I could only hear the chirping of the crickets outside. It was like we were the last couple in the world.

I couldn't wait until he was putting the ring on my wedding finger.

CHAPTER 14

I stood with him on the altar, his presence showing how everyone inside the church sucked up to him. His gaze on them was certain, measured, and controlled. They were all smiling and showing that they were happy with the marriage, but I knew that the truth was anything but.

They were just happy that all the other women in the world were not going to be able to seek him anymore.

His gaze shifted to me, showing me his love. "I love you, Faye. This is the best moment of my life. I want you to know that," he said all of sudden, even while the father, the man that was leading the wedding, was reciting the words in his thick and old book.

The wedding music… it was still ringing in my ears, and I could still feel the hand of the man that took me here. He wasn't my father, though he looked the part. They all knew about his death, with some of them shedding fake tears for him.

Despite the horribleness that followed his passing, I couldn't stop smiling now. There was nothing quite like marrying the man of my life, and he was showing me that. I could feel the love he kept in his heart bathing me with it, and the fuzzy feeling that accompanied it was nothing short of… Well, it was almost hard to describe it.

"I love you too, Artem, and you were right when you said I wasn't going to forget this wedding. It's like a dream of mine coming true."

One of my dreams when I was little and during my teenage

years was marrying a man that I could call mine. I was glad that I could do that now. Despite all the dangers that were going to come after the wedding, one truth was going to remain strong and unchanged – Artem was going to be my husband and nothing and no one would ever change that.

His index finger brushed against the box that he was holding in his other hand. The box where he kept the ring stored, and with which he was going to seal our lives together. I couldn't wait for that to happen, feeling the softness of his skin brushing against mine, his care more than evident…

When the father that was leading the wedding finished his words, his hand that was holding the box opened it, holding it out in front of him. An urge to cover my mouth shot up to my mind, but I kept it in check.

No point in showing the people at the wedding that it surprised me. I wasn't. It was just that everything that was happening here, every little detail was exactly like I thought it was going to be.

His hand finished opening the box and then fished out of it the ring that he was going to gift me. It was beautiful, with small diamonds that rounded the whole frame, shining off the light of the sun coming in through the windows.

Birds chirped outside the church, adding to the coziness and perfection of this place, this atmosphere, and the love that he was showing only he had for me.

Artem slid the ring on my finger, his digital brushing against my skin for a fraction of a second before he dropped his hand. I was also holding a box in my hand now, hiding the other ring that he'd bought for this wedding.

I opened it, my eyes glancing down at the ring for a fraction of a second before proceeding to admire him once more. It didn't matter what happened here, how much time passed, that there were still going to be other women looking to steal him from me – I was forever going to be his.

He showed me his hand, allowing me to slide the ring on his finger, feeling the softness of his skin once more. His grey and steely eyes couldn't hide the love that he had within his heart for me, assuring that there was much more that was going to happen as soon as the wedding ended.

There was still going to be the party, and before that, sipping wine and gossiping about the wedding guests inside his glamorous limousine.

I was almost thinking it wasn't going to happen, that someone was going to come barging in through the entrance to say that this marriage couldn't go on, but then the priest said something about kissing him.

It went over my head, his words coming in through one year and then leaving through the other, but I pulled him to me anyway. I settled one hand on his waist, guiding him to me for a kiss that he was never going to forget.

Having put the rings on our wedding fingers, we could finally kiss each other. His lips self so soft and smooth as I kissed them, and for a moment the urge to use my tongue assaulted me. I only didn't do it because I didn't want the guests inside the church to feel disgusted.

Despite how comfortable and at home I felt here, I didn't want the invitees to have more topics to gossip about as soon as the marriage ended.

Everyone erupted into a series of claps, giving me their congratulations as I sealed my life with his. From now on, there was no escaping his life and spending the rest of my life with him. The concept of divorce was alien and distant to me, as if it was something that would never, ever happen.

And I was pretty sure that he thought the same and would never allow it to happen.

He broke the kiss slowly, his eyes burning me with his intensity, the grey that colored his pupils bathing me with more of his love. For a moment, I felt frozen, incapable of moving as I let his hand continue to rest on the left side of my waist.

"You're looking so beautiful right now, Faye. You're my Queen," he said.

I felt as if there was no more crowd watching us, that we were the only ones inside the church. His extended family was here and I was sure they were looking at this with curious eyes, already wondering when I was going to step outside and throw the bouquet over my head.

That was going to happen soon. They didn't need to worry about it.

I breathed in, taking in the smell of his manly perfume, and couldn't help but say something that corroborated his words.

"I am fully yours now, Artem, and I'm giving myself fully to you."

He smiled, just confirming my words as if he'd been thinking this whole time they were going to come out and were going to corroborate his feelings. His fingers kneaded my skin through the fabric of the dress, teasing me on what he was going to do with me as soon as we were inside his mansion again, with no one to keep us company and bother us, like here inside this church.

His eyes still froze me in place and I didn't know for how much longer his stare was going to last. I wished he could make it last forever, not giving a damn about the guests inside the church and what they were thinking about us now.

I knew what they were thinking, that we were the most unusual couple in the world. How many white Russian men married black Americans like me these years? I couldn't imagine there were many.

Our love was unique in so many ways.

"Well, I guess it's time to acknowledge everyone in here. Wouldn't want to make them feel that we don't like them much."

I giggled softly, still unaware of all the eyes watching us now. They didn't matter one bit. The only thing that was of importance to me now was ending this marriage in style, inside his car, in the sunroof of his limousine while I waved to everyone and showed them that the man of my life was mine now.

I could still imagine the look of disappointment and jealousy on the faces of so many of those women, who all still thought they had a chance with him and that he wasn't happy with me now.

"You're right. No point in delaying that for much longer," I said, keeping my voice low so that the microphones wouldn't pick it up and inform the guests inside the chamber of this baroque church that we were making fun of them.

We turned around, with Artem proceeding to the microphone in front of the altar. The priest cleared his throat and excused himself before proceeding to stand far away from him, as if he knew he would be in deep trouble if he did something that displeased the head of this Russian family.

He cleared his throat, adjusting the microphone before he spoke to everyone. I paid close attention to each of his words as he made his speech look like something straight out of an action movie, right before the moment when the hero was supposed to face a suicide mission.

Everyone stood impressed and mesmerized by his words, as if they couldn't believe there was a man with such a deep and commanding voice speaking to them. His sentences echoed his plans for the future, how much he cared about and loved me, and that he was going to do everything in his power to make our wedded life ever-lasting.

When he finished his speech, I took his place, adjusting the phone as well when a cloud of fear took control of my heart. I wasn't great at speaking in public. During college and high school, I avoided being put in this kind of position like the devil runs away from the cross. And yet, this was a different moment now.

One where I needed to show to everyone that I was better than before and more than determined to do the right thing from now on, including choosing the right words that echoed my uncontrollable thoughts.

And I did that, standing before so many people while quenching the fear in my heart that I was making a fool of myself. I wasn't and there was nothing else I'd rather be doing now.

Everyone inside the chamber of this church kept their attention locked to me. It was almost as if they thought that missing one word – just one – would be enough to rile the hatred that Artem kept locked behind various doors in his mind.

I smiled when I ended my speech, everyone bursting into a round of applause that lasted minutes. The wedding went on for a good while, with me and everyone greeting the others.

We headed to the front of the church, where Artem's huge and luxurious limousine waited for us. But before that, there was something that I needed to do, and given the relevance of this wedding, it couldn't be postponed or skipped.

Throwing the bouquet that I was holding in my hand.

It was beautiful, with all kinds of flowers in it, including roses, long-stemmed orchids, and calla lilies that stole the attention of the eyes of all the women in the church. It was a cascade bouquet that looked like a "waterfall" of flowers that draped down the front of my wedding dress.

Every woman in the wedding positioned themselves behind me before I threw the bouquet over my head, hoping that the right woman was going to grab it mid-air – the right one as in 'the one that was going to find the love of her life too, just like I'd found mine. I didn't know who managed to grab it as the sight of Artem standing by the open door of his black limousine caught my attention.

I bolted to him, eager to drive in circles in this neighborhood and the whole town to make sure that everyone was going to know that I married him.

My future looked so bright I couldn't look at it without feeling like I'd get blind.

CHAPTER 15

Artem popped open a bottle of red champagne, letting the bubbling liquid gush out in a long, hot jet over our heads and the limousine. His smile was a radiant one as he kept holding the bottle, shouting how much he loved me to everyone that could hear him, even the ones that wished to be spending this sunny morning sleeping on their beds.

He offered me the mouth of the champagne bottle, and I couldn't help but loop my fingers around the neck of it and tip it over. The liquid that came flowing down my throat warmed up my insides. I felt like I could make this marriage last forever now.

The limousine took a soft turn as it entered another road, proceeding to downtown Lost Hope. Black sedans followed it, from behind and the front of it, making sure that the wedded couple that was us was safe from everything and anyone that might try to harm us.

Artem and my now deceased father had many enemies, and at least one of them was Sean O'Sullivan, who had to have managed to escape the assault on his estate. I hadn't seen him when Artem met me in his maze, and I didn't think I was ever going to meet him again.

The culprit behind the death of my father was still at large and we didn't know if and when we were going to find him. But hunting him down and finding his location was paramount. Day and night Artem and his soldiers sought him in all kinds of places in Lost Hope and also in Canada. Though I couldn't be sure of this, I was thinking it wouldn't be long now until he was begging for my forgiveness, even though there could never be any for a man that took my father away from me.

I hugged him as his arms looped around me, pushing me to him as his lips looked for mine. The smell and the taste of the champagne, of strawberry mixed with coke, overflowed my senses until I felt like I couldn't resist them for much longer.

His eyes noticed that, feeding me his love once more when his hand settled on my cheek and brushed against it. Time stilled for another moment, with most of all the people that had been inside the chamber of the church now following us.

They were inside their black sedans too, some of them shouting and laughing and talking while standing in the sunroofs. I glanced around the neighborhood, cherishing the view of the buildings, the perfect houses, and how living here might be good for someone like me seeking more peace.

Our lips sealed together one more time, his warmth joining in with the warmth coming from the morning sun. The petals of the Spring flowers flew around us, some of them touching my nose and annoying me a little, but it was okay.

I was so in love with everything that was happening that there was nothing that could bother me now.

His arm, now wrapped around my lower waist, was all I needed to continue feeling safe. I was certain there was nothing and no one in the whole world capable of stealing this man from me.

Nothing and no one.

A gunshot cut through the glee of the morning, his body losing strength all of sudden and falling on me. "Artem? Love? What is happening?" I asked, but it was too late for his mind to make sense of my words.

His eyelids dropped, closing his eyes in front of me as life was sniffed out of them. My blood froze all of sudden, a waterfall of worries and thoughts overflowing my mind.

A gunshot.

Someone had shot my husband while he was still commemorating his marriage with me, as if all the security and safety checks were worthless. They'd speared through it like it was nothing, and now they were showing me they could hurt me even in the best moment of my life.

The best moment of my life that was now turning into a nightmare I couldn't escape from.

His body felt heavy in my arms as I felt forced to drop back down into the backseat of the limousine. I didn't know what was going on, a cascade of gunshots following the one that started this mayhem.

Screams and shouts filled the atmosphere, the limousine we were in swerving as the driver tried to blast it through the black sedans that were supposed to be keeping us safe.

And yet, the armed men inside said vehicles that were sporting their assault rifles and submachine guns not too long ago were now dropping like flies, with so many of the shots striking said targets.

They were getting overwhelmed by snipers from all over the houses and small buildings of this neighborhood, with some of them even positioned in the canopies of the large maple trees.

They'd been planning this attack for a long time, and now they were finally reaping the benefits.

Everything seemed to have been planned for months, as if there had been someone on the inside informing them of my wedding, and that it was going to happen here and today.

I couldn't help but worry about Artem, whose body kept losing its strength by the second. I ran my hand over his face, patted his cheeks, trying to wake him up, but he wouldn't even open his eyes.

My eyes snapped down to the blood soaking through his suit. A pang of pain shot through my heart and I didn't know if he was going to make it or not. Blood was now seeping out through the corners of his mouth, showing me that the shot had cut in deep enough to pierce his stomach and the rest of his digestive system.

I screamed, "Someone, please help him! Artem is dying!"

There were men with assault rifles in the back of the limousine and some of them were trying to do what they could to save Artem, but there was just one place that was going to be able to keep him from dying, and that was that same building they'd taken me when my dad died.

One of the guards inside the limousine fished his phone out as he made one of the most important calls of his life. He was calling the same doctors and nurses from when I visited my deceased father on his deathbed. He was even shouting stuff in Russian, cussing like his life depended on getting this right and making sure that all those people were going to be there already waiting for our arrival.

And yet, the first order of the day was getting rid of the dark green sedans that were chasing us. They sniffed blood and they wanted to make sure that the head of the Yuriev family was going to die here and now.

Dark green sedans… A thought shot through my mind all of a sudden as more and more gunshots peppered the limousine. They were all striking the frame of the car, but it was thick and solid enough to keep us safe.

It wasn't going to be long until all these assailants were surrounding us, if we didn't build a good plan as soon as possible. The fact that this was happening was telling, though. There had to be a snitch somewhere in his mafia family, and he needed to be found and murdered.

And before that, also tortured. I couldn't allow him to come out of this unscathed, as if he hadn't just made the worst mistake of his life. 'He' could also be a woman, but I wasn't going to concern myself with such details now when time was of the essence.

It didn't take too long for the driver to blast through all the dark green sedans still chasing us, the men inside the limousine killing some of them in the process. Each attacker that died was like music to my ears.

I was still holding Artem in my arms, sitting in the seat of the limousine while my other hand clutched the safety belt as hard as I could. The driver was blasting the limousine forward as best as he could, but he was still having to dodge too many cars whose owners didn't know anything of what was going on here.

All they knew was that they needed to get out of the way, even if doing so was easier said than done.

"Love, you're going to be fine. They are going to lose the assholes that are chasing us and we are going to get there safe and sound. I trust these men with my life, and yours too," I said, happy that his chest was still moving.

He was still breathing.

I pressed my hand to the side of his neck slightly and a breath of relief escaped my lungs. His heart was still beating, which could mean that the gunshot hadn't hit an organ of his that, without it, his death would be certain.

One gunshot hit the back glass of the limousine, making me whimper and duck my head. Another cloud of air escaped through my nostrils when time passed and no more gunshots cut through the silence of this morning, the tires of this imperial vehicle still devouring the road until we managed to get there.

I couldn't wait until we found our heaven in the form of that building – or was it a house? I couldn't remember such a frivolous detail now – where all of the best nurses and doctors were going to be.

They were the only ones that could save Artem from certain death.

My heart was hammering against my ribcage when one of the guards, the one sitting right beside me, checked his pulse. Calmness glimmered in his eyes when he managed to feel the beating of Artem's heart.

Artem was tough. He wasn't going to die just because someone managed to land a shot on him. He was going to pull through and come out of this much stronger than ever before. I was so sure of that I could already envision him popping out one of his many handguns and killing the traitor that was still at large.

The driver pulled over, my hands shaking when they took the love of my life from me. But they were only carrying him over to the small house where nobody would guess was owned by one of the most important mafia families in the world – and this one was even capable of influencing national elections.

They kicked open the door, took him into the living room of the small house, and then ushered me inside as their mouths shouted for me to hurry up. And hurry over to where they were going to keep my beloved I did, my mind already getting ready for the hours of operation they were going to be subjecting themselves to.

I didn't know how long it was going to take, and I couldn't help but worry that something vile was going to happen while he was still incapacitated. One of the O'Sullivan could show up here, find this place and call his friends.

Perhaps they all already knew about it and were heading here anyhow, ready to blow it up with an RPG and obliterate the last remnants of Artem's life.

I was biting my nails when they shut the door to the room they were keeping him in, one of them grabbing my arms as he murmured hurryingly, "He's going to be alright and safe. We're patrolling the perimeter. If anything-"

I slapped his face. "How could you be telling me that now? Do you realize that he almost died?"

He opened his mouth, thought about arguing back, but then thought better about it.

And that's when I realized that the hours ahead were going to be arduous and tiresome.

Without Artem, his mafia family was like a fish out of water.

CHAPTER 16

The heart monitoring machine beeped. It was one of the many things telling me he was still alive and that he was going to come out of this much stronger than when he was before. The doctors said that he was going to be okay, but I didn't trust them that much.

The only thing that I fully trusted now was the warmth of his hand.

I was holding it, keeping my eyes closed for as long as I could until every time I had to blink. I felt as if not looking at him for a fraction of a second would be enough for something terrible to happen to him, like him getting shot.

One of the doctors, and he was a nice guy with grey hair, had assured me that Artem was going to pull through. He didn't mention any percentages or anything of the sort, just that he was going to be jumping around and making plans to avenge the attempt on his life in a matter of hours.

I trusted him, though the hours were passing and I still didn't see any change in Artem. His controlled and measured breathing was the only thing telling me that that doctor didn't lie to me to make me feel better.

His mafia soldiers patrolled the perimeter of the building, with most of them keeping their heavier guns hidden from prying eyes. Most of the people that lived in this poor and decaying neighborhood didn't care if there were more shady men hanging out here.

To them, what did it matter what we were planning or doing here? Forgotten by the government and the rest of society, they couldn't care less that criminals hanged out here sometimes.

And that's without mentioning that the Yuriev had more than enough money to keep their mouths shut. They weren't going to rat us out, even though they could. What's more, I guessed that the traitor ended up getting found and killed during our escape.

I still had to ask Artem's soldiers what they knew about that, but so far I could tell that I wasn't mistaken about that assertion of mine. The rat had already been dealt with. One other reason why I knew that was true was that everything was quiet and calm here, as if they hadn't just had a shootout with the O'Sullivan.

The O'Sullivan… Could it be that Sean was alive? I didn't want to think he might be, but also… I couldn't hide that the attack had too many ramifications, and I didn't know how far they extended to.

His hand stirred, eyes opening slowly, as if he was dreaming about something that he'd been wishing to make real for a long time now and didn't want to face the crushing truth of the reality around him.

His eyes meeting mine sent a barrage of shockwaves through my body, my heart beating like a steam machine. I couldn't believe that he was waking up so soon. I believed the doctor when he'd said that it was going to take his body a while to adjust, and this whole time I'd been thinking that I was still far from meeting the warmth of his eyes.

But he was sitting up on his bed now, looking around as he tried to spot anything that might be dangerous, that might lead to another shootout.

He was all tubed up, with smaller tubes going into his nostrils to pump air into his lungs. I worried for a moment that something was going to happen with the machine, like it would go haywire all of sudden and show me that he was going to die.

But he looked alright, his breathing normal, everything else about him looking ordinary to my eyes. I stood up from the chair I was sitting on in a wink and was planning on heading out to tell the doctors and the nurses that he was awake, but his hand grabbed mine all of a sudden.

He didn't speak, his eyes locking with mine. Even though he was choosing not to pronounce a single word now, he was telling me so much about his feelings for me with his stare alone, and what all of this meant to him.

"I missed you, Faye," he said all of sudden, his voice a little throaty, but still with that same commanding tone that only he had. I'd spent a considerable amount of time with his guards and they all sounded less manly than him, as if their subconscious knew that they were below him and that it didn't matter what they did – that fact was always going to remain unchanged.

For a moment, I didn't know what to tell him. His first words were that he missed me, even though he'd been sleeping this whole time and was probably dreaming about things he'd rather not speak about now.

I knew he loved me, and I loved him too, but still… I thought he was going to ask me about who had tried to murder him first.

"What? Cat got your tongue?" He asked, quirking up a corner of his lips.

And there was the playful and cheerful side of his I hadn't seen until I started to warm up to him. His words were enough to un-freeze me as I sat back down, sealing my lips with his for a kiss that should have lasted only some seconds, but ended up con-suming minutes.

"I thought you were going to die," I said, sitting down as relief washed over me. He wasn't going to die. He was alive and he was going to jump off this small and single bed with just one intent in his mind – that of killing the man that had set him up.

"For a moment, I thought that too, but luckily," he said, brush-ing his thumb on the tip of my nose, "I've got someone looking out for me, and I couldn't have asked for a better bodyguard."

"It was nothing," I said, blushing. "I didn't do most of the heavy lifting. Your men helped out too."

"Talking about them, I wonder what happened to the snitch. Someone must have tipped off the O'Sullivan about the wedding and given them instructions on how to open a hole in our defenses."

"I didn't talk to them, but I think they already got him. Otherwise, I don't think we would be having this talk now," I said, leaning in and feeling that temptation again to kiss him.

It felt so right to do that, but there was something else in his eyes – something that was keeping him from immersing himself in this moment and allowing me to soothe his mind.

His eyes looked distant, maybe too focused on the matter of hunting down the last of the O'Sullivan and figuring out how they managed to come back so quickly. The hit on their estate was supposed to have killed most of them and yet they were already back, hunting his men and doing God knew what else.

I didn't feel safe here and neither did he.

He tossed his thin blanket to one side, put his feet on the floor, and tried to get off the bed, but his hand went to the right side of his torso almost at the same moment, his face grimacing.

Pain shot through his body as he cussed and wished he was already feeling much better. I was happy that he wasn't in a coma anymore. When someone is put in that condition, it's difficult to come out, if not impossible, for some cases.

He sat back down on the bed when I scooted over to him, supporting him by helping him put his right arm over my shoulders. He exhaled as he realized that it was going to take him some time to get back to his one hundred percent.

"Fucking hell, I didn't think one gunshot was going to incapacitate me like this," he grumbled, looking outside through the boarded-up window, realizing that he was going to need more patience to get through this.

"You need to rest up some more, love. If not for me, then you need to do it for your family. They are going to love to know that you're alive and kicking."

"I know. I just thought… Sean O'Sullivan. That motherfucker is going to pay with his life after what he did. Ruining our own marriage. I mean, just look at you. You're still wearing your marriage dress, and it looks dirty as fuck. I'm sorry you're having to be facing this kind of shit. You don't deserve it."

I hadn't cared enough about it to put something else on – not that I thought that any of his men patrolling the perimeter of our new hiding place would have gone out to hunt for a shirt and a pair of pants for me to put on anyway.

And even if I'd thought about that before, I would have just ignored it. I was far too worried about Artem making it through his coma, and I couldn't allow such a frivolous thing like this wedding dress and what state it was in worry me.

His hand brushed my knuckles when he opened a smile, kissing me as he pulled me to sit with him on the bed. He pulled me further until I was sitting on his lap, but grimaced a little when another line of pain soared through his body.

Despite that, he could tolerate the pain like no other man in the world could. His love for me bore no limits, and he would do anything to make me feel better, even if only a little.

"When do you think you're going to tell your men and the doctors that they don't need to worry if you're going to die?" I asked, hoping that he was going to take his time with that.

There was no point in setting up plans for his revenge now. He could wait until the time was right, until his body was better and healed.

"Soon, pretty soon. No point in worrying about that now, don't you think?"

The walls of this room were thick enough to keep most sounds contained within. That was not to say that one of the doctors wouldn't come rushing in to check up on him any time soon, though. I was aware that soon one of them was going to, but for now I had all the time in the world to love him some more.

I wouldn't say that my times alone with him were rare or anything like that, but they were not as frequent as I was hoping they were going to be back when I decided to live the rest of my life with him.

"I'm going to smile when Sean is killed. That son of a bitch tried to rape me when I was in his estate."

"You made a mistake by going there. You should have stayed with me. I was the only person that truly cared about you then, and I still am," he affirmed, pecking my lips once before pulling me to him.

I hugged him gently, closing my eyes and allowing the beating of his heart to put me to sleep. It didn't take too long for darkness to encroach my mind, falling into the world of dreams one more time.

And this time, it felt different.

I'd feared that I would never share another night with him.

CHAPTER 17

Artem came back stronger than ever from his wounds, getting off the bed and stepping through the door with a big smile on his face. His men turned their heads to him as the corners of their lips quirked up, finding it impossible that he pulled through so quickly. I shared their sentiment. We'd all assumed that it was going to take him much longer to come out of his coma.

That he did come out in a matter of hours didn't only speak to the absurd amount of luck he had, but also the resilience of his body.

He stood in front of the doorway to the bedroom he was in, looking imperious as he widened his smile even more. Artem was the kind of silent and serious mafia boss, but him having just come out of certain death meant a lot to him.

It fired him up like nothing before did. His objective was just one now. He was going to kill that motherfucker called Sean O'Sullivan. I'd thought that he was a good man willing to help me live in Canada. I'd been so stupid back then.

That I'd come from putting myself under his care and then developed a deep hatred for him like I now had was the kind of change I'd never thought I'd be going through.

The gleam in the eyes of his men was telling. They were all famished for the chance to take the fight back to the O'Sullivan. In truth, they didn't need to worry about them much, though. The old Irish gang was far too crippled to pull off another attack on them.

They were just being cautious was all.

"We're going to kill them. We're going to obliterate each and every one of them, and there's nothing and no one capable of stopping us," he announced, throwing his arms over his head to make his point clearer.

There were some of his men patrolling the perimeter of the house that still didn't even know he was awake and alive, but it was nothing more than a meaningless and unimportant detail.

Word was going to spread and Sean O'Sullivan was going to find out that it was going to take a lot more to kill the head of the Yuriev family.

I grabbed his hand when he dropped his arms, squeezing it. For me, there was nothing more important now than cementing my position as the Queen of his mafia family. No one was going to be calling me that, but the title people came to use for me didn't matter one bit and so I didn't think about it much.

What I was thinking about was how we were going to find Sean. He'd been in hiding this whole time, preparing guerilla attacks against the Yuriev – I couldn't be one hundred percent about that, but I was still pretty sure that was their plan. When they thought they were ready for another skirmish, they were going to show up and cause more havoc, but for now they were going to keep doing the only thing they were good at.

Finding another hiding place somewhere in Lost Hope's underworld.

Still holding my hand, he took me to his limousine. The holes in the frame and the windows of it didn't bother him as he ordered the driver to take him to his estate. There was no need to hide any longer, and now all he needed to do was to pick up the pieces left by Sean in order to find him.

It shouldn't be too hard, for someone like Artem Yuriev.

When the driver turned at the intersection and took another road, he said, "And we're going to have to get you new clothes. Can't have you walking around with garments that don't fit the

Queen you are."

I chuckled, the driver not paying any attention to our conversation. A couple of black sedans followed us from behind, with some also leading us to our destination. They were being more careful this time, and I could see that in the way their eyes surveyed every road we took, examining all the buildings and houses.

It was still dark and silent. The silence was unnerving, but with a man like Artem sitting beside me, holding a small handgun in his hand, I knew that there was nothing and no one capable of hurting him or me.

It happened once and it wasn't going to happen again. Sean O'Sullivan had thought that he could deliver the killing blow on Artem during the wedding, but his plans failed.

It didn't take us too long to reach the estate and just as I'd thought, nobody tried anything against us. Even the police didn't try to stop us to check out what was going on with all these black cars heading in the same direction.

Artem's men paid them well to keep their mouths shut and to worry about other criminals. The Yuriev were far too big for them to deal with. The only way to take them down would be by having inside information on them.

The only person capable of bringing them down was me, and I wasn't going to do that anymore.

The car pulled over in front of his mansion, butlers rushing in to ask him if he was feeling alright or not, if he thought he needed some time to rest up and how they could help him further.

Artem brushed them off, saying that right now he needed time to think and to spend the rest of the night with the only person that mattered to him now – me.

He pushed through the ocean of butlers, their eyes soon realizing that there was nothing for them to do now. They needed to focus on their jobs and less on him.

Artem closed the door behind him, opting to undo his red tie and toss it behind him. "Goddamn, how this thing's been annoying me this whole time since coming out of that shithole."

He chuckled and I chuckled with him, soon turning that into uncontrollable laughter. Tension poured out of our shoulders as he took off the coat of his suit. It was a new one. One of his men had brought it to the house where we were hiding, already foreseeing that he was always going to come out of his coma as a much stronger leader.

I sat on his bed, putting my index finger on my lips, pressing against them a little. "You look stunning, especially after everything that happened."

I needed this moment, the crickets chirping outside his mansion, the need in my heart for him growing by the second. His body still looked so imperious, as if he hadn't been shot not too long ago.

He flashed a smile, saying, "You're tempting me now and making me think I'm doing the wrong thing."

"You're never making the wrong choice when you're spending some quality time with me," I teased when he took off his white office shirt, tossing it into the large wood basket that he kept for used and dirty clothes.

I needed him now, kissing me and devouring me with his lips.

His chest was now fully exposed. The light of the moon snuck through the blinds and the windows, showing me just enough of his body without making it too obscene. I was hoping he was going to take off all of his clothes at once, but I could tell that he was wishing to take his time.

He climbed the bed, putting himself right on top of me, making me feel small. His hands found all the right spots as he kneaded my curves. "Oh, so much to grab onto," he purred, not hiding the lust that he felt for me now.

And he shouldn't be trying to do that. There was no shame in having fallen in love with me.

"This is our wedding night, the one that we deserve," I murmured into his ear, realizing that I'd been thinking about what this moment was going to be like for a good span of my life.

I'd always been thinking about marrying the right man and then having an unforgettable wedding night with him, and yet I'd never thought that it was going to be like this.

I'd never presumed that I would, one day, marry a man like him. A Russian billionaire with more money than he could ever need, and with men willing to follow him to hell if need be.

I felt my ovaries on the verge of exploding when his hand pushed up the skirt of my dress, exposing my thighs for the delight of his eyes. "Oh, someone is a little too excited for her own good," he joked with a sexy tone, kissing my legs and then proceeding to my knees.

When I thought that he was going to kiss my thighs too, he stopped. Dammit. I hated every time he did that. He always tempted me before doing what would push me over the edge.

"I'm going to make you wait," he teased, ripping off my dirty and smelly pair of panties as if the resistance of the fabric didn't mean anything to him, as if this was the moment he'd waiting for his whole life and was finally going to claim me now the only way he knew how.

"Asshole," I moaned, his tongue licking and brushing against my clit. To Artem, there was nothing that was going to make him stop now, and the longer this went on, the closer he was to taking me over the edge, when I would have no choice but to come while he impaled me.

"Now now, there's no need to be using those kinds of words," he advised but did nothing more than flash a smile on his stubbly face.

I brushed the palm of my hand across his beard, trying to push him off me. I needed some time to breathe and think a little about what was happening now, but he was having none of that.

"You're mine now and if you think you can pause this for a mere second, then think again. It's not going to stop. I'm going to keep worshipping you until you're coming and squirming underneath me."

Well, the squirming part was already happening. There was still the coming for him bit, but I was sure that wasn't going to take much longer to happen. As he kept kneading and groping my skin, he was showing how relentless he was.

It didn't take him too long then to take off his pants, whipping out his cock. It was massive, making me wonder how he was going to fit it inside me again. I couldn't believe that he was going to be doing this a second time with me.

Penetrating me with all of his might, and then pounding me over and over again until he was coming at the same time with me.

I moaned and groaned when he pushed it in. I didn't think he was going to fit, but he still found enough space. His eyes locked with mine for a moment, already asking me if I was okay with the direction this was taking.

And I couldn't help but nod.

It was all he needed, moving in and out of me, slow at the beginning but soon picking up the pace. I cried and closed my eyes as I focused only on the pain and pleasure that he was making me feel.

His shaft was thick and long, hitting the back of my tunnel every time he thrust in. When I thought he was going to come, cock twitching, he winked before increasing the speed of his thrusting to levels I never thought possible before.

His sperm came gushing out, coating the walls of my tunnel. I came too, my body squirming and fighting against his when I realized that I could get pregnant from this.

His body plopped down on the bed beside me, pulling me to him as he kissed me.

The kiss was supposed to have lasted nothing more than a couple of seconds, but it lived on for minutes until he closed his eyes one more time and fell asleep.

I fell asleep too, certain that everything was going to be perfect from now on.

Sean O'Sullivan didn't matter anymore. He was soon going to die by my hands.

CHAPTER 18

He closed the door on me. The bastard did that without showing any emotion on his face, as if him doing that didn't matter anything at all.

It mattered. A bit too much, but it mattered. I didn't think he would just have the courage to go out like that with all of his men following him from behind.

He said that he'd found Sean O'Sullivan and that he was going to put an end to all the shootouts and skirmishes they'd been having since the wedding attack.

My heart was beating in my chest like a galloping horse. I couldn't just allow Artem to put himself in danger like this.

It was obscene.

It wasn't like the man I knew at all, and there was a bad feeling creeping up to my heart. A feeling that was trying to tell me he wasn't going to come out of that alive.

The last plan of his life he was putting into practice.

I couldn't allow him to just put himself in danger like that. Something needed to be done, and it seems I was the only one willing to sacrifice herself to tell him that he was making the wrong choice.

He didn't need to go with his soldiers to kill that bastard that tried to take advantage of me. He needed to remain right here with me in his estate, sipping from a glass of wine while saying comforting words into my ears.

Was that too much to ask?

I didn't think it was, so I rushed ahead and threw the door open. One of his men tried to grab my arm and stop me, but I couldn't allow him to do that. I dodged him and kept making my way to the man that needed me the most.

This nagging feeling that he wasn't going to come out of this alive… I needed to quench it before it consumed me.

I slipped through the double door before halting when he stopped. He was getting into the back of his old and trusted limousine but upon noticing me sprinting to him, he couldn't help but question what it was that I was trying to do.

He pushed himself off the vehicle and proceeded to me. His right hand cupped my cheek as he looked into my eyes. "Is there something wrong, love? Don't tell me you're afraid you're thinking I'm going to die. Sean is nothing more than a fool. He's already dead. He just doesn't know that yet."

I grabbed his hand, finding it impossible to let go of it now.

"I don't know what you're thinking now. Maybe you're assuming that he's really nothing more than an idiot who thinks that he can kill you, and that might be right, but still… You don't have to put yourself in danger like this. Nothing good can come out of it."

His other hand cupped my left cheek, gazing into my eyes.

"It's alright. I'm confident that this is going to be one the easiest raids of my life, or do you really think I'd be putting myself in danger this way without knowing what it is I'm stepping into?"

I breathed in and out, trying to control myself. It didn't seem to matter what I was trying to say to him. He didn't seem to want to listen, which in turn was only making me feel more hopeless.

The bad feeling in my heart wasn't going away and the longer this went on, the more certain I was getting that he wasn't going to come here safe and sound.

"Please, don't do this," I begged of him, but he just pulled up a corner of his lips and gave me a short kiss.

His men were still waiting for him inside their limousine and dark sedans. Their expressions showed their discontent that I was delaying him. Perhaps this was one of those assignments in which time was of the essence.

And yet, even if that was true, I couldn't care less. I was selfish and I didn't want him to spend a minute outside his estate, doing God knew what.

I needed him right here with me and telling me that everything was going to be alright.

"Are you going to be okay?" He asked all of a sudden, and I couldn't help but let the first tear come out. It rolled down my cheek as I worried I might be seeing him for the last time and that it didn't matter how hard I tried, I wasn't going to be able to change his mind about staying here.

He had so many loyal men under his command. Did he truly think that he needed to be there at the front lines like everyone else?

I guessed that was one of the many reasons why so many of them followed him.

He was setting the right example, though. By being with them in their moment of need when they were going to be risking their lives for him, he was earning their loyalty that much more.

And that, in turn, made me lower my head and look away from him.

His hand cupped my chin, tilting my head back up.

"Hey, don't worry about it, okay? It's all going to be fine and I'm going to prove that by coming back here with his head in a sack."

I imagined him doing that, my stomach churning.

I smiled without showing my teeth.

"You don't need to do that. I get it. You just feel like you need to be there with your men," I said, pecking his lips. "It's okay, I guess. But I'll be with my phone at all times in case something happens."

"Nothing bad is going to happen," he stated before kissing me one more time and heading back to the back of the limousine.

He signaled with his hand for the driver to head to their destination, my heart stopping for a moment when I wondered if there hadn't been more I could have done to change his stubborn mind.

There wasn't and I'd do well to keep that in mind.

I ignored some of his men that tried to get my attention and comfort me. I wasn't crying anymore. I wasn't. The tears rolling down my cheeks didn't matter. I was going to be strong. For him, for the fact that he loved me like no one else in his life, I was going to be a tough girl.

I crossed the central corridor, took the stairs, and then hurried over to our bedroom. Up there, I could have all the peace and quiet I needed, and right now I needed them like fish need water.

I couldn't stop thinking that something terrible was going to happen to him. Perhaps he was underestimating Sean O'Sullivan, who had managed to shoot and almost kill him during his marriage.

Memories of that still assaulted my mind, and yet I couldn't stop thinking about them. The people I'd befriended in his estate tried to stop me and tell me that he'd put himself in danger many times before, and yet all I could do was to keep ignoring them.

They couldn't predict the future. For all they knew, that was the last time they saw their boss.

Perhaps they were right, though. Artem was taking all the men he could with him, and if they managed to follow their plan almost to the letter, then they should come out of it victorious.

I couldn't wait until he was sitting on the bed, letting me rest my head on one of his shoulders, comforting words of his caressing my ears…

I was going to miss him, even if he ended up being out for not too long.

I ignored some other workers in his mansion before throwing the door of our room open and plopping down on his bed. I closed my eyes and tried to focus on the good things happening around me. Easier said than done, but I was sure I could pull it off.

It didn't take my heart too long to return to its normal beating rate. My phone wasn't ringing or rumbling. It was silent, just like most of all the other things in his estate. Sometimes I could hear Artem's men walking by the window of his room, saying things that didn't matter at all to me and that I couldn't give a rat's ass about, but other than that, I was left with my own thoughts.

Leaving me with my own thoughts wasn't how I thought I was going to be spending the night. I should close my eyes and try to fall asleep soon, but I knew that doing that was going to be almost impossible.

I couldn't fall asleep when he was risking so much to make my life with him safer. I still felt like something terrible was going to happen and that I was never going to see him again.

Knocks sounded on the door, but I didn't open it. I couldn't open the door for anyone right now, for I didn't feel like talking. I wanted some time alone, thinking about everything that was happening here and outside, too.

When I felt I was calm enough to keep going, to open my eyes, I sat up on the bed and looked at nowhere in particular. I knew that I looked like trash now. Disheveled hair, messed up makeup, no bra, feeling my head heavy as if I had a headache.

The longer this went on, the shittier I was going to keep feeling about everything that was happening here, and the more I was going to think that I'd been right when I said to him that it was the last time I was going to see him.

Time passed. How much time? I didn't know and didn't care. I felt that if I grabbed my phone and looked at the clock, I would burst out through all the doors of his mansion, take one of his cars and drive off to where he'd gone with his men, with no intention of coming back here without first making sure that he was alive.

I could see the light of the moon penetrating the windows of the room. I was still thinking about Artem, still hoping that he was going to be alright and that all the presumptions I was making were nothing more than that – paranoia that my mind kept bundling up.

I closed my eyes and lied down on the bed again. More hours ticked by while my mind refused to fall asleep. I felt that I was never going to be able to doze off without feeling his arm tucking me underneath him, telling me that soon he was going to take me to a European country and spend some quality time with me there.

How I'd love to be able to do that, with no worry populating my mind...

"We need to go! Now! Boss is getting surrounded by the O'Sullivan, and if we don't do something about it now- I don't even want to think about it. Let's just fucking go!"

I jumped off the bed, my eyes and mind alert like never before. The worst was happening. All my fears were becoming real. Artem had underestimated the Irish mafia and now he was paying a heavy price for it.

I didn't know what was happening, but it was possible they'd asked some of their friends from Ireland to come here to help them out with their revenge. How likely was that? I didn't know and wasn't going to waste too much time here thinking about it.

I needed to act before it was too late.

CHAPTER 19

Opening one drawer after the other, I could feel sweat drops breaking out on the skin of my forehead. My armpits were sweaty too, my mind thinking about a billion things, with none of them involving Artem coming out alive of the current danger he was facing.

I opened as many drawers as I could, trying to find the key that I was sure he kept somewhere in here. He had another key to one of his many luxurious cars, and I knew I could find it. With it in hand, I'd be able to leave this estate and get to him.

Upon getting there, I didn't know what I'd do, but for sure I'd save him somehow. I didn't trust his men to do it. I felt that they were too stupid and didn't care about him enough to pull it off.

My heart was beating like a galloping horse in my chest, making it impossible for me to think clearly about everything that was going on now. And I needed to think, I needed to put into words in my mind everything that I was going to do.

Find the key, hop into one of his cars, burst through the main gate, and then make my way over to where he was, where the O'Sullivan was surrounding him.

Chances were the rest of his family would chase me with their cars, but I didn't care about that. All I cared about was finding the only man that mattered in my life now. I could still feel his hand caressing mine.

When I thought that I'd been wrong about him keeping one of his keys in the room, I pulled a shirt to the side he kept in his dresser as my eyes met the twinkling of something made of metal.

The key to one of his cars.

I snagged it and didn't bother with putting on better clothes. The only thing I remembered to put on was a bra. I didn't want my breasts bouncing while I hurried over to the huge garage in our mansion.

Nothing could distract me now. I needed my mind one hundred percent focused on the matter at hand.

I wore a pair of flimsy, light pajamas shorts and a yellow shirt when I burst through the door of our bedroom. The guards that were by the door widened their eyes upon seeing me coming out like a hurricane.

I ignored them, their words pleading for me to tell them what in the world I was thinking I was doing. I supposed I should have tried to be sneakier about this, maybe tying a rope to the legs of the bed and then using it to climb down onto the garden by our window, but it was too late to think about that now.

And I wouldn't have had the patience necessary to pull it off anyway.

I ignored them until I reached the garage. They were fast, but not as fast as I was. The door to the room where he kept all of his glamorous cars was thrown open by me. It wasn't closed by a mechanical lock. The keypad connected to a digital and electrical locking mechanism opened it for me. I knew the combination.

I didn't know which car the key belonged to, so I pressed the main button of it until the lights of the vehicle were flashing. My eyes noticed the twinkling of a pair of headlights on the other side of the garage, prompting me to bolt over there.

My face pulled a corner of my lips. I didn't know how this was going to play out, but I was confident that I was going to get to Artem and save him. It didn't matter how I was going to do it, just that I was going to pull it off.

I hurried over to the car whose headlights were still blinking. Men poured into the garage, but it was too late for them. I was already opening the main door, which was the last thing standing in the way of me getting to the love of my life.

I guessed that I could be telling them what I was trying to do, trying to build a plan with them to save the love of my life, but at the moment, I wasn't in the mood for that. They failed in keeping him safe before, and I didn't trust them to do the right thing now.

Even if they had good intentions, they were a far cry from the kind of soldiers that Artem needed now. He needed only the absolute best.

I turned on the engine, put the foot on the gas, and blasted through the main gate of his mansion. His men didn't open fire. They might be stupid, but they weren't that stupid. They knew that if they harmed me, Artem wouldn't hesitate to hunt them down and kill each and every last one of them.

I was driving like a speeding horse through the streets, not even bothering to stop at the red lights. I guessed it was a good thing that the police didn't patrol the streets too hard at night in this part of town.

Before entering this car, I'd searched his office for information on where he'd gone off with most of his men. It was a building somewhere close to downtown, which puzzled me.

Why would the O'Sullivan have been hiding over there, where the police could find them with ease and raid their place for Sean and other criminals? It didn't make much sense to me, and yet I couldn't be bothered by it much.

It didn't matter that this whole thing smelled kind of fishy now. What mattered was finding the love of my life and making sure that he wasn't going to be hurt by the Irish gang.

CHAPTER 20

I was driving as if my life depended on this, my heart thundering in my chest. I sunk my fingers into the steering wheel before turning right and hearing the echoes of the gunshots. Not too long now until I got there.

A car, red and with white decals, honked at me when I swerved the car to the right and entered another road. I couldn't even blink. I couldn't even think straight now. It was all about getting there before the worst happened.

And I was going to reach my beloved before it came to that. There was no way that I was going to allow the love of my life to die. Not tonight, not ever. He was going to come back from this stronger, with a big smile on his face, and telling me that I didn't need to have worried, that I was just being a fool for having thought that he didn't have this whole thing under control.

I looked around when I drove down another straight road, the air kicking up my hair, not finding any signs of the police coming. They were not going to come here. They were understaffed and would be outgunned.

This was a shootout where only the adults could take part in, and they knew that like they knew the back of their hands. Corruption devoured their force from deep within, and with the officers' pockets filled with laundered money, they had almost no reason to show up here.

I pulled over by a block, killing the engine of the car and not wasting even a second before slipping out of it. The cold air of the night kissed my cheeks as I proceeded down to where all the shooting and shouting were coming from.

I did have a gun with me. A simple, small pistol that I was hoping I wasn't going to have to use. I wished to get into that building and slip out of it with the man of my life hugging me. I was going to kill Sean too, but his death already didn't mean a lot to me.

It meant that once he crossed to the other side, he would find peace within his death. There was going to be nothing quite like watching life dissipating out of his eyes, his mind wondering what in the world he'd done wrong to deserve his fate, and what he could have done to prevent it.

Even in downtown Lost Hope, the streets were silent like a desert. I couldn't hear the sound of cars or the police coming over here. The residents that lived inside the buildings were all hoping that the shootout was going to end soon so that they could sleep and wake up tomorrow ready for work.

I rounded the corner of a building when my eyes noticed a pair of men, both wearing dark suits with green ties, running in the opposite direction to the shooting. They were screaming for their lives, making me hope that things were turning around here and that Artem and his men were going to come victorious from this skirmish.

But that was when various SUVs with members of the Irish mafia thundered into the vicinity of the block I was in, their tires screeching and shooting out smoke before men carrying all kinds of guns poured out of them.

I hid behind a wall of a building, my heart still slamming against my chest while I wondered how I was going to fight all those men and win. If Artem and his soldiers were having a hard time, then I stood no chance against them, right?

I clutched my handgun while I breathed heavily, wondering if there was a gap in their plan, something I could make use of to end this shooting once and for all.

I took a deep breath before pushing myself off the wall and proceeding down the block. I didn't know if I was going to enter in through the front door or not, what I was going to do as soon as my eyes found the first member of the Irish mafia I would need to kill, but I was willing to go to hell and beyond to make sure that the love of my life was going to come out of this alive.

I crossed into an alley when my eyes landed on a group of Irish mafia and some Russians shooting at each other, with all of them shouting and trying to make sure their assailants weren't going to come out of this alive.

I froze, my hand almost dropping the gun that I was holding. This was it. I needed to kill all of them and not leave a single one of them alive to make sure that they could never hunt us down again. The only way to make sure that my married life with Artem was going to be peaceful.

They weren't noticing me. They were ignoring me. The Irish were thinking that I was nothing more than an idiotic fool in an alleyway where a shootout was happening.

I snapped my eyes to the right, meeting a sight I didn't think I was going to see here. Sean and Artem, kicking and punching each other not too far from the alleyway I found myself in. Their gazes never once shifted to me. They were both focused on their fight, on killing each other.

Everything was a confusion that I couldn't quite make sense of. I didn't know what I was thinking when I decided to come here I could hear the sound of Artem's guys coming to this place, but it was still going to take them long before storming in and saving the day.

If they could pull it off, that was. More of the Irish were pouring into the area that now became a shooting gallery, their hands holding guns that I thought only the army could use.

This was the right moment, the one begging for me to step in and shoot the asshole that was trying to kill my husband. That Artem could fight him toe to toe, punching and kicking him with all of his might, spoke volumes to his will to keep me safe.

I bolted to them, my slippers almost making no sound as

they touched the cold and rough ground of the alleyway. A light-bulb was the only thing keeping the darkness from engulfing this space, allowing me to see enough to head over to where they were fighting each other.

I ignored the Irish and the Russians shooting one another, focusing on getting to where the important battle was taking place. I almost slipped when I took a small round of stairs that led to the top of the small building where they were fighting.

Sounds of their kicks, grunts, and moans filled the air when I got to the top of it. This was it. The moment I'd been waiting for since making that choice to come here. I didn't need to be here. I knew that Artem was going to snap his head to me and shout that I was doing the wrong thing, that me coming here was a mistake, and yet there was nothing about that he could do.

I came here out of my own volition, and I was going to make sure that I was going to kill Sean.

His eyes bulged wide when he noticed that I was here, pushing Artem off of him and distancing himself from him.

"What the hell is going on here now? You called her to come here and to turn this fight into a joke?"

"Huh? What are you going on about?" Artem was asking when his eyes noticed me here too, something frightening and scary flashing in them. He also couldn't wrap his head around the fact that I'd decided not to wait until one of his men came into my room with news of his death.

Did he think that I was stupid or something of the sort? I was never going to leave this to chance.

"Faye? What are you doing here? I asked you to remain inside your room. It's the only place where you're going to be safe."

"I heard your men gossiping that he was overwhelming you, and I couldn't help but feel that I needed to do something to help."

He almost opened a smile at the thought that I'd managed to break out of his estate and come here, all on my own. His men would only have gotten in the way.

Well, there was no point in wasting any time here. It was time to aim my pistol and shoot at the asshole that stood on the other side of the roof of this short building. It wasn't tall, but a fall from it would still lead to the death of whoever got unfortunate enough to be on the short end of the stick of this battle between the two gangs, and I planned on making sure it wasn't going to be us.

I pulled up my gun, pointing it right at his dirty and bloodied face.

"Woah there, Faye. Are you really thinking that killing me is going to make everything better for you?"

"What do you mean? You're the one trying to ruin my life and kill my husband. Of course it's going to make everything better. Your death is essential for my life."

"Oh, my pretty little one. It doesn't work like that. The whole Irish mafia is going to come here. Did you really think that your husband fucking me up was never going to have some consequences? Well, there are, and they are right here."

"I don't care!" I said, steading my aim. "They can all come here. I'm still going to kill all of them, and they will regret ever trying to kill my husband."

"Kill me now, then. It's over. I always knew that Artem and his men were going to kill me when he managed to survive the wedding. The shot that I took to his heart was supposed to have been lethal."

I bit my bottom lip, remembering everything that happened then. It took a long time, but we finally managed to sniff out this asshole, and if he was presuming that something magical-

A force knocked me off onto the ground of the roof I was on, my small and trusted handgun skidding away toward the ledge. My eyes watched as a man wearing a dark suit with a green tie loomed over me, his hand flying to my neck until he gripped it.

He lifted me off the floor, making me gasp under the weight of his strength. He was massive. His head was devoid of any hair, but he stood like a mountain in front of me. Probably standing at over six feet tall, he made me feel so small and worried that he was going to snap my neck.

I feared he was going to do that before Artem had the chance to sprint over to us, punch his greasy face and end his life before he became a bigger problem to us.

His fingers sunk deeper into the skin of my neck. I couldn't see anything when Artem managed to slip away from Sean's hands, bolting to me as his heart slammed against his ribcage.

Everything happened in slow motion to me when he eased his grip on my neck. My lungs sucked air in as my eyelids slapped up and down. I could see my surroundings again, and my lungs were panting like I'd just finished running a long marathon.

But things were still far from ending.

Sean launched himself to the gun that was nearer him than it was to me. It was two against two now, and considering how light and small I was, I wasn't going to be much of a fighter.

I thought that the gun was going to be enough to tip the scales in my favor. I'd thought wrong and now I was paying the price for my lack of understanding of what was truly going on here.

I tried scrambling to the gun when something heavy and fast hit me in my stomach, making me spin on my own axis before my body stopped a couple of inches from falling off the building.

I snapped my head to the right, finding none other than Sean looming to me, a deep and threatening smile painting across his face. It was the other man whose name I didn't think I was going to learn that kicked me, his reckless act enough to rile up Artem even more, eyes filled with rage.

This was taking a direction I didn't think possible, making me fear the outcome of it. Artem and I were going to come out of this alive, right?

"My little Faye thought that she was going to end this with a small gun. How pitiful," he joked, his tone serious and comical at the same time.

Now that I was thinking better about it, the whole thing about coming here on my own, with nothing but that small pistol to protect me, was kind of dumb.

I just hadn't been able to think about the consequences much before making the choice to rush over here. The fear of Artem dying was too much for me, and I'd never have forgiven myself if he'd died when I could have done something – anything – to stop Sean O'Sullivan from clinching his most sought victory.

I never thought that my slipping away to Canada and then giving myself to Sean's hands would lead to this kind of outcome, that it would rile him up and anger him enough to come hunting the head of the Yuriev family.

I'd assumed that I was doing the right thing, but now I could see that I'd been wrong. Artem had already been looking out for me even back then, and his worry for me didn't change since.

"You're an asshole," I said through gritted teeth, trying to stand up when Sean lifted his leg. He was going to kick me off the roof of the store, his smile widening at the prospect of achieving another dream of his.

"You're going to die now, beautiful, and I hope that God is going to take you up under his wings. You're going to need it."

His eyes burned with a fire I'd never seen before. I shut my eyes, my heart beating like never before when shots screamed through the darkness of the night, flapping my eyelids open.

What the hell was happening here?

A storm of events ravaged the scene, destroying everything that I thought was going to happen here. I assumed that Sean was going to kick me off the building, but now he laid dead on the roof, a pool of blood surrounding his body.

Artem was panting, his hand gripping the gun I'd taken with me here and which I thought was going to end all of this. Well, it turned out that it worked. Kind of, right? Sean and his massive, fat bodyguard laid dead on the floor.

I didn't know how he pulled it off, but upon realizing that

there was no more Sean, I rushed to the safety of Artem's arms.

The rest could be dealt with now. The O'Sullivan family were going to be like headless chickens now that their boss was dead.

And I couldn't wait for what the future held in store for Artem and me.

EPILOGUE

I was holding a huge, heavy bouquet in my hands. His right eye winked, his lips opening to make me the most important question of his life. "Do you like it? Because if you don't, I can always get something else for you."

His words made me blush. He didn't need to get anything else for me. His presence alone was enough to fill my heart with love and also make me think that there was no better life than this. Cherishing the calmness of the ocean and reveling in the cool breeze that accompanied the salty water.

Was there anything more fulfilling than this? Because I couldn't think there was.

His hand grabbed mine, making me put the bouquet so close to my nose that the smell of all the roses and other flowers was flooding my lungs. I closed my eyes and took in a deep breath as I noticed the smell of something else in the air.

The smell of his perfume and what it said about him, that he was indeed the only person in the whole world that had never lied to me.

He'd promised me that I was going to kill Sean one day. It almost happened. Things got out of control and I couldn't pull it off when it meant the most. I was supposed to be the one pulling the trigger and ending his life that night on top of the small store.

Well, I still snagged the gun from Artem's right hand and took the final shot to Sean's head, exploding one of his eyeballs. Artem had looked at me with wide, scared eyes then. He'd never thought that I had it in me to shoot at a man that was already dead.

But he'd soon looped his arms around me and hugged me with the strength of a bear, even when his men had been shooting and killing the rest of the Irish.

We were heading to Ireland now. Artem pondered taking the plane to get over there, but he thought better about it. There was no need to rush his revenge. If the Irish were thinking that they could take on the bratva, then they had a surprise coming their way.

Artem was going to take the fight to them, and he was going to bury each and every one of them. None was going to come out of this alive. It's what he'd promised me and I believed in him. There was no reason to not trust his promise.

It was more of a promise to himself, but also to me.

His eyes gleamed with the light of the sun, his body naked except for shorts that he wore. We were standing at the back of the ship, some couples passing by us as they kissed and cracked jokes.

But while I knew some of them already and thought that they were good people, they were nothing more than background noise to me now. The only thing that my ears could focus on was the gentleness of his voice every time he spoke. And in my opinion, he wasn't speaking enough here on this ship.

The skin of his hand was soft, as if it was made of cotton. His fingers gripping my wrist showed how gentle he could be when he wanted to. His eyes were still looking at me as if he could make this moment freeze, as if he could make it last forever.

"I love it."

"Huh?"

"I love the bouquet. It's beautiful. It reminds me of our wedding."

"I don't think that remembering it now is a good thing."

He was right, but there was still some goodness in it. Everything that happened before the attempted murder had been good, including the dress he'd bought for me, the people in the church, their smiles, and how everyone had been wishing for me to have the best time of my life with him.

Even if many of them had been fake assholes back then, their words still meant something to me. I couldn't forget the wedding music that played when I entered the chapel, the man that was supposed to be faking my father taking me to my fiancé, his hand grabbing mine when he helped me up on the altar.

Even the priest reciting the words from his old and worn book was something that I remembered fondly now, even though at the time I hadn't paid much attention to it.

"Maybe not," I said, my other hand settling on my big and round belly. Ever since my second time with him, I'd been getting some symptoms teasing my pregnancy. I didn't think it was going to happen, but I couldn't deny it. I was pregnant with his baby, and we still had to decide on a name for him.

It was going to be a baby boy, and he was going to grow up happy and without the Irish trying to harm him. Artem had also promised me that the raid on the rest of the O'Sullivan wasn't going to take too long to finish.

"You know, maybe we should choose a name for our little one. Don't you think that he deserves a name already?"

"I'm not sure. There are so many names and I want to make sure that we'll choose the right one for him."

"First and foremost, he's going to be Russian too, so his first name should be Russian. I was thinking of naming him Vlad, after my father."

I almost sighed. I knew that choosing the right name meant a lot to him, but for me, I was thinking there were a couple of things we needed to be thinking about first. And one of them was finding out if I was going to like the house where we were going to stay in Dublin.

I didn't know why, but most of the Irish lived over there. I guessed they needed to be at the forefront of all the businesses and deals the politicians struck. Living in Dublin, though, did mean that finding and exterminating them was going to be easy.

He was looking into my eyes, wondering if I was going to answer his question or not. I'd ghosted him a couple of times since the whole ordeal with the O'Sullivan, so it wouldn't be anything new.

It wasn't that I was thinking that he was pushing me into saying something I didn't want to, but that sometimes he brought up topics I'd rather ignore.

His hand let go of mine, eyes looking at something off in the distance. He realized that at the moment there was no point in discussing the name of the baby. After I thought better about it, then we would have all the time in the world and ponder all the available options.

Our baby boy... I was already wondering what holding him in my arms was going to be like. I'd never breastfed a baby, and I had to admit that pulling out my breast was something that excited me.

His eyes returned to mine, still with the same intensity from before. Artem wasn't going to give up on changing my opinion. He wanted me to choose the same name for the baby. The more I thought about it, the more I wondered if I was going to be able to resist his insistence on said topic or not.

"I want you feeling happy about it too," he said, his voice full of happiness and love, eyes gleaming with how much this moment meant to him.

I couldn't help but peck his lips and grab his hand. There was something here on this cruise that I wanted to see, and it shouldn't be too far from where we were standing. With that thought in mind, I pushed a lock of hair to the side of my face, tucked it behind my ear, and then padded through the double door that led to the interior of the ship.

From there, we entered a hallway littered with paintings depicting the past and the present of the ship. People smiling, laughing, posing for the photos and the like. I guessed that this cruise ship had a deep history behind it, but at the moment, I couldn't care about it.

All I cared about was getting to that big and plentiful dining room that they had in about the middle of the ship. After getting there, I was going to do something that Artem wasn't going to like one bit. He was pretty vocal about it.

"Wait, you're not taking us there, are you?" He asked, smiling while kissing me when a couple passed by us. Artem loved showing me off, and now was no different.

"You're being delusional and naïve if you think I'm not heading over there now," I said, smiling too and kissing him back when another couple speeded by us. They looked at us with disgust and jealousy in their eyes.

They were old, with wrinkled skin, and wore clothes that looked so expensive that once I'd thought I'd never get to touch them. As if to say that I'd been a dumb fool, I could buy as many of those pieces now as I wished, and they complemented my wardrobe like nothing before could.

Just remembering them was enough to make me feel like trying them on, even if I wasn't thinking about taking off the dress that I wore now.

It wasn't too tight, but it did kind of cling to my body. The bottom part of it was peppered with glitter or something that gleamed under the light of the sun and the bright white bulbs from the ceiling. The shoulder straps were thin but not at all uncomfortable, with the waist section giving me enough room to breathe.

My heeled sandals were just the right size for me, complementing to perfection the purpleness of the tall and big dress. I looked imperious before all the women that also expressed their richness through their clothes, and I wasn't denying that being in possession of so much money turned my life into something much better than what it was before.

Bracelets made of pure gold looped around my wrist, complementing my looks and giving off an aura that said that most other people here couldn't touch me in terms of wealth. There was nothing quite like turning my eyes to the right and the left, looking at their faces as they realized that I was black and that I owned not only one of the most powerful men in the world, but that he could also end all of their lives in a wink if he so wished.

We crossed another hallway before entering the promised land. The smell of delicious food, meat, potatoes, and chocolate, and other kinds of desert filled the air, making me close my eyes and focus on it.

Something nudged me on the shoulder, and it was Artem's hand. "You're not going to fall asleep now, right?"

I giggled, covering my mouth. "No, of course not. I was just smelling the food."

He opened his mouth to crack another joke. Artem probably thought that it would be a good idea to say that I was going to get fat or something like that. Well, it wasn't going to happen. I was keeping myself in tip-top shape and even some of my new friends had already pointed out that despite the big belly that I now had, I looked more beautiful than ever before.

And I couldn't help but agree with them.

His hand urged me forward as he said, "Well, no time to waste then. Let's sit down and order something that you and our little one are going to like. And, if you end up being in a good mood, we are going to talk about choosing his name."

People walked around us, cracking jokes and talking so loudly that my beloved had to speak up to be heard. I smiled and said, "Of course, love. If I'm in a good mood, and that's a big if, we're going to talk about his name."

"It's not that big of an if," he joked before choosing a table and sitting down with me. We flipped through the pages of the menu, trying to find the right meal for this unique moment. Although I knew that there were still going to be many times in our life where we were going to be sharing a table on a cruise ship, this trip was still going to hold a special place in my heart.

It was the first time we were on one, after all.

We devoured all the food we could. I did point out to Artem that he complained about me eating too much when he himself had also developed a tendency to eat more than he should. Being the comedian wannabe that he now was, he brushed it off and proceeded to chow down a large piece of his lasagna.

They had lasagna on the menu. As soon as my eyes landed on those words, I couldn't help but point to the waiter that I didn't just want one of it, but two. I was going to take some slices with me to our suite, where I was going to eat them at night.

The rest of the trip happened without anything major happening. We had a good time and when we got off of the ship, I couldn't help but look back at it and wonder what my life was going to be like without it, now that we were going through customs.

The Irish officers cleared us, and minutes later we reached one of the biggest mansions I'd seen my whole life. Artem was married to me, but that didn't mean he was going to change as a man and a person. He was going to continue being his usual rich asshole that liked to show off, always trying to convince he had good intentions behind that.

His hand was holding mine when we stood at the front of the new estate where I was going to live for a couple of months with him.

I didn't know how long it was going to take him to kill every last Irish gang in their country, but I was hoping he was going to be done with it before the baby could understand what was happening around him.

Artem had made a promise to me.

He was going to leave the mafia life behind me and live a normal life with me. One without all the killing and bloodshed.

I couldn't wait until that time came.

The End

Thank you for the reception for my previous books. If you don't mind, I'd like to request you to leave a review for this story on the Amazon store page (or just how many stars you think it deserves). It doesn't take long, and your opinion is very valuable to me. I know some of you leave your reviews on Goodreads, but on Amazon is where they have more visibility, and you'd be helping me a lot, too.

MORE FROM ME

Mafia Vassal: A Dark Italian Mafia Romance Bundle

Beg Me: An Arranged Marriage Dark Mafia Romance

Don't Cry: A Secret Baby Dark Mafia Romance

Seizing her Heart: A Bratva Mafia Romance Collection

Conquering my Queen: A Dark Mafia Romance Bundle

Challenging Destiny: An Arranged Marriage Dark Mafia Romance

Chaining my Queen: A Secret Baby Dark Mafia Romance

Hell is Crying: A Secret Baby Mafia Romance

Beyond Forgiving: A Dark Mafia Captive Romance

Chosen to be Mine: A Dark Arranged Marriage Mafia Romance

Have no Fear: An Enemies to Lovers Academy Romance

Under his Mercy: A Dark High School Bully Romance

Lure Me: A Dark High School Bully Romance

Fallen Angel: A Dark High School Bully Romance

Stop Lying: A Dark High School and College Bundle

Stop Running: A Dark High School Bully Romance

Take Control: A Dark High School Bully Romance

Wounded Soldier: A BBW Romance

Venom Curves: A BBW Alpha Male Romance

Impossibly Curvy: A BBW Alpha Male

Wild Curves: A Western BBW Alpha Male Instalove Romance

Unfair Curves: A BBW Alpha Male Romance

ABOUT THE AUTHOR

Jolie Damman lives with her puppies and many cats on her farmland. She enjoys spending time with nature and tending to her property. When she has some free time, which doesn't happen as often as she would like, she writes her books.

As a writer, she hopes to touch and change the heart of her readers. Her books are not for those weak of the heart, and they tend to be spicier than most. One word after the other, she doesn't stop typing until she has written her idea, and she is very desire-driven when it comes to establishing the connections of her characters.

القوسُ والكِنانةُ

تلقّي السرديّات العربيّة القديمة في النقد الثقافيّ

عامر سلمان أبو مُحارب

القوسُ والكِنانةُ

تلقّي السرديّات العربيّة القديمة في النقد الثقافيّ

إصدارات دائرة الثقافة، حكومة الشارقة 2024 م

الناشر: دائرة الثقافة ـ حكومة الشارقة ـ الإمارات العربية المتحدة

الهاتف: ‎+971 6 5123333

البرَّاق: ‎+971 6 5123303

الموقع الإليكتروني: www.sdc.gov.ae

البريد الإليكتروني: sdc@sdc.gov.ae

813.00923

أ ع. ق   أبو محارب، عامر سلمان

القوس والكنانة: تلقي السرديات العربية القديمة في النقد الثقافي / عامر سلمان أبو محارب. ـ الشارقة، الإمارات العربية المتحدة: دائرة الثقافة، 2024.

266 ص ؛ 23.5x15.5 سم.

يشتمل على إرجاعات ببليوجرافية وكشافات

1 – القصص العربية ـ تاريخ ونقد ـ العصر الحديث

2 – السرد الأدبي (أدب عربي)

أ- العنوان

ISBN: 978‑9948‑760‑382

قولٌ قبلَ القولِ

«وإنّما ذكرنا التآليف المستحقة للذّكر، والتي تدخلُ تحت الأقسام السّبعة التي لا يؤلّف عاقلٌ عالمٌ إلا في أحدها، وهي إمّا شيءٌ لم يُسبق إليه يخترعه، أو شيءٌ ناقص يتمّه، أو شيء مُستغلق يشرحه، أو شيء طويل يختصره دون أن يخلّ بشيء من معانيه، أو شيء متفرّق يجمعه، أو شيء مُختلط يرتّبه، أو شيء أخطأ فيه مؤلفه يصلحه. وأما التواليف المقصّرة عن مراتب غيرها فلم نلتفت إلى ذكرها، وهي عندنا من تأليفِ أهلِ بلدنا أكثر من أن نحيط بعلمها».

(رسائل ابن حزم الأندلسيّ، ج2، ص186)

الإهداء

إلى أبي العزيز ـ حفظه الله ـ

ذي القامة العاليةِ حدَّ السنديانِ الذي لا يُحَدُّ...

إلى أُمَّـي الغاليـة، مكرّمةِ العـشيرِ

صَنَاعِ اليدينِ ـ نسأ اللهُ في أجاها ـ

عـامر

تصدير

د. عبد القادر الرّباعيّ

انشغل النقد العربيّ في الربع الأخير من القرن المنصرم بالنقد الثقافيّ تنظيراً وتطبيقاً. وإن كان الاهتمام قد انصبَّ لبرهة من الزمن على الصدام العنيف الذي طرحته كينونة الشعر، ومسارات التأويل لهذا الوافد الجديد الذي وضع فناءها أولوية من أولوياته. لكنّ الشعر بعبقريّة وجوده، وتاريخه الجذري، أثبت أنه أعلى كعباً من أن يزاح من الآفاق. فالشعر تأبّى ويتأبّى على الفناء؛ لأّنّه باقٍ ما بقي الإنسان، والفنّ، والجمال.

وإيماناً بهذه الحقيقة انزوى النقد الثقافيّ جانباً يفتش له عن أرضيّة تُمكِّنُهُ من نفوذ لطروحاته، بعيداً عن مزاحمة الآخرين. وكان له ما أراد فعالم الثقافة لا ينزاح عن الطريق، لكنه يُستوعب رديفاً للشعر، أو للنثر، أو خليطاً لهما بشكل ما. قد لا يعتمد في وجوده على عمومية الثقافة، لأنها حاضرة في كل فنّ، لكن النقد الثقافيّ بخصوصيته النسقيّة أوجد عنصراً لا يستغنى عن فاعليته في أي نص أدبيّ، وهو ما سمّي (النسق المضمر) الذي أراه نوعاً مما عرف تاريخاً بـ (معنى المعنى) أو المعاني الثواني وما شابه من تأويل.

إنّ هذا العنصر الحيوي المبهم والكاشف معاً، ليشكلُ لغزاً كونه باعث الاحتراق في المغامرات اللدنّية عند الخطابات الأدبيّة الأكثر اشتعالاً. إنه الشكل الآبق للفضول المضاعف لدى البحثة الساعين لحلّ ألغاز المغامرات الأسلوبيّة

في أيِّ نصٍّ أدبيٍّ؛ مهما بعدت إشكالاتُهُ عن ظاهر الكشف، وخبايا الحلّ.

إنني – وأنا أقرأ محطات البحث عند هذا الشاب المغامر (عامر أبو محارب مؤلّف هذا الكتاب) في فكّ شيفرات القراءة الخاصة بالسرديّات العربيّة القديمة – بدا لي أنني أمام باحث حماسي بالغ الأثر في حلّ ألغاز كثيرة. لقد اتّخذ من النقد الثقافيّ السابق الذكر أسلوباً فاحصاً لمسارات متعددة، ومتنوعة، ومختلفة، ومتشابكة، قد تتأبى – لتباعدها – على أن تُلَمَّ معاً، لكن هذا الباحث النابه استطاع فعل ذلك بأريحيّة بالغة التعقيد، والتمحيص، والحفر.

وإذا بدأنا من العنوان فإننا أمام حقل من الطروحات المتشابكة التي احتاجت لتتواءم معاً، إلى رؤية كلية نافذة، وطموح ذاتيّ جامح وغير محدود. وهذا ما كان؛ فعامر – كما ظهر – لم يكن يرضى بالسهل من البحث، وإنما تجاوز ذلك إلى الصعب، والحفر العميق الذي انساق له بعد عصي. لقد انسلكت له قنوات متباعدة، قاصدة جمع التعدد ضمن أفق التوقّع، الذي اعتمدته مدرسة كونستانس الألمانية بعلميها ياوس وآيزر، اللذين رسما دائرة شموليّة يذوب فيها التنوّع بجهد مضاعف قادر عليه ما عرف بالناقد الكفء.

لقد استوعب المؤلف هنا مهمة هذا الناقد الفذّ، بل لقد أصبح هو ذلك الناقد الذي تشعّبت واجباته حسب المقاربات ذوات الاستراتيجيّات المتباعدة والمتقاربة. كما تبعته كل منها ضمن بصيرة فاحصة لمساراتها المعرفيّة، ومداراتها المنهجيّة، تمهيداً للحكم الذي ارتأته وبنت عليه نتائجها المفصليّة. واستجابة للمهمة المعقدة والشائكة ألتي أدار دفتها هذا الناقد الكفء أتت الأحكام على تلك الدراسات لينة حيناً، قاسية حيناً، لكن المرجعيّة في كلّ ذلك هي البصيرة النقديّة الموضوعيّة القاصدة لهذا الباحث المميز، وليس غير.

إنّ من يتابع مجرى هذا البحث ذي المنهجيّة الصارمة الناجزة لدى هذا الباحث الطُّلَعة، وأسلوبه الجازم السابر لكل نامة وعلامة، ليدهش حقاً للثقة العالية

بالنفس التي تقف على مرقبةٍ عاليةٍ للمنطق المسؤول في أسلوب المحاكمات النقديّة، وإدارة العرض لدى كلِّ فصلٍ، وموقع من هذه الدراسة اللامعة.

لقد عولجت السرديّات الحكائية القديمة بكثافة متينة من خلال التحولات وأنماط التلقّي. وكذا الأنساق المضمرة وتجليات التناسخ الأدبيّ، وأيضاً الائتلاف المنهجيّ بين النقد الأدبيّ، والنقد الثقافيّ، ثم تسريد مسارات النقد الثقافيّ وإشكاليات القراءة، وغير ذلك الكثير.

ولعلي أنهي بعض ما في الجعبة من قول مضاعف في هذا التقديم لهذا الكتاب المميز، بالنظر إلى فاعلية الغذاميّ – الناقد السعوديّ – رائد النقد الثقافيّ في المدوّنة النقديّة العربيّة، لأشير إلى أنّ كمّاً لا بأس به من هذه السرديّات توجهت إلى دراسته حول السرديّات الحكائية العربيّة، متخذةً إياه أنموذجاً للمحاكاة الناجحة أو القاصرة. لقد تنبه الباحث هنا إلى مسألة المحاكاة بشكلٍ عام، واضعاً فسحة للخروج على محددات النموذج ونتائجه، مجترحاً بعض المصطلحات خدمة لهذا التوجه العلميّ المستقل، من مثل: الخروج على النموذج، وخرق نمط التلقّي، والخروج عن التعاليم القارة، وفخاخ التقليد، وغير ذلك من المحاذير التي استندت إلى أساسيات الحكم التي هي قيد الذات الباحثة بالتفرد. إن هذا يتم ويلتئم في منطلقات البحث ومنهجياته العلميّة المعروفة، بل إنّ ذلك يستوجب ضرورة الالتزام بكل تلك الاستراتيجيّات لدى كل باحث جاد.

وتبعاً لهذا تراوحت نتائج المقاربات بين السرديّات المعتمة، أو سلطة النموذج، والخروج عليه، والإضمار، والمراوغة، والاحتفاء بدراسات ما بعد الكولونيالية، والانفتاح على الذوق الأدبيّ، وبعض إشكاليات الاعتراض على النقد الثقافيّ، وبروز النسق المضمر، وتمثلات الصورة والبلاغة.

وختاماً، فإنّ هذا الكتاب ليقدم دراسة علميّة أصيلة موثوقة ومُخلصة، من باحث صارم جاد أعدَّ نفسه للبحث الرصين، وسلك إليه طريقاً شائكاً؛ كلّفه جُهداً

مضنياً، ومتابعة حثيثة لكلّ صغيرة وكبيرة، متسلحاً لإنجاز ذلك؛ بعلم غزير، ومصادر أصيلة، ومراجع مسعفة كثيرة: متنوعة ومساندة.

وبناءً على كل ما سبق ذكره أتت مناقشات مؤلّف هذا الكتاب الجاد والجازم، رفيعة المستوى، عالية المقام، متمتّعة بالثقة العلميّة المائزة. ومن هنا فإنني وبكلّ صدق أراه باحثاً أنموذجاً؛ يصلح أن يكون أمثولةً لمن أراد لعلمه الرصانة، والموثوقيّة، والتفوّق.

ولا يفوتني أن أهنّئ هذا الباحث على جهده الكبير، وأن أتمنى له كل توفيق وسداد؛ آملاً أن نرى له في المستقبل القريب مزيداً من الإنتاج الغزير كهذا الإنتاج مناط الاعتزاز والفخار.

والله من وراء القصد، وأهدى سبيلاً

عمّان
السبت 2023/2/15

مقدمة

ينطوي (النقد الثقافيّ) (Cultural Criticism) بوصفه نقداً ما بعدياً على فاعليّة نقديّة في قراءة النصوص قراءةً ثقافيّةً ناجزة، تسعى إلى الكشفِ عن مُضمرات الخِطاب، وأنساقه الثقافيّة المُضمرة؛ بما يمتلكه النقد الثقافيّ من مُقولاتٍ نظريّة وأدواتٍ إجرائيّة، تفسحُ المِراحَ أمام الناقد الثقافيّ على مناوشة جدليّات المضمر وآفاق المتوقّع في بِنى النصّ/ النصوص.

وإذا كانَ منجزُ النقد الثقافيّ ما يَفْتَأُ يمثّلُ موضوعاً سِجاليّاً وفتياً في الآنِ عَيْنِه؛ فإنَّ الدراسة الراهنة تسعى إلى أن تُقدّم مقاربة (نقد نقديّة) تقرأُ من خلالها مجمل القراءات الذي خُصّصَتْ لقراءة السرديّات العربيّة القديمة في إطارِ مقاربات النقد الثقافيّ؛ ذلك أنّها مقاربات تنمازُ بكونها جديدةً وإشكاليّةً وقمينةً في الآن عينه بإنجازِ مُقارباتٍ تُعيد قراءتها من منظورات نقد النقد؛ في سبيل السعي إلى بلورة رؤيةٍ نقديّة سابرة، تكشفُ عن بِناها المعرفيّة، ومرجعياتها الإبستمولوجيّة، وأدواتها الإجرائية.

وتختصُّ الدراسة الراهنة بمنجز النقد الثقافيّ الذي قَرَأَ السرديّات العربيّة القديمة؛ استناداً إلى أنّ النقد الثقافيّ يمثّل على تعدُّدية إبدالاته، وطرائق تلقّيه؛ نسقاً دالاً، وعلامةً فارقةً، وأُفُقاً مُنمازاً، في إطارات النقد العربيّ المُعاصر؛ وذلك بوصفه منهجاً ناجعاً في مكنته أن يختبرَ وأن يكشفَ، والحالُ هذه، عن

الأنساقِ الثقافيّة (Cultural Categories) المنسربةِ عبر أبنية الخطابَيْن الشعريّ والسرديّ.

ولعلّه من مكرور القول الإشارة إلى أنّ النقد الثقافيّ يتأسّسُ على لزوبِ دراسـة النصوص الشعريّة والنثريّة، وفقاً للسياقات الثقافيّة والاجتماعيّة والسياسيّة التي أحاطتْ بالنصّ لحظةَ إنتاجه، في محاولة للخروج من (تيه النصّيّة) الذي طغى كما عبّر عن ذلك إدوارد سعيد (Edward Said)[1]، ذلك التيه الذي فرضته المدرسيّات النقديّة الحديثة[2]، حين مركزتْ خطابها النقديّ حول النصّ، وشيّعت مؤلّفه إلى مثواه الأخير، فكان أن أعلنت موت المؤلف (Death of The Author).

وفي إطار التأسيس السابق فإنّ الدراسة الراهنة تبحثُ في مُفترض مُؤدّاه، أنّ القراءة الثقافيّة (Cultural Reading) للخطاب السرديّ، كما يُسلِّم بذلك أصحابُ المنجز النقديّ المدروس، تؤمن بأنّ النصّ السرديّ – قديماً وحديثاً – يشكّل مَراحاً فسيحاً لمُراوغات الخِطاب أو مُضمراته، بوصفه حادثةً ثقافيّة، تتوسّلُ أو تتزيّا بالجماليّ، وتضمرُ أنساقاً ثقافيّةً مُخاتلةً، بمقدورها التمنع على القارئ أو المُتلقّي، وليس يخفى أنّ هذه الأنساق ليس بالمُستطاعِ استبارها، واستكناهُ دِلالاتها، دون إنجاز قراءاتٍ عميقةٍ، تكشف عنها، وبموجب هذا المُفترض فإنّ هذه الدراسة تنبري للبحث في العلاقة القائمة بين هذه المُنطلقات النظريّة لهؤلاء النقاد وآفاق مُنجزهم النقديّ المدروس.

وتتعاضدُ المُسوّغات المنهجيّة لإجراءِ هذه الدراسة الراهنة؛ أما أولها، فهو أنّ النقّاد، مدارَ الدراسة، التفتوا إلى دِراسة السرديّات القديمة وهُمْ على وعي تامّ بضرورة دراسة الأنساق الثقافيّة في النصّ الأدبيّ عامّةً، والسرديّات خاصّةً، بوصفها أنساقاً مُضمرة ومعلنةً تمارسُ تأثيرها في الكون والحياة دون حسيبِ في حركةٍ لوّابةٍ ومراوغةٍ لا يقرُّ قرارها، وثانيها، أهميّةُ هذا المنهج في قراءة السرديّات العربيّة القديمة؛ وما ينمازُ به من قدرة على قراءة المُضمَر في بِنية

الخطاب السرديّ العربيّ، وهو ما كان غُفْلاً في الدراسات التي شيدتها مدرسيّات النقد الأدبيّ التقليديّة، وثالثها، فمؤدّاه أن خطاب النقد الثقافيّ يمثل اتجاهاً جديداً لما ينتقل إلى فضاءات النقد العربيّ المعاصر بصورة مكتملة؛ ممّا يستوجب بَحْثَ أصوله المعرفيّة، وأدواته الإجرائيّة، وإشكالاته المنهجيّة، إذ إنّه لمّا يَزَلْ كغيره من المناهج النقديّة الجديدة الوافدة نقداً مُلفّعاً «بالغموض والضباب والفتنة» كما يقول (وهب روميّة)(3).

وأما رابعُها فهو أنّ دراسة (نمط التلقّي) (Receiving Mode)، من خلال البحث في تاريخ تلقّي نصٍّ ما، عَبْرَ مراجعة صنوف القراءات المتعاقبة حوله، يسهمُ في تكوين تاريخ لفعل التلقّي في النقد العربيّ، فضلاً عن دور ذلك في إعادة قراءة النصّ، وفَهْمه، وتفكيك بِناه، إذ «فمن منظور جماليّة التلقّي، لا ينفصلُ النصّ الذي يُقرأ عن تاريخ تلقّيه، فتاريخ التلقّيات والقراءات الخاصّ بنصٍّ ما هو الذي يمكننا من فَهْمه بعد أن أُنجز وأصبح ماضياً»(4).

وأما خامسها فهو أنّ هذه الدراسة تجيءُ في سياق فحص بِنية الخِطاب النقديّ العربيّ، الذي يسير منذ فواتح القرن المنصرم في اتجاهيْن لا ثالث لهما، أما أحدهما فنقليٌّ إسقاطيٌّ(5) يرزح نقّاده تحت سطوة المنهج النقديّ الغربيّ، فيتمثلون مفاهيمه وإجراءاته بصورةٍ آليّة مُخلّة، ويَنْظرون إلى «الفكر والنظريّة الغربيين من منظورٍ تقديسيٍّ تصنيميٍّ»(6)، وأما ثانيهما فعقليٌّ التقاطيٌّ يحاور المناهج الغربيّة، ويجتهد المنخرطون في مداراته لاستيلاد منهجٍ نقديٍّ يتواءم مع بنائيّة النصّ العربيّ وخصوصيته.

أسئلة الدراسة:

شكّل النقد الثقافيّ، من خلال حضوره اللافت في مجتليات النقد الحديث، كما سلف، علامةً بارزةً انطوت على إشكالات منهجيّة وإبستمولوجيّة، استأهلتْ نهوضَ قراءة نقديّة فاحصة، تجيبُ عن أسئلة معرفيّة كبرى، وتدير رحى البحث

حول الجدوى المعرفيّة المنشودة من هذا المنهج، ومقولاته النظريّة، وأدواته الإجرائيّة، وطرائق تلقّيه في النقد العربيّ الحديث.

وفي ضَوْء ما تقدّم فإنّ الدراسة الراهنة تحاول صياغة رؤية نقديّة عن هذا الخطاب النقدي، لتجيب من خلالها عن أسئلةٍ يمكن أن تنتظم فيما يأتي:

– ما مفهوم القراءة الثقافيّة عند كل مَنْ قرأ السرديّات العربيّة القديمة من منظور النقد الثقافيّ؟

– ما أبرز آليّات المقاربة النقديّة التي ينتهجُها كلّ ناقد في قراءة السرديّات العربيّة القديمة من أدبيات النقد الثقافيّ؟

– ما طرائق تشكُّلِ العتبات النصيّة وأدوارهـا المنهجيّة في المقاربات المدروسة؟

– ما وجوه التشابه والاختلافِ في تلقّي السرديّات العربيّة القديمة في إطار النقد الثقافيّ، عن تلقّيها في إطار المناهج النقديّة الحديثة؟

– ما أبرز الإشكالات المنهجيّة التي تحفُّ بالنقد الثقافيّ كما تتمرأى في المقاربات المدروسة؟

– ما المرجعيّات النقديّة التي صدر عنها النقّاد كما تبدّت في مراسمهم النقديّ؟

– ما تقييمُ هذه التجربة النقديّة بناءً على محاولة اختبار معطياتها لدى كلّ ناقد؟

لا جرم أنّ هذه الدراسة محفوفةٌ بالعديد من المكاره التي تحيطُ بها في مهمّتها المعرفيّة هذه، وفي رحلتها نحو الإجابة عن هذه الأسلئة الآنفة؛ ذلك أنّها تندرجُ تحت مظلّة دراسات نقد النقد، التي – قطعاً – لم تَنَلْ بعدُ من الناحيتين التأصيليّة المفاهيميّة المنهجيّة الإجرائيّة، حظاً عظيماً ونصيباً مفروضاً من المُمارسة التطبيقيّة الفاعلة في مجتليات النقد العربيّ المُعاصر.

الخطّة والمنهج:

كلُّ دراسة تحترم الحقيقة لا مناص لها من خطة ومنهج، وهذه الدراسة تؤثر أن تؤطّر مسارَها المنهجيّ في أربعةٍ فصولٍ متكاملة متضابطة، يسبقها فصل تمهيديّ، وتردفُ ذلك خاتمة، مذيلة بثبتٍ بالأعلام، ومكمَّلة بمسردٍ بمصطلحات الدراسة وجهازها المفاهيميّ.

وتجلّي الدراسة في الفصل التمهيديّ الموسوم بـ:(أدبيّاتُ الدراسة ومقولاتُها المنهجيّة: مقتربٌ تأسيسيّ) المرجعيّات المعرفيّة التي تأثّثت على أُسٍّ منه أدبيّات الدراسة، ومقولاتها، وقد جاء في مباحث أربعة، أما الأوّل فأصّل لمفهوم (دراسات نقد النقد)، وأما الثاني فانشغل بمدارسة نظريّات القراءة، وصنوف القرّاء، ومساراتهم في القراءة، وأما الثالث فأسّس لمفهوم النقد الثقافيّ، في محاولةٍ لتبيان المسار العامّ لمقارباته، وإشكالاته المعرفيّة، وأما الرابع فقد انشغل بمدارسة مسألتَيْن؛ أما أولاهما فتناولت السرد العربيّ القديم؛ مفهوماً، وتشكّلات أجناسية كُبرى: (مقامة، وحكاية ...إلخ)، وأما ثانيتهما فتتحدّث عن أنماط تلقّي السرديّات العربيّة القديمة في النقد الأدبيّ الحديث.

وتنشغلُ الدراسة في الفصل الأول الموسوم بـ: (تشكلات نمط التلقّي: بين القراءة النموذج ومحاولات الخَرْق)، بمساءلة مسارات التلقّي التي قدّمها الباحثون في إطار النقد الثقافيّ وهم نَهْبٌ بين تقليدٍ للنموذج الغذاميّ وما نقله من الغرب، وثورةٍ على هذه المسلَّمات التي نقلها، وقد خُصّص هذا الفصل لتلقّي السرديّات الحكائيّة عند عبدالله الغذامي، والمقامات عند علي فرحان، والسرديّات السلطانيّة عند محمد المحفليّ.

وتُساءلُ الدراسة في الفصل الثاني الموسوم بـ: (إخصاب نمط التلقّي: النقد الثقافيّ وممكنات ما بعد الكولونياليّة)، المقاربات النقديّة التي أخصبت النقد الثقافيّ بالانفتاح على الدراسات ما بعد الكولونياليّة، وقد عُنِيَ هذا الفصل

بتلقّي السير الشعبيّة عند نادر كاظم، وسرديّات الجنون والسير الشعبيّة عند ضياء الكعبيّ.

وتُباحث الدراسة في الفصل الثالث الموسوم بـ:(انفتاح نمط التلقّي: النقد الثقافيّ ومسارات النقد الأدبيّ)، أبرز مواطن التلاقح المنهجيّ بين النقد الثقافيّ والنقد الأدبيّ، وقد انشغل هذا الفصل بتلقّي الحكايات العجائبيّة والمقامات عند يوسف عليمات، والسرد الأخباريّ عند مصطفى الغرافي، والسرديّات الرحليّة عند مُعجِب العدوانيّ.

وتنشغلُ الدراسة في الفصل الرابع الموسوم بـ: (تفاعلات نمط التلقّي: بين تحليل الخطاب والدرس البلاغيّ)، بالكشف عن علائم التقاعل المنهجيّ بين النقد الثقافيّ وتحليل الخطاب والدراسات البلاغيّة، وقد خُصّص هذا الفصل لتلقي السرد الشطاريّ وسرديّات العشق عند شرف الدين مجدولين، والوصايا السرديّة والسرديّات الجنسانية عند هيثم سرحان، وأقفلتُ الدراسة بخاتمةٍ انطوتْ على زمرةٍ من النتائج، التي اتّضحت من خلالها سيميائية مشهد النقد الثقافيّ في النقد العربيّ، يردفُ ذلك ثبتان للأعلام والمصطلحات.

وإذا كان على الدراسة العلميّة أن تُؤطّر مسارَها المنهجيّ فلا بُدّ من الإشارة إلى أنّ الدراسة الراهنة تنتخبُ منهجاً تفاعليّاً مركَّباً؛ ينهضُ على مفاهيمَ مستمدةٍ من نظرية التلقّي والتأويل ((Receiving Theory ودراسات نقد النقد (Meta – Citicism)، من خلال استقراء الخطاب النقديّ المدروس، ومن ثم تصنيف هذه القراءات، والكشف عن صنوف القُرّاء، ونزوعاتهم، ومساراتهم في البحث عن الأنساق الثقافيّة، ومن ثَمَّ تفكيكِ هذه القراءاتِ، ومعالجتها، وسَبْرها، والكَشْفِ عن بِناها المعرفيّة والمنهجيّة، استناداً إلى منجز الدراسات النقديّة في أطرٍ ثلاثةٍ رئيسةٍ تمثّلُ الأثافيَّ الثلاثَ لكلّ خطابٍ نقديّ وهي: (الجهاز المنهجيّ)، و(المفاهيم المؤسّسة)، و(استراتيجيّات المقاربة النقديّة ومستويات التلقّي)، ولأنّ في طيّات العناوين وبدايات الكتب «فتنةً وعُجباً»[7] كما يقول الجاحظ فقد حاولت

الدّراسة أن تلمع كذلك إلى العناوين الرئيسةِ والفرعيّةِ في هذه المقاربات، وأن تكشف كذلك عن محمولاتها السيميائيّة، وأدوارها المنهجيّة.

وتجبُ الإشارة هنا إلى أنّ هذه الدراسة حاولت أن تجعل محور انشغالها متمركزاً حول استراتيجيّات المقاربة النقديّة كما تتمرأى في الخطاب الإجرائيّ؛ وذلك لأنّها تعبّر عن التحقق الفِعْلي للعمليّة النقديّة، فضلاً عن انطواء هذه الاستراتيجيّات على أبرز الإشكاليّات التي تحفُّ بهذه المقاربات.

وقد فاءت الدراسة في اختيار النقاد الذين مثّلوا مادة الدراسة إلى مفهوم القارئ الكفءِ (Competent Reader)[8] الذي تنمذجه نظريّات التلقّي، بوصفه القارئ الذي يتمثّل بصورة مُنمازةٍ ضوابطَ القراءة، ومفاهيمها، واستراتيجيّاتها، وَفْقاً لمنظورات منهج نقديّ معيّن، وهنا لا بُدّ من الإشارة إلى أنّ هذه الدراسة تعاملت مع هؤلاء النقاد في ظلال مفهوم (نمط التلقّي) الذي يعني تشاركَ جماعةٍ من الباحثين في المنهج، واستراتيجيات القراءة، ومبادئها، ومفاهيمها[9].

وعليه فإن المقاربات التي انتخبَتْها هذه الدراسة تشترك فيما بينها مكوّنةً نمط التلقّي العام، ذلك أنّها تصدرُ عن أفقٍ منهجيّ واحد، وهي جميعاً، منشغلة بالنسق المضمر، والأيديولوجيا، وثنائيّات المركز والهامش، وتجليات الصراع الإنسانيّ[10]، بيد أنّه من الواجب الإشارة إلى أنّ أنماط التلقّي متداخلة تداخلاً لا يمكن أن يؤطر، ومن ذلك مثلاً أنّ سلطة الغذامي منسربة في أبنية جل المقاربات، ولكن بصورةٍ متفاوتةٍ من مقاربة إلى أُخرى، وفي سياق ذلك بدا أن تكون الدراسة في خمسة أنماط رئيسة، فالمقاربات التي يتضمّنها الفصل الأول يجمع بينها خيطٌ ناظم هو سُلطة النموذج الغذاميّ، والتمرد على ما نقله بخصوص فكرة النسق المضمر من جهةٍ أخرى.

وأمّا المقاربات التي يتضمنها الفصل الثاني فإنّها تنزع جميعاً إلى إخصاب نمط التلقّي من خلال توسيع دائرته لتشمل الدراسات ما بعد الكولونياليّة، في محاولة للتأسيس لقراءة نقديّة متكاملة، وأمّا المقاربات التي يباحثها الفصل الثالث

فإنّ موضع اتّساقها يتبدّى في أنّها تتعاملُ مع القراءة الثقافيّة في ضَوْء ضرورات الانفتاح على ممكنات النقد الأدبيّ، وأما المقاربات التي يدور الفصل الرابع حولها فإنّ جِماع القول فيها أنها تتعاملُ مع القراءة الثقافيّة في أتون تقاعلاتها مع مناهج تحليل الخطاب والدرس البلاغيّ ودراسات الصورة.

ويجب إنباه الأنباه هنا إلى أنّ الدراسة استثنت أيَّ مقاربة جعلت من النقد الثقافيّ رديفاً هامشياً، كمقاربة جمال مقابلة حول (المقامة الموصليّة)[11]، ومقاربة صالح الحجيلان حول (قصص الأمثال)[12]، وكذلك استثنيت المقاربات التي قرأت الأنساق التي يتضمنها تلقّي السرديّات في النقد القديم من مثل مقاربة أحمد آل مريع حول (خطاب الجنون)[13]، وقد تبيّن أنّ يوسف عليمات وضياء الكعبيّ قد قدّما أكثر من مقاربة حول السرديّات العربيّة القديمة، بيد أنّ مقاربات كلّ ناقدٍ منهما صدرت عن أُفُق منهجيٍّ واحد، حدده كل ناقد منهما في دراسته جميعها، ولذا فقد اقتصرت هذه الدراسة على قراءة أو اثنتين لكلٍ منهما، نأيا عن التكرار والاجترار[14].

الدراسات السابقة:

لمّا تنلْ القراءات الثقافيّة التي خصصت لقراءة السرديّات العربيّة القديمة حظّها من الدرس النقديّ الجادّ، ولمّا تجد من يحسر لها عن ذراعه؛ ليحاول أن يسبر أغوارها، ويفكّك بناها، وأن يعمل معوله فيها قراءة ومُدراسة، وهو ما تحاول الدراسة الراهنة أن تستوفيه، بيد أن ذلك لا يعني أنه ليس ثمّة دراساتٍ انبرتْ للبحث في هذا المُشْكل، ومن هذه الدراسات السابقة يُذْكَرُ مثالاً لا حصراً:

– دراسة ضياء الكعبيّ (السرد العربيّ القديم: دراسة في الأنساق الثقافيّة وإشكاليّات التأويل)[15]، وهي دراسة رنت الباحثة خلالها إلى استشراف آفاق تلقّي السرد العربيّ القديم في النقد الحديث، والإشكاليّات التي انتظمت هذا التلقّي، بدءاً بتلقّي القدماء، ومروراً بالتلقّي الإحيائيّ مطلع القرن المنصرم

عند محمد رَوحي الخَالديّ، مروراً بتلقّي طه حسين وزكي مُبارك وتوفيق الحكيم، وانتهاءَ بتلقّي النقد الجديد بمساراته الأربعة، وهي: النقد التأصيليّ، والنقد البنيويّ، و النقد التأويليّ، والنقد الثقافيّ، وفي الحديث عن التلقّي في إطار النقد الثقافيّ اقتصَرت الكعبي على عرض موجزٍ لتجربتيْن نقديتيْن عربيّتيْن هما تجربتا: عبدالله الغذّاميّ، وعبدالفتاح كيليطو، وقد استغرق عرضهما خمس صفحات فقط.

– دراسة أميرة القَفاريّ (النقد الثائر: قراءة النقد الثقافيّ للتّراث الأدبيّ)[16]، وهي دراسةٌ عامّة وجزئية تناولت الباحثةُ خلالها خمساً من المقاربات التي شيّدها النقاد حول التراث العربيّ سَرْداً وشِعْراً في إطار النقد الثقافيّ، وهي مقاربات: عبدالله الغذّاميّ، ويُوسف عُليمات، ومريم عفانة، وأحمد المرازيق حول الشعر، ومقاربات نادر كاظم، وصالح الحجيلان، وأحمد آل مريع حول السرد، وإذا استثنيت مقاربة أحمد آل مريع؛ لأنّها في دراسة أنساق تلقّي سرديّات الجنون لا السرديّات ذاتها، ومقاربة الحجيلان، لأنّها تتخذ النقد الأدبيّ المحض منهجاً لها كما تعترف بذلك الباحثة، فإن الباحثة تكون بذلك قد تناولت في هذه الدراسة مقاربة واحدة في السرد، وهي مقاربة نادر كاظم.

ويشبه أن يكون هذا الكتاب إلماعةً أولى مُهمّة في التأريخ لتلقّي الأدب العربيّ في إطار نظرية النقد الثقافيّ، وهي حلقة في سلسلةِ دراساتٍ يجبُ أن تكون، وفي هذا السياق فإنّ دراستي تختصُّ بدراسة هذه الخطابات النقديّة التي تلقّت السرديّات العربيّة القديمة وحسب، دون غيرها.

وفي ضَوْء ذلك فإن الدراسة الراهنة تختلفُ عن هذه الدراسات جميعاً في مناحٍ منهجيّة وإجرائيّة ذواتي عَدَدٍ، أمّا أوّلها فإنّها مُختصّة بدراسة النقد الثقافيّ الذي تناولَ السرد وحسب دون الشعر، في حين أنّ هذه الدراسات اختصّتْ بدراسة القراءات التي قرأت السرد والشعر بصورةٍ عامّة، بصورة تجعلُ دراستي تتمازُ بكونها تمتلك حدوداً مُضاءة أو كاشفة للمتن النقديّ المدروس، وأما ثانيها، فأنّها

لم تأتِ على جُلّ بحوثات النقاد الثقافيّيْن ودراساتهم في دراسة التراث العربيّ عامّةً، والسرديّات العربيّة القديمة خاصّةً، مدارِ موضوع الدراسة الراهنة.

وأما ثالثها فهو أنّ هذه الدراسات لا تُفيد منهجياً من أدوات (نظرية التلقّي والتأويل) ومفاهيمها في التأريخ لفعل التلقّي، الذي مارسه هؤلاء القرّاء في قراءة السرديّات العربيّة القديمة[17]، إذ تبدو مفردات التلقّي والتأويل في هذه الدراسات مرتبطةً بسياقهما المعرفيّ العامّ، دون الإفادة الحقيقية من مقولاتها، في تصنيف هذه القراءات، والكشف عن نزوعات القراء أثناء ارتحالاتهم في البحث عن أنساق الخطاب المضمرة، وهو ما تحاول الدراسة الراهنة أن تستوفيه.

وعليه فإنّ هذه الدراسة انتحتْ منهجاً يتقاطع مع الدراسات السابقة في بعض من مناحيها، ويفترق عنها في مناحٍ أخريات، على أنّها حرصت على أن تفيد من هذه الدراسات قَدْرَ المستطاع، لظنّها الراسخ أنّها تشترك معها في مهمةٍ معرفيّة واحدة، مرومُها هو التأريخ لتلقّي الأدب العربيّ في إطار النقد الحديث، ومراجعة الأصول المعرفية للنظريّات التي يُستعان بها لقراءة هذا النصّ.

آخر القول:

لا مريةَ في أنّ اتساع المدوّنة النقديّة التي تشكّل متن الدراسة الراهنة تمثّل، والحالُ هذه، تحدياً معرفياً، تضطلعُ به هذه الدراسة، فقد تعدّدت القراءاتُ التي وظفت أدوات النقد الثقافيّ لقراءة السرديّات العربيّة القديمة: مقاماتٍ، وسرديّات جنون... إلخ، وقد تشابكتْ، مع حقولٍ معرفية أخرى، في مسعاها إلى أن تخالف المألوف من القراءات التقليديّة السائدة، على أنّ الدراسة الراهنة، تنطوي على ما في المكنة بأن يتسمّى بـ(قراءة المُتعة)، التي تحاولُ، وهي تدركُ وعورةَ مسالكها، أن ترصد ارتحالات النقد الثقافيّ من الغرب إلى الشرق، من خلال مُدراسة منجز النقّاد المُنشغلين بمقارباته، في ظِلالِ كفاحهم التائه أحياناً، والمُسْتنير في أخرى، في محاولة التأصيل للنقد الثقافيّ، ووضع قواعده الأُولى؛

التي يمكن الركون إليها في قراءة النصّ العربيّ، سردياً كان أم شعرياً، قراءةً ثقافيّة ناجزة.

وأخيراً، فإذا كان النقد الثقافيّ لا يزالُ نقداً فتياً، لمّا ينضجْ ولمّا يحترقْ ولمّا تَقَرَّ قواعده بعدُ، فإنّ ذلك ممّا يزيدُ في ثقل المهمّة المعرفيّة التي تنوءُ بها هذه الدراسة؛ ذلك أنّها تندرج في سياقات الكلام على الكلام كما يقول (أبو حيّانَ التوحيديّ)، ولكنَّ حسبَنَا أنَّا رمينا، وربما فرسٍ تظلُّ دون السابقة.

والله وليّ التوفيق والسداد

عامر سلمان أبو محارب
الزرقاء، الجمعة، 2024/1/5

هوامش المقدمة:

1 – سعيد، إدوارد، العالم والنصّ والناقد، ترجمة: عبد الكريم محفوض، منشورات اتحاد الكتاب العرب، دمشق، سوريا، ط1، 2000م، ص7.

2 – يُنظر: عصفور، جابر، نظريّات معاصرة، دار المدى للثقافة والنشر، دمشق، سوريا، ط1، 1998م، ص89. وكاظم، نادر، الهُويّة والسرد: دراسات في النظريّة والنقد الثقافيّ، دار الفراشة، الكويت، ط2، 2016م، ص13.

3 – رومية، وهب، شعرنا القديم والنقد الجديد، سلسلة عالم المعرفة، منشورات المجلس الوطني للثقافة والفنون والآداب، الكويت، العدد (207)، مارس 1996م، ص37.

4 – كاظم، نادر، المقامات والتلقّي: بحث في أنماط التلقّي لمقامات الهمذاني في النقد العربي الحديث، المؤسسة العربيّة للدراسات والنشر، بيروت، لبنان، ط1، 2004م، ص13.

5 – ينظر في سياق ذلك: البازعيّ، سعد، استقبال الآخر: الغرب في النقد العربيّ الحديث، المركز الثقافيّ العربيّ، بيروت، الدار البيضاء، لبنان، المغرب، ط1، 2004م، ص156.

6 – صالح، فخري، أزمة النقد العربيّ في الوقت الراهن وفواتنا الحضاريّ، مجلة علامات في النقد، النادي الأدبيّ الثقافيّ بجُدّة، جُدّة، المملكة العربيّة السعودية، الجزء (76)، 2013م، ص20.

7 – الجاحظ، عمر بن بحر (ت150هـ)، الحَيَوان، تحقيق وشرح: عبدالسلام هارون، مطبعة مصطفى البابي الحلبي، ط2، 1965م، القاهرة، مصر، ج1، ص 88.

8 – باعشن، لمياء نظريّات قراءة النصّ، مجلة علامات في النقد، النادي الثقافيّ بجُدّة، جُدّة، المملكة العربيّة السعودية، المجلد (10)، الجزء (39)، 2001م، ص119. وكاظم، نادر، المقامات والتلقّي...، (م.س)، ص31.

9 – يُجسّد مُصطلحُ «نمط التلقّي» مُصطلحاً رئيساً من مصطلحات نظريّة التلقّي، وهو اتّفاق ضمني بين زمرة من النقاد على الانخراط في ممارسة العمليّة النقديّة وفقاً لمنهجيّة معيّنة. يُنظر: كاظم، نادر، المقامات والتلقّي...، (م.س)، ص13.

10 – آيزابرجر، أرثر، النقد الثقافيّ: تمهيد مبدئي للمفاهيم الرئيسية، ترجمة: وفاء إبراهيم ورمضان بسطاويسي، المشروع القومي للترجمة، القاهرة، مصر، ط1، 2002م، ص31. والرويلي والبازعي، ميجان وسعد، دليل الناقد الأدبيّ: إضاءة لأكثرَ من سبعين تياراً ومصطلحاً نقدياً معاصراً، ط3، 2002م، المركز الثقافيّ العربيّ، بيروت، الدار البيضاء، لبنان، المغرب، ص231.

11 – مقابلة، جمال، وعي النقد ونقد الوعي في المقامة الموصليّة: قراءة تداوليّة ثقافيّة، المجلة الأردنية في اللغة العربيّة وآدابها، جامعة مؤتة، الكرك، الأردن، المجلد (2)، العدد (2)، 2006م.

12 – الحجيلان، صالح، الشخصية في قصص الأمثال: دراسة في الأنساق الثقافيّة للشخصيّة العربيّة، ط1، 2009م، المركز الثقافيّ العربي، بيروت، الدار البيضاء، لبنان، المغرب.

13 – آل مريع، أحمد، خطاب الجنون: الحضور الفيزيائيّ والغياب الثقافيّ (الاستبعاد والنفيّ)، ط1، 2014م مكتبة العبيكان، الرياض، المملكة العربيّة السعوديّة.

14 – ذلك أنّ عليمات يصدر في كل مقارباته عن أفق منهجيّ واحد يجمع بين النقد الأدبيّ والنقد الثقافيّ، أما الكعبيّ فالأفق الذي تصدر عنه أُفُقٌ يسعى إلى تجنيس النوع السرديّ ومن ثم استخراج أنساقه الثقافيّة. ينظر: عليمات، يوسف، أنساق الخطاب الحكائي

15 – يُنظر: الكعبيّ، ضياء، السرد العربيّ القديم: دراسة في الأنساق الثقافيّة وإشكاليّات التأويل، ط1، 2005م، المؤسسة العربيّة للدراسات والنشر، بيروت، لبنان، ص518 – 522.

16 – وهذه الدراسة في أصلها أطروحة أكاديميّة تقدّمت بها الباحثة لنيل درجة الماجستير في الأدب والنقد في جامعة الإمام محمّد بن سعود الإسلاميّة بالسعودية بعنوان: «قراءة النقد الثقافيّ للتراث الأدبيّ» عام 2016م. يُنظر: القفاري، أميرة، النقد الثائر: قراءة النقد الثقافيّ للتّراث الأدبيّ، ط1، 2019م دار الانتشار العربيّ، بيروت، لبنان. وقد استلت القفاريّ من مقاربتها بحثها هذا، وقدّمته في الندوة الدولية الثانية الموسومة بـ «قراءة التراث الأدبيّ واللغوي في الدراسات الحديثة»، جامعة الملك سعود، السعودية، 2014م، ص17 – 44.

17 – وذلك يشبه ما فعله نادر كاظم مثلاً في التأريخ لأنماط قراءة المقامات في النقد العربي الحديث. يُنظر: كاظم، نادر، المقامات والتلقّي...، (م.س)، ص11 – 19.

الفصل التمهيديّ:
أدبيّاتُ الدراسة ومقولاتُها المنهجيّة؛ مقتربٌ تأسيسيّ

ويشتمل هذا الفصل على أربع إضاءات:

المبحث الأول: نقد النقد: الحدُّ وآليّات الاشتغال.

المبحث الثاني: نظريّات القراءة: القارِئ ومسارات التلقّي.

المبحث الثالث: النقد الثقافيّ: المتن والمقولات وآفاق التنظير.

المبحث الرابع: السرديّات العربيّة القديمة: الأنواع وفضاءات التأويل.

فاتحة أولى:
في تحريرِ مُصطلحات الدراسة

يتكوّن الجهاز المفاهيميّ لهذه الدراسة الراهنة من مصطلحاتٍ أربعةٍ هي: النقد الثقافيّ، والسرديّات العربيّة القديمة، ونقد النقد، ونظريّات القراءة؛ ولعلّه من الحَسَنِ تحرير مصطلحات الدراسة؛ خشيةَ الوقوع في مغبّات فوضى الاصطلاح – إذا كان التعبير جائزاً – إذ تحاولُ الدراسة من خلال هذا البساط النظريّ أن تؤصّل نظرياً للمنطلقات المعرفيّة والمفاهيميّة التي تصدرُ عنها في جانبها الإجرائيّ.

أما نقد النقد؛ فيمكن أن يُعرَّف بأنّه ممارسة نقديّة تتعالى على القراءة الأولى التي يشيّدها النقاد حول ظاهرة/ نصّ ما، بوصفه يمكن أن يكون مُسباراً لمراجعة الخطابات النقديّة/ ومساءلة مرجعيّتها، والكشف عن مفاهيمهما الرئيسة، ومشحوناتها الإيديولوجيّة؛ فضلاً عن مدارسة مدى ملاءمة منطلقاتها الرؤيويّة التنظيريّة لأدواتها التطبيقيّة الإجرائيّة، أما نظريّات القراءة فهي نظرياتٌ تتصل بسُؤالات التلقّي، ونظريّات التأويل، وصنوف القُرّاء ومساراتهم في البحث عن المعاني النصّيّة، فضلاً عن انشغالها بمعاينة فِعْل التلقّي، والتأريخ له.

ويقصد بالنقد الثقافيّ الممارسةُ النقديّة التي تبحث في الأنساق الثقافيّة المُضمرة، والمعلنة كذلك كما يتبدى لدى بعض الدارسين، وهي أنساقٌ تضمرها النصوص في بنيتها العميقة، متكئةً علىِ مكر التمثيل ومراوغاته، ومجازات

اللغة واستعاراتها، في حين أنّ مفهوم السرديّات العربيّة القديمة يتحدّد بوصفها نوعاً أدبياً؛ ابتدأ منذ عصر ما قبل الإسلام (العصر الجاهليّ) في صورةٍ مرويّاتٍ وأخبارٍ وقصص، يرويها الناس عن بعضهم، وقد استمرّ حتى تبلورت الأجناس السرديّة الجديدة كالرواية والقصة والمسرحيّة في مطلع القرن الفائت.

نقد النقد: الحدُّ وآليّاتُ الاشتغال

1 – نقد النقد: المفهوم وفوضى الاصطلاح:

يمثل نقد النقد (Meta – Citicism) على اختلافِ تسمياته[1] مفهوماً فاعلاً في الدرس النقديّ المعاصر، منذ ثمانينيّات القرن المُنصرم، لا سيّما الغربيّة منها، التي اتكأت على تنظيرات (تزفيتان تودوروف Tzvetan Todorov) و(نورثروب فراي Northrop Frye) وغيرهما[2]، وفي سياقات هذا الخلاف أو (الفوضى الاصطلاحيّة)، التي أحدثها الخلاف على مسمّىً يُؤطّر مفهوم نقد النقد، بصورته العامة، فإن الدراسة الراهنة تذهبُ إلى ترادف مُصطلحي نقد النقد والميتا نقد في المدوّنة النقديّة العربيّة، فالوظائف التي تحدّدها المعاجم الأجنبيّة للميتا نقد هي ذاتها الوظائف المعرفيّة التي يعمل المنشغلون في حقول نقد النقد على تحقيقها في أثناء انشغالهم بممارسة نقد النقد[3].

وفي ظلّ هذا السياق، يرى محمد الدغموميّ، وهو كذلك أحد أبرز المنشغلين بحقول نقد النقد، أنّ نقد النقد «يتموضعُ في مكان آخر يجعله إبستمولوجيّةً نوعيّةً خاصّةً بموضوع معرفيّ هو النقد الأدبيّ، ويقفُ على عتبة العِلْم»[4]، وهو بوصفه مفهوماً معرفيّاً «ما زالَ يشيّدُ ويُبنى»[5]، على أن عدم الاكتمال هذا «لا ينفي اعتباره مشروعاً معرفيّاً متطوّراً»[6].

2 – نقد النقد ومدارات البحث:

يختصُّ النقد الأدبـيّ عموماً بدراسة النصوص الأدبيّة، ودراسـة مدى صلاحيتها وَفْقاً للفسلفة الكانطيّة، بيد أن نقد النقد، انطلاقاً من وظائفه المعرفيّة

وأدواته المنهجيّة، يتموضعُ بوصفه قراءةً عُليا، تتعالى بأدواتِها المنهجيّة على القراءة الأولى، أي قراءة النقد الأدبيّ، وتُسهمُ في إنتاج معرفةٍ جديدةٍ، من خلال الاستعانة بجهازٍ مفاهيميّ وعلميّ نوعي؛ وبذلك فإنّ نقد النقد «يختلف عن النقد في الكينونة والهُويّة والبِناء المنهجيّ والتوظيف المفاهيميّ»[7].

وإذا كانَ تزفيتان تودوروف (Tzvetan Todorov) أحدَ الأسماء الفاعلة في مِراس نقد النقد، تنظيراً، وتطبيقياً، في النقد الغربيّ، فلعلّ على الدراسة الراهنة أن تُشير إلى أنّ مفهوم نقد النقد يتحدّد لديه بوصفه ممارسةً قمينةً بأن يُنْهَدَ أَجْلَ الدفاع عن مشروعيتها العِلْميّة، وتخليصها من الأوضار التي قد تقدحُ في فعاليتها، أو في وظيفتها المعرفيّة[8].

وتتحدثُ المدوّنات النقديّة العربيّة التي حاولت التأصيل لنظريّة أو منهج نقد النقد عن أنّ خطاب نقد النقد يُعدُّ ضرورة معرفيّة، تستوجبُ الانخراط في مداراته؛ ابتغاء قراءة الخطابات النقديّة، وتفكيكها، وإعادة تقييمها، ويسجّلُ عمر زرفاوي عدداً كبيراً من هذه الأسباب، التي تستعلن لتؤكد ضرورة إنجاز مقاربات تفحص الخطاب النقديّ من منظور علميّ منهجيّ، وهي أسبابٌ يمكن أن تُجمل في التراكم النقديّ الذي يشهده الخطاب النقديّ في النقد المُعاصر دون إنبراء مقاربات تساءلُ هذه التيارات النقديّة، وتفحصها، وتراجعها، على الرغم من حضورها المركزيّ والممتد في الفضاء العربيّ[9]؛ ذلك أنّ ترك الخطاب النقديّ دون مراجعة ومساءلة يجعلُه عُرضةً «إلى نوعٍ من التكلُّس، والنمطيّة، والركود في الحياة النقديّة»[10].

وهكذا فإنّ خطاب نقد النقد يسعى إلى امتحان نجاعة النظريّات النقديّة التي يُستعان بها لقراءة النصّ الأدبيّ العربيّ، بوصفها (بناءات معرفيّة) وفقاً لتعبير محمد الدغموميّ[11]، فضلاً عن دورها المركزيّ في تصحيح مساراته النظرية النقديّة العربيّة، والوقوف على تحوّلاتها، ومعاينة إشكاليّاتها، ويشيرُ عمر زرفاوي إلى أنّ نقد النقد ينقسمُ من الناحيّة المنهجيّة إلى قسمين اثنيْن: أما أولاهما

فهو (نقد النقد التنظيريّ)، وأما ثانيتهما فهو (نقد النقد التطبيقيّ)[12].

وفي سياق هذا السابق يمكن القول: إنّ نقد النقد التنظيريّ هو الخطاب النقديّ الذي يمحور عمليّة المدارسة النقديّة للخطابات النقديّة النظريّة التي يدشّنها النقاد في فواتح دراستهم بغية الاتّكاء إليها في الإجراء التطبيقيّ، إذ «ينشغلُ هذا الفرع بمناقشة الأسس النظريّة والمعرفيّة للخطاب النقديّ، موضع الدرس، والبحث في مرجعيّاته الفكريّة، والفلسفيّة، والجماليّة، والسيسيولوجيّة، والزّمانيّة، وحتى الإيديولوجيّة»[13]، وأمّا خطاب نقد النقد التطبيقيّ فهو الخطاب الذي يسعى إلى قراءة الخطابات النقديّة التطبيقيّة الإجرائيّة، في تحقُّقها الفِعْلي، إذ «يركّز هذا القسمُ على الممارسة التطبيقيّة عند ناقد بعينه أو مجموعة من النقاد»[14].

وينبه الدغموميُّ إلى أنّ ثمّة إشكالات معرفيّة أو (معوقاتِ انتظام) يمكن أن تنحرفَ بخطابات نقد النقد عن مروماتها الأصيلة من مثل: الانتقائيّة، والاحتذاء، والتعميم، والادّعاء، والتحول أخيراً[15].

ولعلّ هذه الإشكالاتِ التي ينبه إليها الدغموميُّ تؤكّد أنّ الخطاب النقديّ الذي تُشيّده خطابات نقد النقد أو الدراسات الميتا نقديّة لا يسعى إلى تأسيس خطابٍ للمناوأة والاختلاف بمعنى الخِلاف، كما يتبدى ذلك في منجز الأسماء الفاعلة في مراس نقد النقد، وإنّما تتحدّدُ وظائفه بوصفه ممارسةً نقديّةً تُسهم، بسهمةٍ وافرةٍ، في إغناء العمليّة النقديّة، والكشف عن مرتكزات النظريّة النقديّة، وتحوّلات مساراتها.

ويرى باقر جاسم أن نظريات القراءة، التي فتحت أمام القارئ مراحاتِ التأويل على مصراعيها، خلّقت إشكاليّة تتمحور في ترسيخ حصانة القارئ/ الناقد من المساءلة، أو النقد؛ ذلك أنها «تدافع بشراسةٍ عن حقوق القارئ إزاء ما يمكن أن نسميه بحقوق النصّ؛ فهي في محصّلَة الأمر، تحصّن قراءة الناقد إزاء أيّ مساءلةٍ علميّةٍ أو أخلاقيّة»[16]، مما يجعل الخطاب النقديّ مَصُوناً عن

المراجعة العلميّة، والانخراط في حواريّة نقديّة، مرومها دفع الخطاب النقديّ، وتطويره، والأخذ بيده إلى سواء السبيل.

3 – نقد النقد وآليّات الاشتغال:

تختلف آليات الاشتغال المنهجيّ التي تؤطّر القراءة المعرفيّة لنقد النقد، وهي – بالطبع – آليات تسعى إلى أن تكون ضابطةً لوظيفته، على أنها لا تزال قَيْدَ التشكل عند مختلف الباحثين والدارسين، وليس في الحوزة آلياتٌ ضابطة قد اتفق عليها، ويمكن النظر إليها بوصفها نموذجاً يُحتذى.

ويؤمن زرفاوي بأنّه ينبغي على نقد النقد أن يهدفَ إلى دراسة النقد من خلال محاور تباحثه لغةً، ومقولاتٍ معرفيّة، ومرجعياتٍ علميّة، وتحولاتٍ منهجيّة، وملائمةً، ومحمولاتٍ معرفيّة[17]، وفي هذا السياق يقترح عبدالرحمن التمارة أن تتمحور حول سبع خطوات وهي على الترتيب: اعتمادُ مدخلٍ ملائم لمحمولات النصّ النقديّ، وتوضيحُ هندسته البنائيّة، والكشفُ عن غاياته، وتوصيفُ محمولاته، وإظهارُ مرجعيّاته، وتحديدُه، وإبرازُ عناصر الممارسة النقديّة خلاله[18]، ومن خلال هذه الآليات يمكن القول: إن فاعليّة نقد النقد تظلُّ مرهونة بأن يقدّم نصاً ثالثأ، يعقبُ تراتبياً النصّ الأوّل /المنقود، والنصّ الثاني /النقد؛ أجلَ فتح محجّاتٍ جديدة، يمكن أن تعين في محاولة الإلمام بمسارات الخطابات النقديّة، وتحوّلاتها.

4 – نقد النقد بوصفه تفكيكاً:

يشتبكُ تفكيكَ النقد بنقد النقد أو الميتا نقد، اشتباكاً معرفياً في الأصول المعرفيّة ومرومات البحث، وفي هذا السياق السابق ذاته يرى عبدالنبي اصطيف أن نقد النقد يَستعملُ – في مفهومه العامّ – استراتيجيّة التفكيك في قراءته للخطابات

النقديّة، ذلك نقد النقد هو «تفكيك النصّ النقديّ من أجْلِ إعادته إلى عناصره المشكّلة له، وتبينِ العمليّة التي أنشئ من خلالها في محاولةٍ جادة لتحديد الذّهنيّة التي أنتجته»[19]، وهو ما يؤكّده محمد البنكيّ في دراسته عن تجليّات حضور مشروع دريدا في النقد العربيّ، إذ تغدو وظيفة تفكيك النقد الرئيسة لديه هي «الكشفَ عن آليّات التفكير، واستراتيجيّات بناء المعرفة، بغية بلورة شروط الإمكان، وفحص حدود الصلاحيّة»[20].

وتجدرُ الإشارة إلى أنه قد تقرّر في البحثِ النقديّ والفلسفيّ أنّ مُصطلح التفكيك ينمازُ بكونه مصطلحاً أو مفهوماً سلبياً، فلقد فَكَّكَ دريدا، والتفيكك يفيدُ الهَدْمَ والبناء كليهما معاً، أهمَّ المُرتكزات التي تتكئ إليها الثقافة الغربيّة[21]، وإذا كانَ التفكيك كما قد قرَّ في أصوله الإصلاحيّة الفرنسيّة هدماً وتشتيتاً فإنّه يمكن أن يغدو، كذلك، وفقاً لدريدا فِعْلاً بنيوياً، أي بنائياً، يُفيد منه القارئ أو المُتلقّي في إعادة بناءٍ ما تَمَّ هدمه من النصوص بناءً جديداً؛ فيجعلها خلقاً آخر، وعليه فالتفكيكية (Deconstruction) لا بُدّ ألا تكونَ هدماً، على طولِ المسار، وإنما يجبُ أن تكون بناءً وتخليقاً كذلك[22].

– تركيب:

يمكن في ضَوْء الطرح السابق القول: إنّ مفهوم نقد النقد يتأطر بوصفه ممارسة نقديّة تتعالى على القراءة الأولى التي يشيّدها النقاد حول ظاهرة أو نصٍّ ما، وينتظم في خطوات منهجيّة ضابطة تجعله يمثّل مِسباراً لمراجعة الخطابات النقديّة، ومساءلة مرجعيّتها، والكشف عن مفاهيمهما الرئيسة، ومشحوناتها الأيديولوجيّة، وهندساتها البنائيّة، فضلاً عن مدارسة مدى ملاءمة منطلقاتها التنظيرية لإجراءاتها التطبيقيّة، وعليه فإنّ نقد النقد يمثّل اتّجاهاً أو حقلاً نقديّاً حداثيّاً جذب الأنظار إليه في الدرس النقديّ الحديث في الغرب والشرق؛ استناداً إلى فاعليته في تفكيك النصوص النقديّة، ومراجعتها، ومساءلتها.

المبحث الثاني:

نظريّات القراءة:
القارِئ ومسارات التلقّي

1 – التلقّي في نظريات القراءة؛ إلماعة في الإطار المفاهيميّ:

تتجدل نظريّات القراءة ونظرية التلقّي[23] ونقد استجابة القارئ[24] وغيرها في إطار منهجيّ موحّد يُباحث التلقّي النقديّ، ويجعل من التلقّي بوصفه موضوعاً مراحاً للمساءلة والمدارسة، ذلك أنّها تتفق على أنّه ينبغي أن تمنح القراءة النقديّة التي يفرزها التلقّي النقدي فضل مباحثة ومدارسة، بوصف وظيفة القارئ/ الناقد تمثل، والحال هذه، وظيفةً تكون مركزيّة في قراءة النصوص.

ولعل ذلك يجيء في ظلال تَغَيُّبِ المُتلقّي عن مُجتليات النقد والبحثِ سنينَ طويلةً، حين كانت سطوةُ المُؤلّف ضاربةً بأطنابها على ميادين النقد في الشرق والغرب، ولا محيص من الإشارة إلى أن نظرية التلقّي ترتبط بما يُعرف في المدرسيات الغربية بنقد استجابة القارئ، ويمكن القول: إن جل هذه النظريات أعادت للقارئ (المتلقّي) السلطة، إذ كان مصطلح (سلطة القارئ/ المتلقّي) أحد أبرز إفرازاتها المعرفيّة والنقديّة، ولذا فإننا نجد أن هذا المصطلح بدأ يتموضع؛ ليحلّ بوصفه بديلاً منهجياً ومعرفياً عن مصطلح (سُلطة المؤلّف) الذي أصّلت له البنيويّة فيما مضى من تاريخ النظريّة النقديّة الحديثة.

2 – القارئ وصنوفُ القرّاء ومساراتُ البحثِ عن المعنى:

تمحورُ نظريّات القراءة جميعُها عمليّة التلقّي النقديّ حول المُتلقّي، الذي يضطلعُ بمهمة القراءة؛ ذلك أن وظيفة المتلقّي القارئ لدى (ستانلي فيش) تنحصر بمَهمّة إعادة تخليق المعنى النصّي، وفقاً لاستراتيجيات معيّنة، تحتكمُ

إليها قراءته للنّصّ[25]؛ فالقراءة النقديّة للنّصّ ليستْ مرهونة بهتك الحُجُبِ التي تُغطي أو تسترُ المعنى النصيّ، وإنما تظلّ مرهونة «بصناعة المعاني والنصوص، وليس استخلاصها أو كشف الحجب عنها»[26].

وفي هذا السياق يطرح جيرالد برنس (Gerald Prince) ثلاثة أصناف من القرّاء، تختصُّ بالقارئ، ومنها: القارئ الحقيقيّ (Real Reader) وهو القارئ «الذي يمسك كتاباً بيديه»[27]، والقارئ الفِعْليّ (Tule Prince) «وهو نوع من القرّاء يعتقد المؤلف بأنه يكتب له، قارئٌ يمنحه المؤلف رسائل وقابليات وميولاً معيّنة»[28]، والقارئ المثاليّ (Ideal Reader) «وهو القارئ الذي يفهم النصّ فَهماً تاماً، ويتذوق كل دقائقه»[29]، ويشير هارولد بلوم (Harold Bloom) إلى القارئ القويّ (Strong Reader)[30]، وهو القارئ/ الناقد الذي لا يتقيّد في أثناء قراءته بشروط آفاق التلقّي القارّة التي يتبنى هذا القارئ/ الناقد مسلماتها وتعاليمها، أما القارئ الكفء (Competent Reader) فإنّه القارئ الذي يَصْدُرُ عن أفق منهجيّ، ويحقق شروط الإتقان والاستيفاء لمقولات هذا الأفق المنهجيّ الذي يشتغل عليه، أو يقوم بتجريبه[31].

ويتحدث الناقد تزفيتان تودوروف (Tzvetan Todorov) عن ثلاثة أنواع من القراءات التي يمكن أن تشيّد حول النصوص، وهي: القراءة الإسقاطية، والقراءة الشارحة، والقراءة الشعريّة، والقراءة السطحية[32]، ويتحدّث حسين خَمري عن ضروب مختلفة من القراء، الذين يشير إليهم رولان بارت، فمنهم من يمارسون في قراءتهم على النصّ عنف القراءة، ومنهم من يمارسون على النص القراءة السطحيّة، ومنهم من يحاولون أن تكون قراءتهم ناسخةً تنسخ القراءات السابقة للنّصّ، وتجدد في نُهُجِ قراءته[33].

3 - نمط التلقّي: من التلقّي الفرديّ إلى الجماعيّ:

يجسّد مُصطلحُ (نمط التلقّي) مصطلحاً رئيساً من مصطلحات نظريّات

القراءة، ويعرّف نمط التلقّي بأنّه اتّفاق ضمنيٌّ بين مجموعة من النقاد على الانخراط في ممارسة العملية النقديّة وفقاً لمنهجيّة نقديّة معيّنة، وهو بذا حالة من التلقّي الجماعيّ المشترك، الذي يتواضع خلاله مجموعة من النقاد على منهجيات ومواقف ومفاهيم واستراتيجيّات واحدة.

وتأسيساً على السابق فيمكن القول: إنّ (نمط التلقّي) هو تشاكلُ القراءات أو صدورها عن أفق معرفيّ وتاريخيّ واحد، ودراسة نمط تلقّ أو أنماط تلقّ، من خلال البحث في تاريخ تلقّي نص ما عبر مراجعة صنوف القراءات المتعاقبة حول ظاهرة أدبية معينة، يعدُّ «من منظور جماليّة التلقّي، دراسة لا ينفصلُ فيها النصّ الذي يُقرأ عن تاريخ تلقّيه، فتاريخ التلقّيات والقراءات الخاص بنص ما هو الذي يمكننا من فهمه بعد أن أُنجز وأصبح ماضياً»[34] .

ويتحدث نادر كاظم في سياق تأصيله لمصطلح نمط التلقّي عن مفهومَيْن يتداخلان أو يتشابكان عند الحديث عن نمط التلقّي، وهما: مصطلح (الجماعة التفسيريّة) (Interpretive Communities)، عند ستانلي فيش (Stanley Fish) في كتابه (هل هُناك نص في هذا الفصل؟) (Is There a Text in This Class?)، ومصطلح (النموذج الإرشاديّ) عند توماس كون (Thomas Kuhn)[35]، ويقصد ستانلي فيش بمصطلح (الجماعة التفسيريّة) (Collective Interpretation) الجماعةَ التي يتشاركُ أعضاؤها باستعمال أعراف قراءة واستراتيجيّاتٍ تفسيريّة واحدة، أو متقاربة، حيث ينتهون في أغلب الأحيان إلى نتائج واحدة، وهم يتحرّكون في مدارات بحثية متشابهة، ويهجسون بتسآلات معرفية متساوقة؛ بصورة تغدو خلالها «استراتيجياتُ جماعةٍ مُؤوّلة خاصةٍ مرتبطة بتقرير عمليّة القراءة برمتها»[36]، أما بالنسبة إلى (النموذج الاستبداليّ أو الإرشـــاديّ) فإنّ توماس كون (Thomas Kuhn) اقترحه في كتابه (بُنية الثورات العلميّة)، وهو يعني لدى كون، النموذج الذي يُحتذى به، ويُسار على منواله، ويُلْتَزَمُ بضوابطه، وهو النموذج القرائيّ، الذي يمثّل قاسماً مشتركاً بين

جماعة من القراء، ويُعرّف كون النموذج الإرشادي بوصفه «هو تلك النظريات المعتمدة كنموذج لدى مجتمع من الباحث العلميّ»[37].

– تركيب:

تنجدل نظريّات القراءة ونظرية التلقّي وجمالية التلقّي ونقد استجابة القارئ بخيطٍ شفيف، يقوم على معاينة فعل التلقّي، ومن ثم الكشف عن ممارسات القارِئ ومسارات التلقّي في العمل/ الخطاب النقدي، وقد تبين أنّ ثمة ضروباً من القرّاء من مثل: القارئ الكفء، والقارئ القويّ، والقارئ المقلد، والقارئ الأجناسيّ...إلخ.

ولا مشاحة في أن مُصطلحَ (نمط التلقّي) يتموضع بوصفه مصطلحاً رئيساً في إطار هذه القراءات جميعها، وهو اتّفاق ضمني بين مجموعة من النقاد على الانخراط في ممارسة العملية النقديّة وفق شروطٍ ومحددات وضوابط مخصوصة.

المبحث الثالث:

النقد الثقافيّ:
المتن والمقولات وآفاق التنظير

1 – النقد الثقافيّ: ملابسات النشأة ومدارات المفهوم:

يعدُّ النقد الثقافيّ بوصفه نقداً ما بعديّاً أحدَ أبرز نتاجاتِ مركز الدراسات الثقافيّة المُعاصرة (Center for Contemporary Cultural Studies) في جامعة بيرمنجهام بإنجلترا في ستّينيّات القرن المُنصرم؛ وهو كذلك أحدُ أبرز الاتّجاهات النقديّة التي تتموضعُ في طليعة الاتجاهات النقديّة التي قرّت تسميتُها، شرقاً ومغرباً، بالمابعديات؛ أي ما بعد الحداثة أو ما بعد البنيويّة[38].

وهكذا فقد ارتبط النقد الثقافيّ برباطٍ وثيق العُرى بالدراسات الثقافيّة (Cultural Studies)[39]، بصورةٍ يغدو أمرُ الفَصْل بينهما أمراً عسيراً وشائكاً؛ ذلك أنهما كما تقرّر في معظم مدوّنات النظرية الحديثة، يمثّلان اتجاهيْن نقديين يؤطّران لممارسات نقديّة تتقارب فيما بينها؛ تهتَمُّ بدراسة الثقافة ومُنتجاتها من مناظيرَ معرفيّة مُتعددة؛ مثل: الأنثربولوجيا، وعلم الاجتماع، والنقد الأدبيّ[40]، وترفضُ بعض الأسماء الفاعلة في النظريّة النقديّة الحديثة أن تعترف بالنقد الثقافيّ بوصفه منهجاً قائماً بذاته، ذلك أنه يتحدّد لديها بوصفه نشاطاً معرفياً، ومن هذه الأسماء النقديّة البارزة آرثر أيزا برجر (Arthur Asa Berger) الذي يمثل النقد الثقافيّ لديه «نشاطاً وليس مجالاً معرفياً خاصاً بذاته»[41].

وفي سياق ذلك يتمثل صعود تيارات الدراسات الثقافيّة كما يرى رونان ماكدونالد صاحب كتاب (موت الناقد) في نشر (رايموند ويليامز) (Raymond Williams) لكتابه المشهور (Culture and Society)[42]، الذي مثّل إرهاصاً بشّر بولادة هذه الدراسات، التي تحولت «إلى مشروع سياسيّ يزدري الشكلانيّة

والوَلَعَ بالآداب الرفعية»[43]، وفي سياق ذلك يضطلع النقد الثقافيّ عند (فنسنت ليتش) (V.Leitch)، الذي بدء بالدعوة إلى (نقد ثقافيّ ما بعد بنيويّ) (Post Structural Cultural Criticism –) في كتابه المهم (النقد الثقافيّ، النظرية الأدبيّة، ما بعد البنيوية) (Post , Literary Theory , Cultural Criticism) Structuraslim[44]، بمهمة إيديولوجيّة تحدّد بقراءة النصّ، بوصفه وثيقةً إيديولوجيّة (Ideological)[45].

إنّ مفهومَ النقد الثقافيّ – في ضَوْء السابق – يتحدّدُ بوصفه منهجاً نقدياً ما بعدياً أو ما بعدَ حداثي أو ما بعد بنيويّ، ينمازُ باشتغال مُنظّريه والمهتمين بمقارباته بمحاولة القَبْضِ على الأنساق الثقافيّة المُضمرة/ المعلنة في بِنى الخِطاب العميقة، أو الماكرة بحسب تعريف ستيفن غرينبلات (Stephen Greenblatt)؛ ذلك أنَّ النصّ يمثّلُ لديهم بنيةً مخاتلةً تتسمُ بالمفارقة والمراوغة والاختلاف، لما تخلّقه المجازاتُ والاستعاراتُ والصّور الشعريّة في النصّ شعرياً كان أم سرديّاً من طاقاتٍ لغويّة وشعريّة تعمل على تعمية النصّ، وجعله بنية ماكرة ومراوغة[46]، وعليه فإنّ هذه المجازات والتوترات تجعلُ النصّ منمازاً على الدوام بتعدّدية المعنى أو لا نهائية التأويل في ظل مفهوم خيبة التلقّي والتأويل، فقد عادت (سُلطة المتلقّي) في النقد الثقافيّ إلى التوهج بعد خُفوت (سلطةِ المُؤلّف) (Author Authority).

ويلحظُ المستبصر في المرجعيّات المعرفيّة والتنظيريّة للنقد الثقافيّ أنّ النصّ في ضَوْء القراءة الثقافيّة، بنيةٌ تتشكلُ، والحال هذه، من أنساقٍ تحتاجُ إلى إنجاز قراءة واعيةٍ، تستأهلُ – ضرورةً – (ناقداً مُختلفاً) (Dissident Critic) يكون بوَسْعِهِ الجَوْسُ خلال شِعاب النصّوص ووهادها، بُغية القبض على هذه الأنساق، ومن ثَمَّ الكشف عن آليّات تشكّلها، وتمظهراتها في ثنايا النصوص، وعليه فإنّ في المُكنةِ القول: إنّ النصّ الأدبيّ قد غدا في ضَوْء المقاربات النقديّة الثقافيّة نصّاً ثقافيّاً؛ أي نصّاً تشرّب أو امتصّ قيم المجتمع والثقافة اللتين أُنتج في مطاويهما.

2 – النسق الثقافيّ: إلماعة في آفاق المصطلح:

يمثّلُ مصطلح النسق (Category) مصطلحاً محوريّاً مركزيّاً في النقد الثقافيّ والدراسات الثقافيّة وأخيراً في النقد النسقيّ؛ ذلك أنّ نظريّة النقد الثقافيّ تختصُّ بمساءلة الأنساق الثقافيّة المُضمرة في بنى النصوص الأدبيّة، وهي تُعنى بطبيعة تحوّلات هذه الأنساق، وتشكُّلاتها، ووظائفها، ومُمارساتها، وفاعليتها، ومحمولاتها الثقافيّة، ولا ريب أنّ النسق بوصفه مفهوماً نقديّاً لمّا ينزلْ مثار نزاعٍ واختلاف، وهو يُمثّل عُنصراً مركزيّاً في الحضارة والمعرفة والثقافة والسياسة، وهو مراوغ وزئبقيّ وخدّاع[47]، إذ إنّه «يتسمُ من حيث هو نظامٌ بالمُخاتلة، واستثمارِ الجماليّ والمجازيّ؛ ليكرّر جدليّاته ومضمراته التي لا تنكشفُ إلا بالقراءة الفاحصة»[48]، وهنا يرى نيكلاس لومان أنّه «بإمكان النسق أن يتكرر بداخل نفسه»[49].

ولعلّ التأصيل التاريخيّ وكذا المفاهيميّ لمُصطلح النسق يقتضي الإشارة إلى أنّ النسقَ بوصفه مصطلحاً مفاهيمياً قد بدأ يتشكّلُ على يد اللغويّ السويسريّ دي سوسير، فقد كان «أكثر اللسانيين شغفاً بالنسق»[50]، فقد تردَّد هذا المُصطلح «مراراً في محاضرات سوسير؛ بل كاد يمثّل المحور الجوهريّ في نظريته»[51]، بيد أنّ مصطلح النسق كان يعني عند سوسير البِنية أو النظام؛ وهو يستخدمُ عند سوسير في إطار تعريفه مصطلح اللغة[52]، ويلحظُ أنّ ثمة وشيجة تربط بين المعنى الاصطلاحيّ والمعنى اللغويّ لمفردة (نسق)[53].

إنّ مُصطلح النسق، وإن كان يحتفظ في إطار النقد الثقافيّ بهذا المعنى العامّ، أقصدُ البنية أو النظام، إلا أنّه قد مرّ بتحولات مفاهيميّة واصطلاحيّة جذريّة في سياق النقد الثقافيّ؛ وبفعل هذه التحولات فقد أمسى مفهوم النسق يكتسي بُعداً ثقافيّاً، وبذا فقد غدا النسق الثقافيّ من خلاله «نسقاً معرفيّاً اجتماعيّاً فكريّاً، يحملُ كلّ ما تفرزه الثقافة في النصّ أو الخِطاب»[54]، ويذهبُ نادر كاظم إلى أنّ

تحديد لحظة ولادة أو نشوء مصطلح النسق الثقافيّ يعدُّ أمراً عسيراً، إذ يرجعُ نشوءه إلى تداخل حقلينِ مَعْرفيّينِ كبيرينِ هما: الأنثروبولوجيا والنقد الأدبيّ الحديث(55)، وعيله فإنّ النسقَ في النصّ الأدبيّ ينمازُ في إطار النقد الثقافيّ بوصفه يظلّ نزاعاً إلى المخاتلة؛ إذ يغدو أمرُ القبض عليه أمراً صعباً؛ يستطلب جهازاً نقدياً متكاملاً، يتسلّح به الناقد الثقافيّ، كما أُشِيرَ سابقاً، للدخول في هذا الرهان المعرفيّ الصّعب.

3 – ارتحالات النظريّة: تلقّي النقد الثقافيّ في مُجتليات النقد العربيّ:

لا محيصَ من القول: إنّ الناقد عبدالله الغذّامي بوصفه ناقداً مجدداً ومختلفاً في الآن عينه؛ قد انبرى ليكون في طليعة الذين أقبلوا على تلقّي نظريّة النقد الثقافيّ، تنظيراً وتطبيقياً وترجمةً؛ ممّا أسهم في تبلور مشروعه النقديّ الخاصّ في إطارات النقد الثقافيّ، بصورة تحوّل خلالها مشروعه إلى مدرسة نقديّة، تحلّقتْ حولها زمرٌ من الباحثين المنبهرين بها؛ مثل: (نادر كاظم وضياء الكَعبيّ)، والمُعادين لها؛ مثل: (عبدالنبي اصطيف)(56)، والمنتقدين لها كما يبدو في نَقَدات: (عبدالله حامد وعبدالله إبراهيم وعبدالقادر الرباعيّ)(57)، ولذا فلا مراء في القول: إنّ الغذامي قد غدا «ظاهرة يتحلّق حولها معجبون كثر، ويتربّصُ بها غرماءُ أكثر»(58).

وقد أثارَتْ مقولاتُ الغذّاميّ إشكالاتٍ منهجيّة وإبستمولوجيّة بدعوته إلى موت النقد الأدبيّ، وإحلال النقد الثقافيّ بديلاً منهجياً له، وبناءً عليه فإنّ الغذّاميَّ يمثّل أحدَ الباحثين القلائل الذين أخلصوا – في ظلال تجاربهم النقديّة – لنظريّة من نظريّات النقد الحديث، فما برحوا يُوصّلون لها، ويُساجلونها، ويدرسون النصوص وفقاً لمنظوراتها، فالنقد الثقافيّ تَمثَّلَ لديه بوصفه منهجاً ناجعاً، في مناوشة النصوص، ومحاولة سَبْرها، والنفاذ إلى بِناها العميقة.

وتجدرُ الإشارة إلى أن مقاربة الغذّاميّ تفصح عن تمثيلاتِ قارئٍ مُختلف، أو عن تجليات مفهوم القارئ الثائر [59]، على أنّ الحكم على صحّة ذلك الاختلاف من خطئه ليستْ من مرومات الدراسة الراهنة، فقد استطاع الغذّامي – وهو يعي ما يريد – أن يُفيد من منجزات النقد الثقافيّ في إنجاز مقاربة إشكاليّة منهجياً ومفاهيمياً وتطبيقياً، جعلت مشروعه موضوعةً سجاليّة ومعرفيّة، جذبتِ الأنظار إليها، مشرقاً ومغرباً، وأدّت وظيفة إشهاريّة وتسويقيّة، جعلته – مع تقادم السنين – نموذجَ التلقّي المعياريّ.

ولعلّه من مكرور القول الإشارة إلى أنّ مشروعه هذا قد حَظِيَ بمراجعات ونَقَداتٍ لا تُكاد أن تُحصى، تتلخّص في أغلبها على مختزل مؤدّاه أن الغذّاميّ قد وَقَعَ في شِراك القراءة التعميميّة، ومعضلة اجتزاء النصوص من سياقاتها، وممارسة حريّة القراءة، ممّا أوقعه وفاقاً لذلك في ما يمكن الاصطلاح على تسميته بـ(فوضى التأويل)[60].

ويرى عبدالعزيز حمودة أنّ وظيفة النقد الثقافيّ تتجلّى في الكشف عن وظائف الأيديولوجيا في الخِطاب الأدبيّ، ولذا فإنّ هدفه الرئيس عند حمودة يتمحورُ في «استكشاف الوظائف الأيديولوجيّة للنصوص في مراحل تاريخيّة متنوعةٍ، وفي ممارسات ثقافيّة متباينة»[61]؛ وتتماثلُ وظيفة النقد الثقافيّ عند عامة المنشغلين به، فهو يُعنى بالأيديولوجيا والأفكار والسياسة.

4 – معضلة النقد الثقافيّ: جدل الجماليّ والقُبحيّ:

تمثل جدليّة الجماليّ والقُبحيّ معضلة منهجية عند عامة المنشغلين بنظريّة النقد الثقافيّ في مُجتليات النقد العربيّ الحديث، فقد تفرّقوا شِيَعاً في دراسة النصّوص وفقاً لآليّات النقد الثقافيّ، أمّا الفريق الأوّل فقد ذهب إلى أنّ النقد الثقافيّ كما تأسس في مراجعه الأصليّة نقدٌ يُعنى بدراسة القبحيات، ومُضمرات الثقافة في النصوص، مُتسترةً بعباءات الجماليّ، وأما الاتجاهُ الآخرُ فقد نحى

منحىً مختلفاً في هذه المسألة، وقد ذهب منظّروه إلى أنّ مهمة الناقد الثقافيّ لا يمكنُ أن تكونَ مقصورةً على دراسة قُبحيّات الثقافة، وألاعيبها، بل إنّ فضاءات البحثِ لا بُدّ من أن تُفْسَحَ للبحث عن الجماليّات الثاويّة في بِنى هذه النصوص؛ ذلك أنّ الدراسة الثقافيّة الناجزة للنُّصوص يجب أن تنطلق من منظورات اتّجاه معرفيّ اصطلح على تسميته بـ(جماليّات التحليل الثقافيّ)[62].

ولا شك أن جدل الجمالي والقبحي امتدَّ إلى أن شكّل مدرستين نقديتين مختلفتين ومتضادتين وسمها الباحث هشام زغلول بالتيار الغذامي نسبة إلى عبد الله الغذامي والتيار الربّاعيّ نسبة إلى عبدالقادر الربّاعي وهو يقول في هذا السياق: «من يراجع النقد الثقافيّ في المدونة العربيّة ـتنظيراً وممارسة ـ يجده موزعاً بين تيارين كبيرين؛ أحدهما: ثقافي محض، يتخذ من القبحيات وحدها مدخلاً للنقد الثقافيّ، ولا ينفكُّ يقتفي قرائن تمرير النسقي/القبحي عبر الجماليّ؛ وهذا ما أسميه التيار الغذامي. والآخر: ثقافي ـ أدبي/جمالي، يضفر الجماليّات بمقارباته الثقافيّة، ولا يرى تعارضاً بين ما هو ثقافي وما هو جمالي/أدبي. وينطلق من رؤية جمالية محايثة لا تعارِض النقد الثقافى في بنيته الصلبة، فتطرح الخطاب عوضاً عن النسق المضمر (القبحي)؛ وهذا ما أسميه التيار الربّاعيّ»[63].

إنّ هذين التيارين شكّلا مدرستين نقديتين مركزيّتين في النقد الثقافيّ على امتداد الوطن العربي، ولكل مدرسة أتباعها، ومقولاتها النظرية، وأدواتها النقديّة.

وعلى أيّة حال؛ فإنّ هذه المساءلة تعدّ معضلة إبستمولوجيّة وإشكاليّة منهجيّة، وهي لا تزالُ مثارَ نزاع في النقد الثقافيّ، على أنّ الدراسة الراهنة تذهب إلى أن القراءة الثقافيّة لا بُدَّ أن تنفتح انفتاحاً واعياً على النصوص، وأن تقرأ أنساقها قراءةً واعيةً دون الاكتراث لمسألة القبحيّات والجماليّات، وألّا تجعل استخراج الأنساق القبحيّة أو الجماليّة منطلقاً مسبقاً؛ يحوّل القراءة الثقافيّة للنصوص إلى قراءة آليّة تتغيّا أن تستخرج هذه الأنساق، بإكراه النصّ، أو لي عنقه؛ ليتساوق مع المنطلقات التي تحددها مسبقاً.

- تركيب:

يعدُّ النقد الثقافيّ نقداً ما بعدياً نشأ في ظلال الدراسات الثقافيّة في مركز برمنغهام ببريطانيا، وهو يسعى إلى الكشف عن الأنساق الثقافيّة المضمرة في الخطاب، وقد أثار سجالات وصراعات معرفيّة في مجتليات النقد العربيّ الحديث، تختصُّ بفاعليته، وجدواه، وحقيقة وجوده، ووظيفته التي تراوحُ بين الكشف عن ألاعيب الثقافة أو جماليّاتها، وينهضُ النقد الثقافيّ على مفترض مؤدّاه أن القراءة الثقافيّة تكشفُ أنّ النصوص وإن كانت تتوسّلُ بالجماليّ والمجازيّ، فإنها تبدو من وجهة نظر أخرى نصوصاً غيرَ بريئةٍ، تخاتلُ المتلقّي، وتراوغه؛ ذلك أنّ حركة الأنساق الثقافيّة فيها لوَّابةٌ، ومخاتلةٌ، ومُضلِّلة، لا يقرُّ قرارها، ويصعبُ القبض عليها؛ فهي تستطلب قارئاً خبيراً، وناقداً مُثقَّفاً، يكون قادِراً على أن يَقْبِضَ على بِنى النصّ العميقة، ودِلالاتها، وتمثيلاتها، وأبعادها.

المبحث الرابع:

السرديّات العربيّة القديمة:
الأنواع وفضاءات التأويل

1 - في السرد والسرديّة: تشييد مفاهيميّ:

لـمّا يتشكّلُ مفهوم السرد (Narration) بتجلياته الموضوعيّة والإصطلاحيّة والمفاهيميّة، بصورته الراهنة سوى في قرونٍ مُتأخّرة، على أنَّ السردَ عموماً هو صِنْو الشعر، وقَسيمه، وذلك وفاقاً للقولةِ الرائجة في نظريّة الأدب، التي مؤدّاها أنّ الأدب ليس إلا فنّ الشعريّات والسرديّات[64]، وفي سياقِ التأصيل الإصطلاحيّ لمُصطلح السرد، فلعلّ من اللازب الإشارة إلى معاني الجذر (سَرَدَ) في المعاجم العربيّة القديمة؛ ذلك أنّ مفهوم السرد في تلك المعاجم يرتبطُ بوشائج مفاهيميّة مع مفهوم السرد في النقد الأدبيّ الحديث، إذ تشير الجذريّة المُعجميّة (السرد) لمفردة في المعجمات العربيّة إلى معانٍ عدة تتمحور في ظلال مفاهيمَ رئيسةٍ من مثل: الكلام المتتابع، والحدث المسرود[65].

وبناءً على هذا فإنّ لفظة (السرد) تتواشج معجمياً من ناحية المعنى مع كلمة (سرد) كما ترد في معاجم النظرية السردية الحديثة، إذ يُعرّف جيرالد برنس (Gerald Prince) السرد بأنّه: «خطابٌ يقدّم حدثاً أو أكثر، ويتمُّ التمييز تقليدياً بينه وبين الوصف والتعليق؛ سوى أنّه كثيراً ما يتمُّ دمجُهما فيه..»[66]، ولـمّا يزل الاختلاف قائماً ومثاراً بين النقاد حول الركون أو الاتّفاق على اسم واحد يتّصفُ به هذا النوع الأدبيّ، ومن هذه التسميات: السرد، والسرديّة، والسرديّات؛ بيد أنّ المتبصّر فيها يلحظ أن بوناً ينقام فيما بينها[67]، فالسرد «هو مجموعُ الكلام الذي يؤلّف نصّاً يتيح للكاتب أن يتّصل بالقارئ»[68]، أما السردية فهي منهج نقديّ، وهي «لا تعنى بالمتون السرديّة ذاتها، إنّما بكيفيّات ظهور مكوناتها سردياً، أي

بالممارسة السرديّة التي اتخذتها مكوّنات السرد ضمن البِنية السرديّة»[69].

ولا مرية أنّ السردَ لم يَعُدْ في النظريّة النقديّة الحديثة مجرّد متواليات حكائيةٍ تؤدّي وظائفَ إمتاعيّةً وحسبُ، إذ يعد السرد «مظهراً من مظاهر الإنتاج الأدبيّ؛ ولم يعُد مجرّد شكلٍ أو بناء أدبيّ، بل أصبحت ثقافةُ ما بعد الحداثة تتحدث عن السرديّات الكُبرى، التي يُشار بها إلى الأنساق الفكريّة الكبرى بما تقدّمه من تفسيراتٍ كُليّة للظواهر»[70].

وانطلاقاً من هذا التصوّر تُمْكِنُ الإشارة إلى مركزيّة الخطاب الشعريّ في الثقافة العربيّة، الأمر الذي حَدَا بالنقد العربيّ إلى محورةِ الخطاب النقديّ، أوّل الأمر، حول هذا الخطاب، استناداً إلى الفكرة المركزيّة، والرائجة كذلك، التي مفادها أن الشعر ما فتئ يُمثّل للأمة العربيّة ديوانها، بوصفه الخطاب الرسميّ /المركزيّ في الثقافة العربيّة[71]، على أنه لا بُدَّ من الإشارة إلى صعود منزلة الكاتب مقابل تخلخل مكانة الشاعر المادح[72]، إذ لم تَعُدْ مكانة الشاعر مكانةً سَنيّة مثلما كانت في السالف السابق، ولعلّ ذلك يجيءُ اتساقاً والتحولاتِ الجذريّة التي مرّت بها الثقافة العربيّة، ولعلّ أمارات هذا التحول قد ظهرت في فواتح عصر بني أميّة، حين غدتْ وظيفة الكتاب وظيفة مركزيّة، ذلك أنّه بالكتابة «ينتظم المُلْكُ، وتستقيم للملوك أمورهم»[73] كما قال عبدالحميد الكاتب في رسالته الشهيرة إلى الكتّاب.

2 – السرديّات العربيّة القديمة: مدخل إلى الأجناس السرديّة:

يتحدّد مفهوم السرديّات العربيّة القديمة بوصفها نوعاً أدبياً ابتدأ منذ عصر ما قبل الإسلام (العصر الجاهليّ)، واستمرّ إلى أن تبلورت الأجناس السرديّة الجديدة في بواكير القرن المنصرم، وإذا كان مُصطلح السرديّات لم يقرَّ بعدُ في المدوّنة النقديّة الحديثة، فإنّ الدراسة الراهنة تحاول أن تُؤطّر مفهوم السرديّات العربيّة القديمة؛ بوصفها أنواعاً أدبيّة، تنماز عن قسيمها الشعر، الذي يشترط

الوزن والقافية، بوصفهما معيارَيْن أجناسيَّيْن يتحدد وينمازُ بهما النوع الشعري، وبناءً على التأطير المفاهيميّ السابق فإنّ الدراسة الراهنة تميل إلى مُصطلح السرديّات القديمة، وهي تقصد بذلك الأنواع السرديّة، التي شاعتْ في السرديّات العربيّة القديمة، من مثل: المقامة، والحكاية، ولعلّ في اختيار هذا الاسم منأىً عن الإشكاليّات المفاهيمية والاصطلاحيّة التي تُثيرها تلك التسميات الأخرى، وترى ضياء الكعبيُّ أنّ ثَمّة مقترحاتٍ عديدةً يمكنُ أن يُوسمَ بها الموروث السرديّ مثل: السرديّة العربيّة، والموروث الحِكائيّ العربيّ، والتراث القصصيّ، والأدب القصصيّ، والسرد العربيّ القديم [74].

وتغدو الإشارة لازبةً في صَدْرِ الحديث عن السرديّات العربيّة القديمة إلى أنّ الباحثين يرون أن النثر العربيّ ينشعبُ إلى قسمين اثنين؛ أما أولاهما فهو الذي ينطوي في تضاعيفه على بعد سرديّ من مثل؛ الحكاية، والمقامة... إلخ، وأما ثانيتهما فيكون خِلْواً من هذا البُعد من مثل: الخطبة، والمَثَل، ويستدعي الحديث عن السرديّات العربيّة القديمة الإشـارةَ إلى أنها من منظور عبدالله إبراهيم تنشعبُ إلى نمطين هما: النمط الشفويّ، والنمط الكتابي/ المدوّن [75]، ويتحدّث إبراهيم عن عددٍ من الموجّهات التي أثّرت بصورةٍ بارزةٍ في مسارات السرديّات العربيّة القديمة، وهي: الشفاهيّة، والإسلام، والحكاية التفسيريّة [76]، وعليه فإن بِنية هذه السرديّات تتنشكّل في تشكُّلات أجناسية كبرى من مثل: المقامة، وسرديّات المجانين، ويُشير مُحمّد عبيد الله إلى أن الأجناس السردية في هذه السرديّات تنوف في عددها عن العشرين نوعاً [77].

3 – تلقّي السرديّات القديمة في النقد الأدبيّ الحديث؛ مدخل إلى أنماط التلقّي:

لا مرية في القول: إنّ السرديّات العربيّة القديمة قد غدت مراحاً للتساؤل المعرفيّ والدراسة البحثيّة في ظلال المقاربات المابعدية كما أشرتُ سابقاً في

مفتتح الدراسة؛ ويمكن أن يتأكّد هذا المزعمُ عند إبعاد النظر في القِراءات النقديّة المتعددة للسرديّات القديمة من منظورات النقد الأدبيّ الحديث[78]، وإذا كانت الدراسة الراهنة تبحث في آفاق تلقّي السرديّات العربيّة القديمة من منظورات النقد الثقافيّ، الذي يعدُّ منهجاً ما بعدياً، فإنّ الدراسة معنيّةٌ بأن تبسط القول في آفاق تلقّي السرديّات العربيّة القديمة في ضَوْء المناهج الحديثة، ولكنها ليستْ معنيّة باجترارِ القراءات البنيويّة والتاريخيّة والاجتماعيّة السابقة؛ أو إعادتها صَوْغ مضموناتها، ذلك أنّ ثمة دراساتٍ رصينةً تصدّت للبحث في مسألة تلقّي الموروث السردي العربيّ في النقد العربيّ الحديث في ضَوْء هذه المناهج، ويمكن أن يُذكر منها: دراسة ضياء الكعبيّ الموسومة[79]، ودراسة هيثم سرحان[80]، ودراسة محمّد مسالتيي[81].

وفي هذا السياق اقترح سعيد يقطين تصنيفاً للدراسات النقديّة التي جعلت السرديّات العربيّة القديمة موضوعها؛ وهي قراءات ثلاث: القراءة التاريخيّة، والقراءة الإيديولوجيّة، والقراءة النقديّة[82]، وترى الكعبيُّ أن عبدالله إبراهيم يُعدُّ أبرز مَنْ قرأ السرديّات العربيّة القديمة من منظور بنيويّ، ممثلة بالحكايات الخرافية والمقامات والسير الشعبية[83]، وفي سياق ذلك تمثِّل مقاربات كيليطو من مثل: (الغائب: دراسة في مقامة الحريريّ) أبرز المقاربات التي تمكن أن تنطوي في إطار النقد التفكيكي، كما يذهب إلى ذلك سامي عبابنة، وذلك من خلال الأمارات التي تبدت في خطابه النقديّ، التي تؤكد نزوعه إلى النظريّة التفكيكيّة[84]، وتعدُّ مقاربة هيثم سرحان أبرز المقاربات التي تندرجُ في إطار التلقّي في إطار النقد السيميائيّ، وقد استثمرَ سرحان في دراسته (الأنظمة السيميائيّة: دراسة في السرد العربيّ القديم)[85] مُنْجَزَ اللسانيّات السيميائيّة، ابتغاء استخراج الأنظمة السيميائيّة التي تنتظم السرديّات العربيّة القديمة، وذلك في تمثُّلات موضوعيّة أربعة هي: الأسطورة، والأنسنة، والسلطة، والجنس.

أما بما يتعلّق بالتلقّي التأويليّ فتعدُّ مقاربة سعيد الغانمي (الكنز والتأويل:

قراءات في الحكاية العربيّة)[86] إحدى أهم المقاربات التأويليّة للسرديّات العربيّة القديمة، وترتكز هذه المقاربة على تصوّر مؤداهُ أن المعنى الثاوي في النصوص، يظل مُنفلتاً، وهو معنىً يتجدّد في كلّ اشتباك بين النصّ والقارئ؛ وينبغي الإشارة إلى أن الغانميّ يتّخذ من التأويلية منهجاً لقراءاته في بضع حكايات، يغدو خلالها التأويل «القراءة التي تتجولُ في الكنوز»[87].

– تركيب:

لقد أفضى الحديث عن السرديّات العربيّة القديمة في هذا المبحث إلى خلاصات معرفية مؤداها أن هذه السرديّات مرّت بتحوّلاتٍ مفصلية انتظمت أجناسها في إطار (جدلية النثر والشعر)، وتبيّن برجع النظر في المدونات النقديّة التي انشغلت بمهمة (تجنيس النص السردي القديم) أنّ ثمة أنواعاً سردية متعددة تمثّل الأنواع السردية الكبرى أو المركزيّة في السرديّات العربيّة القديمة.

وقد أشار هذا المبحث إلى أنّ البحث في أنماط التلقّي تلقّي السرديّات العربيّة القديمة في النقد العربيّ الحديث قد أظهر أنّ السرديّات العربيّة القديمة تمثّل نصوصاً أو خطاباتٍ تظلُّ منفتحةً أمام آفاق القراءة والتأويل، بوصفها بناءاتٍ سرديّة رامزة، مما يجعلُ من تأويلها تأويلاً نهائياً فِعْلاً يدخل في إطار الاستحالة المعرفيّة.

هوامش الفصل التمهيدي:

1 – يلحظُ الباحث في مدونات النظرية النقديّة المُعاصرة أنّ نقد النقد يتسمّى بغير ما مُسمّى، إذ تتباينُ ترجماتـه من باحثٍ إلى آخرَ من مثل: «النقد الشـارح، والميتـا نقد، والنقد الحِواريّ، وما بعدَ النقد، وقراءة القراءة ...إلخ». للاستزادة في هذه المسـألة ينظر: ابن تميم، علي، النقاد ونجيب محفوظ: الرواية؛ من النوع السـرديّ القاتـل إلى جماليّات العالم الثـالـث، ط1، 2008م، هيئة أبوظبي للثقافة والتراث، إمارة أبوظبي، الإمارات، ص42 – 52.

2 – تودوروف، تزيفيتان، نقد النقد، ترجمة: سامي سويدان وليليان سويدان، ط2، 1996م، دار الشؤون الثقافيّة العامة، بغداد، العراق، ص16.

3 – ومـن تجليـات هذه الفوضى ما يسـوقه علي بن تميم مـن البراهين ليؤكّـد أنّ كلّ مصطلحٍ من هذه المصطلحـات يأخذ بُعـداً مفاهيمياً معيّناً؛ استنادًا إلى تعريفـه الخاصّ في معاجم النظريّة النقديّة الغربيّة. يُنظر: ابن تميم، علي، النقاد ونجيب محفوظ...، (م.س)، ص52.

4 – الدغمومـي، محمد، نقد النقد وتنظير النقد العربيّ المُعاصر، ط1، 1999م، منشـورات كلية الآداب والعلوم الإنسانية بالرباط، الرباط، المغرب، ص113.

5 – المرجع السابق، ص61 – 80.

6 – القسـطنطيني، نجوى، في الوعي بمصطلح نقد النقد وعوامل ظهوره، مجلة عالم الفكر، منشـورات المجلس الوطني للثقافة والفنون والآداب، الكويت، المجلد (38)، العدد (1)، 2009م، ص37.

7 – التمـارة، عبدالرحمـن، نقد النقد: بين التَّصوّر المنهجيّ والإنجـاز النصيّ، ط1، 2017م، دار كنوز المعرفة للنشر والتوزيع، عمان،ـ الأردن، ص18.

8 – تودوروف، تزيفيتان، نقد النقد، (م.س)، ص16.

9 – زرفاوي، عمر، نقد النقد: مقاربة إبسـتيمولوجيّة، مجلة كليّة الآداب بجامعة الملك سعود، الرياض، المملكة العربيّة السعودبة، المجلد (28)، العدد (2)، 2016م، ص11.

10 – زرفاوي، عمر، نقد النقد...، (م.س)، ص11.

11 – الدغمومي، محمد، نقد النقد وتنظير النقد العربيّ المُعاصر، (م.س)، ص61 – 80.

12 – زرفاوي، عمر، نقد النقد...، (م.س)، ص211 – 212.

13 – المرجع السابق، الصفحات نفسها.

14 – المرجع السابق، الصفحات نفسها.

15 – الدغمومي، محمد، نقد النقد وتنظير النقد العربيّ المُعاصر، (م.س)، ص295 – 329.

16 – محمـد، باقر جاسـم، نقد النقد أم الميتا نقد؟، مجلة عالم الفكر، منشـورات المجلس الوطني للثقافة والفنون والآداب، الكويت، المجلد (37)، العدد (3)، 2009م، ص37.

17 – زرفاوي، عمر، نقد النقد...، (م.س)، ص213.

18 – يُنظر: التمارة، عبدالرحمن، نقد النقد: بين التّصوّر المنهجيّ...، (م.س)، ص14 – 35.

19 – اصطيـف، عبدالنبي، نحو تجديد لمفهوم النقد الأدبيّ، مجلة مواقف، لبنان، العدد (47)، 1983م، ص164.

20 – الدغمومي، محمد، نقد النقد وتنظير النقد العربيّ المُعاصر، (م.س)، ص11.

21 – يُنظر: دريدا ودي مان، جاك وبول، وآخرون، مداخل إلى التفكيك (البلاغة المعاصرة)، تحرير وترجمــة: حسـام نايل، تصديـر: محمد بـدوي، ط1، 2013م، الهيئة المصريــة العامة للكتاب، القاهرة، مصر، ص187 – 227 .

22 – عليمات، يوسـف، الرباعيّة الجديدة، صحيفة الرأي، عمان، الأردن، 14 ربيع أوّل 1440هـ – 23 نوفمبر 2018م، ينظر الرابط:

تاريخ الدخول: 2020/10/10م (http://alrai.com/article/10460147)

23 – هولــب، روبــرت، نظرية التلقّي: مقدَّمـة نقديّة، ترجمة: عز الدين إسـماعيل، المكتبة الأكاديمية، القاهرة، مصر، ط1، 2000م، ص 105.

24 – ينظـر: يـاوس، هانس، جماليّة التلقّي: من أجل تأويل جديد للنّصّ الأدبيّ، تقديم وترجمة: رشـيد بنحـدو، ط1، 2016م، الـدار العربيّــة للعلوم ناشـرون (بيـروت/ لبنان)، منشـورات الاختلاف (الجزائر العاصمة/ الجزائر)، دار الأمان (الرباط/ المغرب). تومبكنز، جين، نقد استجابة القارئ من الشـكلانيّة إلى ما بعد البنيويّة، ترجمة: حسـن ناظم وعلي حاكم، مراجعة وتقديم: محمد جواد محسن الموسويّ، ط1، 1999م، المشروع القوميّ للترجمة، القاهرة، مصر، ص17 – 18 .

25 – حمّودة، عبد العزيز، الخُروج من التيه: دراسـة في سُلطة النصّ، العدد (298)، نوفمبر 2003م، سلسلة عالم المعرفة، المجلس الوطنيّ للثقافة والفنون والأدب، الكويت، ص116.

26 – المرجع السابق، الصفحة نفسها.

27 – تومبكنز، جين، نقد استجابة القارئ من الشكلانيّة ...، (م.س)، ص21.

28 – تومبكنز، جين، نقد استجابة القارئ من الشكلانيّة ...، (م.س)،

29 – المرجع السابق، الصفحة نفسها.

30 – يُنظر: بلوم، هارولد، خريطة للقراءة الضّالة، ترجمة: عابد إسـماعيل، ط1، 2000م، دار الكنوز الأدبيّة، بيروت، لبنان، ص7.

31 – باعشن، لمياء نظريّات قراءة النصّ، (م.س)، ص119.

32 – تودوروف، تزيفيتان، الشــعريّة، ترجمة: شـكري المبخوت ورجاء بن سلامة، ط2، 1990م، دار توبقال للنشر، الدار البيضاء، المغرب، ص20 وما بعدها.

33 – خمـري، حسـين، نظريّات القراءة وتلقّـي النصّ الأدبيّ، مجلة العلوم الإنسـانية، جامعة منتوري قسنطينة، الجزائر، العدد (12)، 1999م، ص173 – 184.

34 – كاظم، نادر، المقامات والتلقّي...، (م.س)، ص13.

35 – كاظم، نادر، المقامات والتلقّي...، (م.س)، ص13.

36 – سلدن، رامان، بروكس، بيتر، النظريّات الموجّهة إلى القارئ، ترجمة: محمد نور النعيمي، مجلة الآداب العالمية، منشـورات اتحاد الكتاب العرب، دمشـق، سـوريا، المجلد (26)، العدد (106 – 107)، حزيران 2001، ص116.

37 – كون، توماس، بُنية الثورات العلميّة، (م.س)، ص11.

38 – الرويليّ والبازعيّ، ميجان وسعد، دليل الناقد الأدبيّ، ص305 – 309.

39 – للاستزادة حول الدراسات الثقافيّة ينظر:

John Storey, Cultural Studies: An Introduction; in What is Cultural Studies: A Reader, edited by: John Storey, New York: Arnold, 1997,

40 – إذ يتثشــابكُ «النقـد الثقافيّ» معرفياً مع حقول معرفيّـة أخرى مثل: علم الاجتماع، واللسـانيّات، والسـيميائيّات، ومناهج النقد الأدبيّ الحديث، فضلاً عن الفلسـفة، وعلم النفس، والأنثروبولوجيا، ونظريات الفنّ، والتاريخ، وعلم النفس، والاقتصاد، والسياسـة، ووسـائل الاتصالات. يُنظر: آنغ، إيـن، النقـد الثقافيّ وتداخل الحقـول المعرفيّة الآن، ترجمـة: عطارد حيدر، مجلـة اتحاد الكتاب العرب، دمشق، سوريا، السنة (34)، العدد (138)، 2009م.

41 – Arthur Asa Berge, Cultural Criticism: A Primer of Key Concepts, California: Sage Publications, 1995, P.2

وفـي هذا السـياق يرى عبدالقادر الرباعـيّ أننا «أمام حراك نقديّ لم تكتمل صورته، ولم يسـتقر قـراره بعدُ». الرباعي، عبدالقادر، جماليات الخطاب فـي النقد الثقافيّ، ط1، 2015م، دار جرير، عمّان، الأردن، ص204.

42 – ينظـر: ماكدونالد، رونان، مـوت الناقد، ترجمة وتقديم: فخري صالح، ط1، 2014م، منشـورات المركز القومي للترجمة، القاهرة، مصر، ص125 – 159.

43 – المرجع السابق، ص147.

44 – وهذا الكتاب من الدراسات المعتمدة في النقد الثقافيّ، ينظر:

Vincent B. Leitch, Cultural Criticism, Literary Theory, Post Structuraslim, New York: Columbian University Press, 1992,

45 – الموسـوي، محسـن جاسـم، النظرية والنقد الثقافيّ، ط1، 2005م، المؤسسـة العربيّة للدراسات والنشر، بيروت، لبنان، ص 20.

46 – عليمات، يوسف، النسق الثقافيّ: قراءة ثقافية في أنساق الشعر العربي القديم، ط1، 2009م، دار عالم الكتب الحديث، إربد، الأردن، ص1.

47 – يُنظر: الغذاميّ، عبدالله، النقد الثقافيّ...، (م.س)، ص84.

48 – الخليل، سمير، دليل مصطلحات الدراسات الثقافيّة والنقد الثقافيّ...، (م.س)، ص294.

49 – لومـان، نيـكلاس، مدخـل إلى نظريّة الأنسـاق، ترجمة: يوسـف فهمي حجـازي، ط1، 2010م، منشورات الجمل، بغداد، كولونيا، العراق، ألمانيا، ص37.

50 – يوسـف، أحمد، القراءة النسقيّة: سُـلطة البنية ووَهْم المحايثة، ط1، 2007، الـدار العربيّة للعلوم ناشرون (بيروت/ لبنان)، منشورات الاختلاف (الجزائر العاصمة/ الجزائر)، ص117.

51 – يوسـف، أحمد، القراءة النسقيّة: سُلطة البنية ووَهْم المحايثة، (م.س)، ص117.

52 – يُنظر: سوسـير، فريدناند، علم اللغة العام، ترجمة: يوئيل يوسـف عزيز، ط1، 1985م، دار آفاق، العراق، ص34.

53 – إذ يوئّق اللسـان في مادة نسق: «النَسَقُ من كل شـيء: ما كان على طريقة نظامٍ واحد، وقد نَسقْتُه تَنْسـيقاً (...) قال ابن سيده: نَسَقَ الشيء يَنْسُقُه نَسْقاً، ونَسَّقه نظَّمه على السواء» ابن منظور، لسان العرب، (م.س)، مادة (ن س ق).

54 – الخليل، سمير، دليل مصطلحات الدراسات الثقافيّة والنقد الثقافيّ...، (م.س)، ص294.

55 – كاظم، نادر، تمثيلات الآخر: صورة السـود في المتخيّل العربيّ الوسيط، ط1، 2004م، المؤسسة العربيّة للدراسات والنشر، بيروت، لبنان، ص92.

56 – يُنظـر: الغذّامـي، عبدالله، واصطيف، عبدالنبي، نقد أدبي أم نقد ثقافيّ، ط1، 2004م، دار الفكر، دمشق، سوريا.

57 – يُنظـر: حامد، عبدالله، النقد الثقافيّ للغذاميّ: سـؤال المرجع وإشـكالات النسـق، السـجل العلمي للـدورة الثانيـة من ملتقى النقد الأدبـيّ: الخطاب النقدي المعاصر في المملكة العربيّة السعودية، النـادي الأدبيّ بالرياض، الرياض، السـعودية، 2008م، ص7. وإبراهيـم، عبدالله، الثقافة العربيّة والمرجعيّات المُستعارة، ط1، 2010م، الدار العربيّة للعلوم ناشرون (بيروت/ لبنان)، منشورات الاختلاف (الجزائر العاصمة/ الجزائر)، ص97 – 111. والرباعي، عبدالقادر، جماليات الخطاب في النقد الثقافيّ، (م.س)، ص79 – 147.

58 – كاظم، نادر، الهُويّة والسرد...، (م.س)، ص225.

59 – يمكـن القول: إنّ «القراءة المُختلفة» أو «القراءة الثائرة» هي القراءة التي تهدف إلى كَسْـرِ آفاق التلقّي، وقد مثَّلت مسلكاً معرفياً اختطه عددٌ من النقاد العرب في القرن المُنصرم، وفي فواتح قرننا هذا، ومن تلك التَّجارب تجربة طه حُسين في قراءته للشّعر الجَاهليّ. يُنظر: القفاري، أميرة، النقد الثائر...، (م.س)، ص121.

60 – إبراهيم، عبدالله، الثقافة العربيّة ...، (م.س)، ص97 – 111.

61 – حَمَودة، عبد العزيز، الخُروج من التَّيه...، (م.س)، ص264.

62 – يُنظر: غرينبلات، ستيفن، الثقافة والشعرية الثقافيّة، ترجمة: معتز سلامة، مجلة فصول، الهيئة المصرية العامّة للكتاب، القاهرة، مصر، المجلد (3/25)، العدد (99)، 2017م، ص303 وما بعدها.

63 – يُنظر: زغلول، هشام، (الناقد الثقافيّ وأفق التلقّي: من التيار الغذامي.. إلى التيار الرباعيّ) ضمن: (نَمارقُ مَصْفوفةٌ دراسات – مقالات – شهادات تكريماً للأستاذ الدكتور عبدالقادر الرباعيّ بمناسبة نيله لقب «أستاذ شرف» من جامعة اليرموك)، ط1، 2014م، دار المؤسسة العربيّة للدراسات والنشر، بيروت، لبنان، ص62.

64 – سرحان، هيثم، الأنظمة السيميائية دراسة في السرد العربيّ القديم، ط1، 2008م، دار الكتاب الجديد المتحدة، بيروت، لبنان، ص62.

65 – ابن منظور، لسان العرب، (م.س)، مادة: (س ر د).

66 – برنس، جيرالد، المصطلح السردي: معجم مصطلحات، ترجمة: عابد خزندار، مراجعة: محمد بريري، ط1، 2003م، منشورات المشروع القومي للترجمة، القاهرة، مصر، ص145.

67 – يُنظر: القاضي، محمد وزملاؤه، معجم السرديات، ط1، 2010م، دار الفارابي ومؤسسة الانتشار العربي، بيروت، لبنان، ص254.

68 – ابن منظور، جمال الدين بن مكرم (ت711هـ)، لسان العرب، (د.ط)، 1978م، الدار المصريّة، مصر، ص122.

69 – المرجع السابق، ص254.

70 – العشيري، محمود، الشعر سَرْداً: دراسة في نصّ المُفَضَّلِيّات، ط1، 2014م، المؤسسة العربيّة للدراسات والنشر، بيروت، لبنان، ص33.

71 – عبدالحميد بن يحيى الكاتب وما تبقّى من رسائله ورسائل سالم أبي العلاء، دراسة وإعداد: إحسان عباس، ط1، 1988م، دار الشروق، عمان، الأردن، ص281.

72 – يُنظر للاستزادة في هذا السياق: يقطين، سعيد، الكلام والخبر: مقدمة للسّرد العربيّ، ط1، 1997م، المركز الثقافيّ العربيّ، بيروت، الدار البيضاء، لبنان، المغرب، ص127 – 135.

73 – عبدالحميد بن يحيى الكاتب وما تبقّى من رسائله ...، (م.س)، ص281.

74 – الكعبيّ، ضياء، منهجية النقد الثقافيّ وتطبيقاته: السرد العربي القديم أنموذجاً: تصوُّر مقترح، بحث محكَّم في الندوة العلميّة: قضايا المنهج في اللغة والأدب، النظريّة والتّطبيق، جامعة الملك سعود، السعودية، 2010م، ص842.

75 – إبراهيم، عبدالله، موسوعة السرد العربيّ، ج (1)، (م.س)، ص26.

76 – للاستزادة يُنظر: إبراهيم، عبدالله، النثر العربيّ القديم: بحث في السرديّة العربيّة، ط1، 2002م، منشورات المجلس الوطني للثقافة والفنون والتراث، الكويت، ص8 وما بعدها.

77 – ومنها: القصة، والخبر، والحكاية، والسير الشعبيّة. يُنظر: عبيد الله، محمّد، السرد العربيّ القديم: من الهامش إلى المركز، المجلة العربيّة للعلوم الإنسانيّة، جامعة الكويت، الكويت، المجلد (25)، العدد (98)، 2007م، ص53 – 85.

78 – يمكن القول: إنَّ هذه القراءات يمكنُ أن ينتظم شـتيتها في مسـالك بحثيّة كُبرى من مثل: السرديات البِنيويّة عند فلاديمر بروب «Wladimir Propp»، والسـرديات السيميائيّة عند جوليان غِريماس «Julien Greimas»، والسرديات الثَقافيَة عند هومي بابا «Homi K. Bhabha». يُنظر للاستزادة على سـبيل المثال: بروب، فلاديمير، مورفولوجيا القصّة، ترجمة: عبدالكريم حسـن وسميرة بن عمَّو، ط1، 1996م شِـراع للدراسـات والنشر والتوزيع، دمشق، سـوريا. وبعدها. وبابا، هومي، موقع الثَقافة، ترجمة: ثائر ديب، ط1، 2004م، منشورات المجلس الأعلى للثَقافة، القاهرة، مصر. وغريماس، جوليان، سـيميائيّات السرد، ترجمة: عبدالمجيد نوسي، ط1، 2018م، المركز الثَقافيّ العربيّ، بيروت، الدار البيضاء، لبنان، المغرب.

79 – الكعبي، ضياء، السرد العربيّ القديم: دراسة في الأنساق الثَقافيّة...، (م.س)، ص433 – 524.

80 – سرحان، هيثم، الأنظمة السيميائيّة...، (م.س).

81 – يُنظر: مسالتي، محمد عبد البشير، السرد العربيّ القديم وآفاق التأويل، (م.س)، ص93 – 106.

82 – يُنظر: يقطين، سـعيد، قراءة التراث الأدبيّ: التراث السردي أنموذجاً، الندوة الدولية الثانية قراءة التـراث الأدبيّ واللغوي في الدراسـات الحديثة، جامعة الملك سـعود، الرياض، المملكة العربيّة السعودية، 2014م، ص319.

83 – إبراهيم عبدالله، السردية العربيّة: بحث في البنية السردية للموروث الحكائي العربي، ط2، 2000م، المؤسسة العربيّة للدراسات والنشر، بيروت، لبنان.

84 – عبابنـة، سـامي محمد، التفكيكيـة وقراءة الأدب العربي القديم: عبد الفتـاح كيليطو نموذجاً، مجلة دراسـات للعلوم الاجتماعية والإنسـانية، الجامعة الأردنية، عمان، الأردنّ، المجلد (42)، الملحق (1)، 2015م، ص1079 – 1081.

85 – يُنظر: سرحان، هيثم، الأنظمة السيميائية...، (م.س).

86 – الغانميّ، سعيد، الكنز والتَأويل: قراءات في الحكاية العربيّة، المركز الثَقافيّ العربيّ، ط1، 1994م، بيروت، الدار البيضاء، لبنان، المغرب.

87 – المرجع السابق، ص8.

الفصل الأول:
تشكلات نمط التلقّي:
بين القراءة النموذج ومحاولات الخَرْق

ينتظمُ عقد هذا الفصلِ في ثلاثِ مقاربات تمثّل المقاربة الغذاميّة نقطة ابتدائها وتوسُّطها، أما المقاربتان الأُخريان، فأولاهما تمثّل القراءة المنتمية، التي تبنت مقولات المقاربة الغذاميّة، وما نقلته من مقولاتٍ غربيّة، وأما ثانيهما فتحاول أن تشقّ مسارها المنهجيّ الخاص، الذي يسعى إلى خَرْقِ النموذج والعبث به، أو قل: التعديل والتبديل في مقولة مركزيّة من المقولات التي نقلتها المقاربة الغذّاميّة، وهي المقولة التي مؤداها أنّ النسق لا يعمل إلا في حالات الإضمار والمراوغة.

وفي هذا السياق ارتبط اسم عبدالله الغذّامي منذ مطلع الألفية الراهنة بوجوب تحرير قراءة النصّ الأدبيّ العربيّ من إسار النقد الأدبيّ، والتحوّل عوضاً عن ذلك إلى القِراءة الثقافيّة، ابتغاء نقد الأنساق الثقافيّة الثاوية في أغوار هذه النصوص، لا الانشغال ببنيتها الخارجيّة، المتمأسسة على الجماليّ البلاغيّ، تأثراً بالطّرح الغربيّ حول النقد الثقافيّ.

وفي مقاربته موضع الدراسة، حول حكاية غنيّة وابنها عَرَامة، يغدو الجاحظ بحسب منظور الغذامي سارداً منتصراً للهامش، الذي تمثله المرأة، وأيديولوجيات هذا الهامش، وسردياتّه التي تعاني من أبويّة الثقافة، وتقاليدها الرصينة، وهو في ذلك يخالف الرأي القارّ، بأن الجاحظ مارس فعل الكتابة تحت رعاية السلطة.

ولا ريب أن ذلك يقود مسارات التأويل عند الغذامي إلى التأويل الجموح،

الأمر الذي يمثّل على امتداد مقاربته أرضاً خِصبةً وحافزاً مثيراً للخلاف والجدل والاختلاف حول تأويلاته، المتصفة – دوماً – بالحريّة، والجموح، وكسر آفاق التلقّي النقديّ، وأُطُره، ومسلّماته، وعليه فإنّ الجاحظ والحريريّ يمثلان معادليْن موضوعيين لغنية في حكاية الجاحظ عند الغذاميّ، ولأبي زيد السروجيّ في المقامات الحريريّة عند فرحان، مما يؤكد أنّ مقاربة فرحان تسعى إلى استيلاد القراءة من القراءة، والاندغام مع النمط المؤسس اندغاماً منتجاً.

وفي هذا السياق ستتماثل مواقع التبئير بين أطروحتي الغذاميّ وعلي فرحان حول (الأنساق الثقافيّة في مقامات الحريريّ)، بصورة يغدو تشابههما تشابهاً كليّاً، ينحازُ خلالها الناقد الكفءُ وهو علي فرحان، في المنهجيّة البحثيّة، والتصور النظريّ لمفهوم النسق، والمضمر، والجمالي، إلى المفاهيم المطروحة في النموذج الغذامي، بوصفه الصوى التي يهتدي القراء بأضوائها الكاشفة، في اشتباكهم الدائب مع النصوص من منظور النقد الثقافيّ.

وبرغم نزوعات التأبّي والخَرْق والتمرد التي تمثلها مقاربة المحفلي حول (الأنساقُ الثقافيّةُ في كليلة ودمنة) إزاء فكرة النسق المضمر الناسخ للنسق الظّاهر المنسوخ، التي نقلها الغذامي من النقد الغربيّ، فإنّ مقاربته ستظلُ متواضعة مع القواعد القارة في تلقّي الخطاب الأدبيّ في إطار النقد الثقافيّ، بل إنّها في ضَوْء هذا التمرد تخلق لنفسها إشكالية كبرى، استناداً إلى زئبقيّة الأنساق الثقافيّة، ومخاتلتها، التي تظهر تارة، وتستر تارة أخرى، وهو ما أشكل على المحفليّ ذلك أنّه راح يصنّف الأنساق الثقافيّة إلى أنساقٍ مضمرة وأنساقٍ معلنة، وهو عملٌ مشروع، بل إنّه يمثّل موضع جِدة، وتميّز، وخروجاً حقيقياً على النموذج الأبويّ، بيد أنّه انتخب لنفسه مدونة صعبة القِياد، هي كليلة ودمنة، التي ارتحلت بين ثقافات ثلاث، واغتنت بأنساق متباينة، وغدا أمر تصنيفها أمراً يكاد يكون مستحيلاً في ظلّ هذه الإشكاليّة.

وعليه فيمثّل هذا الفصل لحظة تأسيس نمط التلقّي من خلال النموذج الغذامي،

ولحظتين نقديتين يمثلان حال كثيرٍ من المقاربات النقديّة المنطوية في إطار النقد الثقافيّ العربيّ، لحظة التقليد، وسُلطة النموذج، ولحظة محاولة الانعتاق من سُلطة النموذج، وإن كان هذا الانعتاق جزئياً ومنطوياً على غير قليلٍ من الإشكالات الكبرى.

1 – مدخل: نمط التلقّي وإشكاليّة التقليد والتجديد:

تتأسس مقاربة عبدالله الغذّامي الموسومة بـ(النقد الثقافيّ: قراءة في الأنساق الثقافيّة العربيّة) على مقولة مركزية مفادها أن النصّ السرديّ الجاحظيّ، نصّ مراوغ وخدّاع، ذلك أنه يؤسس في نماذج حكائية لثقافة السلطة، ومن ثم فإنه ينقضها، ويلغيها في نصوص حكائية أُخرى، ومن هنا فإن سرديّات العصا لدى الجاحظ إنما هي سرديّات يلفُّها الغموض والمراوغة والتداخل، الذي لم يكن الاستطراد هو سببه الحقيقيّ كما تواضع كثير من الباحثين على ذلك، إذ يبدو الاستطراد عند الغذاميّ قناعاً يمرِّر من خلاله الجاحظ رسائله المشفَّرة، وأنساقه المضمرة.

وتنتمي مقاربة علي فرحان الموسومة بـ(مقامات الحريريّ حجاجية السرد والنسق الثقافيّ: دراسة في البِنية والخطاب)[1] إلى سياقات المقاربات التي تنقام على محاولة قراءة مقامات أبي القاسم الحريريّ قراءة ثقافية فاحصة، إذ يحاولُ علي فرحان في مقاربته هذه أن يكشف عن عددٍ من الأنساق الثقافيّة المُتعاضدة، التي تشكل البنية النسقية التي تنتظمُ هذه المقامات، بيد أنها تقع في فخاخ التقليد، حين تقدم أنموذجاً للقراءة النقديّة المقلِّدة.

وتحاول مقاربة محمد المحفليّ الموسومة بـ(الأنساقُ الثقافيّةُ في كليلة ودِمنة)[2] تأكيد فكرة مختزلها أنّ كتاب كليلة ودِمنة يشكّل مراحاً للأنساق الثقافيّة الظاهرة والمضمرة، وليس المضمرة وحسبُ، كما تواترَ في مدونات النقد الثقافيّ شرقاً ومغرباً، وذلك على اعتبار أن النصّ الأدبيّ يضمر أنساقاً

ثقافية ويظهر أنساقاً أخرى، مخالفاً في طرحه المنهجيّ هذا السواد الأعظم من المشتغلين بالنقد الثقافيّ العربيّ، الذين تأثروا بالطّرح الغذاميّ، وكرّسوه، وأعادوا إنتاجه من خلال مقارباتهم.

2 – سيمياء القارئ: من القارئ البكر إلى القارئ القويّ:

1 – 2 – الغذامي: القارئ البِكْر وتشكّل نمط التلقّي:

تُمثّل مقاربة الغذاميّ نموذج القراءة المعياريّة أو القراءة القياسيّة[3] التي ستُمسي فيما بعدُ النموذجَ المُحتذى، والمرجعيّة الكُبرى، والقراءة البِكْر، التي تمثّلُ المعينَ الذي يظلُّ النقادُ الثقافيون يمتحون منه ما من شأنه أن يؤطر قراءاتهم، من الناحية المنهجيّة، بوصف تلك القراءة هي القراءة المنهجيّة المعياريّة، التي تُؤسّس لآفاق الانتظار عند القارئ في مدارات النقد الثقافيّ[4].

ولقد عمد الغذاميُّ في مقاربته المعياريّة هذه إلى تكسيرِ آفاقِ التلقّي القارّة عند جمهرة الدارسين العرب في مُفتتح القرن المنصرم، وذلك حين تجاسرَ على القول بنسقيّة الخطاب الأدبيّ، وإضماريته السالب والقبيح، وتزيّه بالجماليّ البلاغيّ، وإسهامه بفاعليّة جليّة في تصنيع أنساق الفحولة، والشاعر الهَجَّاء، والذّكورة، والعصبيّة، والرجعيّة، وتتضافرُ في المنجز النقديّ لدى الغذّامي ميزتان قلما تجتمعان عند غيره من النقاد، وهما الجسارة المعرفيّة، والاقتران بقضية الحداثة العربيّة النقديّة[5].

وفي هذا السياق فلا بُدّ من الإشارة إلى أنّ الغذّامي لما يزل منذ عقود ثلاثة يسعى بدأب إلى محاولة السمهة في التأسيس لنظريّة نقديّة، تتجاوب مع نسقيّة الأدب العربيّ، ودوره في التأسيس لأنساقٍ ثقافيّةٍ مضمرة، لما تنفكّ تمارس تأثيرها المُستتر في الوعي الجمعيّ العربيّ، وعادات المجتمعات العربيّة، ونُهُج تفكيرها، منذ بدء تكوينها، وحتى اللحظة الراهنة من التاريخ العربيّ المعاصر.

وتأسيساً على السابق فقد ارتبط اسم عبدالله الغذاميّ منذ نهاية القرن المنصرم بوجوب تحرير النصّ الأدبيّ من سطوة النظريّة النقديّة الحديثة، أو نظريّات النقد الأدبيّ الكلاسيكيّة، التي تَرين، من منظور الغذاميّ، على قلوب المتلقّين، وتجعلهم غارقين في سياقات العَمَى الثقافيّ، من خلال المجازات والبلاغات، التي تزنّر النصوص، وتسترُ خلف بلاغاتها أنساقاً مُضْمَرَةً لا يمكن أن تُرى سوى عند الاشتباك بقراءة النصّ من منظور الناقد الثقافيّ المُخْتَلِف.

وعليه فإن القراءة الثقافيّة الغذاميّة تغدو، والحال هذه، هي القراءة القادرة على تغيير مسارات النظرية النقديّة العربيّة من محورة العمليّة النقديّة، بكل تجلياتها ومستوياتها، حول إبراز جماليّات النصّوص، وأضْرُبِ بلاغتها، ومواطن بيانها، إلى الالتفات إلى المعائب/ المثالب النسقيّة التي تتضمنها هذه النصوص، على اختلاف أسيقتها وأضربها⁽⁶⁾.

2 – 2 – علي فرحان: القارئ المحاكي والنموذج الإرشاديّ:

يبدو علي فرحان في هذه المقاربة ملتزماً بمرتكزات النقد الثقافيّ كما تقرّرت في التنظيرات المنهجيّة والإجرائية التي نقلها عبدالله الغذامي تنظيراً وكرّسها تطبيقاً؛ إذ يقرر فرحان بداية مقاربته أنه «يختبئ خلف جمالية نص المقامات وشعبيته وجهٌ قبيحٌ يتستر بالجماليّ والأدبيّ، إنه هيمنة الأديب وسطوته»⁽⁷⁾.

ويمكن في هذا السياق الإشارة إلى مفهوم (النموذج الاستبداليّ أو الإرشاديّ) عند المفكر الأمريكيّ توماس صاموئيل كون (Thomas Samuel Kuhn)⁽⁸⁾، إذ يمثل النموذجُ الغذّاميُّ بالنسبة إلى فرحان النموذجَ الإرشاديّ، ولعلّ النموذجَ الغذّاميَّ يمثل رأس (الجماعة العمليّة) عند فرحان كذلك، إذ تعرف الجماعة العمليّة بأنّها «تتألف من أعضاء يشتركون في معارفَ، وخبراتٍ، وطرائقِ بحثٍ، وتحليل، واستنتاج مشتركة، أي يشتركون في نموذج إرشاديّ واحد»⁽⁹⁾.

ويغدو فرحان هنا، وفاقاً لذلك، متأثراً بفكرة النسق المضمر/ القبيح التي

طرحها الغذّامي، ذلك أنّها قد تموضعت في المشروع الغذاميّ بوصفها النواة المركزيّة له، إذ إنّ الغذّامي ظلُّ يلحُّ عليها في كتابه النقد الثقافيّ[10]، ولا ريب أنّ هذه المقولة التي تلقفتها أيدي النقاد العرب من الغذّامي، شرق البلاد العربيّة وغربها، وراحوا يَقْرأون النصوص من خلالها، أو من منظوراتها، فضلاً عن تبنيه لمقولة إقصاء الجماليّات، وما تنطوي عليه من أنساقٍ مضمرة سالبة، تكرّس نسقية الثقافة العربيّة كما يرى الغذّاميّ[11].

وبتعبير آخر يمكن القول: إنّ قراءة علي فرحان للمقامات الحريرية في مقاربته هذه تمثل ضرباً من أضرُبِ (القراءة المتنمية)، التي تتبنّى نموذجاً استبداليّاً أو تفسيريّاً، بكل ما ينطوي عليه هذا النموذج من استراتيجيّات قرائية، ومقولات تنظيريّة، ومفاهيمَ، وأفكارٍ، ومن ثم فإنّها تستعمله على نصٍّ آخر، أو نصوصٍ أخرى[12]، ويتموضع مصطلح (النسق الثقافيّ) في هذه المقاربة بوصفه المفهوم الذي يدير رحاها، ويوجه مساراتها، وتمثل الاستراتيجيّات التي ابتدعها الغذّامي في مقاربته كوى كاشفة يستعين بها فرحان.

ويسترشد فرحان بالمقاربة الغذاميّة، مأتثأً مقاربته على مقولاتها منذ مُفتتح دراسته، لكنه مع ذلك يرجع إلى مصادر رئيسة في النقد الثقافيّ بلغتها الأصليّة، وهذا عمل منهجيّ وتأصيلي انمازت بها هذه المقاربة، في محاولة تعديل الأفق الغذامي وتوسيعه.

وعليه يمكن القول: إن مبتدأ التفرد ومنتهاه في هذه المقاربة يتجلّى في تفعيلها لمبدأ الانتخاب الثقافيّ، أقصد، أنها وطأت أرض المقامات، بوصفها أرضاً بِكْراً، لم تطأها أقدام النقاد الثقافيّين من قبل، ومن ثَمَّ محاولة قراءتها قراءة ثقافية.

3 – 2 – المحفليّ: القارئ القويّ وخرق نمط التلقّي:

يتمثل محمد المحفليّ في مقاربته هذه نمطاً خاصاً من القرّاء، وهو نمط

القارئ القويّ (Strong reader) [13] عند هارولد بلوم (Harold Bloom)، وهو القارئ/ الناقد الذي لا ينسجم في قراءته مع آفاق التلقّي القارّة في الاتجاه النقديّ الذي يتبناه هذا القارئ/ الناقد.

ولا ريب أنّ محمد المحفليّ ليس قارئاً قويّاً [14] بهذا المعنى المتمأسس على المخالفة المحضة، أو الرفض التامّ، إذ إنّه قارئ/ ناقد يتمثّل مفهوم القارئ القوي من خلال جسارته على التفلّت من إسارِ سلطة نمط التلقّي المعياريّ الذي نقله الغذامي وكرّسه.

لقد مثّل رفض المحفليّ لفكرة النسق المضمر المتداولة بشأن النسق الظاهر والنسق المضمر كسراً لآفاق التلقّي المعهودة في القراءة الثقافيّة، ويبدو أن المحفليّ متأثرٌ بفكرة الأنساق الواعية واللاواعية، أو المفكَّر فيها واللامفكّر فيها كما يرى ليتش، الذي مثل لدى الغذّاميّ مرجعية كبرى، تأسست مقاربته في كثيرٍ من مناحيها على أسٍ منها [15].

ولذلك فإنّ مقاربة المحفلي تجلّي نموذج القراءة الجسور، التي تُكَسِّر آفاق الانتظار التي تواضعتْ قواعدها على امتداد القراءات الثقافيّة المتعددة، وهي قراءات ومقاربات لا يمكن إحصاؤهنّ عدداً؛ لكثرتها وتشعُّبها.

وإذا كان النموذج الغذامي هو النموذج المحتذى، أو النموذج البؤريّ – إذا جاز التعبير – ممثلاً مفهوم (النموذج الاستبداليّ أو الإرشاديّ) عند توماس كون، ومفهوم (الجماعة التفسيرية) ستانلي فيتش، أو مفهوم (القارئ القياسيّ) عند صالح بن زياد، فإنّ هذه المقاربة تنطوي في بعضٍ من تجلّياتها على مفهوم الثورة والخروج على مرتكزات هذه المقاربة الأبويّة [16]، وهو ما يؤكد أنّ هذه المقاربة تتمثّل فكرة القارئ القويّ الذي يدأب على تطوير النظريّة النقديّة التي يشتغل عليها خلال مراسه النقديّ.

وتأسيساً عليه فيبدو أنّه قد غدا مركوزاً في ذهن المحفليّ أن النسق الثقافيّ

مرتهنٌ بالزئبقية، وبجدليات التخفي والظهور، أو الإضمار والإظهار، وفقاً لرغبة صاحب النص/ الخطاب الذي ينطوي عليه، أو دون رغبةٍ منه، مما حفزه على معاودة النظر إلى الأصول المنهجيّة التي بنيت عليها المقاربة الغذامية.

3 – المتن المنهجيّة والجهاز المفاهيميّ:

1 – 3 – الغذامي والمرجعيّة الغربية:

ولعلَّ الإشارةَ تغدو لازبةً إلى أنّ الغذاميّ قد أقام مشروعه في النقد الثقافيّ على مقولاتٍ مركزيّة كبرى مؤدّاها أن النقد الثقافيّ مشروع بحثيّ يرتكز في أصله، على البحث في الأنساق المضمرة في الخطاب، وهي تبدو على وشيجةٍ بالطرح المنهجيّ الرائج حول النقد الثقافيّ في الغرب، إذ تشير مدونات النظرية النقديّة إلى اهتمام النقد الثقافيّ بالنسق المضمر، ومخاتلاته[17].

ولا مشاحة في أنّ أفكاراً من قبيل: النسق المضمر والمخاتلات والتمثيلات الثقافيّة هي أفكار غريبة خالصة اشتغل عليها عددٌ كبيرٌ من النقاد واستنبتها الغذامي في البيئة العربيّة، وتبدو إفادة الغذامي من المنظور الليتشي، نسبة إلى ليتش (V.Leitch)، وطروحات غرينبلات، إفادة ظاهرة جليّة، وفي هذا السياق يذهب ليتش إلى أن موضوع الدراسة/ القراءة الثقافيّة عند البريطانيين هو «ليس الأدب وإنما الممارسات الخطابية في معناها التاريخيّ، كأبنية بلاغيّة ترتبط بالمعرفة والقوة»[18]، وهي الفكرة ذاتها، التي يكررها الغذامي عن المضمرات التي يتضمنها البلاغي المجازي.

ويغدو الغذامي في هذا السياق ناقلاً لها إلى النقد العربيّ، ومجرياً عليها تعديلاً يربط بين النسق المضمر ومثالب الثقافة العربيّة، وإذا كان النقد الثقافيّ، بحسب رؤية الغذّامي، يعملُ على الكشف عن الأنساق المُتوارية في بنى النصوص النثريّة والشعريّة، خلف ستارات الجماليّ البلاغيّ، فإنّ كُلّ نصّ ينطوي على

نسقيْن اثنيْن: أما أحدهما فظاهر، وأما الآخر فمضمرٌ ينسخ الظاهر [19]، وعليه فإن الغذامي يجعلُ البحثَ في وظيفة النسق مدار البحث والمدارسة، بوصف النسق هو البؤرة المفاهيميّة لمشروعه النقديّ [20].

تتأسّس مقاربة الغذّاميّ حول السرديّات العربيّة القديمة ممثلة بحكاية (غنية وابنها عرامة) في كتابه (النقد الثقافيّ: قراءة في الأنساق الثقافيّة العربيّة) [21] على فكرةٍ مختزلها أنّ الثقافة العربيّة ما فتئت تدأبُ على ترسيخ أنساق ثقافيّة سالبة، منذ ما قبل الإسلام (العصر الجاهليّ)، وحتى أبرز شُعراء الحداثة العربيّة (أدونيس)، مؤسس الحداثة الرجعيّة عند الغذّاميّ، بُعيد منتصف القرن المُنصرم، وفي هذا السياق يؤطّر الغذّاميّ مقاربته بعناوين دالّة تشبتك مع رؤيته المنهجيّة وهي [22]: (الفرز الثقافيّ)، و(البيان الثقافيّ)، و(الحكاية الناسخة)، و(المأزق النسقيّ)، و(العصا الرمزيّة)، و(لعبة الاستطراد أو طرد المتن).

وإذا كان الغذامي يقيم أود عناوينه على فعل الدهشة أو الاسترداد من سياقات العمى، فإنّه يكرّس العنوان، ليقوم بالوظيفة الإغرائية الإدهاشية [23]، التي تنطوي على ضَرْبٍ من المفارقة، إذ تعمل هذه العنوانات فيما يبدو على تكريس المقولة المنهجيّة التي يتبناها الغذامي، وهي نسقية الخطاب ومخاتلته من جهة، ودعوتها للقارئ إلى المبادرة بالبدء بتفكيك شفرات هذه العنوانات.

ويقرأ عبدالله الغذّاميّ الأنساق الثقافيّة المضمرة في حكاية (غنية وابنها عَرَامة)، التي يتضمنها كتاب العصا في كتابه (البيان والتبيين)، بوصفها حكاية تؤسّس لثقافة الهامش (Margin) أو الثقافة الشعبيّة (Popular Culture)، في مقابل ثقافة السلطة (High Culture)، ثقافة السلطة المهيمنة، وذلك على الرغم من كونها تنتمي في ظاهر الأمر إلى أدب الثقافة العالمة، أو ثقافة السلطة المهيمنة.

2 – 3 – علي فرحان والمرجعيّة الغذّاميّة:

أما مقاربة علي فرحان فتتشعب في بابين اثنين، أما أولهما فيقرأ مقامات

الحريري قراءة ثقافية، ابتغاء الكشف عن أنساق الثقافة بوصف مقامات الحريري نصّاً ثقافيّاً، وقد وسمه فرحان بـ(البنية والنسق الثقافيّ: دراسة معرفية)[24].

وأما ثانيهما فقد حاول فرحان خلاله أن يفحصَ البنية الحجاجية أو المحمول الحجاجي الذي ينتظم في بنية هذه المقامات، وقد وسمه فرحان بـ: (مقامات الحريري بوصفها دالاً)[25]، وعليه فإن العنوان في هذه المقاربة كانَ منسجماً مع موضوعها، ودالاً عليه[26].

وإذا كان العنوان الرئيس دالاً وواضحاً كما سلف فإنّ العنوانات الفرعية تتمثل المفاهيم الدارجة في النقد الثقافيّ، ما يشي بانغماس الناقد في مقولات المنهج الذي يتّبعه انغماساً كلّياً، وذلك من قبيل العنوانات الآتية[27]: (كسْر تابو الثنائيّات)، (ما ترك السابق للاحق من شيء)، و(فحولة البيان)، و(سُلطة النموذج)، و(سُلطة الأديب).

ويبدو الخطاب العَتَبيُّ عند فرحان في العموم ذا وظيفة تواصلية، إذ تُستخدَمُ اللغة في مستواها الوظيفيّ، دون العمل على تحفيز القارئ أو شدّه إلى الدخول في مراحات النصّ النقديّ، فهي عنوانات مكشوفة، ولعلّ في ذلك خروجاً على نمط التلقّي، الذي انمازت أغلب أطاريحه بأنها ولّت وَجْهها إلى الخطاب العتبيّ، وعملت على تنميقه، وتزيينه[28].

وينتخبُ فرحان لمقاربته هذه منهجاً تفاعليّاً مركبّاً، يجنبها مسالك الرؤية الأحادية، كما يزعم هو بذلك، بيد أنه فرحان وإن كان يحاول أن يتجنب مسالك الرؤية الأحادية، التي تفرضها مقاربة النصّ وفقاً لأدوات منهجٍ نقديّ واحد، فإنه ظلّ مثل غيره من الباحثين في السرديّات العربيّة القديمة أسيراً للقراءة الغذاميّة[29].

واتساقاً مع ذلك فيغدو مصطلح النسق المضمر القبيح، هو المصطلح المركزيّ في هذه المقاربة، وهو نوعٌ من المواضعة مع نمط التلقّي السائد، أو

نمط التلقّي التأسيسيّ على وجه التعيين. فضلاً عن ما يرتبطُ به من مصطلحات تأتي في ذات السياق من قبيل: (جماليات النص)، و(أنساق مراوغة)، و(النسق المضمر)، (المضمر).

إنّ مقاربة علي فرحان يمكن أن تدرج ضمن المقاربات التي تظلّ رهينة الأطر العامّة التي قررها الغذامي في مقاربته التأسيسة، بصورة تغدو خلالها القراءة النقديّة اللاحقة قراءة تنسجم واستراتيجيات القراءة السابقة/ الأولى.

3 – 3 – المحفليّ والقراءة المغايرة:

تنشعب مقاربة محمد المحفليّ، مدار المدارسة، إلى عدة مسالك مبحثية هي [30]: (مقدمة القراءة)، و(النقد الثقافيّ)، و(في النقد الثقافيّ والنقد الأدبيّ)، و(أهمية النقد الثقافيّ)، و(كيف يكون النقد الثقافيّ فاعلاً؟)، و(النسق الثقافيّ).

وفي (مقدمة القراءة) يجلّي المحفليّ فكرة مقاربته ومقولاتها المعرفيّة وآلياتها المنهجيّة، وفي مبحث (النقد الثقافيّ) يشير خلاله المحفليّ إلى مركزيّة مقولة النسق في النقد الثقافيّ، كما يتجلى ذلك في مقاربات ليتش (V.Leitch) وعبدالله الغذّامي، فضلاً عن الإشارة في سياق ذلك إلى الانفتاح المعرفيّ الذي ينماز به النقد الثقافيّ من الحقول المعرفيّة الأخرى.

ويبحث المحفلي في (في النقد الثقافيّ والنقد الأدبيّ) وشائج الاتّصال وعلائق التكامل بين النقد الثقافيّ والنقد الأدبيّ؛ محاولاً أن يؤلّف بينهما، بوصفهما نقدين يتكاملان ولا يتعارضان، وفي (أهمية النقد الثقافيّ) [31]، يشيرُ المحفليّ إلى مكامن الأهميّة المعرفيّة التي يضطلع بها النقد الثقافيّ، بوصفه نقداً مرتبطاً بآفاق الثقافة.

ويناقشُ المحفليُّ في (كيف يكون النقد الثقافيّ فاعلاً؟) [32] المسالكَ التي يمكن انتهاجها في تطوير مفهوم النقد الثقافيّ ومقولاته المعرفية وإجراءاته المنهجيّة.

وفي (النسق الثقافيّ)[33] يقدم المحفليّ تصوراً منهجياً مغايراً لجدليّة الأنساق الظّاهرة والأنساق المُضمرة في النقد الثقافيّ؛ إذ يحاول المحفليّ أن يؤسس لمسلكيّة بحثية جديدة؛ تنقام في أصولها على المواءمة بين البحث في المضمرات والمظهرات النسقية؛ وفي المبحث الموسوم بـ(الأنساقُ الثقافيّةُ في كليلة ودمنة)[34] يجلّي المحفليّ الأنساق الظاهرة والمضمرة في كتاب كليلة ودمنة، على اعتبار أنه يمثل نصّاً يضمر هذين النسقين كليهما، على خلاف ما قررته المقاربات السابقة في إطار النقد الثقافيّ.

وتبدو هذه العنوانات التي كوّنت المسار المنهجيّ لمقاربة المحفليّ مفصحةً عن منهجيّتها، التي تسعى إلى إعادة النظر في المنهجيّة المتبعة/ القارة عند النقاد الثقافيّين، وذلك بضرورة التفريق بين النسق المضمر والنسق المعلن.

ويبدو أنّ المحفليّ لا يؤمن بأنّ النسق المُعْلَن هو نسقٌ جماليّ، مراوغ، لا ينطوي على دلالات ثقافيّة ـ كما يرى الغذاميّ ـ إذ يمكن أن تكون النصوص منطويةً على أنساق ظاهرة، وأنساق مضمرة، يرتبطان بالثقافة وتقاليدها.

وهنا فلا يمكن أن يكون النسق المعلن ساتراً خلفه نسقاً مضمراً واحداً «وقد يكون التأويل جزءاً من هذه المهمة الصعبة، وهنا نكون إزاء نسقين ظاهرٍ جميل، ومضمرٍ نسقيّ، وذلك لا يمنع وجود أنساق أخرى، على اعتبار وجود أنساق ظاهرة تشترك في بنية النص، لا سيما النص الفني الغني بدلالته وتكثيفاته»[35] .

ولا مشاحة في أن المحفلي يبدو متأثراً أو مطوراً للمقاربات التي يطرحها يوسف عليمات ومعجِب العدوانيّ في تنظيرهما لمفهوم النسق الثقافيّ، إذ ينقل المحفلي لأفكارهما، ويناقشها، ويخلص منها إلى أنّ الأنساق الثقافيّة في النص تكون معلنةً ومضمرة.

وفي هذا السياق ينقل المحفلي عن عليمات نصّاً يرفض فيه عليمات مقولة الغذّاميّ حول النسق المضمر، إذ إنّه يرى أن: «النسق الظاهر بما هو وجود

متعيّن في النص الأدبيّ لا يمكن أن ينتج نسقاً أحاديّاً مضمراً ـكما أشار الغذّاميّ ـ، بل إنّ هذا النسق الظاهر يتميّز بالمخاتلة التي تفرض على المؤول الثقافيّ التحصّن بكفاءاتٍ وخبراتٍ لفحص هذا النسق ومساءلة إضمارته، مما يمنح المؤول الثقافيّ، وكما هي الصورة في الدائرة التأويليّة، يكتشف أن النسق الظاهر ينتج سلسلةً من الأنساق المضمرة اللامتناهيّة»[36]، ويؤكد المحفليُّ هذا الطرح بنقله عن العدوانيّ نقضه لمقولة الغذاميّة، إذ يقول العدواني: «فتاريخ المعرفة، وواقع الثقافات البشريّة، كلّها يفيدان بأن الأنساق الثقافيّة متنوعةٌ مختلفةٌ متعارضةٌ متناقضةٌ متغيرةٌ متطورة، وقابلةٌ للحياة والموت لحُسْنِ الحظّ»[37].

4 – استراتيجيّات المقاربة النقديّة ومستويات التلقّي:

1 – 4 – الغذّاميّ بين تحوّلات القراءة وتشكيل نمط التلقّي:

– القبض على النسق المضمر والاسترداد من سياقات العمى:

يمثل الكشف عن النسق المضمر والتأويل المجنح والاسترداد من سياقات العمى الاستراتيجيّتين اللتين تؤطّران استراتيجيات المقاربة النقديّة في مقاربة الغذّامي، وتقود هاتان الاستراتيجيّتان الغذّاميّ إلى فتح أبواب التأويل على مصراعيها في هذه الحكاية، إيماناً منه بأنّ تلقّي النصّ يمكن أن ينفتح أمام المتلقّي على تعدديّة المعنى والتأويل، بوصف المعنى النصيّ (معنى مفتوحاً)، إذ يعترفُ الغذّامي بأنّ التأويل الذي سيقدمه في هذه المقاربة، وإن انطوى على ربطه لأمورٍ لا يربط بينها رابط، يمثل نوعاً من استرداد القارئ من سياقات العَمَى الثقافيّ، الذي ران على قلبه سنين عدداً، محاولاً أن يُريَ القارئ كيف يمكن أن يضمر النص ما لا يتوقعه هذا القارئ، وكيف يمكن أن تنسج الثقافة خطابها المضاد.

إن الجاحظ من منظور الغذّامي غدا من خلال لعبة الاستطراد قادراً على

الانفلات من سطوة السلطة، والهُزْء بالقارئ العادي الذي لا يدرك مضمرات الخطاب أو إشارياته الرامزة، ولعلّ هذه اللغة الغذامية الحجاجية، يمكن أن تتسمى بـ(بلاغة النقد)، التي تنتزع له تأييداً ومناصرة[38].

ولا يماري المرء أنّ العصا كانت تمثل الذّات العربيّة بعد أن نالت الثقافة الفارسيّة من العصا، وجعلتها إحدى أبرز مثالب العرب، ولكن الربط المتعسف بين العصا بوصفها رمزاً للسلطة، وبين الخروج عن المتن أو لعبة الاستطراد بوصفها تمرُّداً وتدميراً لأنساق السلطة، أو انتصاراً للهامش، أو بوصف الاستطراد نَسْخاً للنّصّ الأصليّ، يغدو ربطاً بعيداً، ولكن الغذامي استطاع بقدرته النقديّة الفذة أن يبرره، وأن يسوقَ الحجج والبراهين في تأكيده.

ويرى الغذّاميّ أن كتاب العصا عند الجاحظ يؤدّي وظيفة نسقيّة في كتاب البيان والتبيين، تتمثّلُ في صناعة مفهوم الفَحْل، وترسيخ قيم الذّكورة، والرجولة؛ بوصف العصا لازمةً من لوازم الذّكورة أو الفحولة العربيّة[39] قُبيل أن تتحوّل في حكاية (غنية وابنها عَرَامة)، الحكايةِ الناسخة، إلى حكايةٍ تحتفي بالهامشيّة والهامشيين[40].

إنّ الغذّامي يمثّل في هذه المقاربة مفهوم القراءة بوصفها تَرحالاً في الفضاء المفتوح، بصورة تمسي خلالها نوعاً من اللعب مع النصّ، كما يعبر عن رولان بارت، ذلك أنّ الغذّامي يصغي إلى صوت النصّ، الذي يسمعه هو وحده، إذ يمكن للقارئ الحرّ/ الغذاميّ – بحسب أهوائه ونزواته – أن يقرأ النص بالإجهاز عليه، أو بالقفز على بعض مناطقه[41].

– الحكاية الناسخة ولعبة الاستطراد والتأويل المفتوح:

تمثل العصا بدءاً في كتاب الجاحظ علامة دالّة على نسقية الثقافة العربيّة، وذلك بوصفها «رمزاً ثقافياً، لها علاقةٌ عضويّة بالمفهوم النسقيّ لشخصيّة الفَحْل»[42]؛ ذلك أنّ الجاحظ ينمذجها في كتابه بوصفها قيمةً فحوليّة، وآلةً للبيان

والبلاغة، ورمزاً للكمال، قبل أن ينقلب على هذه الفكرة فيما يتلو، فالجاحظُ يسعى إلى ترسيخ أنساق الثقافة العربيّة «حيث يَجْري تقديم العصا في كتابٍ خاصٍ بها، يرسخها كقيمةٍ فحوليّة بيانيّة، لا تتحقّق الرجولة والخطابة إلا بها»[43].

ويذهبُ عبدالله الغذّاميّ إلى أنّ الجاحظ كان يَعْمَدُ إلى أن يتحايل على المتن أو الثقافة المركزيّة من خلال ترسيخ أنساقها، ومن ذلك امتداحه العصا، آلتها الأثيرة، التي يتباهى بها ذو الخلافة والسلطان، ومن ثَمَّ التحول عن ذلك إلى الاحتفاء بالهامشيّة في حكاية (تفاريق العصا)[44]، من خلال الانتقال بها من نسقيّة المتن إلى نسقيّة الهامش، إذ يتحدّث الجاحظ عند فوائد تفاريق العصا بصورة «يتكسّرُ [فيها] شرف العصا»[45] بُعيد أن كانتْ رمزاً للبلاغة والفحولة.

ولا يفوت عبدالله الغذّاميّ الإنباةُ إلى ما يُمكن أن يتسمّى بـ(مفارقات التسمية)، التي يستعين الغذامي بإشارياتها السيميائية، وإن كان لا يُصرّح بذلك، فغنية في القصة امرأة فقيرة، بخلاف ما يشي به اسمها، الذي يحمل معاني الغِنى واليَسَار، وهو ما تدأب عليه السلطة المصابة بالعمى الثقافيّ، المُقصية للهامش، والمُحتفية بالمركز، وفي ظلال الإشارات السيميائية التي يَحمِلُها اسم عَرَامة، بوصفه اسماً غير مخصّص لشخص بعينه يبدو أنّ الجاحظ اتخذه نموذجاً للإشارة إلى فحولة الرجل أو الذّكر العربيّ عموماً، ولذا فإن (تحوّل العصا إلى تفاريق) و(تقطيع وجه عَرَامة) يمثلان عند الغذّامي انتصاراً لـ(الهامش)، وتكسيراً لرموز المركزيّة المُهيمنة[46].

وفي سياق ذلك وسعياً إلى ترسيخ هذا الانقلاب في رؤية الجاحظ للعصا يتحدث الغذامي عن (حكاية غنيّة)، التي تؤدي لديه وظيفةً نسقيّة مخاتلة كذلك، بوصفها حكايةً ناسخة، تؤسّس لثقافة مُضادّة، تمتهنُ ثقافة السلطة المُهيمنة، من خلال سُخريتها اللاذعة من (الذّكورة)، بوصفها قيمة مركزيّة لنموذج الثقافة العالِمة، وذلك من خلال رسمها «صورةً هزلية للفحل النسقيّ/ الشعريّ»[47] (عَرَامة)، من منظور الهامش (غنيّة)، فهو فحلٌ يخسرُ أطرافه جرّاء وقوعه

في مآزق سَلاطَتِهِ وشُرُوْرِه، وفي ضَوْء هذا المعنى يغدو تقطيع وجه (عَرَامة) ابن (غنيّة) صورةً من صور ثورة الحكاية على المركزيّة النسقيّة الفحوليّة، إذ إنّ (عَرَامة) هو الذّكر العربيّ، الذي يمثّل (المتن) أو (المركز) في هذه الثقافة، وذلك يتجاور نسقياً مع تهشيم العصا إلى تفاريقَ ذات فائدةٍ كفائدة العصا بصورتها الأولى.

والحقيقة أنّ الغذاميّ لا يقدم دليلاً ينفع الغُلّة ويشفي العِلّة يؤكد خلاله أن الجاحظ مارس المخاتلة والمراوغة على السلطة في سرديّته هذه، وقد وقع في هذه الإشكالية؛ لأنّه أراد أن يصنع تساوقاً بين المرجعيّات الكُبرى اللائي انطلق منها بخصوص إضمارية الخطاب للمضمرات النسقيّة، وإشكالية الذات العربيّة، وشعرنتها، إلى غير ذلك مما أسّس له في مقاربته هذه، وعليه فإنّ هذا الربط الذي اجترحه الغذامي يُفضي في نهاية الأمر إلى التسليم بأنّ كلّ خروج أو استطراد هو بالضرورة تحايلٌ على المتن/ السلطة، وهذا افتراضٌ تسقطه الاستطرادات ذاتها، التي تكاد يكون بعضها أبعدَ شيءٍ عن الحديث عن الهامش والسلطة وغيرها، مما يؤكد صحة المأخذ الذي وسم به عبدالله إبراهيم مقاربات الغذامي، وهو تعميم النتائج من خلال نصوص مفردة[48].

– الجاحظ والتأرجح بين الهامش والمركز:

تمثّل مسألة تصنيف الجاحظ وتأطير موقفه بوصفه معبّراً عن صوت الثقافة العالمة أو منتمياً إلى ثقافة الهامش معضلةً حقيقيّة، تحتاج إلى فضل مباحثةٍ ومدارسة، وقد بيّن مُصطفى ناصف أنّ الجاحظ لا ينتمي إلى ثقافةٍ واحدة، سواءً الثقافة المركزيّة أو الثقافة غير المركزيّة، بل إنّه كان يراوح بين هاتين الثقافتين، ويعبّر عنهما كليهما[49]، ولا ريب أنّ هذه الحكاية يمكن أن تقرأ بوصفها حكاية الانتصار لنسق المرأة/ الأنثى في الثقافة العربيّة، إذ إنّ مآلات القصّة تنتهي في مختتمها لصالح المرأة التي تغتدي غنيّةً ذات يَسَار؛ من خلال المال الذي تأخذه

ديّاتٍ على تقطيع وجه ابنها وأطرافه، وعليه فإن هذه الحكاية «تتضمّن الانتصار للأنثى المُهمّشة، منذ جاءت صيغة الحبكة لصالح المرأة»[50].

ولعلَّ هذه الحكاية يمكن أن تكون من منظور مختلف انتصاراً للهامش اتساقاً مع احتفاء الجاحظ بالهامشيين في عددٍ من كتبه: و(فضل السودان على البِيضان) [51]، ولعلّه من فُضُول القول: إنّ التراث السرديّ الجاحظيّ قد أسال حبراً كثيراً من أمداء المنشغلين بمناهج النقد الأدبيّ، إلا أنّ الناظر فيها لا يجد ائتلافاً بين ما انتهتْ إليه تلك الدراسات، وما انتهت إليه مقاربة الغذّاميّ؛ فقد مثّلت مقاربته خروجاً صارخاً على آفاق تلك القراءات[52]؛ ذلك أنّ (فكرة المتن والهامش)، التي جعلها مدار البحث والمساءلة في مقاربته، هي أحد تجلّيات النقد الثقافيّ التي سلك الغذامي في طريقه[53].

– الغذاميّ وتجليات النزعة التفكيكيّة:

يفاجئ الغذامي القارئ في مقاربته هذه بالقول في مختتمها: إنّ قراءته تظلّ قراءة محتملة أو لا نهائيّة من إحدى القراءات التي يحتملها النصّ الجاحظيّ المُراوغ، على الرغم من أن لُغته النقديّة كانت تشي بأنه الناقد الذي استطاع ملامسة لباب المعنى النصيّ، وكشف أنساق الخطاب.

وهو بذلك ينزعُ عن قوسٍ تفكيكيّة، تظلُّ مسكونةً بفكرة إرجاء المعنى، ولا حدوديته[54]، بصورة تغدو فيها النزعة التفكيكية/ التشريحية التي صدر عنها الغذامي في دراسته الذائعة الموسومة بـالخطيئة والتكفير: من البنيويّة إلى التشريحيّة 1986م[55]، هي نزعة مطّردة في الخطاب النقديّ عنده، ولعلّ هذا يرجّحُ مذاهب القائلين بالتشابه بين التفكيكيّة والنقد الثقافيّ[56].

وفي ضَوْء السابق فلا ريب أنّ مقاربة الغذامي هذه تنجدل برباطٍ وثيق بالمقاربات التي دأبَ على تقديمها منذ عُرِفَ ناقداً «إذ إنّها [مقاربات] تُفاجئ،

وتدهشُ وتستفزّ، وتجعله يكسّر في أيدينا آنية استيعابه»[57]، فقد حاول في مقاربته هذه إعادة إحياء مفهوم سلطة المُتلقّي، الذي يضطلعُ بمهمة القراءة والتأويل، إذ تناط بالقارئ المُختلف مهمة تخليق المعنى النصّي، وفقاً لاستراتيجيات معيّنة[58].

2 – 4 – علي فرحان: مركزيّة النموذج الغذّاميّ وقوة المحاكاة:

– تعرية الأنساق الثقافيّة المضمرة:

يمثل الكشف عن النسق الثقافيّ المضمر أبرز استراتيجيّات المقاربة النقديّة في مقاربة فرحان، حتى ليغدو هو المحور الركين الذي يدير مقاربته هذه، بوصف هذه المقامات كما يتجلى من منظور القراءة الفاحصة سروداً مفعمة بالشيفرات النسقيّة، والمحمولات الإيديولوجيّة، والمرجعيّات الفكريّة؛ التي تهدف إلى التعبير عن تسخط الحريري على مجمتع، وتحديه له، وفي ضَوْء هذا السابق تحتشدُ في مقامات الحريري، وفقاً لمنظور علي فرحان، أنساق التضاد، والفحولة، والذّات، بصورةٍ لافتة للنظر، وهي أنساق مضمرة، تحتاجُ إلى أدوات النقد الثقافيّ، وذلك لِسِبْرها، وتبيانها[59].

ومن الملاحظ أن فرحان يفترضُ أنّ النسق في مقامات الحريري لا يكون إلا مضمراً، مما جعله لا ينتبه إلى أنّ أغلب الأنساق التي ذكرها هي أنساق ظاهرة أو معلنة، وإن كانت غير ظاهرة كلَّ الظهور، ولعلّ هذا التوجه في القراءة هو من إملاء التأثر بمقاربة الغذاميّ، التي كرست مقولة النسق المضمر، الذي يكون ناقضاً للظاهر وناسخاً له كما هو معلوم.

ويشير فرحان إلى أنساق الفحولة التي تتضمنها مقدمة الحريري؛ ذلك أنها تعكس سيمياء الحريري الكاتب الفذّ، الذي يتمرد – وهو يتقصّد ما يريد – على قوانين مجتمعه حول قانون الإبداع الشعريّ، حين يتجاسرُ على تخليق نوع / جنس أدبيّ جديد، يؤمن كلّ الإيمان بأنه لم يؤئتَ بمثله من قبل، تجسّدُه هذه

المقامات التي ألّفها لا على مثال سابق، خارج إطار «الصراع على شرف الوجود بين الشعر والنثر»[60].

ويلمح فرحان إلى أنّ فنّ المقامة عند الحريري والهمذاني يضمر نسقاً مخاتلاً بوصف المقامات فنّاً لا يمكن أن يندرج ضمن أقنومي الكتابة الشعر والنثر، فالمقامات فنٌّ (لا هو بشعرٍ ولا هو بنثر)[61]، ولعلّ في اختيارهما هذا النوع الهجين إشارةً صريحةً إلى رغبتهما المضمرة في تحطيم (الثنائيّات الضّديّة)[62] التي تنتظم هذا الوجود، وتَحْكُمُ حركة الإبداع في ذلك العصر، وهي تمثل «إعلاناً سافراً عن كسر قانون الثنائيات المتضادة»[63]، ولعل هذه القولة التي يفتتح بها فرحان مقاربته لا تندرجُ في سياق تحطيم الثنائيات، وإنما تمثل إشارةً إلى قدرة الذّات على الإبداع، والتفرد، وتبرز في المقامتين الكوفية والحجرية أنساق الذات والاستعلاء، التي يكسر بها الهمذاني النموذج، ويرى فرحان أنّ السروجي في (المقامة المراغيّة)[64] كسر النموذج الهمذاني حين تجاسر على رفضه قولة ندمائه، الذين أقروا أن الآخرين عِيالٌ على الأوائل في كلّ فن، فما كان منه إلا أنّ قرّعهم أشدّ تقريع، وأسمعهم من القول ما لا يسرّهم، فقال: «لقذ جئتم شيئاً إدّاً، وَجُرْتُمْ عن القَصْد جداً، وَعَظمتمُ العظام الرفات، افْتَتُّمْ في المَيْلِ إلى مَنْ فات، وغمصتم جيلكم الذين فيهم لكم اللذت»[65].

ويتحدَّث فرحان عن تجلٍّ آخر لأنساق الذّات في مقامات الحريري، التي ينكسر فيها النموذج الهمذاني مرّةً أخرى في المقامة الكوفية؛ ذلك أن أبا زيد السروجي، بطلَ مقامات الحريري، يبزّ سحبان وائل، ويتفوّق عليه، في غير ما موضع من هذه المقامة، مما يضفي إلى البطل أبي زيد السروجيّ إحساساً بفاعليته المؤثرة في الوجود من حوله[66].

– الحريريّ والهمذانيّ والتخاصم القديم:

يرى علي فرحان أنّ هذه الخروجات التي يخرُجُ من خلالها الحريري،

المؤلّف، عن النسق العامّ، تسعى، والحال هذه، إلى تكسير مسلّمات الثقافة الجمعيّة، التي كرّست النموذج الهمذاني، وسلطة المتقدّم، وفضلَ الأوّل، التي رسّختها مقولات رائجة في الثقافة العربيّة من قبيل: (ما ترك الأوّلُ للآخِر شيئاً) و(ذهب العلماءُ فلم يبقَ إلا المتعلّمون)، وفي ضَوْء هذا المعنى المشار إليه آنفاً يرى فرحان أن المقامات قد تبنت ثقافة التجاوز فقد «انكسر إذن ذلك النسق الذي يتخفى تحت قناع الثقافة الجمعيّة، إنّ اللاحق لا يقلّ شأناً عن الأوائل، بل قد يفوقهم براعةً وفضلاً»[67].

وهنا تبرزُ إشكاليّة كبرى انتظمت مقاربة فرحان والمقاربات الأخرى في النقد الثقافيّ، وتتجلى في افتراض علاقة أكيدةٍ غير قابلة للنقض أو التشكيك بين المؤلّف وإبداعه، أو بلغة أخرى، بين المؤلف وحُضوره في نصّه، إذ يغدو أبو زيد السروجيّ هو الحريري عَيْنَهُ أو قناعه[68].

ولا مراءَ في أنّ قراءة المقامات وأنساقها وربط ذلك بمؤلفها يمثل نوعاً من الاعتساف، وهو ما أكّده عبدالمنعم الخفاجيُّ في مقاربة كاملة، أقامها لمناقشة هذه الإشكالية، وحاول خلالها التشكيك في هذه المُسَلَّمة، وبحث طويلاً عن حقيقة أبي الفتح الإسكندري بطلِ مقامات الهمذانيّ، وأبي زيد السروجيّ بطلِ مقامات الحريريّ[69].

ولا ريب أنّ الإشارات التي قدمها فرحان حول فحولة الذات في هاتين المقامتين هي إشاراتٌ ممكنةٌ في ضَوْء ممكنات التأويل، ولكن موضع الإشكالية يتّضح في أنّ الناظر في بينة المقامتين يلحظ أنّهما لا تشيران، في حال من الأحوال، إلى انكسار النموذج الهمذانيّ، إذ لا يمكن أن يكون كل خروج على السابق في مقامات الحريريّ هو خروجاً على الهمذاني كما يرى فرحان، وهو ما لا تؤيده كذلك قراءة نصوص المقامات ذاتها، وتَحْسُنُ الإشارة هنا إلى القراءة البارعة التي قدمها حسن النعْمي التي تخلّص فيها من هذه العُقْدة، ودرس المقامة

البغداديّة بوصفها نصّاً ثقافياً، واجتماعياً، دون أن يسقطه على الحريريّ، أو يربطه بحياته، أو يجعله تجلياً من تجلياتها[70].

إنّ الأنساق التي تضمرها هاتان المقامتان لا يجب، كما ترى الدراسة الراهنة، أن تُقْرَأ في سياقات الثورة على النموذج الهمذاني أو انكسار هذا النموذج، دون وجود دليل نصيّ واضح، يمكن أن يُتَّكَأ إليه، بل تجب قراءتها في سياق إبرازها لمظاهر الثورة والثقة والاستعلاء، التي ينفتحُ بها التأويل، على أن تكون مخصوصةً بالحريريّ مؤلّفها، أو بالمجتمع الذي تُصَوِّره هذه المقامات، بوصف المقامات نصّاً يقدّم تصويراً لسياقات الصراع الذي يمورُ به مجتمع الحريري دون أن يكون شريكاً فاعلاً فيه، أو تعبيراً عن موقفه الخاص منه.

ولا ينبغي أن يُفْهَمَ من القول السابق: إنّ الدراسة الراهنة تُنادي بموت المؤلف، «لأنها مقولة أُحادية وعاجزةٌ عن فَهْمِ الظّاهرة الإبداعيّة بكلّ شمولها»[71]، بيد أنها تزعم أنّ قراءة هذه السرديّات المقامية لا ينبغي أن يكون مشروطاً بأن مؤلفها قد أراد منها بثّ أنساق خاصة به، أو العكس من ذلك، ولعلّ هذا يمكن أن يكون ناجعاً في النقد الثقافيّ الذي ينبري لقراءة الخطاب الشعريّ، الذي يكون تعبيراً غنائياً عن الذات، بوصفه خطاباً يحملُ في ثناياه أصداء التجربة الإنسانيّة التي يعالِجُها الشاعر في حياته، في حين يكون الخطاب السرديّ أكثر تعقيداً، إذ تمتزج في أتونه رُؤى المؤلّف برؤى المجتمع، بصورة يمسي أمر نَخْلِ هذه الرؤى، وتصنيفها أمراً صعباً.

ولعلّ فرحان لم ينتبه إلى أن هذا الافتراض تُسْقِطُهُ قولة الحريري في مفتتح مقاماته، وهي قولة تكرس سلطة النموذج الهمذانيّ، ولا تكسّره، أو تخرجُ عليه، إذ يقول الحريريّ عن مقامات الهمذاني: «هذا مَعَ اعترافي بأن البديع – رحمه الله – سبّاقُ غايات، وصاحبُ غايات، وأن المُتصدّي بعده لإنشاء مقامة ولو أوتي بلاغة قدامة لا يغترف إلا من فضالته ولا يشرى ذلك المشرّى إلا بدلالته...»[72].

والواضح أنّ فرحان متأثرٌ بالنص الذي نقله عن القلقشنديّ الذي مؤداه أن مقامات الهمذاني كسرت هذا النموذج، يقول القلقشنديّ عن الحريريّ: «عَمِلَ مقاماته الخمسين المشهورة، فجاءت نهايةً في الحُسْن، وأتت على الجزء الوافر من الحظّ، (...) حتى أنستْ مقامات الهمذانيّ، وصيّرتها كالمرفوضة»[73]، ولا ريب أنّ هذا النص يمثّل رؤية القلقشندي، التي لا يمكن أن تعكس – بالضرورة – رؤية الحريريّ.

ويبدو أنّ فرحان ليس رأساً في ذلك، إذ إنّ زُمْرَةً من الدارسين للمقامات قالت بذلك، ومنهم نادر كاظم، وهيثم سرحان، وهما – قطعاً – متأثران بمقاربة كيليطو، إذ إنّه أشار إلى أنّ الحريري أضمر رغبةً في تكريس ثقافة التجاوز، أو قتل الأب[74]، إذ يرى كيليطو أنّ الحريريّ كان يضمر رغبةً في التجاوز «مع إظهاره لتقديرٍ كبير نحو الهمذانيّ، فقد استطاع إزاحته إلى مركز ثانويّ»[75]، ويؤكد ذلك سرحان بقوله: «إنّ طموح الحريري [في مقاماته تَمَثَّلَ في] أن يفتح فتحاً جديداً، وأن يعلن أفقاً إبداعيّاً قائماً على قتل الأب»[76].

ومن الأنساق الثقافيّة المضمرة الأخرى التي تضمرها مقامات الحريري أنساق من قبيل: نسق فحولة البيان في عددٍ من المقامات، من مثل: المقامة الشعرية، والمقامة الحلبيّة، وغيرها[77]، وكذلك نسق سلطة الأديب، الذي يتجلّى في عددٍ من المقامات كـالمقامة الرميلية والنصيبيّة[78]، ويبدو أن هذه المقاربة وقعت في فخاخ التقليد فأرادت أن تمارس على النص القراءة المتعسفة، التي تنطلق من حقيقة تريد إثباتها، على الرغم من امتلاكها لأدوات المنهج، وقدرتها على تشقيق مسارٍ خاص بها.

– النسق الثقافيّ في مقامات الحريري نسقٌ مضمرٌ أم مخاتِلٌ؟:

لا يماري المرءُ في القول: إنّ هذه الأنساق التي تناولتها هذه المقاربة ليست مضمرة كل الإضمار، بل بدت مخاتلة أو مراوغة، تلك المقامات تطرح

أنساق التعالي والفحولة بصورة ظاهرة، وهنا تبرز إشكالية أخرى هي إشكالية المراوغة والإضمار، وهي إشكالية لا تكاد تخلو منها مقاربة من المقاربات المدروسة، ولكنّها تمسي واضحةً في هذه المقاربة، فالأنساق التي يتحدّث عنها فرحان، بوصفها أنساقاً مضمرة، تظهرُ على سطح النص السردي، وهي ليست بحاجة سوى إلى قليل تأمّل لإدراكها، ولعلّ مأتى هذه الإشكالية يرتدُّ إلى أن اللفظين، أقصد الإضمار والمراوغة، يدلّان عند عامة المنشغلين بالنقد الثقافيّ على معنىً واحد، والحال أن الأمر ليس كذلك، فالأنساق المخاتلة تختلف عن الأنساق المضمرة المخفيّة، أي أنّ النسق المضمر الذي يكون بحاجةٍ إلى حَفْرٍ في طبقات النصّ للقدرة على الكشف عنه، في حين أنّ النسق المخاتل، هو الذي يحمل أماراتٍ يمكن الكشفَ عنه من خلالها.

وفي هذا السياق تحتاج الفكرة التي ينطلقُ منها فرحان في مفتتح مقاربته، التي مؤداها أن الأنساق الثقافيّة التي تكشفت عنها قراءته لمقامات الحريري قراءة ثقافية هي أنساق مضمرة، زاعماً أنّ جمالية المقامات تخفي وجهاً قبيحاً لسطوة الأديب وسطوته[79]، وهنا، وفي ضَوْء إشكاليّة المضمر واللامضمر، فتنبغي الإشارة إلى أنّ ثمّة تقاطعات واضحةً بين النتائج التي انتهى فرحان في قراءة المقامات الحريرية من منظور النقد الثقافيّ، والنتائج التي انتهت إليها المقاربات التي تناولت المقامات من منظور المدرسيات النقديّة التقليديّة[80].

وعليه فإن الناظر في مدونات النقد الأدبيّ، الذي اهتمت بدراسة مقامات الحريريّ وفقاً لمنظوراتها، يلحظ أنها تمحورت في جلاء صورة المجتمع كما يتبدى في هذه المقامات، منيخةً مطايا البحث عند الصّراعات الاجتماعية، التي تَحْفَلُ بها المقامات، فقد نظرت هذه المقاربات إلى هذه المقامة بوصفها نصاً ثقافياً واجتماعيّاً، يعكسُ صراعات المجتمع، وكشفت عنها منذ سنوات طويلة ماضيات، وجاءت القراءة الثقافيّة لتقولبها في صورةٍ جديدة، بوصفها أنساقاً متضادة ومضمرة.

93

3 – 4 – محمد المحفليّ: القارئ القويُّ ومـحاولاتُ خـرق نمط التلقّي:

– الأنساق الظاهرة وإشكاليّات النسق المضمر:

يمثّل البحث في النسقين الظاهر والمضمر استراتيجيّات المقاربة المركزيّة التي يستعملها المحفليّ في مقاربته هذه، إذ إنّه يرى بأن ثمة أنساقاً ثقافيّة ظاهرة تكون مُدْرَكَةً من لدن القارئ / المتلقّي، وأنساقاً مضمرةً تتزيّا بعباءات الجماليّ المُراوغ والمخاتل[81].

وفي هذا السياق ينطوي كتاب كليلة ودِمنة كما يتمرأى في هذه المقاربة على أنساق ثقافيّة مركبّة، وهي أنساقٌ ترتبط بمؤلّف الكتاب الأصليّ، وأنساق مخصوصةٌ بترجمته الفارسية عن الهنديّة، لغته الأصليّة، وأنساقٌ بثّها ابن المقفّع خلال ترجمته لهذا الكِتاب إلى العربيّة[82]، وهي أنساق ترتبط بالجدليّة التي تنتظم علاقة المثقف بالسلطان، أو علاقة السيف بالعقل، بصورة تتجلى خلالها ثيمات الصراع الإنسانيّ والمجتمعيّ.

ويقرّرُ المحفليّ أنّ هذه الأنساق الثقافيّة المركبّة تتساوق والاختلافاتِ الفكريّة والثقافيّة والمجتمعيّة التي مرّ بها كتاب (كليلة ودمنة) عبْر ارتحالاته بين ثقافاتٍ مركزيّة ثلاث، تمثّل، والحال هذه، الثقافات الإنسانيّة المركزيّة في أنظار عددٍ من المنشغلين بالدراسات الحضارية والكونيّة، وهي: العربيّة، والفارسيّة، والهنديّة، ولعلّ هذه الإلماعة تمثّل وعياً بنسقية الترجمة، بوصف الترجمة فِعْلاً غير بريء، يعيدُ صياغة النصّ من منظور جديد، هو منظور المترجم[83].

ويشير المحفليّ إلى أنّ نسق التزلّف إلى السلطة[84] يمثّل نسقاً ظاهراً في كتاب كليلة ودمنة على الرغم من كونه نسقاً مخاتلاً، يميلُ إلى الاستتار والتخفّي، وهذا النسق هو نسق الرعية المتزلّفة، التي تحيطُ بالسلطة الحاكمة، وتُزيّن لها ممارساتها العنيفة، من خلال تزيّنها بثوب الوعظ والنصح والإرشاد في حكاية ابن آوى.

ويبدو أنّه فات المحفليّ الإنباه إلى أنّ هذه الحكاية يمكن أن تضمر نسقاً آخر هو نسق القوّة والبطش والفجور التي تسيطر على السلطة وحاشيتها، بصورةٍ دائبة، إذ يقرن ابن آوى في حديثه خدمةَ السلطان بالفجور، ولا ريب أنّ في ذلك لمزاً بالسلطة، ونقداً لطرائقها النمطية وشروطها الفاسدة في اختيار رجالها، ولعلّ هذا يؤكد، بصورة ما، صحة الطرح القائل بزئبقية النسق الثقافيّ، وانفتاحه على عددٍ من الدلالات، ووجوب إعداد عدّة معرفيّة متأسسة على معارف شتى في ارتحالات الناقد في البحث عنه.

ومما يَعْضُدُ هذا القول، أي إضمار الحكاية السابقة لنسقٍ مضاد، أنّ بيدبا حين خاطب الملك أول مرة «انزعج من جرأته، وتسلّط لسانه في التنكيل بالسدة العالية فأمر بسجنه، وتقييده»⁽⁸⁵⁾، وهو وعيٌ من السلطة بالنسق الثقافيّ، أو بالخطاب المضاد، الذي يتضمنه هذا الخطاب السرديّ، الذي يتأسّس على فَضْح العمى الذي يحكم مسارات السلطة، وقراراتها.

ولعلّ هذا النسق هو النسق المضمر، الذي أراد السارد أن يبثّه في هذه الحكاية، ذلك أن فحولة هذه السلطة، وقوتها، وبطشِها، هي التي تجعل من التزلّف، النسقِ الظاهر، مهيمناً على هذه السرديّة، وناسخاً لنسقِ نقد السلطة، بنمطق النقد الثقافيّ، وتبدو هذه الأنساق كذلك في حكاية الغراب الذي يمثل البطانة الفاسدة، التي تسعى إلى جعل الملك مُلكاً مقدّساً يحرمُ الخروج عليه⁽⁸⁶⁾.

لقد عَبَّرَ السارد عن هذا النسق المضمر، ولكنْ بطريقةٍ مراوغة، تُفيد من إغراءاتِ الخطاب السرديّ، الذي يستندُ إلى جماليات القصّ، التي تجعلُ من المؤانسة والإمتاع هي وظيفة الخِطاب السرديّ، وتجرّده من وظائفه النسقيّة، ممّا يسمح للكتاب بتمرير خطابه حول أنساق البطش السلطويّ، والفتك بالخُصوم والأعداء، ويبدو أنّ السارد تقنّع بألسنة الحيوانات لتمرير رسائله الرامزة إلى السلطة، لأنّه ينأى بنفسه عن الصدام المباشر معها، خوفاً من فتكها به؛ لأنّها تملك قوة السيف، فقد برزت في هذه السردية مفارقات القوّة والعَقْلِ ــ إذا كان

95

التعبير جائزاً ــ فالعقلُ نسقُ المثقّف دمنة، قناعِ المؤلّف، وهو يتفوّق على نسق القوّة الذي يعكس الأسد السلطان.

ولا ريب أنّ احتواء كليلة ودمنة على عديد الأنساق الثقافيّة الأخرى وزئبقية النسق الثقافيّ، قد تأتى بسبب رحلة الكتاب، وانتقالها بين الثقافات، ذلك أن الناظر فيها يجد أنها أو قل: يمكن أن يقرأها بوصفها مُمالئةً للسلطة، ومروجةً لها في أحيان، وهي في أحيان أخرى سرديّات تهدف إلى صَوْغِ خطاب مضادّ يمثل تيار وعي النقد لخطاب القوّة الذي تتمترس به السلطة، ويشيرُ المحفليّ إلى أنّ كتاب كليلة ودمنة يحفلُ عبر تجلّياته السردية بتمثيلات لنسق/ أنساق المكر والخداع في أتون الصّراع على السلطة الذي يسميه المحفليّ بـ(صراع الأنساق للاقتراب من السلطة)، وذلك كما يتبدّى من خلال الصراع الذي يدور بين ابن آوى والثور [87].

إن المحفليّ كما يبدو تعامل مع هذه الحكايات بالتأويل المباشر، غير أنّ هذه السرديّة وأن كانت تعبّر عن هذا المعنى النسقيّ، فإن التأويل يظلّ منفتحاً إلى إضمارها أنساق الذّات المتمركزة حول نفسها، وهي أنساق مُضمرة خفيّة، إذ إنّ الذات تغدو من خلال هذا الصّراع راغبةً في بلوغ حظوةٍ لدى السلطة، وبذا التغلبِ على غيرها ممن ينافسها في سياق صراعاتها على تحقيق المكانة السلطويّة، وكذلك يمكن أن تعبّر عن تجليات الصراع الإنساني المجتمعي، الذي يومئ إليه السارد.

ويبدو أنّ المحفليّ قد أدرك حجاجية النسق الثقافيّ، المعلن أو المضمر سواءً في كتاب كليلة ودمنة، فقد بيّن أن هذه الأنساق قد لاذت الحجاج؛ أجلَ تبرير مشروعيتها، وإضفاء بعدٍ إقناعيّ لمضموناتها، وهو ما يؤكد أنّها كانت تعبّر عن ذاتية محضة، أجبرتها على القول بذلك.

ــ الأنساق المُضمرة والنقد الأدبيّ وتجليات التناسخ:

إذا كان النقد الثقافيّ معنياً بمساءلة الأنساق المضمرة [88]، فإن المحفليّ يحاولُ

أن يُجلي الأنساق المضمرة في كتاب كليلة ودمنة، وهي: نسق الترميز، والنسق الديني، والنسق الاجتماعيّ(89)، وتبدو نتاجات استخراج هذه الأنساق على تماسٍ واضح مع ما انتهت إليه في النقد الأدبيّ، الذي قرأ كليلة ودمنة، إذ إنها أشارت إلى تجلّيات الرمزيّة في هذا الخطاب.

ويتحدث المحفليُّ عن الأنساقِ الثقافيّةِ التي تتضمنُها نسقيّة الترميز في هذا الكتاب، فالكتابُ يشير في مقدّمته إلى أنه يقدّس أنساق الخاصّة، أو أنساق السلطة، في مقابل النيل من أنساق العامّة(90)، وينطوي كتاب كليلة ودمنة كما يرى الباحث على أنساق اجتماعيّة، تربط والحال هذه، بالبيئة الاجتماعية، وهي: أنساق المرأة التي تعبّر عن دونيتها(91)، بوصفها مخلوقةً من ضلع أعوج، في مقابل تفضيل الذَّكر عليها، الذي يمثل رمز الفحولة والشرف والفخار، كما يتمرأى في المخيال الجمعيّ للثقافة العربيّة.

ويتحدث الكتاب عن مخادعة المرأة ومكرها، ومحاولتها الإطاحة بالذّكر الفَحْل، كما في حكاية القنبرة والفيل(92)، فكتاب كليلة ودمنة يفيضُ «بإشارات نسقيّة تؤكّد رسوخ نظرة معيّنة نحو الأنثى، ابتداءً من تفضيل الذّكر عليها، وانتهاءً بجعلها مصدر المكر والخديعة»(93)، فضلاً عن ترسيخ «ثقافة الكيد النسائي وذلك في باب القِرْد والغيلم»(94).

وإذا كان هذا المؤدّى أحد أبرز الإفرازات المعرفيّة التي توصّل إليها المحفليّ في مقاربته هذه، فإنه من الواجب الإشارة إلى أنّ تمثيلات صورة المرأة في كليلة ودمنة إحدى أبرز الخلاصات التي توصّلت إليها الدراسات النقديّة الكلاسيكيّة في النقد الأدبيّ الحديث؛ مما يجعل هذه النتيجة نتيجة منسوخة يتفق فيها النقد الثقافيّ مع ما انتهى إليه النّقد الأدبيّ.

ولعلّ هذه الأنساق التي تنال من المرأة، تمثل أنساقاً ظاهرة، ليست بحاجةٍ إلى مضاعفة عمليـات التأويل والحفر، في هذا الخـطاب، وعليه فلعلّ هذه

الأنساق يجب أن تكون تحت أنساق الخطاب المعلنة وليس المضمرة كما ذهب محمّد المحفليّ.

ويشيرُ المحفليُّ إلى إفادة السلطة من النسق الدينيّ، الذي يجمعُ بين القَدَرِ والمُلْك، إذ يغدو تفرّد السلطة بالمُلْك قدراً مقدوراً، لا فكاك منه كما يتجلى ذلك في الحكاية التي يتضمنها باب ابن الملك وأصحابه من كتاب كليلة ودمنة[95]، وينتهي المحفليُّ بالإشارة إلى نسق الإعلاء من شأن الخديعة والمكر والخداع، إذ إنه قد تقرّر في المخيال الجمعيّ أن الدهاء والمكر والخديعة، تمثل قيماً نسقيّة، تساعد في تحقيق الغايات والمرومات على اختلاف أنواعها، كما يتمثّل في باب البوم وملك الغِرْبان[96].

– تركيب:

يتجلّى مفهوم القراءة الثقافيّة لدى عبدالله الغذامي بوصفها القراءة التي تكشف ألاعيب الثقافة، ونسقية الخطاب الأدبيّ، فهي تمثل لديه بديلاً نقديّاً فاعلاً لأدوات النقد الأدبيّ التي لا تستطيع أن تخلص بممكناتها إلى ما يمكن الخلوص إليه عند الاستعانة بممكنات القراءة الثقافيّة.

وتنماز هذه المقاربة بوصفها تمثّل لحظة تكوّن نمط التلقّي حول السرديّات العربيّة القديمة، ولعلّ ذلك يتجلّى فيما لقيه مشروع الغذامي من استقبال، واحتفاء، مما جعل مقاربته تتموضع بمثابة نمط تلقٍ يشكّل لدى القارئ في النقد الثقافيّ أفق انتظار تنقاس إليه التلقّيات التالية في النقد الثقافيّ.

ولا ريب في القول: إنّ هذه القراءة وقعت في محظور عنف القراءة[97]، حين لوت عنق النص، وأدخلته في سياق تأويليّ متعسف، دون دليل قاطع، يقنع أو يشفي، وعليه فإن قراءة الغذامي هذه قراءة استعمالية، أرادت أن تثبت سلبية موقف الجاحظ من السلطة، ولذا فإنها لتحقيق مأربها هذا لم تتورع في فرض

تصورات مسبّقة على النص، فلقد أراد الغذامي أن يبين تحيزات الثقافة العربيّة ضد المرأة والهامش، فبنى مقاربته جلها على فكرة مؤداها أن جماليات السرد، تخبّئ وراءها أنساقاً قبيحة، والحقيقة أن مقاربة الغذاميّ حول حكاية عَرَامة تفيءُ إلى مفهوم القراءة الحرة، التي تكسبُها لُغته النقديّة المجنّحة حجاجيّة ترين بها على قلب المتلقّي، حين تظل تلح على القارئ بأنه مصابٌ بالعمى الثقافيّ.

وبدا أن الغذّامي ظل يعيشُ تحت سطوة نظريّات النقد الأدبيّ الحديث، التي كان منشغلاً بها قبل انتحائه سُبَلَ النقد الثقافيّ، ويغدو مصطلح (النسق) وما تفرع منه من مصطلحات كـ(النسقية) و(المضمر) بؤرةً مركزيّة في سياق هذه القراءة الغذّاميّة، ولا ريب أن مصطلحات ومفاهيم من قبيل: (الهامش) و(النسق المضمر) التي مثلت الجهاز المفاهيمي الذي اتكأ إليه الغذامي، ستغدو في المقاربات التالية حقلاً مفاهيميّاً يمتح منه المنشغلون بالنقد الثقافيّ، ويدورون في فَلَكه.

وعليه فإنّ الغذامي يمثل في قراءته للنص الجاحظي خروجاً على النسق المتواتر من القراءات النقديّة العربيّة، حين حاول أن يستنطق النص السردي، بوصفه مكمناً للأنساق الثقافيّة المُخاتلة، من خلال البحث في مضمرات الخطاب، وأنساقه المخاتلة، واطّراح جماليّات البلاغة، التي تتوسلُ بها الثقافة العالِمة أو الشعبية لتمرير أنساقها.

لقد بلغ النموذج الغذاميّ كما أشارت الدراسة سابقاً أمداً قصيّاً من الشهرة ومحاولات المضارعة أو التقليد، ولعلّ ذلك كان وبالاً حقيقياً على النقد الثقافيّ، أو عاملاً يساعد على تصدُّع قواعده فيما يستقبلُ من أيام؛ ذلك أنّ سطوة المقاربة الغذاميّة، يعضُدُه التلقّي الإنبهاريّ لهذه المقاربة، ينضاف إلى ذلك عدمُ بروز نماذج كثيرة استطاعت أن تختطّ للنقد الثقافيّ مساراتٍ جديدة، أسهم في ترسخ النسق الغذّاميّ، وفحولته، بصورة أصبح خلالها الكثيرُ من المنشغلين بالنقد الثقافيّ يدورون في مداراته، دون قدرةٍ حقيقية على الخروج عن نموذجه، أو النفوذ من سُلطانه، وهنا يبدو أنّ فرحان مأخوذ بطقوس القراءة الثقافيّة، التي لم

يحاول أن يخرق أنساقها أو أن يخرج عن آفاقها التي تراكمت بفِعْل المقاربات الثقافيّة المتعاقبة حول التراث العربيّ، على الرغم من تصريحه في مفتتح مقاربته بأنها من تمتح منهجياً من مرجعيات مختلفة.

ولا مندوحة من الإشارة إلى أنّ ذلك جعل مقاربته تقع في إشكالية المنهج، فهي تطبيقاً تنتمي انتماء صريحاً للنمط السائد من القراءات في النقد الثقافي، الذي يُطلق عليه نمط التلقّي الغذامي، ولكنها تنظيراً، تدعي إفادتها المنهجيّة من مرجعيّاتٍ مختلفة، وفي هذا السياق ينجدلُ مفهوم القراءة الثقافيّة عند علي فرحان بالمفهوم المعياريّ الذي تبنّاه عبدالله الغذّاميّ، وهو مفهوم يقرأ النصّ من منظور ثقافي، بوصفه نصّاً ثقافياً، يحفل بعديدٍ من الأنساق التي تحتاج إلى قراءةٍ فاعلةٍ فاحصةٍ. ولعلّه من الموجِبَاتِ الإشارة إلى أنّ فرحان وقع في إشكاليّة المضمر والمعلن، التي مثّلت إشكاليّةً من إشكاليّاتِ القراءة الغذامية، إذ يبدو أن فرحان لم ينبه إلى أن هذه الأنساق تمثل أنساقاً غير مضمرة إضماراً تاماً، حيث يمكن للقارئ الضمني إدراكها، وفهمها، دون الحاجة إلى الحفر المعرفيّ العميق في بِنى هذه المقامات، ذلك أنّها تمثل أنساقاً معلنة، تعكس بجلاء ووضوح تامّين موقف الحريريّ من مجتمعه، وأنساقه، وأنظمته.

وعليه فإنّ مقامات الحريري أضحت في ضَوْء القراءة الثقافيّة التي قدمها علي فرحان نصّاً ثقافياً، حافلاً بالأنساق الثقافيّة، التي عبرت عن الحريري، ومفارقاته، وموقفه من الناس، والسلطة، والأعراف القارة في مجتمعه.

لقد أسس المحفليّ في مقاربته هذه منهجيته الخاصة، التي لا تتفق مع غيرها من القراءات، التي تعاقبت ضمن إطار النقد الثقافيّ، في محاولة لكسر نمط التلقّي الذي شيده الغذّاميّ، بيد أنه لم يستطع أن يكشف اللثام عن أنساق الخطاب السردي في كليلة ودمنة، دون التأثر الواعي، وربما غير الواعي، بما خلصت إليها مدرسيات النقد الأدبيّ، التي تصدت لقراءة كليلة ودمنة، ومحاولة سبر أغوارها.

ولا مراء أنّ المحفلي حاول في مقاربته هذه أن يؤسس لمسلكيّة بحثية جديدة،

يكون مدار البحث فيها، النسق الظاهر المعلن، والنسق الخفيّ المضمر، وهو تجلٍّ من تجليات الخروج الصريح على أدبيات النقد الثقافيّ، التي انعقد القول عليها منذ سنين طوال ماضيات، وعليه ينبني مفهوم القراءة الثقافيّة في مقاربة محمد المحفليّ على فكرة مركزيّة مؤداها أنّ القراءة الثقافيّة تمثل ضرباً من القراءة التي تكشف عن أنساق النصّ، المعلنة والمضمرة.

وبذا فإن مقاربة المحفلي هذه تمثّل صورة من صور التجاسر المعرفيّ وكذا المنهجيّ على الخروج على نسق القراءة العامة، الذي كوّنته القراءة الغذّامية، وما تلتها من قراءات، وتكاد تكون مقاربة المحفلي هي المقاربة الوحيدة التي أنبهت إلى إشكالية النسق في مشروع النقد الثقافيّ، على أن هذا الخروج لم يمثل خروجاً نهائياً عن نمط التلقّي، أو طلاقاً بائناً لمقولاته، فقد ظلّ نمط التلقّي حاضراً في هذه القراءة، حضوراً خافتاً، لا يقارن بسطوة حضوره في مقاربات أخرى.

ويمثل مفهوما (النسق المعلن) و(النسق المضمر) مرتكزاً مفاهيميّاً رئيساً تنبني مقاربة المحفليّ هذه على أسٍ منهما، وعليه فإنّ الأنظار التي قدّمها المحفلي في هذه المقاربة تنطوي على مزية خاصة هي محاولة التأسيس لمفهوم القراءة الثقافيّة المتكاملة، التي تجوب النصّ، وتكشف عن أنساقه، دون الاندغام بنمطيّة تظلُّ تدافعُ القارئ في أثناء قراءته.

وعليه فقد بدا أن السرديّات التي يتضمنها كليلة ودمنة تؤكد أنه نصٌّ نسقيٌّ، بوصفها سرديّات محملة بالأنساق الرائجة في الثقافة العربيّة، فهي تقف من الأنثى موقفاً دونيّاً، وتروج لمواقف السلطة المختلفة، وتشيع في الناس أنساق الذل والاستكانة.

هوامش الفصل الأول:

1 – فرحان، علي، مقامات الحريريّ حجاجية السـرد والنسـق الثّقافيّ دراسة في البنية والخطاب، ط1، 2017م، منشورات الجامعة الأهلية، المنامة، البحرين، ص149 – 190.

2 – المحفليّ، محمّد، الأنساقُ الثقافيّةُ في كِليلة ودمنة، مجلة سِمات، جامعة البحرين، البحرين، المجلد (4)، العدد (1)، 2014م، ص18 – 36.

3 – يُنظـر: زيّاد، صالح، القارئ القياسي: سـلطة القصد والمصطلح والنمـوذج: مقاربات في التراث النقدي، ط1، 2009م دار الفارابي، بيروت، لبنان.

4 – يُعَدُّ «ولفغانـغ آيـزر» «Iser Wolfgang» و«هانس روبرت يـاوس» «Jauss Robert Hanz» قُطبي مدرسة «كونستانس» النقديّة الألمانيّة «School Konstanz» التي كرّست اهتماماتها للبحث والتّأصيل المعرفيّ لنظريّة التلقّي؛ تنظيراً وتطبيقاً. للاسـتزادة يُنظر: ياوس، هانس، جماليّة التلقّي: من أجل تأويل جديد للنّص الأدبيّ، تقديم وترجمة: رشيد بنحدو، ط1، 1996م، الدار العربيّة للعلوم ناشرون (بيروت/ لبنان)، منشورات الاختلاف (الجزائر العاصمة/ الجزائر)، دار الأمان (الرباط/ المغرب)، ص55. وهولب، روبرت، نظرية التلقّي...، (م.س)، ص16.

5 – الغذاميّ، عبدالله، النقد الثّقافيّ...، (م.س)، ص7 – 8.

6 – المرجع السابق، ص8.

7 – فرحان، علي، مقامات الحريريّ: حجاجية السرد والنسق الثّقافيّ...، (م.س)، ص71.

8 – ينظـر: كون، توماس، بُنية الثورات العلميّة، العدد (168)، 1992م، سلسـلة عالم المعرفة، المجلس الوطني للثقافة والفنون والأدب، الكويت، ص246. والمرجع السابق، ص13.

9 – كاظم، نادر، المقامات والتلقّي ...، (م.س)، ص41.

10 – الغذاميّ، عبدالله، النقد الثّقافيّ...، ص7.

11 – فرحان، علي، مقامات الحريريّ: حجاجية السرد والنسق الثّقافيّ...، (م.س)، ص7 – 8.

12 – المرجع السابق، ص8.

13 – يُنظر: بلوم، هارولد، خريطةٌ للقراءة الضّالة، (م.س)، ص7.

14 – يـاوس، هانس، جماليّة التلقّي: من أجل تأويل جديد للنّصّ الأدبيّ، (م.س) ص55. وهولب، روبرت، نظرية التلقّي...، (م.س)، ص16.

15 – الموسـوي، محسـن جاسـم، النظرية والنقد الثقافيّ، (م.س)، ص20. وليتش، فنسنت، النقد الأدبيّ الأمريكي ...، (م.س)، ص410 وما بعدها.

16 – كـون، تومـاس، بُنية الثورات العلمية، ص246. وفيتش، سـتانلي، هل يوجد نصّ في هذا الفصل؟ سـلطة الجماعات المفسّـرة، ترجمة: أحمد الشـيمي، ط1، 2004م، منشورات المشروع القومي للترجمة، القاهرة، مصر، ص411. وزياد، صالح، القارئ القياسيّ: سلطة القصد ...، (م.س).

17 – يوسـف، أحمد، القراءة النسـقيّة...، (م.س)، ص204. والرويلي والبازعي، ميجان وسـعد، دليل الناقد الأدبيّ...، (م.س)، ص231. ولومان، نيكلاس، مدخل إلى نظريّة الأنساق، (م.س)، ص37.

18 – ليتـش، فنسـنت، النقد الأدبيّ الأمريكيّ من الثلاثينيات إلـى الثمانينيات، ترجمـة: محمد يحيى، مراجعة وتقديم: ماهر شـفيق فريد، ط1، 2000م، منشـورات المشروع القومي للترجمة، القاهرة، مصر، ص410.

19 – الغذاميّ، عبدالله، النقد الثقافيّ...، (م.س)، ص83.

20 – وفـي هـذا السـياق يقول الغذامي: «إنّ النسـق يتحدّد عبـر وظيفته، وليس عبر وجوده المجرّد، والوظيفة النسقية لا تحدث إلّا في وضع محدّد ومقيّد، وهذا يكون حينما يتعارض نسقان أو نظامان مـن أنظمة الخطاب، أحدهما ظاهـر والآخر مضمر، ويكون المُضمر ناقضاً وناسخاً للظاهر». ينظر: الغذاميّ، عبدالله، النقد الثقافيّ...، (م.س)، ص77.

21 – الغذاميّ، عبدالله، النقد الثقافيّ...، (م.س)، ص83.

22 – المرجع السابق، ص221 – 242.

23 – بلعابـد، عبـد الحق، عتبات: جيرار جينيـت من النص إلى المنـاص، ط1، 2008م، الدار العربيّة للعلوم ناشرون (بيروت/ لبنان)، منشورات الاختلاف (الجزائر العاصمة/ الجزائر)، ص88.

24 – فرحان، علي، مقامات الحريريّ: حجاجية السرد والنسق الثقافيّ...، (م.س)، ص66 – 72.

25 – المرجع السابق، ص66 – 72.

26 – المرجع السابق، ص66.

27 – المرجع السابق، ص66 وما بعدها.

28 – بلعابد، عبد الحق، عتبات: جيرار جينيت ...، (م.س)، ص87.

29 – فرحان، علي، مقامات الحريريّ: حجاجية السرد والنسق الثقافيّ...، (م.س)، ص71.

30 – المحفليّ، محمّد، الأنساقُ الثقافيّةُ في كليلة ودمنة، (م.س)، ص18 – 24.

31 – المرجع السابق، ص22.

32 – المرجع السابق، ص22 – 23.

33 – المرجع السابق، ص23 – 24.

34 – المحفليّ، محمّد، الأنساقُ الثقافيّةُ في كليلة ودمنة، (م.س)، ص24 – 35.

35 – المرجع السابق، ص18 – 24.

36 ــ عليمات، يوسف، عليمات، يوسف، النسق الثّقافيّ: ...، (م.س)، ص68 ــ 69.

37 ــ العدوانيّ، معجب، مفهوم «النسق الثّقافيّ» من منظور المعرفة، جريدة الرياض، الرياض، المملكة العربيّة السعودية، الخميس 11 ذي القعدة 1425 هـ ــ 23 ديسمبر 2004م، العدد (13331). ينظر الرابط:

تاريخ الدخول 2020/10/10 (http://www.alriyadh.com/11617)

38 ــ العشّي، عبدالله، بلاغة النقد: النصّ النقديّ خارج خطابه، مجلة أنساق، تصدر عن كلية العلوم والآداب، جامعة قطر، الدوحة، قطر، المجلد (1)، العدد التجريبي، 2017م، ص54.

39 ــ تعدّ موضوعة الفحولة العربيّة موضوعةً مركزيّة في الخطاب النقديّ عند الغذّامي. يُنظر: عشّا، علـي مصطفى، الفُحـولـة فى الوعي الثّقافيّ العربيّ: كتاب المرأة واللغة نموذجاً، المجلة العربيّة للعلوم الإنسانية، جامعة الكويت، الكويت، المجلد (37)، العدد (147)، 2019م، ص159 ــ 190.

40 ــ ويتجلى ذلك في عدد من الحكايات ومنها حكاية أعرابي سُئل عن تفاريق العصا: «قيلَ لأعرابيٍّ: مَـا تَفاريقُ العَصا، قالَ: العَصا تُقْطَعُ سـاجوراً فتَصيرُ أوتاداً، ويُفرّقُ الوَتـدُ، ثُمَّ تَصيرُ كلُّ قِطْعَة شِظاظاً: فإذا جُعِل لرأسِ الشِّظاظِ، كالفُلْكة صَار للبختيّ مِهاراً، وَهُوَ العـودُ الّذي يُدْخَلُ في أنفِ البُخْتيّ». الجاحظ، عمر بن بحر (ت150هـ)، البيان والتبيين، تحقيق: عبدالسلام هارون، ط7، 1998م، مطبعة الخانجي ومطبعـة المدنـي، القاهرة وجدة، مصر والسـعودية، ص49 ــ 51. والغذاميّ، عبدالله، النقد الثّقافيّ...، (م.س)، ص231.

41 ــ بنحدو، رشـيد، قراءة في القراءة، مجلة الفكـر العربي المعاصر، مركز الإنماء القومي، بيروت، لبنان، العددان (48 ــ 49) 1988م، ص20.

42 ــ الغذاميّ، عبدالله، النقد الثّقافيّ...، (م.س)، ص230.

43 ــ الغذاميّ، عبدالله، النقد الثّقافيّ...، (م.س)، ص231.

44 ــ «وذلك إنّه كان لها ابن شـديد العَرامة، كثير التّفلّت إلى الناس، مع ضَعْفِ أسْـر ودِقّةِ عظم، فواثَبَ مـرة فتـى من الأعراب فقطَع الفَتى أنفَه، فأخذَت غنيّة دِيَة أنفِه، فحَسُنَت حالُهـا بعدَ فقْرٍ مُدْقِعٍ. ثُمَ واثَبَ آخرَ فقطَع أُذُنَه فأخذت الدية فزادت دية أذنه في المال وحسن الحال. ثم واثب بعد ذلك آخر، فقطع شـفته فأخذت دِيَة شفته، فلما رأت ما قد صار عندها من الإبل، والغنم، والمتاع، والكسـب بجوارح ابنها حَسُنَ رأيها فيه، فذكرته في أرجوزة لها تقول فيها: أحلِفُ بالمَرْوةِ حقّاً والصّفا*إنّك خيرٌ من تَفاريقِ العَصا». معاني الألفاظ الغريبة: العرامة: الشراسة والشدة. يُنظر: الجاحظ، عمر بن بحر (ت150هـ)، البيان والتبيين، (م.س)، ج2، ص49 ــ 51.

45 ــ المرجع السابق، ص235.

46 ــ الغذاميّ، عبدالله، النقد الثّقافيّ...، (م.س)، ص229.

47 ــ المرجع السابق، ص228.

48 ــ إبراهيم، عبدالله، الثّقافة العربيّة والمرجعيّات المُستعارة، (م.س)، ص97 ــ 111

49 ــ ناصِـف، مصطفى، محـاورات مع النثر العربيّ، العدد (218)، 1997م، سلسـلة عالم المعرفة، منشورات المجلس الوطني للثقافة والفنون والآداب، الكويت، ص55.

50 – الغذاميّ، عبدالله، النقد الثقافيّ...، ص235.

51 – المرجع السابق، ص240.

52 – وفي سـياق ذلك تُراجع المقاربة الجامعيّة الضخمة التي قدمها محمد عبدالبشـير مسـتالي فعرض فيها جل الدراسـات النقديـة التي تناولت التـراث الأدبيّ الجاحظي من منظورات النقد الأدبيّ على تعدد مناهجها واختلاف مقولاتها. يُنظر: مسالتي، محمد عبدالبشير، الجاحظ في قراءات الدارسين المحدثين، رسالة ماجستير (غير منشورة)، 2014م، جامعة سطيف (2)، الجزائر.

53 – القفاري، أميرة، النقد الثائر...، (م.س)، ص125.

54 – يُنظر: دريدا ودي مان، جاك وبول، وآخرون، مداخل إلى التفكيك ...، (م.س)، ص187 – 227 . وحمّـودة، عبد العزيز، المرايا المُحدّبة: من البنيويّة إلـى التّفكيك، العدد (232)، إبريل 1998م، سلسلة عالم المعرفة، المجلس الوطنيّ للثّقافة والفنون والأدب، الكويت، ص362.

55 – ينظـر: الغذّامـي، عبـداله، الخطيئة والتكفير من البنيوية إلى التشـريحية: نظريـة وتطبيق، ط4، 1998م الهيئة المصريّة العامة للكتاب، القاهرة، مصر.

56 – تجدر الإشـارة إلى أن مقاربة نزار السـعوديّ هذه لم تكشـف عن تلك الملامح التّفكيكيّة في نماذج تطبيقيّة تمثلت النقد الثقافيّ منهجاً لها، وتكتفي بتبيان هـذه الملامح في التنظيرات المفاهيمة لتلك المقاربات. يقول السـعوديّ: «أقام النقد الثقافيّ كثيراً من مقولاته النظرية وفرضياته اعتماداً على القـراءة التفكيكية، التي أرسـى قواعدها وأصولها جاك دريدا J.Derrida))». ينظر: السـعوديّ، نـزار جبريل، الملامح التّفكيكيّة للنّقد الثقافيّ، المجلة العربيّة للعلوم الإنسـانيّة، جامعة الكويت، الكويت، المجلد (37)، العدد (147)، 2019م، ص12.

57 – البنكي، محمد، قراءة في نموذج للتّسويق الثقافيّ: الغذّامي بوصفه مسـوّقاً، بحث منشـور ضمن كتاب (عبدالله الغذّامي والممارسة النقديّة الثّقافيّة)، (م.س)، ص200.

58 – حمّودة، عبد العزيز، الخُروج من التّيه...، (م.س)، ص116.

59 – فرحان، علي، مقامات الحريريّ: حجاجية السرد والنسق الثقافيّ...، (م.س)، ص66 – 72.

60 – المرجع السابق، ص66.

61 – المرجع السابق، الصفحة نفسها.

62 – المرجع السابق، الصفحة نفسها.

63 – المرجع السابق، الصفحة نفسها.

64 – الشريشـي، أبو العباس، كمال الدين أبو العباس أحمد بن عبد المؤمن (ت619هـ)، شرح مقامات الحريـري، 2004م، تحقيـق: محمد ـبوالفضـل إبراهيم، المكتبة العصرية، بيـروت، لبنان، ج1، ص225 – 228.

65 – الشريشي، أبو العباس، شرح مقامات الحريري، (م.س)، ص225.

66 – المصدر السابق، ص225 – 228.

67 – فرحان، علي، مقامات الحريريّ حجاجية السرد والنسق الثّقافيّ...، (م.س)، ص68.

68 – الشريشي، أبو العباس، شرح مقامات الحريري، (م.س)، ص225 – 228.

69 – الخفاجي، عبدالمنعم، أبو الفتح الإسكندريّ: بطل مقامات بديع الزمان وشخصيته المجهولة، ط1، 1996م، مكتبة الإنجلو المصريّة، القاهرة، مصر، ص53 – 130.

70 – يُنظر: النعمي، حسن، غواية السـرد: قراءة في المقامة البغداديّة للحريريّ، المجلة العربيّة للعلوم الإنسانيّة، جامعة الكويت، الكويت، المجلد (19)، العدد (73)، 2001م، ص140 وما بعدها.

71 – ثامر، فاضل، اللغة الثانية: في إشكاليّة المنهـج والنظريّة والمُصطلح في الخِطاب النقديّ العربيّ الحديث، ط1، 1994م، المركز الثقافيّ العربيّ، بيروت، الدار البيضاء، لبنان، المغرب، ص131.

72 – الشريشي، أبو العباس، شرح مقامات الحريريّ، (م.س)، ص225.

73 – القلقشنديّ، أحمد بن علي (ت821هـ)، صبح الأعشى في صناعة الإنشا، شرحه وعلق عليه وقابل نصوصه: محمد حسـين شـمس الديـن، ط1، 2012م، دار الكتب العلمية، بيـروت، لبنان، ج14، ص125.

74 – كيليطو، عبدالفتاح، المقامـات: السـرد والأنسـاق الثقافيّـة، ط2، 2001م، ترجمـة: عبدالكبير الشـرقاوي، دار توبقـال للنشـر، الـدار البيضـاء، المغرب، ص163. وكاظم، نـادر، المقامات والتلقّي...، (م.س)،ص. وسـرحان، هيثم، إشـكاليّة المعارضة والانتحـال في مقامات الحريريّ، (م.س)، ص136.

75 – ينظر: كيليطو، عبدالفتاح، المقامات: السرد والأنساق...، (م.س)، ص163. ويبدو أن كيليطو يلحُّ على هذه الفكرة فهو يعيده برمته في كتابه بحبر خفي. ينظر: كيليطو، عبدالفتاح، بحبر خفي، ط1، 2018م، دار توبقال للنشر، الدار البيضاء، المغرب، ص36.

76 – سرحان، هيثم، إشكاليّة المعارضة والانتحال في مقامات الحريريّ، (م.س)، ص136.

77 – فرحان، علي، مقامات الحريريّ حجاجية السرد والنسق الثقافيّ...، (م.س)، ص69.

78 – المرجع السابق، ص70.

79 – فرحان، علي، مقامات الحريريّ: حجاجية السرد والنسق الثقافيّ...، (م.س)، ص71.

80 – يمكن في سـياق ذلك الإشـارة إلـى الأنظار التي تناولت قـراءة المقامة في ضَـوْء «النقد الأدبيّ الحديث». ينظر: الجديع، خالد بن محمد، الدراسـات السـرديّة الجَديدة: قـراءة المقامة أنموذجاً، ط1، 2007م، مركز بحوث كليّة الآداب بجامعة الملك سعود، الرياض، المملكة العربيّة السعودية.

81 – المحفليّ، محمّد، الأنساقُ الثقافيّةُ في كليلة ودمنة، (م.س)، ص25.

82 – المرجع السابق، ص25 – 26.

83 – المرجع السابق، ص24.

84 – يتجلّى هذا النسـق في حديث ابن آوى باب الأسـد والشـغبر الناسـك: «قال ابن آوى: إنما يستطيع خدمة السلطان رجلان لستُ بواحدٍ منهما: إما فاجرٌ مصانع ينالُ حاجته بفجوره ويسلم بمصانعته وإما مغفلٌ لا يحسده أحد». يُنظر: ابن المقفع، كليلة ودمنة، ص158.

85 – الداهي، محمد، السلطة العمياء في كليلة ودمنة، مجلة الكوفة، مجلة علمية محكمة تصدر بدعم من جامعة الكوفة، العراق، العدد (10)، 2016م، ص59.

86 – «قال الغراب: إني لأعرف ما يقول الملك؛ ولكن النفس الواحدة يفتدى بها أهل البيت؛ وأهل البيت تفتدى بهم القبيلة؛ والقبيلة يفتدى بها أهل المصر؛ وأهل المصر فداء الملك». يُنظر: ابن المقفع، أبو مُحمّد عبد الله (ت142هـ)، كليلة ودمنة، دار الهلال، القاهرة، مصر، 1999م، ص78. والمحفليّ، محمّد، الأنساقُ الثقافيّةُ في كليلة ودمنة، (م.س)، ص27.

87 – المحفليّ، محمّد، الأنساقُ الثقافيّةُ في كليلة ودمنة، (م.س)، ص27.

88 – يوسف، أحمد، القراءة النسقيّة...، (م.س)، ص204. والرويلي والبازعي، ميجان وسعد، دليل الناقد الأدبيَ...، (م.س)، ص231.

89 – المحفليّ، محمّد، الأنساقُ الثقافيّةُ في كليلة ودمنة، (م.س)، ص31 – 35.

90 – المحفليّ، محمّد، الأنساقُ الثقافيّةُ في كليلة ودمنة، (م.س)، ص31 – 35.

91 – المرجع السابق، ص34.

92 – «يحكـى أنَّ قنبـرةً اتخـذت أدخيةً وباضت فيها على طريق الفيل؛ وكان للفيل مشـرب يتردد إليه. فمر ذات يوم على عادته ليرد مورده فوطئ عش القنبرة؛ وهشم بيضها وقتل فراخها. فلما نظرت ما سـاءها، علمت أن الذي نالها من الفيل لا من غيره. فطارت فوقعت على رأسـه باكيةً؛ ثم قالت: أيها الملك لم هشـمت بيضي وقتلت فراخي، وأنا في جوارك، أفعلت هذا اسـتصغاراً منك لأمري واحتقاراً لشأني. قال: هو الذي حملني على ذلك. فتركته وانصرفت إلى جماعة الطير؛ فشكت إليها ما نالها من الفيل. فقلن لها وما عسى أن نبلغ منه ونحن الطيور؟، فقالت للعقاعق والغربان: أحب منكنّ أن تصرن معي إليه فتفقأن عينيه؛ فأجبنها إلى ذلك، وذهبن إلى الفيل، ولم يزلن ينقرن عينيه حتى ذهبن بهما». ابن المقفع، أبو مُحمّد عبد الله، كليلة ودمنة، (م.س)، ص13.

93 – المرجع السابق، ص31 – 35.

94 – المرجع السابق، الصفحتان نفسهما.

95 – المحفليّ، محمّد، الأنساقُ الثقافيّةُ في كليلة ودمنة، (م.س)، ص31 – 32.

96 – المرجع السابق، ص33.

97 – خمري، حسين، نظريّات القراءة ...، (م.س)، ص179.

الفصل الثاني:

إخصاب نمط التلقّي:
النقد الثقافيّ وممكنات ما بعد الكولونيالية

- فاتحة أولى:

تُوصف المقاربات التي يضمنها هذا الفصل بأنهما أخذت على عاتقهما إخصاب نمط التلقّي من خلال تخصيب مسارات القراءة الثقافيّة، إذ ينفتح النقد الثقافيّ، بمفهومه الوافد، الذي تمثله الغذّاميّ، على ما اصطلح على تسميته في المدونات النقديّة بدراسات ما بعد الكولونياليّة أو دراسات ما بعد الاستعمار (Post – Colonial Studies)، التي تمثّل أحد أبرز التوجّهات التي برزت في ثنايا الدراسات الثقافيّة (Cultural Studies)[1].

ويجدر الإنباه إلى أنّ نمط التلقّي هذا لا يتضاد مع نمط التلقّي العام، وإنما يسعى إلى تشييد فعل الإخصاب، وتوسيعه، وتفتيق أكمامه فقد «انفتح النقد الثقافيّ على خطاب ما بعد الكولونيالية؛ ليستمد منه رؤى ثقافيّة جديدة، تتعلق بدراسة كل أغراض العنصرية والإمبريالية، والهُويّة، والتهجين، والهيمنة، والمركزيّ، والهامشيّ والآخر»[2]، ويبدو الإنباه لازباً إلى أن الدراسات ما بعد الكولونياليّة مثلت لدى الباحثين في هذا المسار القرائيّ منهجاً مفترعاً من النقد الثقافيّ، والحال أنهما حقلان يتداخلان تداخلاً كبيراً، بصورة يصعب تأطيرهما بأُطرٍ جليّة، أو تسويرهما بحدود ضابطة[3].

ولعلّ هذا الاشتباه يعود في أصله إلى أن هذه التجارب، مثلت تجارباً مبكرة، لم يستقم في أوقات صدورها أمرُ النقد الثقافيّ، وبذا فإنهم يكونون قد مارسوا فعل الإخصاب من حيث يعلمون ومن حيث لا يعلمون، حين استعانوا على كشف أنساق الخطاب السرديّ، مدار النقد الثقافيّ، ومدار مقارباتهم، بمدارسة

التمثيلات الثقافيّة، وآليات الإقصاء، وطرائق التخييل الجماعي ...إلخ، التي تعد أو تمثل محاضن الأنساق الثقافيّة، مدار البحث في النقد الثقافيّ.

ويبدو للناظر في السيرورة التاريخية التي انتظمت هذا التوجه في إخصاب نمط التلقّي، أن مقاربة نادر كاظم تمثل تاريخيّاً نقطة التأسيس لهذا النمط/ الأفق، الذي بدأ يتشكل عام 2004م عُقب إصدار مقاربته حول المؤسِّسة (تمثيلات الآخر: صورة السود في المتخيَّل العربيّ الوسيط)، وفي هذه المقاربة تتشابك مفاهيم عديدةٌ، في تشكيل منهجيّة، لا تؤمن بالأحادية، وترى أن الممارسة النقديّة في النقد الثقافيّ يجب أن تنجدل بأربطة وثيقة مع الدراسات الثقافيّة عموماً ودراسات ما بعد الكولونيالية خصوصاً، على اختلاف حقولها، ومنازعها.

وتبدو مقاربة ضياء الكعبيّ (خطابُ التحامق والجنون في السرد العربيّ القديم: قراءةٌ في التمثيلات الثقافيّة) حول سرديّات الجنون/ الهامش، ومقاربتها حول (السرديّات الشعبيّة) إلماعةً تكاد تكون الأولى ثقافياً في النقد الثقافيّ العربيّ حول خطاب الجنون والسيرة الشعبيّة، وقد بدا أنّ القراءة الثقافيّة لا يمكن أن تستكمل شرطها دون العمل على وضع حدودٍ أجناسيّة ضابطة، تؤطّر خلالها سرديّات الجنون، وهو ما يبدو مركوزاً في وعي كلّ من تصدّى لقراءة السرديّات المهمشة، إذ إنّ وعي التجنيس ضرورةٌ لا مناص عنها، تأتي تراتبياً في المرحلة الأولى، ومن ثم تتبعها القراءة الثقافيّة التي تلتفت إلى آليات تكوين التمثيلات والتمثيلات المضادة.

وإذا كان النقد الثقافيّ فتيّاً، كما أسلفت، فإن هذه الأطرحات انطوت على إشكالية مركزيّة، تتجلى في عدم مقدرة هذه المقاربات على سكّ منهجيّة قرائيّة ضابطة، تمتلكُ جهازاً معرفيّاً مؤطَّراً، ومقولات نقديّة مؤسِّسة، واستراتيجيات قرائية ثابتة، بيد أنها وعلى الرغم من ذلك فلا مراء في أنها قد أسهمت، بسهمة وافرة، في تصنيع مسارٍ منهجيّ يبقى لافتاً للنظر، ومحفّزاً على الاشتباك به، ومساءلته.

1 – مدخل: ما بعد الكولونياليّة وإخصاب مسارات القراءة:

تنطوي مقاربة نادر كاظم (تمثيلات الآخر: صورة السود في المتخيّل العربيّ الوسيط)[4] ضمن منظومة القراءات الثقافيّة، التي تعتمدُ على منجز النقد الثقافيّ، في مساءلة الأنساق الثقافيّة المُضمرة والثاوية في بنى النصوص، إذ إنّها تُشكّل لديه تأويلاً مُفارقاً ذلك أنها تتجاوز الفكرة القارة إزاء السيرة الشعبية (Popular Folktales)، التي مؤدّاها أنّ السيرة الشعبيّة العربيّة على تعددها لانطة بالقصّ والحكي والإمتاع والمُؤانسة وحسب، إذ يختزل وظيفتها بذلك دون تأديتها لدورٍ أيديولوجيّ محدّد، أو دون تحقيق دور آخر.

وتعدُّ مقاربات ضياء الكعبي حول (خطابُ التحامق والجنون في السرد العربيّ القديم: قراءةٌ في التمثيلات الثقافيّة)[5] و(السير الشعبية)[6] من أبرز المقاربات التي خُصّصت لمساءلة سرديّات التحامق والجنون (Narratives of Madness) والسير الشعبية في السرديّات العربيّة القديمة، وقراءتها قراءة ثقافيّة ناجزة، تكشف تشكُّلاتها ومحمولاتها وجدلياتها؛ وهي تبحث في المضمرات النسقيّة في خطاب التحامق والجنون والهامشية، وخصوصاً في تمثيلات البطل الشعبي المجنون بوصفه هامشاً أو مُهمّشاً في ظلال السطوة المركزيّة للسُّلطة الاجتماعيّة والسياسيّة والدينيّة.

2 – سيمياء القارئ: من القارئ المُخْصِب إلى القارئ المؤصّل:

1 – 2 – نادر كاظم: القارئ المُخْصِب وتجربة البدايات:

تجلّي مقاربة نادر كاظم صورةَ المقاربة التي تهدف إلى إخصاب نمط التلقّي، الذي أسّسه الغذامي، ذلك أنّها حاولت إخصابه من مرجعيّاتها ذاتها، من خلال المتح من مرجعيات الدراسات الثقافيّة عامة، ممثلة بالدراسات ما بعد الكولونياليّة (Post – Colonial Studies's) والدراسات الأنثروبولوجيّة

(Anthropological Studies)، وإدماجها بأفق /نمط التلقّي، بهدف إخصابه[7].

وإذا كان النقد الثقافيّ نقداً بينيّاً أو عابراً للتخصصات (Interdisciplinary Studies)[8]، فإنه يبدو على تماسٍّ مَعَ فروع معرفية كثيرة، بصورة تغدو خلالها هذه الفروع عصيّة عن التأطير المنهجيّ، فقد غدتِ ـ اليوم ـ حقلاً معرفياً واسعاً، ومتداخلاً مع كثيرٍ من الحقول العمليّة الأخرى.

ويبدو نادر كاظم على وعْي جليّ بهذه الحقيقة، أو بهذه المَيْزة التي ينمازُ بها النقد الثقافيّ، إذ يمثل النقد الثقافيّ لدى نادر كاظم، حقلاً أو فرعاً من الدراسات البينيّة، التي تستنهض سؤالات الإبداع، والابتكار، والتكامل، وذلك حسب تعبير سعد البازعي[9]، ويمثل فعل الإخصاب هنا بالانفتاح المنهجيّ الحرّ على مختلف الأسيقة المنهجيّة أو الحقول البحثيّة التي تنتظم ما بعد الكولونيالية، بوصفها مظلّة ينطوي تحت ظلالها فروع معرفيّة من مثل: دراسات التابع (Subaltern's Studies)[10]، أو القراءة الطّباقيّة (Contrapuntal Reading)[11].

وفي هذا السياق يمكن الإشارة إلى أن مقاربة نادر كاظم من الناحية التاريخية هي المقاربة الأولى، التي انطوت على تجليات هذه التجربة، أي أنّها أوّلُ تجربةٍ حاولت أن تقوم بفعل الإخصاب المنهجيّ لمقاربات النقد الثقافيّ في عقب المقاربة الغذامية[12].

ولعلّ ذلك يجيءُ على اعتبار أنَّ النقد الثقافيّ يشترك مع هذه المناهج في المرجعيّة الكُبرى، التي يمثلها النقد الثقافيّ، ولا ريب أن المقاربة التي قدمها كاظم تمثل تجربة البدايات، التي تقود فيما تلا سلسلة اهتزازات ستصيب نمط التلقّي إخصاباً، وتوسيعاً[13].

ويمكنُ الإشارة في سياق هذا إلى العدة المعرفيّة التي تسلح بها نادر كاظم، من خلال إفادته من مقاربات الدراسات ما بعد الكولونياليّة، التي ترتبط برباطٍ وثيق العُرى مع النقد الثقافيّ، بصورة غدا خلالها منهجه منهجاً تفاعلياً مركّباً[14].

2 – 2– ضياء الكعبيّ: القارئ الأجناسي وإشكاليّات أُلفة التلقّي:

تنزعُ ضياء الكعبيُّ عن قوسٍ تجنيسيّة – إن كان التعبير جائزاً – فهي مُشغولة في أطروحتيها بهواجس التأصيل لسرديّات الجنون والسير الشعبية بوصف كل منهما نوعاً أدبيّاً خاصّاً، وذلك أنّها تموضعها من الناحية المنهجيّة بين التلقّي التجنيسيّ، نسبةً إلى الانشغال بالعمل على تجنيس الأنواع الأدبيّة، والتلقّي في إطار النقد الثقافيّ، الباحثِ في أنساق الخطاب السرديّ، وتشكُّلاته، وتمثيلاته[15].

ويبدو تلقّي ضياء الكعبي لسرديّات الجنون والسير الشعبية تلقّياً مفارِقاً يتجاوز الفكرة المكرورة، التي مؤدّاها أنّ هذه السرديّات سرديّات متعةٍ وإحماض، إذ تمثّل هذه السرديّات في ضَوْء النقد الثقافيّ، مراحاً فسيحاً يمكن للناقد أن يجوس خلالها لتميطُ اللثام عن عديد الأنساق الثقافيّة المُضمرة في بنيتها العميقة، إذ يغدو القارئ الأجناسي المتتبع للخصائص الأجناسية لهذه السرديّات قادراً على كَسْرِ المسلّمات القارة، التي شكلتها ألفة التلقّي حول هذه السرديّات[16].

وتأسيساً على السابق فإن رؤية الكعبي تقوم على الوعي بالازورار والتهميش الذي لحق بالسرديّات العربيّة القديمة عامّة، وبسرديّات الجنون والسير الشعبية على وجه الخصوص، ذلك أن من يرقُبُ المقاربات المنشغلة بهذه السرديّات بوصفها أجناساً سرديّة مستقلّة، ينماز كلُّ نوع منها بخصائص، وبنىً حكائية، يحدها مقاربات قليلة عدّاً.

وهنا فإنّه لا شيةَ في أن الكعبيّ قد سلكت المساراتِ التي اختطها نادر كاظم، حين أخصبت النقد الثقافيّ، بممكنات الدراسات ما بعد الكولونيالية، بصورة استوفت من خلالها الكعبيّ شروط الإخصاب المنهجيّ، بما استدخلته من مفهومات عُمَدٍ في الدراسات ما بعد الكولونياليّة إلى حياض النقد الثقافيّ، وذلك باستيلاد وشائج منهجية تربط هذين الفرعين المعرفيين بوصفهما فرعيْن

ينطويان عند جمهرة من الباحثين في ظلال الدراسات الثقافيّة، التي تضم إليها عدداً كبيراً من الفروع المنهجيّة الأخرى.

وعليه فإنّ هذا التدبير المنهجيّ التي اتخذته ضياء الكعبيّ في مقارباتها الراهنة يبدو تدبيراً سديداً، يجعل من تجنيس النصّ، وإشكالات هذا التجنيس، وهي إشكالات ما زالت موضوعة خصيبة للبحث والمدارسة، فضلاً عن تخصيب النقد الثقافيّ بممكنات الدراسات ما بعدالكولونيالية، مدخلاً لقراءة الخِطاب السرديّ، واستيعابه، بما ينطوي عليه هذا الخطاب من أنساق وتمثيلات[17].

3 – المتن المنهجيّة والجهاز المفاهيميّ:

1 – 3 – نادر كاظم والمرجعيّة المتعدِّدة:

ينتظمُ عقد مقاربة نادر كاظم في بابيْن كبيريْن: أما الأول (مرجعيات المتخيل والتمثيل الثقافيّ)، فيتناول فيه كاظم الصورة النمطية للسُّودان والزّنوج والأحباش، كما جاءت في مرجعتين هما: التاريخ والأنساق الثقافيّة غير التخيلية: (الرمز) و(الدين) و(اللغة)[18]، ومن خلال الفصل الأوّل يحاولُ أن يتوقَّف عند جذور المرجعيّة التي كانت – ولا تزال – تتحكم بصورة السودان، وتمثيلاتها في المخيال العربي.

ويسعى نادر كاظم في الفصل الثاني: (مستويات المغايرة وقوة التمثيل) إلى إعادة تركيب ما اختزنه المتخيّل العربيّ عن الأسود، من صورٍ نمطيّةٍ انتقاصية[19]، وأما في الباب الثاني: (الأسود والتمثيل الثقافيّ التخييليّ)، فقد صبّ فيه جهوده على تقديم مقارباتٍ ثقافيّة لتمثيلات السودان في الإنتاج العربيّ الأدبيّ السرديّ والشعريّ.

ويلحظ أنّ العناوين التي اختارها كاظم لمقاربته ذاتُ أبعادٍ سيميائيّة، فهي فضلاً عن مجيئها شعريّةً، ولافتةً للنظر، ومغريةً للقارئ في الغالب، وهي متسقةٌ

مع طرحه المنهجيّ، إذ يمكن من خلال قراءة هذه العناوين توليد دلالات النصّ النقديّ من خلال فعل التكثيف[20]، وفي هذا التفت عناوين الجزء المخصص للسرد في مقاربة كاظم كما يأتي: (المولود الأسود وصدمة الولادة)، و(الأسود بين التاريخيّة والآخريّة العجائبيّة)، و(سيرة سيف بن ذي يزن: نبوءات مُحتشدة وكذبة مرعبة)، و(ألف ليلة وليلة: السودان والشهوانيّة المفرطة).

وهي عنواناتٌ انعكست على صفحتها مجالات الانشغال المنهجيّ الذي يحكم عمل كاظم النقدي في كلّ سيرة، وهنا فلا بُدَّ من الإشارة إلى مقاربة نادر كاظم تتأسس على ائتلاف منهجي مُزدوج لُحْمَتُهُ الدراسات ما بعد الكولونياليّة وسَداه النقد الثقافيّ.

وتجدرُ الإشارة إلى أن مقاربة نادر تتأسَّسُ على مفاهيم ثلاثة هي: (التمثيل) و(الآخر)، و(المتخيّل)[21]، يعدُّ مصطلح النسق الثقافيّ بؤرتها، بوصفه «شبكة من الدلالات والأدوات الرمزيّة التي هي عبارة عن تعليمات وقواعد تتحكم في سلوك الأفراد وتصوراتهم وتضبطها على وجه ينزع نحو الثبات والاستمراريّة والتناسق»[22].

ويبدو كاظم منشغلاً بضرورة إزالة اللَّبْسِ الواقع بينها؛ لتداخلها، وترابطها، وتقارب الحقول المعرفيّة التي ينتمي إليها كلّ واحدٍ منها إليه، فالتمثيل هو: «ضرب من التعليمات التي تدور حول طريقتنا في النظر إلى أنفسنا وإلى الآخرين»[23]. أما المتخيل فهو: «عبارة عن نسقٍ مترابطٍ من الصّور والدلالات والأفكار والأحكام المسبقة التي تشكلها كلّ فئةٍ عن نفسها وعن الآخرين»[24]. في حين أن الآخر هو: «الكائن المختَلِفُ عن الذات، وهو مفهوم نسبي، ذلك أن الآخر لا يتحدّد إلا بالقياس إلى نقطة مركزيّة هي الذات»[25].

وإذا كانتْ الدراسات ما بعد الكولونياليّة تدأبُ في تجلّياتها النقديّة، بصورتها العامّة، إلى محاولة إبراز صوت المهمّشيْن والتابعين والمعذّبين والمستعمَريْن

في الأرض، وإعادة دراسته من منظوراتٍ جديدةٍ مختلفة فإنّ كاظماً انتخب، الإنسانَ الأسود، بوصف تمثيلاته موضوعاً بحثياً خصيباً.

ويبدو أن نادر كاظم في هذا السياق كان يملكُ وعيّاً نقدياً منتخِباً[26] حين كان أول من يختارُ أن يستثمر أدواتِ النقد الثقافيّ، والدراسات ما بعد الكولونياليّة، التي ترتبط برباطٍ وثيق العُرى مع النقد الثقافيّ، في توليفة نقديّة مركّبة، ذلك أنّ النقد الثقافيّ من منظور كاظم يتقاطعُ مع حقول معرفية عديدة[27]، غير أنّ المصطلحات اللواتي يقيم عليهنَّ أود مقاربته (التمثيل) و(الآخر)، و(المتخيّل) تنتمي إلى الدراسات ما بعد الكولونياليّة انتماءً صريحاً[28].

2 – 3 – ضياء الكعبيّ بين المرجعيّة الأجناسية والثقافيّة:

جاءت مقاربة الكعبي حول سرديّات الجنون في محورَيْن اثنيْن، أما أولهما في دلالة المصطلح ثقافيّاً، وأما ثانيهما في آليّات التمثيل السرديّ، وقد اتّسقت الموضوعات/ العنوانات التي انتخبتها الكعبي، مع نزوعات الباحثة في مقاربتها، حول البحث في التمثيلات الثقافيّة، والعمل على تجنيس سرديّات الجنون، والعنوانات هي[29]: (التحامق والجنون: في دلالة المصطلح ثقافيّاً)، و(في التمثيلات الثقافيّة لسرديّات التحامق والجنون)، و(آليّات التمثيل الثقافيّ في سرديّات التحامق والجنون)، وبحثت الكعبي (التحامق والجنون: في دلالة المصطلح ثقافيّاً) تمثيلات مصطلحي التحامق والجنون، في مدوّنات عربيّة ثلاثٍ هي: كتب التراث اللغوي، والمعاجم، وكتب عقلاء المجانين، وقد خَلُصَتْ إلى أنّ المعجمات قد حفلتْ بعددٍ وافرٍ من الأسماء التي وسم بها (المجنون)[30]، أما في المبحث الثاني فعرّفت الكعبيّ بالمسارد الحكائيّة التي تضمّنت في مطاويها خطاب التحامق والجنون في السرديّات العربيّة القديمة[31]، أما في المبحث الثالث[32]، فقد تناولت تمثيلات التحامق وما تضمره من أنساقٍ ثقافيّة.

ومما يبرز في موضوعات/ عنوانات المبحث الثالث، وهو الأهمّ، أنها تزنر

العنوانات الفرعية بشعرية طافحة تحتاج من القارئ مزيدَ تأمّل وتحديق في سبيل فكّ معمياتها، والقبض على إشارياتها، وهي: (بلاغة التحامق والجنون: مجاز الاختلاف والمغايرة) ويضم: (بلاغة المفارقة)، و(الحجاج)، و(مجاز الطّعام)، و(إبانة الصّمت)، و(التحامق والجنون وبلاغة الصمت).

ويمثل ذلك صورة من صور وعي الكعبي بوظيفة العنوان، إذ لا محيص من القول: إنّ العتبات النصيّة، بوصفها فواتحَ أولى، يمكن أن يُتَّكَأَ إليها في قراءته للنص النقديّ، فهي لا ريب تمثل، والحال هذه، صوىً تكشف للمتلقّي المنهجيّة التي تنتظم هذه المقاربة(33).

وبالنسبة إلى تلقّي السرديّات الشعبية فتسخّر ضياء الكعبيّ جهدها البحثيّ في مقاربته هذه بغية فهم آليات تشكّل الأنساق الثقافيّة في السير الشعبية العربيّة؛ استناداً إلى أنّها تمثّل، أي السير الشعبية، نصاً ثقافياً، مفعماً بالتمثيلات الثقافيّة، فضلاً عن كونها «تتوفر في نصوصها على محمولاتٍ ثقافيّة في غاية الخطورة، ولذا فإن القراءة الثقافيّة أداة يتمكن بواسطتها الباحث من الكشف عن أعماق هذه الخطابات»(34)؛ وتمثّل مفاهيم المرتكزات المفاهيمية التي تقيم أود هاتين الأطروحتين ومن قبيل: التمثيلات الثقافيّة (Representations)، والجماعات المتُخَيَّلة (Imagined Communities)، والهامش (Margin)، والمقدّس (Holy)، والمدنّس (Profane)، و(النسق)، و(الثقافة العالِمة)، و(الثقافة الشعبية)، و(السرديّات الكبرى)، و(الأنساق الثقافيّة).

ولا ريب أن الجهاز المفاهيمي عند الكعبيّ في أطروحتيها هاتين ينفتح بها على المقولات المؤسسة لدراسات ما بعدالكولونيالية (Postcolonial Studies)، إذ تمثل هذه العناوين علامة مائزة لهذا الحقل، وفي سياق ذلك تتخذُ الكعبيّ هذه الدراسة من النقد الثقافيّ بوصفه منهجاً ما بعدياً فاعلاً في اكتناه النصوص، والكشف عن الأنساق الثقافيّة المندسّة في ثناياها، في عدد من السير الشعبية، إذ إنها تمثّل نصوصاً تسعى على الدوام إلى التّفلُّت من ضغوطات وإكراهات

السلطة الحاكمة المتربصة؛ ذلك أن هذه الجماعات التي أنتجت السير الشعبية قد حاولت أن تنتج «أنساقاً مضادّاً للأنساق الحاكمة المسيطرة»[35].

وعليه فإن الكعبي تسلك مذهباً خاصّاً في قراءة السرديّات الشعبية سرديّات الجنون من منظور النقد الثقافيّ، ذلك أنها تحاول بدءاً أن تجنّس النوع الأدبيّ الذي تشتغل عليه، ومن ثَمّ فإنها تستثمر خواصّ هذا الجنس الأدبيّ، في قراءتها للنَّصّ، ويمكن للناظر في المنجز النقدي المتراكم الذي أنجزته الكعبيّ حول السرديّات العربيّة القديمة نزوعها عن هذه القوس ذاتها.

4 – استراتيجيّات المقاربة النقديّة ومستويات التلقّي:

1 – 4 – نادر كاظم: القراءة عبر متوسطات الدراسات الثقافيّة:

– القراءة الثقافيّة وتعدد الاستراتيجيات:

تتعدد استراتيجيّات المقاربة النقديّة في مقاربة نادر كاظم تعدداً لافتاً، مما سوّغ أن تُوسم مقاربته بالقراءة بين متوسطات النقد الثقافيّ والدراسات ما بعد الكولونياليّة، على أن هذه الآليات – وإن تعددت – فإنها تظلُّ منشدة إلى سياق منهجيّ واحد، هو الدراسات ما بعد الكولونياليّة، وإن كانت تندُّ عنه في أحايين إلى النقد الأدبيّ المحض، أو إلى النظرية السردية تحديداً، إلا أن ذلك لا يلغي أن مبدأ التحليل الثقافيّ هو المبدأ المهيمن في المقاربة، وقد مثل مبدأ (الحفر المعرفيّ) (The Archaeology of Knowledge)[36] الذي استعاره كاظم من فوكو، و(مبدأ الانتقاء)، و(مبدأ التنظير)، الذي أفاض كاظم في مراسهما، هي المبادئ المركزية إلى جانب استراتيجيّات تفكيك التمثيلات الثقافيّة[37]، وتأسيساً على السابق يحاولُ كاظم أن يتعرّف إلى صور السودان في المتخيل العربيّ الوسيط، في محاولة لاستخلاص جملةِ التمثيلاتِ التي شكَّلها المتخيلُ العربيّ في السير الشعبية عن السودان، وتحليلها، واستنطاق دلالتها الثقافيّة[38].

وتدخلُ هذه المقاربة في سياق نَقْدِ المسكوت عنه في الثقافة العربيّة، وهو ما يعطيها أهميّةً جُلَّى، وخطورةً كُبرى، إذ إنَّها تجمعُ إلى جدَّة الموضوع وطرافته، وعيَ كاظم بضرورة تجلية صورة الآخر (الأسود) التي هي انعكاسٌ لصورة الذات، ومؤشّر على وعيها، ولعلَّ اختيار كاظم للعصور الوسطى يمثّلُ صورةً من صُور وعيه بأهميّة الانتخاب الثقافيّ، إذ إنَّ الفترة الوسطية من تاريخ الثقافة العربيّة والإنسانيّة هي أكثر الفترات ثراءً وإنتاجاً للنصوص على المستويين السرديّ والشعريّ، ويتوقف نادر كاظم عند أربعٍ من المدونات التي كان السودان يؤدّون في أحداثها أدواراً رئيسةً هي: (سيرة بني هلال)[39]، و(سيرة الأميرة ذات الهمّة)[40]، و(سيرة عنترة بن شدّاد)[41]، و(سيرة الملك سيف بن ذي يزن)[42]، ومرويّة واحدة من كتاب (ألف ليلة وليلة)[43]، ويبدو أنّ اختيار كاظم لهذه المرويات جاء عن قصدٍ وغايةٍ، إذ إن ذلك يرتبط بمناحٍ منهجيّةٍ، أما أولها الحُضور البارز لمسألة الآخر/الأسود على وجه الخصوص، وأما ثانيهما لأنَّها شعبيةٌ، وشفهيةٌ، وتنسبُ في غالب الأحيان إلى غير ما مؤلفٍ، إذ «لا تحظى هذه السير بمؤلفٍ واضح بل هي من إنتاج الشعب»[44]، حيث جعل هذان المسوغان هذه السير عند كاظم مادةً غنيّة للبحث والدراسة، إلا أنّ اختياره للسير الشعبية يوقعه في إشكالية الانتقاء، أو النظرة غير الشاملة، وذلك باطراحه المنامات والمقامات وغيرها، دون الإفصاح عن سبب ذلك.

– سيرتا الهلاليّ وعنترة وتفكيك آليّات التمثيل الثقافيّ:

يرى نادر كاظم أنّ خصائص المرويّات الآنفة الذكر، مهّدت أمام المتخيل الثقافيّ الجماعيّ الطَّريق، لكيما يمرّر تمثيلاته الانتقاصيّة والعنصريّة تجاه الآخر الأسودِ دون مراقبةٍ أو من أحد، ويشير كاظم إلى أن صورة السود في المدونة السرديّة العربيّة كانت في الغالب صورةً سيئةً وانتقاصيّةً، إذ إنها قليلاً ما تحدثت عن الأسود بشكلٍ إنسانيّ محايد، سوى في نماذج قليلة من مثل «سيرة

الأميرة ذات الهمة»[45]، ويشير كاظم إلى أن الناظر في معمارية البناء السردي في السير الشعبية يلحظ أن ثمة مشتركاً بينها، يتمثّل في كون أبطالٍ ثلاثٍ منها كانوا (سوداً)[46]، فضلاً عن محورية (صدمة الولادة)[47]، التي يمرُّ بها أبطال هذه السير، ذلك أنّهم يولدون (سوداً) على الرغم من أنّ آباءهم بيض.

ويؤكد نادر كاظم أنّ إلحاح السارد في هذه السير على تذكير القارئ بقضيّة السواد والسود إنما هو انشغالٌ بقضيتهم، وتعبيرٌ عن الإشكالات الاجتماعيّة التي تحفُّ بحياة الإنسان الأسود في البيئة العربيّة، ويمكن القول: إن السيرة الشعبية عموماً حفلت بمعضلة السواد، كما يسمّيها عبدالله إبراهيم، بخلاف ما يذهب إليه كاظم، إذ يرى أنّ صدمة الولادة في سيرة (بني هلال) لم تكن عند كاظم سوى تقنية التجأ إليها السارد، بوصفها (معضلة عابرة)، فالسواد لم يكن موضوعاً مركزياً فيها، إلا أنها تكشفت عن موقف متحيّز من الأسود، وذلك ما يتجلى في غير موضع منها، ولعل ذلك يتجلى في الأبيات التي أنشدها الأمير رزق، بُعيد أن ولد له أبو زيد الهلالي، مما كسر لديه ولدى القارئ آفاق التوقعات[48].

ويذهب كاظم إلى أنَّ عقدة اللون تمثل بؤرة مركزيّة في سيرة (عنترة بن شدّاد) الذي يظلّ طوال حياته رازحاً تحت إشكالية هذه العقدة، فهو على امتداد سيرته «دَعِيٌّ وولد سِفاح وزنا ومعلولُ النسب»[49]، وينبهُ كاظم في فاتحة تأويله إلى إشكالية التأليف التي تنتظم سيرة (عنترة بن شدّاد)، ويقرر كاظم أن توظيف (عنترة بن شدّاد) بادئ الأمر كان توظيفاً أيديولوجياً «يهدف إلى الانتصار للعدنانيين على القحطانيين»[50]، وذلك في ظلال حمأة الصراع القبليّ الذي أذكته السلطة الأمويّة، وفي سياق ذلك يشير كاظم إلى التناصية (Intertextualiy) التي تربط سيرة (عنترة بن شدّاد) بالمرويات المذكورة في كتاب (ألف ليلة وليلة)، ذلك أنّ السارد يستعير من كتاب (ألف ليلة وليلة) أوصافاً لعالم السودان، وأسراره[51].

وينقض كاظم الفكرة القارّة التي مؤداها أن (سيرة عنترة) هي سيرة النضال

ضدّ العبودية، كما يذهب فاروق خورشيد في دراسته الموسومة بـ(أضواء على السيرة الشعبية)[52]، ويرجح كاظم فكرته بالإقرار بأن سيرة عنترة تحفلُ بعددٍ غيرِ منتاهٍ من الصور والتمثيلات الانتقاصية التي يختزلها المخيال العربيّ حول الأسود والسودان في هذه السيرة[53]، وهنا يمكن الإشارة إلى رجاحة رأي كاظم الذي يذهب إلى امتلاء سيرة عنترة بالأنساق الثقافيّة الإقصائيّة.

ــ ألف ليلة وليلة والأسود وجدل الهامشيّة:

يناقش نادر كاظم إشكاليّة البحث في حقيقة مؤلف ألف ليلة وليلة، بوصفها مروياتٍ (عابرة للثقافات)، ولا يمكن الجزم أو القطع بحقيقة أصل تأليفها، ولكنّ كاظماً يخرج من هذا المأزَق بالتأكيد أن مرويات (ألف ليلة وليلة) وإن كانت قد ألفت في محاضن ثقافيّة أخرى غيرِ المحضن العربيّ فإنّ دخولها إلى الثقافة العربيّة، جعلها تصطبغ بالتمثيلات السائدة في هذه الثقافة[54].

ويلتمس نادر كاظم في (نموذج غريماس) منهجاً مسانداً في قراءة هذه المرويات، والكشف عن تمثيلات الآخر الأسود في مرويات (ألف ليلة وليلة)، إذ يرى كاظم أن المرأة والأسود يمثلان مِحور الرغبة في هذه المرويات، ويتحدّث كاظم عن الهيكلة الثابتة لحكايات الخيانة، التي يكون الأسود والمرأة طرفيها في مرويات (ألف ليلة وليلة)، وهو ما يمكن أن يُطلَقَ عليه (الحكاية الإطارية)[55]، إذ يستبين ذلك في حكايات متوالدة، تتناسل من بعض، ويرى كاظم أنّ هذه الحكايات تسبتطن نسقيْن ينتظمان الثقافة العربيّة «الأولى وهي القائلة بشهوانية السود المفرطة، والثانية وهي القائلة برغبة المرأة الجنسيّة غير المحدودة[56]، وهما يبرزان نسقيْن، هما نسقُ الانتقاص من الأسود، ونسق الانتقاص من المرأة، ويمرّ نادر كاظم سراعاً على حوداثَ يواقع الأسود خلالها زوجات الأمراء في عددٍ من المرويّات، التي تعبّر عن نَسَقٍ مضمر، هو نسق الفحولة والفاعليّة، التي لا تعترف بها السلطة، فتصرُّ على جعل السود خَدَماً أو عبيداً[57]،

ذلك «أنّ العبد الأسود حين يكون معشوق السيدة وسيّدها فهو بذلك يهينُ كرامة السيد، ويهدّد أعراف المجتمع السياديّة والذّكوريّة»⁽⁵⁸⁾ .

وتتكشفُ عددٌ من المرويَّات التي يتضمنها كتاب (ألف ليلة وليلة) عن تصوير الثقافة السائدة الأسودَ دائماً مأخوذاً بالشهوة الجنسية المُفرطة، فالجنسُ في مرويات (ألف ليلة وليلة) أعزُّ على الأسود من رُوحه، ونفسه، وهو علاوةً على ذلك لا يملك شيئاً ذا بالٍ غيره⁽⁵⁹⁾، وتجبُ الإشارة إلى أنّ ثمة نسقاً فحولياً مضاداً لم ينتبه إليه نادر كاظم في دراسته لتمثيلات الأسود في هذه السير، ويتمثل في أنّ انتخاب الأميرات للقيام بفعل الخيانة، هو تمثيل رامزٌ، يسعى إلى الطَّعن في السلطة، بصورة مخاتلة، فهي سلطة لا تستطيع منع العَبْدِ الأسود من حريمها، على الرغم من امتلاكها مقاليد السلطة والسيادة.

ـ سيرة الأميرة ذات الهمّة والتمثيل المضاد:

يذهب كاظم إلى أنّ السارد الشعبيّ في سيرة (الأميرة ذات الهمّة) كان مناصراً للإنسان الأسود، إذ إنّها تجعل من السودان «جنوداً مجنّدة من عساكر الإسلام»⁽⁶⁰⁾، الذين هم مستعدون للتّضحية بدمائهم نُصرةً للإسلام⁽⁶¹⁾، ولعلّ كاظم لم ينبه إلى أن ربط صورة السود بالإسلام، وبالبعد الديني، يرتبط برغبة مبيّتةٍ عند السارد بالإفادة من قدسية الدين عند المتلقّي، في انتزاع مناصرة وتأييد للأسود، الذي يدافع عن هذا الدين، بوصفه عصب (عساكر الإسلام).

إن السارد، وفاقاً للسابق، ظلّ في هذه السيرة مشغولاً بمحاولة ترسيم تمثيلاتٍ ناصعة لهؤلاء السود، الذين يقترنُ ذكرهم بالصّفات الإيجابيّة، فالسود كما يصورهم السارد هم: (الأوفياء) (الأنجاد) (الأبطال) (الكِرام) (الأنجاب)⁽⁶²⁾، في حين أنّ السارد لا يتوانى عن تجريم أعداء السود الذين ينمازون بـ(الكذب والظّلال)⁽⁶³⁾، وتقترنُ تمثيلات الأسود المضادّة في سيرة (الأميرة ذات الهمّة) بمحمول حجاجيّ، أشار إليه كاظم سراعاً، فقد حاول السارد خلخلة

التمثيلات الانتقاصيّة للأسود من خلال الحجاج الكلاميّ، الذي يجيء على لسان (الشريف المرتضى)[64].

ــ السيرة الشعبية والقراءة الثقافيّة وخلق مسارات جديدة:

تذهب ضياء الكعبيّ[65] إلى أن الناظر في مدونات النقد الأدبيّ الحديث يجد أنّ سعيد يقطين وعبدالله إبراهيم[66]، هما أوائل النقّاد العرب الذين حاولوا أن يطبقوا مناهج النقد الأدبيّ الحديث على هذه السير الشعبية، وقد اهتمّ هؤلاء النقّاد بدراسة البنى الحكائية التي تنتظم هذه السرديّات من مثل: بنية الفضاء المكانيّ، وبنية الفضاء الزمانيّ، وبنية الفعل الحكائيّ، وبنية الشخصيّات أو العوامل، ولا ريب أنّ هذه المقاربة اشتبكت في بعضٍ من مناحيها مع منجزات النقد الأدبيّ، الذي خُصّص لقراءة هذه السرديّات، ذلك أنّ كليهما ناقشَ بنائيّة شخصيّة البطل في هذه السير، وخلص إلى أن السيرة احتفت بهذه الشخصية، على أنّ النقد الأدبيّ لم يتلفت بصورة كبيرة إلى جدليّات الهامشيّة والفاعليّة التي تنتظمُ هذه السرديّات الشعبيّة[67]، وعليه فإن النقد الثقافيّ كان رائداً في الالتفات إلى السيرة الشعبيّة، وإخضاعها للبحث والمدارسة، بوصفها سرديّات تنطوي على تجلّياتٍ نسقيّة، بخلاف النقد الأدبيّ، الذي يظلُّ ينظر معظم نقّاده إلى السير الشعبية من منظورٍ إقصائيّ تهميشيّ[68].

2 ــ 4 ــ ضياء الكعبي: وعي التجنيس ووظائف القراءة الثقافيّة:

ــ تفكيك التمثيلات المُضادة ووعي التجنيس:

يمثل تفكيك التمثيلات الثقافيّة (Representation)، والوعي بالتجنيس[69]، مبدأين يحكمان استراتيجيّات المقاربة النقديّة في هاتين المقاربتين، انطلاقاً من أن المجنون وبطل السيرة يحاولان بوسيلةٍ ما أن يعبرا عن نظرتهما الخاصة

إزاء العالم من حولهما، وفقاً لمنظورهما الخاصّ، وهو ما تهتمُّ به استراتيجيّة تفكيك التمثيلات الثقافيّة بوصفها آلية قرائية، تحاول إعادة اعتبار للرّؤى التي تنتجها الأقلّيات[70]، من خلال محاولة اصطفاء هذه التمثيلات المضادة من خلال الوعي بالمحددات الأجناسية التي تميز هذه السرديّات.

ولعلّ من الواجب الإشارة كذلك إلى أن سرديّات عقلاء المجانين والسير الشعبية تغدو وفقاً لمقاربة الكعبيّ، وإن لم تكنْ الكعبيّ قد أشارت إلى ذلك، على تماسٌ مع فكرة التابع، كما تتجلى في الدراسات ما بعد الكولونياليّة عامّةً (Post Colonial Studies —)[71]، وإذا كان يوري لوتمان يقسّمُ الكونَ السيميائيَّ من الناحية الثقافيّة إلى مركزٍ نطلق عليه اسم النواة، وهامشٍ أو محيطـ[72]، فاتّساقاً مع السابق فإنّ ضياء الكعبيّ تنمذجُ صورة المجنون بوصفه هامشاً، للبحث في تمثيلاته النسقيّة في سرديّات الجنون.

وفي هذا السياق تجيءُ مقاربة ضياء الكعبيّ أجل قراءة أو استكناه المرويات المنسوبة إلى عقلاء المجانين والمتجانّين أو السرديّات الدائرة حولهم قراءةً ثقافيّةً، بوصفها سرديّات يقصد أصحابها إلى إعادةِ تحبيك التاريخ، ومناوأةِ السلطة، وتغير أسس المُتخيّل القارّ، وخلخلة الأنساق القارّة[73]؛ بوصفها أنساقاً متوافقاً عليها من سنينَ خلتْ، فخطاب الجنون جاء «لمناوأة خطاب السلطة من خلال إخضاع التاريخ للتحبيك والتحويل السرديّ لإيجاد تاريخ جماعة عقلاء المجانين المفارق للتاريخ الرسميّ»[74].

وفي سياق هذا السابق حاولت الكعبي أن تكشف عن تمثيلات التحامق والجنون في هذه المدوّنات جلّها، على ما في هذه التمثيلات من ائتلافٍ واختلاف، يصلُ في بعضها حدّ التعارض والتناقض، إذ يغدو المتحامق في بعض هذه المدوّنات ذا هيبة وحكمة آسرة، ناطقاً بالحكمة والموعظة الحسنة، اتّساقاً مع رؤية الثقافة التي تتبناها الثقافة الشعبية، في حين يغدو في غيرها من هذه المدوّنات هامشاً لا يلتفتُ أو يُنظر إليه، اتّساقاً مع رؤية الثقافة التي تتبناها الثقافة العالِمة.

ولا مراءَ في أنّ ثمة حقيقةً ماثلةً للعيان تطالع القارئ في الخطاب النقديّ الذي قرأ سرديّات الجنون مؤداها أن هذه السرديّات ظلت من منظور مدرسيّات النقد الأدبيّ الحديث سرديّات غيرَ قمينةٍ بالدراسة أو المباحثة، على اعتبار أنّها رُويت بهدف الإمتاع والمؤانسة، أو بوصفها آداباً هامشية، لم يحفل بها النقد الأدبيّ، كما لم يحفل بغيرها من الآداب الهامشية، خلا إشارات محمد رجب النجار إليها بوصفها آداباً تتبنى (السخرية الهادفة)[75].

تبحثُ ضياء الكعبيّ في مقاربتها هذه آليّات التمثيل والأنساق الثقافيّة المخبوءة في عدد السير الشعبية العربيّة؛ وتشير الكعبيّ إلى أن سير ألف ليلة وليلة والسيرة الشطارية تحفل بصورة الحاكم، الذي يملك في يده مقاليد الحكم المُطلق، وهي بذلك سرديّات تقوم على ترسيخ نسق السلطة، الذي ينقام على مقولة مؤداها أنّ الحاكم هو ظل الله على الأرض، استناداً إلى نظم الرعوية القائمة على ثنائية الراعي والمرعيّ، أو ما يمكن أن يسمى بـ(السلطة الرعوية)[76]؛ ولذلك فإنّ هذه السير تحفل بالعبارات التي ترسّخ هذه الثقافة، ومن ذلك قول الإسكافيّ بعد أن صار ملكاً: «والناس تخاف مني، ولا أخاف إلا من الله». ومن ذلك أيضاً:

وتتحدث ضياء الكعبيّ عن أنّ هذه السرديّات الشعبية حاولت تهشيم أنساق التاريخ الرسميّ، ونقضها، والعملَ على إنتاج أنساق التاريخ الشعبيّ، تاريخ الهامشيين الخاصّ، حول بعض الحكام والأمراء من مثل[77]؛ هارون الرشيد، والظاهر بيبرس، والملك الصّالح نجم الدين أيوب، وشجرة الدرّ، وغيرهم؛ إذ تختلف سِيَرُ هؤلاء الأشخاص في السيرة الشعبية، عن سيرهم في السرديّات الرسمية، بوصف هذه سرديّات بديلة أو مضادّة؛ حاولتْ أن تُبرز وأن تنتج كذلك من خلال هذا السرد البديل أو المضادّ صورة جديدة لهؤلاء الأمراء والخلفاء والحُكّام[78].

ــ الهامش والردّ بالسرد[79]: التقويض وتحبيك التاريخ:

تشير الكعبي إلى أنّ سرديّات الجنون والسرديّات الشعبية يمكن أن تندرج

ضمن السرديّات التي تسعى إلى تحبيبِك التاريخ، وصناعة تاريخ جديدٍ للجماعات المتخيّلة، وفي ضَوْء ذلك يمكن القول: إنّ هذه السرديّات، تنطوي كذلك على فاعلية تقويضيّة مضادّة، بوصفها يمكن أن تنطوي، في ظن هذه الدراسة، تحت مظلة (السردّ التقويضيّ) أو (السرديّات المُضادّة) (Alternative Narratives) [80]، الذي تؤسّسه سرود الثقافة الشعبيّة، في مواجهةٍ غير مُعلنة مع السرود التي تُنتجها الثقافة العالِمة، ذلك أن هذه السرود الشعبيّة تنطوي في بواطنها إلى إنتاج تأريخ جديد، إذ تختلف تمثيلات هؤلاء الأشخاص في السرديّات البَلَاطيّة، عن سيرهم في السرديّات الشعبية[81].

وتبدو الإشارة هنا لازمةً إلى أن وعي التجنيس مثّل إحدى أبرز المميّزات المنهجيّة لأطروحتي الكعبيّ[82]، بيد أن هذا الوعي الذي تمثل في إلماعتها المهمة إلى ضرورة تجنيس/ تأطير سرديّات الجنون، وتقديمها تصوّراً أولياً لذلك، لم يوظف توظيفاً معرفيّاً، يفيد من طرائق رواية سرديّات الجنون، والسرديّات الشعبية، ومساردها الحكائية، بوصفها يمكن أن تكون متضمّنة لإشاراتٍ يمكن الإفادة منها في قراءة النص قراءة ثقافيّة ناجزة[83].

– التمثيل المضاد والنسق المُخاتِل:

تنطوي التمثيلات المضادة في سرديّات الجنون والسيرة الشعبية على أنساق مخاتلة، تجلّي تمثيلات الهامش، ومفارقاته، وموقفه من الناس، والسلطة، والأعراف المركوزة القارّة في مجتمعه، وسيتضح أن كل هذه التمثيلات كانت تتبلور في ملامح أجناسية مخصوصة، تضمر أنساقاً مخاتلة مراوغة.

وهنا يمكن القول: إن الكعبي لم تُنِلِ الأنساق الثقافيّة فضلَ بحثٍ ومدارسة، فقد سخّرت جَهْدها في هذه المقاربة لفهم ما تسميه بآليات التمثيل السرديّ للهامش في سرديّات الجنون والسير الشعبية، ذلك أنّها، أي هذه السرديّات، كما يتمرأى في مقاربة الكعبيّ، تمثل خطاباً خاصّاً، ومفارِقاً، ومراوغاً في الآن عينه[84].

وفي هذا السياق تتمأسسُ مقاربة الكعبيّ على مختزلٍ مؤداه أنّ سرديّات التحامق والتجانن تنهضُ على فكرةٍ مؤداها المفارقة والمغايرة، أي كَسْر آفاق الانتظار، ابتغاء التحايل على السلطات السياسيّة والدينيّة والثقافيّة المُحيقة بالإنسان وقتذاك، ولذا فتساوقاً مع ذلك يمكن القول: إنّ خطابهم ينماز بعددٍ من الخصائص المائزة له من غيره من مثل: بلاغة المفارقة، والحِجاج، ومجاز الطّعام، وإبانة الصمت، والتحامق والجنون ببلاغة التسمية[85]، وتبرز أنساق التضاد في ما تسميه الكعبيّ بـ(مجاز الاختلاف والمُغايرة)، إذ يتحدث المجانين بلغة خاصّة، تعكس رُؤاهم، وتمرُّدهم على القانون اللغويّ العام، ومن أمثلة ذلك حكاية أبي القاسم البغداديّ الذي يقول: «أنا الفيل المُعتلم، أنا الدهر المُصطلم، أنا العُسْرُ اللزوم، أنا السبع الغشوم»[86]، وعليه فإن هذه اللغة المفارقة التي تمثّل خصيصة مائزة لهذه السرديّات كشفت عن نسق التضادّ، الذي تحفل به هذه السرديّات، بغية التفلُّت من ضغوطات السلطة الحاكمة المتربصة وإكراهاتها.

ويتحقق مبدأ مركزيّة الذّات (Center – cism) في سرديّات المجانين من خلال قانون المفارقة، الذي يكسر آفاق التلقّي، فيغدو كسر هذا الأفق، علامة أجناسية فارقة في سرديّات الجنون، تنماز بها هذه السرديّات، وتسهم في تخليق مبدأ المفارقة، ويتجلى ذلك في المقامة المارستانية، التي تصور أبا الفتح الإسكندريّ «متنكزاً مسيطراً ومهيمناً في حين تعتري عيسى بن هشام (الراوي)، وأبا داود المتكلّم الحُبسة البلاغيّة، فيبدون عاجزين عن الجدَلِ والحجاج»[87].

ولا ريب أنّ مبدأ المفارقة هذا يضمرُ أنساق التفوق والفحولة، وهو ينفتح على السياسيّ، والأيديولوجيّ، ذلك أنّ انتخاب المتكلّم/ أي المعتزلة، يمثل اختياراً واعياً من السارد، لمناوأة هذا الفريق، وربما يمثل تأكيداً لمبدأ المركزيّة هذا، ذلك أنّ اختيار أبرع الناس في المجادلة، ومن ثم التغلب عليهم، يمثّل نسقاً فحوليّاً، وهما ما لم تشر إليه الكعبيّ مطلقاً. ويمثل (الحِجاج) ملمحاً أجناسياً ثالثاً يميز سرديّات الجنون، وفي هذا السياق تبدو الأخبار التي يوردها صاحب عقلاء

المجانين، رافضة لقانون التحيز والإقصاء، الذي تمارسه السلطة في ميلها إلى المعتزلة، وإعراضها عن السنة[88]، وعليه فإن الحجاج يسهم في إنجاز فرادة الذات، وخصوصية تجربتها، فضلاً عن فاعليته الكبيرة في التعبير عن إنتاج المضمرات الخطابية التي تفيضُ بها هذه السرديّات، وهو يضمر نسقياً نسق القوّة، التي تمثله الفاعلية الحجاجيّة للمجنون، وهو معزِّزٌ للنسق المضاد الذي أشرت إليه في الحديث عن السرد التقويضيّ.

ويغدو الصمت إبانة[89] في هذه السرديّات، بوصف (إبانة الصمت) ملمحاً بارزاً في كثير منها، إذ يفضل الصمت خوفاً من السلطة أو نأياً عن التلاقي المباشر بها كما ترى الكعبيّ، ولعلّ هذه الخصيصة لا تضمرُ ذلك، إنما تضمر موقفاً مناهضاً للسلطة، يترفع من خلاله المجنون عن حوار السلطة، إذ يبدو الصمت داحضاً لمقاربة الخصم[90]، ولعّل إبانة الصمت تضمر نسق الاستعلاء، الذي يترفع به المجنون عن النقاش مع الجهلة.

ويبدو ذكاء المرأة في هذه السرديّات ملمحاً أجناسياً آخر، يكسر أُفُق التوقّع، ويروج لأنساق الوعي بقيمة المرأة، ومنزلتها، على الرغم من ذكوريّة الثقافة العربيّة، التي يَسِمُ المرأة بقلّة العقل، واتّباع الهوى، وتنكُّب سبل الرشاد، متكئين على نصوص شرعيّة لا تثبتْ أمام التمحيص والبحث في أسانيدها ورُواتها في الغالب، ومفادها أنّ أكثر أهل النار من النساء[91].

وقد بيّنت المقاربة أنّ المجنون في هذه السرديّات كثيراً ما يكون (أسودَ)، وهو ما يتساوق مع نظرة الثقافة العربيّة الرسمية وموقفها من الأسود، بوصف الإنسان الأسود أقلّ منزلة وقدراً وبشريّة كذلك من الإنسان الأبيض، وبذا تكون سرديّات الجنون ملتزمة بالمشترك الاجتماعي، الذي تؤسسه الثقافتان العالمة والشعبية[92].

لقد استطاعت الكعبيّ أن تميط اللثام على تمثيلات المجنون في السرديّات التي تنسب إليهم، ولكنها لم تحدد الأنساق الثقافيّة، التي تضمرها هذه التمثيلات،

ذلك أن تمثيلات مجاز الاختلاف والمُغايرة تضمر أنساق التضاد، كما تضمر تمثيلات الحجاج والماحجة نسق القوّة، في حين أن إبانة الصمت تضمر نسق الاستعلاء، أما تمثيلات المرأة المجنونة الذكيّة فإنها تمثّل أنساق الوعي، الذي تفتقده الثقافة العربيّة في موقفها من المرأة.

أما بالنسبة إلى تمثيلات المهمش في السيرة الشعبية فإذا كانت سيرة هارون الرشيد في مدوّنات التاريخ الرسميّ تلبسه لَبوس الحاكم الظالم، فإنها ما تلبث أن تنقلب إلى عكس ذلك في سيرة الظاهر بيبرس الشعبيّة، إذ يمسي هارون الرشيد في هذه السيرة الخليفةَ العادلَ «الذي يحقّق العدل، ولا يتوانى عن أخذ الثأر لمن ظلم حتى لو كان الظالم ابنه الأمين كما في حكاية (الحمال والبنات الثلاث)» (93)، وهي بذلك سيرةٌ تُبْرِزُ صورة هارون الرشيد المظلوم في مرايا التاريخ الرسميّ؛ وترسّخ بدلاً من ذلك سيرة الحاكم العادل، الذي ما فتئ، عمره كلَّه، يحجُّ عاماً ويغزو عاماً كما تشير إلى ذلك كثير من المدوّنات الرسمية والتاريخية.

وتسجّل سيرة بيبرس، في سياق ذلك، تاريخاً مفارِقاً ومختلفاً لـ(شجرة الدرّ)؛ فقد نصّت المصادر التاريخيّة الرسميّة على أنّها كانت جارية السلطان الملك الصالح نجم الدين أيوب؛ في حين أنها في هذه السيرة هي ابنة الخليفة المقتدر بالله، وهي كذلك امرأة غيور (94).

وفي سياق فكرة السرد النقيض تتناول (سيرة الحلّاج) الشعبية قصّة حُسين الحلّاج (95)، الإمام الصوفيّ، الذي ترسخت صورته في المرويّات الرسمية عند ابن الخطيب البغدادي، وابن خلّكان، وابن كثير (96)، بأنها سيرته تحفل بشتى ممارسات الكفر والشعبذة والتهويمات، إذ تحاول هذه السيرة الشعبية نقضَ هذه الفكرة، واستيلاد تأويل آخر له؛ يتساوقُ والإيدلوجيّات، إذ تغدو هذه الشعبذات التي يقوم بها الحلّاج، كما يتقرّر ذلك في مدوّنات التاريخ الرسميّ، كراماتٍ عَرْفانيّة وهبها الله تعالى لحُسين الحلّاج، في سياق تصوّفه؛ وذلك لصَلاحه، وصفائه، ونقاء سريرته (97).

وفي سياق الفكرة السابقة ذاتها تتحدث الكعبيّ عن سيرة بني هلال أو السيرة الهلالية[98]، فالمتخيّل الشعبيّ يصنع لهم سيرته الخاصة، التي تخالف سيرة الثقافة الرسميّة العالِمة، وهي سيرة «تؤسس للجماعة الهلالية نسباً أسطورياً يصلهم بالأوس بن تغلب جدهم الأكبر المزعوم»[99]؛ فضلاً عن إضفاء «الراوي على الجماعة الهلالية، وانتقالاتها في الفضاءات المختلفة طابع القداسة»[100]، إذ إنّ السيرة الهلاليّة في مدوّنات التاريخ الرسميّ تعكس لهم صورةً سالبةً، وهي تحتفي كذلك بمرويات دينية مأثورة عن النبيّ الكريم ـصلى الله عليه وسلم ـ مؤدّاها أنه قد دعا عليهم بأن يتشتت شملهم ويفرّق أمرهم.

وتغدو السيرة الشطارية سيرةُ (علي الزّيبق)[101] سيرةً أدبيّةً مُضادّة، تحتفي بالهامشيّين والشطار والعيّاريْن؛ على الرغم من كونها تحظى برعاية السلطة السياسيّة، ممثلة بهارون الرشيد، إذ إنها تحتفي بسيرة عدد من هؤلاء الشطار والعيارين من مثل؛ علي بن أحمد الزّيات، وعلي البسطي، وعمر الخطّاف، وعلي بن فارس الشيباني، الذين يعجب بهم هارون الرشيد، ويأمر بأن تحفظ تجربتهم التي صاغها الزبيق في خزانة الملك؛ ليكما تغدو تذكاراً ونبراساً هادياً للمنخرطين في دواليب السلطة من ورائه، على الرغم من أنّ هذه السيرَ كانت سيراً مقصاةً من التاريخ الرسميّ التي نصّ كُتّابه ومؤرخوه على أن أبطالها شطار وزعار وقُطّاع طرق[102].

ولعلّ ما تنبغي الإشارة إليه أنّ هذه السرديّات، وإن كانت تحاولُ أن تبثّ وترسّخ أنساقها الخاصّة كما ترى الكعبيّ، أي أنساقَ الهوامش، فهي تقوم بوعي منها وبلا وعي كذلك على ترسيخ أنساق السلطة كذلك، على الرغم من كونها تنتمي إلى أدب العامّة، أو أدب الثقافة غير العالِمة عند عموم الباحثين والدارسين، مما يجعل البحث فيها بحثاً شاقاً وشائكاً، ولعلّ ذلك يرجعُ إلى طبيعة هذه السير المخاتلة والمراوغة؛ ذلك أن خوفها من بطش السلطة؛ جعلها تأتي على هذه الصورة المراوغة؛ فهي سيرٌ مزدوجة، تتساوق مع أنساق السلطة حيناً، وتحاول

نقضها في أحايين، ذلك أن هذه السير الشعبية كانت تتخذ من المخاتلة النسقية منهجاً ناظماً لها.

– تركيب:

أشارت مقاربة نادر كاظم إلى أنّ السيرة الشعبية لمّا تزلْ مراحاً متسعاً لقراءات جديدةٍ، وفق المناهج النقديّة الحديثة، التي تحاول أن تكشف عن بِناها العميقة، وأنساقها المضمرة، مما أعانه على تشقيق مسالك ممهدة إلى تلك السرديّات، على الرغم مما يحفُّ بها من إشكالات كبرى، تنتظم طرائق روايتها، وحقيقة مؤلفها، وزمنه، ومقاصده، إلى غير ذلك.

ولا بُدَّ من الإشارة أن مفهوم القراءة الثقافيّة يمثل لدى نادر كاظم تفكيكاً لآليات التمثيل التي ينتجها المتخيّل، على أنّها في الوقت ذاته كشفٌ عن الأنساق الثقافيّة المضمرة، التي تمررها الثقافة بحيلها الماكرة، وأدواتها المختلفة، وهو بذلك لا ريب يظل مشدوداً لآفاق القراءة الغذامية إذا كان التعبير جائزاً، ولا فكاك من القول: إن هذه مقاربة تتكشف عن تجليات القارئ الذي يتّخذ من اندماج الآفاق مذهباً له، فقد استطاع كاظم بثقافته الموسوعية وجَلَده البحثي، أن يستنطق تراثاً سردياً كبيراً يتمثل بالسرديّات الشعبية، ليكشف عن موقفه من الإنسان الأسود، ورؤاه المتراحبة حِيال ذلك. ويبدو أنّ كاظماً قد بنى هذه المقاربة على ائتلافٍ منهجيّ، يحاول من خلاله أن يسبر بِنى النصوص، ويحفر في طبقاتها عميقاً، على هيئة أركيولوجية، تفيد من الدرس الأنثربولوجي.

ولا ريب أن نادر كاظم ينتحي فجاجاً جديدةً في قراءة النصّ السردي قراءةً ثقافيّة تفيد من أنظار الدراسات ما بعد الكولونياليّة، وتمثل مفهومات من قبيل: التمثيل والحفر المعرفي والنسق الثقافيّ مفهوماتٍ مركزيّة في مقاربته. وتمثل الحفر المعرفيّ وتفكيك آليّات التمثيل والتمثيل المضاد استراتيجيتين رئيستين تكونان مجتمعتين إلى بعضهما استراتيجيات القراءة التي ينتحيها نادر كاظم في

مقاربته هذه. وتغدو هذه السير وقفاً لهذه المقاربة مكمناً للأنساق المتخيَّلة إزاء الأسود، فقد انسربت هذه الأنساق إلى أبنية الخطاب السردي، وكرست نمطيّة الذهنية العربيّة حوله، بصورة غدت خلالها بتعاقب السنوات، حقائق، أو ثوابت، لا مراء أو جدال فيها.

تأتلف القراءة عند الكعبي في هذه المقاربة مع المشروع المعرفيّ الذي انشغلت به الكعبيّ منذ إنجاز مقارباتها لمرحلة الدكتوراه حول السرد العربيّ القديم، إذ إن الكعبي ظلت تحاول منذ سنوات طوال أن تنجز قراءات ثقافية لمختلف أجناس السرد العربيّ القديم، وفي سياق ذلك يبدو أنّ الكعبيّ تؤطّر مشروعها النقديّ في سياقين، أما أحدهما يقرأ أنساق هذه السرديّات، ويكشف عن بِنياتها، ومصادرها، وبلاغتها، وثانيهما يختصّ بتجنيس النوع السردي، وبذا فإنّ أطروحتها ظلت تراوح من الناحية المنهجيّة بين التلقّي التجنيسي والتلقّي الثقافيّ، لأن دراسة السرد في ضَوْء ممكنات النقد الثقافيّ، ومحاولة ربط هذه القراءة بخصوصية الجنس الأدبيّ المقروء، يسفر عن فتوح تأويليّة جديدة..

وتنماز تلقّي الكعبي، بمحاولتها تغيير مواقع فعل التبئير، وذلك من صرف النظر عن التركيز على ألاعيب الثقافة، إلى النظر إلى أنساق النص، وعليه فإن التحولات التي لحقت بفعل التبئير أعانت الكعبي على التأسيس لمفهوم اختلاف القراءة بالنسبة إلى نمط التلقّي الغذّامي، وتبدو مصطلحات (النسق) و(القراءة الثقافيّة) و(الثقافة العالمة) هي المصطلحات التي تؤطّر مقاربة الكعبي مفاهيميّاً.

وتغدو استراتيجية تفكيك آليّات التمثيل والتمثيل المضادّ هي الاستراتيجية التي تتكئ في مناحي الدراسة جلها، استناداً إلى الرائجة في النقد الثقافيّ بأن نص السيرة الشعبية، يمثل نصاً ثقافيّاً، يمكن أن يكشف من خلال دراسته وفقاً لأدوات النقد الثقافيّ أنساقه، وهُويّاته، وأنظمته، التي تعكس، والحال هذه، بنية المجتمع الذي تصوره هذه السير.

كما أنّ تلقّي ضياء الكعبيّ لسرديّات الجنون ينطلق من فكرة القراءة المُختلفة،

إذ إنّ هذه القراءة تحاولُ أن تكسر آفاق التلقّي التي شيّدتها القراءات النقديّة الكلاسيكيّة المُتعاقبة حول هذا الجنس الأدبيّ.

ولا مرية في أنّ هذه المقاربة تمثّل إلماعةً ذكيّةً إلى سرديّات المجانين، والسيرة الشعبية، ومحاولة جادة لقراءة هذه السرديّات قراءة مفارقة، تبطل القول القارّ بأن هذه السرديّات هي سرديّات الإمتاع والإضحاك والمؤانسة، وتثبت أنّها سرديّات أيديولوجيّة، تتزيا بالإضحاك، والخارق، بوصفه أداةً تُهشّم أنساق التاريخ الرسميّ، وتنقضها، وتعمل على إنتاج أنساق التاريخ الشعبيّ، تاريخ الهامشيين الخاصّ.

هوامش الفصل الثاني:

1 – تعرف الدراسات الثقافيّة بأنها دراسات متداخلة، تهتمُّ بدراسة ثقافة الروك، والموسيقى، والإعلانات، والمسرح، والعولمة، ...إلخ. ينظر: ديورنغ، سايمون، الدراسات الثقافيّة: مقدمة نظرية، ترجمة: ممدوح يوسف عمران، العدد (425)، يونيو 2015م، سلسلة عالم المعرفة، المجلس الوطني للثقافة والفنون والأدب، الكويت.

2 – السعودي، نزار، تفاعل النقد الثقافيّ مع المناهج النقديّة والمعارف المتعددة: قراءة لأهم المفاهيم الرئيسة، مجلة جامعة الشارقة للعلوم الإنسانية والاجتماعية، الإمارات العربيّة المتحدة، المجلد (14)، العدد (2)، 2017م، ص211.

3 – ينظر: أبو شهاب، رامي، الرسيس والمخاتلة: خطاب ما بعد الكولونيالية في النقد العربي المعاصر: النظريّة والتّطبيق، ط1، 2013م، المؤسسة العربيّة للدراسات والنشر، بيروت، لبنان، ص220 وما بعدها. الجرطي، أحمد، النصّ الأدبيّ في ضَوْء إبدالات النظريّة الأدبيّة المعاصرة: استراتيجيات التأويل ورهانات الدراسات الثقافيّة، مجلة تبيُّن للدراسات الفكرية والثقافيّة، المركز العربيّ للأبحاث ودراسة السياسات، بيروت، لبنان، المجلد (6)، العدد (23)، 2018م، ص59.

4 – كاظم، نادر، تمثيلات الآخر...، (م.س)، ص1 – 587.

5 – الكعبي، ضياء، خطابُ التّحامق والجنون في السرد العربيّ القديم...، (م.س)، ص11 – 59.

6 – الكعبيّ، ضياء، السرد العربيّ القديم: دراسة في الأنساق الثقافية وإشكاليّات التأويل، (م.س)، ص240 وما بعدها.

7 – المرجع السابق، ص15.

8 – البازعي، سعد، الدراسات البينية وتحديات الابتكار، مجلة كلية الآداب، جامعة الملك سعود، الرياض، المملكة العربيّة السعودية، المجلد (25)، العدد (2)، 2013م، ص221 – 230.

9 – يُنظر: البازعي، سعد، الدراسات البينية وتحديات الابتكار، (م.س)، ص221.

10 – ينظر: شاكر اباري، ديبيش: دراسات التابع والتأريخ ما بعد الكولونيالي، ترجمة: ثائر ديب، مجلة سطور، المركز العربي للأبحاث ودراسة السياسات، الدوحة، قطر، العدد (3)، كانون الثاني 2016م، ص8.

11 – ينظر: سعيد، إدوارد: الثقافة والإمبرياليّة، نقله إلى العربيّة وقدّم له: كمال أبو ديب، ط1، 1997م، دار الآداب، بيروت، لبنان، ص20.

12 – كاظم، نادر، تمثيلات الآخر...، (م.س)، ص المقدمة.

13 – المرجع السابق، الصفحة نفسها.

14 – المرجع السابق، ص24.

15 – ينظر حول مفهوم «ألفة التلقّي»: فيدوح، عبدالقادر، ألفة النصَ ومستويات التلقّي، مجلة علامات في النقد، النادي الأدبيّ الثقافيّ بجُدَة، جُدَة، المملكة العربيّة السعودية، المجلد (10)، المجلد (34)، 1999م، ص131 – 144.

16 – الكعبـي، ضيـاء، خطابُ التَّحامق والجنون في السـرد العربيّ القديـم...، (م.س)، ص11 – 12. والمبخـوت، شكري، جماليّـة الألفة: النـصَ ومنتقبّله في التـراث النقـديّ، (د.ط)، 1993م، بيت الحكمة، منشورات وزارة الثقافة، تونس، ص17 – 49.

17 – المناصـرة، عزّ الدين، إشـكالات التجنيس الأدبيّ، مجلـة البصائر، جامعة البترا الخاصة، عمان، الأردن، المجلد (9)، العدد (2)، 2005م، ص75.

18 – كاظم، نادر، تمثيلات الآخر...، (م.س)، ص92 – 145.

19 – المرجع السابق، ص161 – 255.

20 – قطّوس، بسّـام، سـيمياء العنوان، ط1، 2001م، منشورات وزارة الثقافة الأردنية، عمان، الأردن، ص101.

21 – يُنظـر: كاظم، نـادر، تمثيلات الآخر...، (م.س)، ص19 – 20. والخضـراوي، إدريس، المتخيّل والتَّمثيل الثقافيّ للآخر: قراءة فى كتاب تمثيلات الآخر لنادر كاظم، مجلة العلوم الإنسانيّة، جامعة البحرين، البحرين، 2006م، ص344 – 369.

22 – كاظم، نادر، تمثيلات الآخر...، (م.س)، ص92 – 101.

23 – المرجع السابق، ص19.

24 – المرجع السابق، ص20.

25 – المرجع السابق، الصفحة نفسها.

26 – ينظر حول «مفهوم الانتخاب»: فوج، أجنر، الانتخاب الثقافيّ، ترجمة: شوقي جلال، ط1، 2005م منشورات المشروع القومي للترجمة، القاهرة، مصر.

27 – ومن هذه الحقول هي: «المادية الثقافيّة، والتعددية الثقافيّة، والدراسـات الثقافيّة، ودراسـات ما بعد الكولونيالية، وما بعد الحداثة...». كاظم، نادر، تمثيلات الآخر...، (م.س)، ص19.

28 – المرجع السابق، ص24.

29 – الكعبي، ضياء، خطابُ التَّحامق والجنون في السرد العربيّ القديم...، (م.س)، ص11 – 59.

30 – المرجع السابق، ص14 – 16.

31 – المرجع السابق، ص22 – 28.

32 – المرجع السابق، ص29 – 46.

33 – قطّوس، بسّام، سيمياء العنوان، (م.س)، ص57.

34 – الكعبيّ، ضياء والعدواني، معجب، السرديات الشعبيّة العربيّة؛ دراسة في التمثيلات الثقافيّة، دار الانتشار العربي، بيروت، لبنان، ط1، 2014م، ص57.

35 – الكعبيّ، ضياء، السرد العربيّ القديم: دراسة في الأنساق الثقافيّة وإشكاليّات التأويل، (م.س)، ص245.

36 – يُنظر: موسى، عبدالله، في المنهج الأركيولوجيّ: الحفريّ: قداسة النصّ وجدوى المنهج، مجلة الجمعية الفلسفية العربيّة، القاهرة، مصر، المجلد (25)، العدد (25)، 2016م، 291 – 299.

37 – يُنظر: ميشيل فوكو وآخرون، التحليل الثقافيّ، تحرير: إيدث كريزويل، ترجمة: فاروق أحمد مصطفى وآخرون، ط1، 2008م منشورات المركز القومي للترجمة، القاهرة، مصر.

38 – يُنظر: التمارة، عبدالرحمن، نقد النقد: بين التّصوّر المنهجيّ...، (م.س)، ص24.

39 – سيرة بني هلال، ط1، 1981م دار الكتب الشعبيّة، بيروت، لبنان.

40 – سيرة الأميرة ذات الهمّة وولدها عبدالوهاب، (د.ط)، 1980م، المكتبة الثقافيّة، بيروت، لبنان.

41 – سيرة عنترة بن شدّاد، نسّقها وهذّبها: عمر أبو النضر، (د.ط)، 1993م، المكتبة الشعبيّة، منشورات مكتبة المعارف، بيروت، لبنان.

42 – سيرة الملك سيف بن ذي يزن فارس اليمن، المكتبة الثقافيّة، بيروت، لبنان، ط2، 1986م.

43 – ألف ليلة وليلة، منشورات دار مكتبة الحياة، بيروت، لبنان، (د.س).

44 – شبانة، ناصر يوسف، أنماط السرد في تراثنا العربيّ، مجلة جامعة النجاح للأبحاث/ العلوم الإنسانية، جامعة النجاح الوطنية، رام الله، فلسطين، المجلد (21)، العدد (2)، 2007م، ص425.

45 – كاظم، نادر، تمثيلات الآخر...، (م.س)، ص329.

46 – المرجع السابق، ص312.

47 – يُنظر للاستزادة: الحجاجي، أحمد شمس الدين، مولد البطل في السيرة الشعبيّة، ط1، 1990م، مؤسسة دار الهلال، القاهرة، مصر.

48 – كاظم، نادر، تمثيلات الآخر...، (م.س)، ص312.

49 – المرجع السابق، ص357.

50 – المرجع السابق، ص362.

51 – ويتحدّث نادر كاظم عن إشكاليّة الهُويّة التي يعيشها عنترةُ في هذه السيرة بين «اضطراب الهُويّة» و«الذّات الممزّقة»، فهو يعيش في «جدلية البياض والسواد، والعربيّة والحبشيّة، والسيادة والعبوديّة». المرجع السابق، ص374.

52 – خورشيد، فاروق، أضواء على السيرة الشعبية، منشورات اقرأ، بيروت، لبنان، (د.ط)، (د.س)، ص32.

53 – كاظم، نادر، تمثيلات الآخر...، (م.س)، ص379.

54 – المرجع السابق، ص399.

55 – المرجع السابق، ص402.

56 – المرجع السابق، ص404 – 405.

57 – ينتخب كاظم عدداً من المرويات التي تمثل حكاية الخيانة، وهي حكاية شهريار وشاه زمان وزجتيهما الخائنتين، وحكاية الشيخ الثالث صاحب البغل ويظهر هذا النسق في الحكاية التي أوردها نادر كاظم من كتاب النفراوي «الروض العاطر في نزهة الخاطر» تتماثل مع «الحكاية الإطاريّة» عن مواقعة عبد أسـود يُدعى ضر غام نسـوةً كبراء الناس، من مثل: زوجة الوزيـر الأعظم، وزوجة القاضي، وامـرأة الكاتـب. يُنظر: النفراوي، أبو عبدالله عمـر بن محمد، الروض العاطر فـي نزهة الخاطر، تحقيـق: جمــال جمعـة، ط2، 1993م دار رياض الريس، لندن، بريطانيا. وكاظـم، نادر، تمثيلات الآخر...، (م.س)، ص409.

58 – المرجع السابق، ص422.

59 – كاظم، نادر، تمثيلات الآخر...، (م.س)، ص409.

60 – المرجع السابق، ص333.

61 – المرجع السابق، ص336.

62 – المرجع السابق، ص335.

63 – المرجع السابق، ص342.

64 – إذ يقول: «فاللهُ لا يفعل الشـرّ، ولا يصدر عنه النقص والقصور، وما دام السـواد من خلقة الله فهو خيّر، ولا يجوز وصفه بالشرّ أو النقص أو القصور او التَّشوه». المرجع السابق، ص336 – 337.

65 – وفي سـياق ذلك عقدت الكعبي فصلاً خاصاً لبحث تلقّي موروث السـرديّ في النقد العربي الجديد في النصف الثاني من القرن المنصرم وسمته بـ«تلقّي الموروث السرديّ في النقد العربي الجَديد». يُنظر: الكعبيّ، ضياء، السرد العربيّ القديم: دراسة في الأنساق...، (م.س)، 472 – 522.

66 – يُنظر: يقطين، سعيد، الكلام والخبر...، (م.س). وإبراهيم عبدالله، السردية العربيّة: بحث في البنية السردية للموروث الحكائي العربي، (م.س).

67 – يُنظـر: ذياب، صفاء، السيرة الشـعبية في النقـد المُعاصـر، ط1، 2020م، دار الرافدين للطباعة والنشر والتوزيع، بيروت، لبنان.

68 – يُنظر: الكعبيّ، ضياء، السرد العربيّ القديم: دراسة في الأنساق...، (م.س)، 472 – 522.

69 – ولا منـاص من الإشـارة هنا إلـى أنّ التجنيس يمثّل معضلة عند عامة النقّاد، وقد نشبت خلافات كبيرة حولها خصائص الأنواع الأدبيّة. إبراهيم، عبدالله، التلقّي والسياقات الثقافيّة: بحث في تأويل الظّاهرة الأدبيّة، العدد (93)، 2001م، منشورات سلسلة كتاب الرياض، مؤسسة اليمامة الصحفية، الرياض، المملكة العربيّة السعودية، ص62 – 64.

70 – انظر: إبراهيم، عبدالله، موسوعة السرد العربيّ، (م.س)، ج8، ص 286 وما بعدها.

71 – لومبا، آنيا، نظريّة الاسـتعمار وما بعد الاسـتعمار الأدبيّة، ترجمة: محمد عبد الغني غنّوم، ط1، 2017م، دار الحوار، اللاذقيّة، سوريا، ص231 – 245.

72 – بريمي، عبدالله، الكون السيميائيّ والكون الثقافيّ (يوري لوتمان)، مجلة فصول، الهيئة المصرية العامّة للكتاب، القاهرة، مصر، المجلد (3/25)، العدد (99)، 2017م، ص47.

73 – ينظر حول مفهوم «الجماعات المُتخيَّلة» عند بندكت أندرسن. ينظر: أندرسن، بندكت، الجماعات المتخيَّلة: تأمُّلات في أصل القومية وانتشارها، ترجمة: ثائر ديب، تقديم: عزمي بشارة، ط1، 2009م، شركة قدمس للنشر والتوزيع، دمشق، سوريا، ص49.

74 – المرجع السابق، ص46 – 47.

75 – يُنظر: طاهر، حامد، نوادر جُحا: تراث شعبي ونقد اجتماعي، مجلة دراسات عربية وإسلامية، مركز اللغات الأجنبية والترجمة، جامعة القاهرة، القاهرة، مصر، الجزء (74)، 2015م، ص166.

76 – الكعبيّ، ضياء، السرد العربيّ القديم: دراسة في الأنساق الثقافيّة وإشكاليّات التأويل، (م.س)، ص246.

77 – سيرة الملك الظّاهر بيبرس، مكتبة التربية للطباعة والنشر والتوزيع، بيروت، لبنان، ط1، 1983م.

78 – الكعبيّ، ضياء، السرد العربيّ القديم: دراسة في الأنساق الثقافيّة وإشكاليّات التأويل، (م.س)، ص246 – 254.

79 – ينظر حول مفهوم «الردّ بالسرد»: اشكروفيت وجريفيث وتيفين، بيل وجاريث وهلين، الردُّ بالكتابة: النظرية والتطبيق في آداب المستعمرات القديمة، ترجمة: شهرت العالم، ط1، مارس 2006م، المنظمة العربيّة للترجمة، بيروت، لبنان، ص15 وما بعدها.

80 – وجديرة الإشارة إلى أنّ السرديات البديلة بوصفها مفهوماً نقديّاً قد نشأت في أحضان الدراسات ما بعد الكولونياليّة، وبذلك فإنّ سرديّات الجنون، تغدو وفقاً لهذه الفكرة سرديّات مضادة تؤسّس لتاريخ جديد، هو تاريخ الهامشيين في الأرض. يُنظر: الطّائي، معن، السرديات المضادة: بحث في طبيعة التّحولات الثقافيّة، ط1، 2014م، المؤسسة العربيّة للدراسات والنشر، بيروت، لبنان.

81 – ينظر الفصلان الموسومان بـ«تلقّي الجنون في اللغة» و«تلقّي الجنون في منطقة المفاهيم» في: آل مريع، أحمد، خطاب الجنون: الحضور الفيزيائي والغياب الثقافيّ...، (م.س)، ص149 – 212.

82 – انظر: تودوروف، تزيفيتان، نظريّة الأجناس الأدبيّة: دراسة في التّناص والكتابة والنقد، ترجمة: عبدالرحمن بو علي، ط1، 2016م، دار نينوى للدراسات والنشر والتوزيع، دمشق، سوريا، ص11 – 44.

83 – الكعبي، ضياء، خطابُ التّحامق والجنون في السرد العربيّ القديم...، (م.س)، ص46 – 47.

84 – الكعبي، ضياء، خطابُ التّحامق والجنون في السرد العربيّ القديم...، (م.س)، ص46 – 47.

85 – المرجع السابق، ص27.

86 – حكاية أبي القاسم البغداديّ، تحقيق: آدم متز، ط1، (د.س)، مطبعة المثنى، بغداد، العراق، ص137.

87 – الكعبي، ضياء، خطابُ التّحامق والجنون في السرد العربيّ القديم...، (م.س)، ص31.

88 – المرجع السابق، ص32.

89 – المرجع السابق، ص34.

90 – يُنظر: البهلول، عبدالله، في بلاغة الخطاب الأدبيّ: بحث في سياسة القول في نصوص من الأدب العربي القديم، ط1، 2007م، التسفير الفني، تونس، ص50.

91 – تبحث الكعبيّ في تمثيلات المرأة في قصّة مثل «حُسَبُها حَمْقَاءَ وَهيَ باخِسٌ» التي يرويها الميداني

بقولــه: «تَحْسَــبُها حَمْقَــاء وَهْيَ بَاخِسٌ». ويروى «باخِسـة» فمن روى باخِس أراد أنها ذات بَخْس تَبْخَسُ النَاسَ حقوقَهم، ومن روى «باخسة» بناه على بَخَسَتْ فهي باخسة. يقال: إن المثل تكلم بــه رجــلٌ من بني العَنْبَر من تميم، جاورته امرأة فنظر إليها فحسـبها حمقاء لا تعقل ولا تحفظ ولا تعرف مالها، فقال العنبري: ألا أُخْلِطُ مالي ومَتَّاعي بمالها ومتاعها ثم أقاسمها فآخذ خيرَ متاعها، وأعطيها الرديء من متاعي، فقاسـمها بعد ما خَلَط متاعه بمتاعها، فلم ترضَ عند المُقَاسَمة حتى أخَذَتْ متاعها، ثم ناز عته وأظهرت له الشكوى حتى افْتَدَى منها بما أرادت، فعُوتِبَ عند ذلك، فقيل له: اخْتَدَعْتَ امرأة، وليس ذلك بِحَسَنٍ، فقال: تحسَبُها حَمْقَاء وهي باخسة. يضرب لمن يتباله وفيه دهاء». يُنظر: الميدانيّ، أبو الفضل النيسابوريّ، مَجْمَعُ الأمثال، (د.ط)، 1995م، دار مكتبة الحياة للطباعة والنشر والتوزيع، بيروت، لبنان، ص170.

92 – «حدَّثنا إبراهيم بن الأدهم قال: رأيت في المنام كأن قائلاً قال لي: ميمونة السوداء زوجتك. قال فكنت أطلبهــا حتــى وجدت أثرها بحمص، فطلبتها فقيل: إنّها مجنونــة لا تألف أحداً. قلت فأين هي؟ قيل: دفعنــا إليها أغناماً فهـي تكون الجبابين. فخرجت إلى الجبانة فإذا هي قائمة تصلي ... قال: فتعجّبت من فطنتها فقلت: يا سبحان الله! قالت: سلّمتها إلى منشـئها، ثم ولت». النيسابوريّ، ابن حبيب (406)، عُقلاء المجانين، تحقيق: عمر الأسعد، ط1، 1987م، دار النفائس، بيروت، لبنان، ص292.

93 – الكعبيّ، ضياء، السرد العربيّ القديم: دراسة في الأنساق الثقافيّة وإشكاليّات التأويل، (م.س)، ص249.

94 – الكعبيّ، ضياء، السرد العربيّ القديم: دراسة في الأنساق الثقافيّة وإشكاليّات التأويل، (م.س)، ص254 – 255.

95 – السيرة الشعبيّة للحلّاج أو سيرة حسين الحلّاج، تحقيق: رضوان السح، دار صادر، بيروت، لبنان، ط1، 1998م.

96 – الكعبيّ، ضياء، السرد العربيّ القديم: دراسة في الأنساق الثقافيّة وإشكاليّات التأويل، (م.س)، ص265.

97 – الكعبيّ، ضياء، السرد العربيّ القديم: دراسة في الأنساق الثقافيّة وإشكاليّات التأويل، (م.س)، ص257.

98 – سيرة علـي الزَّيبـق المصريّ أو مدير الشـرطة في عهـد الدولة العبّاسـيّة، دار عمر أبو النصر وشركاؤه، بيروت، لبنان، ط1، 1971م.

99 – الكعبيّ، ضياء، السـرد العربيّ القديم: دراسـة في الأنسـاق الثقافيّة وإشـكاليّات التأويل، (م.س)، ص246.

100 – الكعبيّ، ضياء، السـرد العربيّ القديم: دراسة في الأنسـاق الثقافيّة وإشكاليّات التأويل، (م.س)، 257.

101 – يُنظر: سيرة علي الزَّيبق المصريّ أو مدير الشرطة في عهد الدولة العبّاسيّة، (م.س).

102 – الكعبيّ، ضياء، السـرد العربيّ القديم: دراسة في الأنسـاق الثقافيّة وإشكاليّات التأويل، (م.س)، 261 – 263.

الفصل الثالث:

انفتاح نمط التلقّي:
النقد الثقافيّ ومـــسارات النقد الأدبيّ

تلتقي هذه المقاربات التي يتضمنها هذا الفصل على محورٍ عريضٍ مشتركٍ، يحاول تجسير الفجوات بين النقد الثقافيّ والنقد الأدبيّ، وفض الاشتباك، الذي مثّل شرقاً وغرباً، جدليّةً أمسى أمرُ حلّها أمراً صعباً ومعقّداً، ولذا فإن هذه المقاربات الثلاث، تمثل دوالاً شواهد، على انفتاح النقد الثقافيّ على ممكنات النقد الأدبيّ، وإمكانية إدماجهما.

ولا ريب أنّ هذا الاتجاه الذي تمثّله هذه المقاربات يسيرُ في توازٍ وانسجامٍ مع اتجاه غربيّ، يروم أن يدشن هذا الائتلاف، وأن ينهي الخلاف الذي ينقدح أوراه كلّ حين بين النقد الثقافيّ والنقد الأدبيّ، ومن هنا جاء تساؤل جون باتنز: «ماذا لو حاولنا أن نتصور تحالفاً جديداً بين الدراسات الأدبيّة والدراسات الثقافيّة، بدلاً من النظر إليهما بوصفهما عدوين طبيعيين؟ بحيث ندرسهما دفعة واحدة، وليس ما تفعله إحداهما في الأخرى، أي ندرس ما يمكن أن تسهم به الدراسات الثقافيّة في الدراسات الأدبيّة، والعكس بالعكس...»[1].

وفي ذات السياق تبرز مقاربة يوسف عليمات الموسومة بـ(العَجائبيّة وثقافة الإشهار: قراءة ثقافية في حكاية أبي القاسم الطّنبوريّ)، التي تنحاز منهجيّاً لمقولات النقد الأدبيّ، كالسيميائية، ونظرية التلقّي، والنظرية السرديّة، والحال أن مقاربة عليمات يمكن أن تنتظم ضمن مسار قرائي، لا يؤمن ببراءة الجمالي، ويرى وجوب الالتفاتِ إلى جماليات النص، المقصاة عند السواد الأعظم من المنشغلين بالنقد الثقافيّ.

وقد آخى مصطفى الغرافي بين النقد الثقافيّ ونظرية التلقّي في مقاربته (السرد والمُضمر: دراسةٌ في أخبار ابن قتيبة)، إذ نفث الغرافيّ في رَوْع المؤلّف من جديد، فكان أن قرأ الأنساق التي تتضمنها هذه الأخبار، بوصفها نصوصاً غير معزولةٍ عن سياقاتها اللائطة بها لحظة إنتاجها، على أن ذلك جعله رازحاً تحت سلطة التاريخ، مما حبس مقاربته عن التحليق في عوالم القراءة والتأويل.

وتجلو مقاربة معجب العدواني الموسومة بـ(مرايا الآخر: مقاربة ثقافية لرسالة ابن فضلان وانعكاساتها في الثقافة الغربية) صورة القراءة الثقافيّة التناصيّة، التي تخيرت النظريّة التناصية للإفادة من مرونتها المنهجيّة، وانفتاحها، وإشكالية تلقّيها في النقد العربيّ المعاصر، جاعلة من ذلك مدخلاً، لتأسيس أُفق قرائي يسهم، بحظٍ وافرٍ، في إخصاب نمط التلقّي.

وتغدو التناصيّة الثقافيّة، منهجيّة مركّبة مِطواعاً، يمكن لها أن تكشف اللثام عن وسائل تشكل الصّور/ التمثيلات الذّهنية، في إطار علاقة الأنا بالآخر، أو المركز بالهامش، أو التابع بالمتبوع، وهي تجربةٌ بِكْر، يمكن لها أن تفيد في بناء منهج يسائل الأنساق الثقافيّة من منظور تناصيّ مقارِن يجعل من النقد الثقافيّ والتناصية محاور جهازه المنهجيّ.

وبعد فقد مثلت لحظة التلقّي في هذا الأُفُق أقصد الأفق القائم على انفتاح نمط التلقّي على النقد الأدبيّ لحظةً فارقةً في تاريخ التلقّي، بوصفها لحظةً منطويةً على محاولات نقديّة جادة، تبنت موقفاً وسطاً لا ينزع منزعاً أحادياً، وإنما يجسّر الفجوات المنهجيّة بين النقد الثقافيّ والنقد الأدبيّ. أعلى النموذج

1 – مدخـل: النقد الثقـافيّ والنقد الأدبيّ والتأسيس لائتلاف منهجيّ:

تندرجُ مقاربات يُوسف عُليمات (العَجائبيّة وثقافة الإشهار: قراءة ثقافية في

حكاية أبي القاسم الطّنبوري)[2] في سياقات المقاربات التي تسعى إلى إعادة قراءة حكاية مداس أبي القاسم الطّنبوريّ العجائبيّة والمقامة البشرية قراءة جديدة، إذ يحاول عليمات أن يكشف عن المضمرات النسقيّة المتوارية خلف جماليّات السرد، أو فِتْنَتِهِ في حكاية الطنبوريّ، والمقامة البشرية بوصف الحكايات العجائبية والمقامات كذلك خطاباً نسقيّاً، يعكسُ موقفي الطنبوريّ والهمذاني من مجتمعهما، وتوتّر علاقتهما معهما.

وتنتسبُ مقاربة مصطفى الغرافيّ (السرد والمُضمر: دراسةٌ في أخبار ابن قتيبة)[3] إلى إطار القراءات الثقافيّة التي تتوسل بمقولات النقد الثقافيّ ممثلة بالأنساق الثقافيّة ونظرية التلقّي ممثلة بالقارئ الضمني، وذلك أجل قراءة نماذج منتخبة من لدن مصطفى الغرافي من السرود التي يتضمنها كتاب (عُيون الأخبار) لابن قتيبة الدينوريّ، وتنقام مقاربة الغرافي على مفاهيم رئيسة هي: الأنساق الثقافيّة، وسلطة التاريخ، والقارئ الضّمنيّ، في صورة من صور الائتلاف المنهجيّ والمعرفيّ مع نظرية التلقّي.

وتنقامُ مقاربة معجِب العدوانيّ (مرايا الآخر: مقاربة ثقافيّة لرسالة ابن فضلان وانعكاساتها في الثقافة الغربيّة)[4] على فكرة مركزيّة كبرى مؤدّاها المعرفي أنّ السرديّات العربيّة القديمة الرحليّة تمثل سرديّات تنطوي في أجزاء كبيرة منها على أنساق ثقافيّة مضمرة ترتبط بمركزيّة الأنا وهامشية الآخر، ذلك بوصف الخطاب الرحليّ عند ابن فضلان، والرحالة العرب ممن سواه، يمثل خطاباً يسفرُ بجلاء عن موقف ابن فضلان أو موقف العربيّ من الآخر، وتصوّراته له، ومواقفه منه.

2 – سيمياء القارئ: من الناقد الأدبيّ إلى الناقد التناصي:

1 – 2 – يوسف عليمات: الناقد الثقافيّ ومنازع الناقد الأدبيّ:

تنطوي مقاربات يوسف عليمات على سمةٍ بارزةٍ تكمن في كونها ممثلةً

لانفتاح نمط التلقّي في النقد الثقافيّ على مناهج النقد الأدبيّ، وتضافره مع أدواته، وذلك بالتحول من الخطاب النقديّ في إطار النقد الثقافيّ من مساءلة الأنساق المضمرة، وإهمال جماليّات النصوص، إلى محاولة قراءة أنساقه وجمالياته في الآن عينه، ولذا فيمكن القول: إنّ عليمات سعى إلى العمل على انفتاح نمط التلقّي من خلال التفاته إلى جماليات النصّ بالتزامن مع قراءته لأنساقه[5].

وهنا لا بدّ من الإشارة إلى ذلك أنّ عليمات قد مثّل اتجاهاً نقدياً يتضادُ مَعَ مشروع الغذّاميّ، ويتّسق معه في الآنِ عينه، فقد اهتمّ عليمات بقراءة الأنساق الثقافيّة وتشكُّلاتها في بنية النص الأدبيّ، في ضَوْء الإفادة المنهجيّة الصريحة من أدوات النقد الأدبيّ الحديث، ومناهجه المختلفة[6].

ولا ريب أنّ يوسف عليمات في صنيعه هذا حاول أن يسلتهم مقولاتٍ نقديّة يزدحم بها الفضاء النقدي الغربيّ، وهي مقولات تسعى إلى فضّ الاشتباك القائم بين النقد الثقافيّ والدراسات الثقافيّة، من جهة، والنقد الأدبيّ من جهة أخرى، كما يعبّر عن ذلك جون باتنز بقوله: «ماذا لو حاولنا أن نتصوّر تحالفاً جديداً بين الدراسات الأدبيّة والدراسات الثقافيّة...»[7].

فقد طغى تيه النصية في مدارات البحث النقديّ في الغرب، فكان أن أعلن الكثيرون موت المؤلّف، ونهاية التاريخ، إلى غير ذلك، مما حدا بزمرةٍ من النقاد إلى القول بحياة النص، في سياقات نقديّة مختلقة، من مثل: (تيارات النقد الثقافيّ)، و(الدراسات الثقافيّة)، و(التاريخانية الجديدة)، إذ اتفقت هذه التيارات على أن «الأدب له قاعدة تاريخية، والأعمال الأدبيّة ليست نتاج وعي فردي، بل نتاج عدد من القوى الاجتماعية والثقافيّة»[8].

وعليه فتغدو القراءةُ الثقافيّةُ التي تطمحُ مقاربة عُليمات إلى تقديمها حول السرديّات العربيّة القديمة، مقارباتٍ تستعين بالنقد الأدبيّ، وترفض القطيعة المنهجيّة المفترضَة بين النقد الثقافيّ ومناهج النقد الأدبيّ، ولعلّ المطلع على

نتاج عليمات النقدي برمّته يجد أنه يتفق مع ما قرّ في نمط التلقّي بصورته العامة، ولكنه ما ينفكُّ يحاول أن ينفتح به على النقد الأدبيّ، ليقيم تحالفاً جديداً بين النقد الثقافيّ والنقد الأدبيّ⁽⁹⁾ .

2 – 2 – مصطفى الغرافيّ: القارئ الثقافيّ الضمّني وهوس المؤلَّف:

تنتمي مقاربة الغرافيّ بكلّيتها إلى سلطة نمط التلقّي المتعارف عليه في النقد الثقافيّ، إذ إن الغرافي منتمٍ إلى طقوس القراءة الثقافيّة انتماءً ظاهراً، يتجلى في عنوان مقاربته، إذ إنّه يمضي في مقاربته هذه دون خرقٍ لآفاقها التي تراكمت بفِعْل المقاربات الثقافيّة المتعاقبة حول التراث العربيّ عامة، والسرديّات العربيّة القديمة خاصة، ولكنه يبدو مع ذلك رازحاً تحت وطأة سلطة المؤلف، وتمثيلات القارئ الضمني⁽¹⁰⁾ .

وعليه فهو مسكونٌ كغيره من النقاد المنخرطين في إطارات النقد الثقافيّ بالكشف عن الأنساق الثقافيّة، ولكن انتماءه لهذا النمط المترسخ لم يمنعه من أن ينفتح على منهج آخر، يقيم به تحالفاً مع النقد الثقافيّ، أو يستنبت به منهجاً مركّباً جديداً.

ولعل هذا التحالف لا يظهر في الإطار المنهجيّ لهذه المقاربة، وإنما يلحظ عند النظر في الممارسة النقديّة عند الغرافي، حيث يوظف الغرافي مفاهيمَ مختلفة من هذين المنهجيّن في ثنيات فعل القراءة لديه⁽¹¹⁾ .

وعليه فإن مصطفى الغرافيّ يعمل مبضعه النقديّ في تأويل التاريخ المضمر الذي تنطوي عليه هذه الأخبار بوصفها سرديّات أيديولوجية، ولا ريب أن الغرافي يستعين هنا بمفهوم رائج هو (القارئ الضمنيّ((Implied Author) الذي يقابل مفهوم المؤلَّف الضمني.

وهو القارئ الذي يظلّ منتصباً عند بوابة النصّ لحراسة المعنى، أو لتأطير

مسارات القراءة، بوصف النصوص متضمنة لأنساق مقصودة ورسائل معيّنة، يريد المؤلف أن يلقيها في رَوْعِ قارئه أو متلقّيه، من خلال بثها بصورة مخاتلة أو بطرق فنية تنأى بها عن الطرح المباشر الفج.

وعليه فإنّ هذا الاستيلاد المنهجيّ، الذي نبت من رحم الاندغام المنهجيّ بين النقد الثقافيّ ونظرية التلقّي، لهو دليلٌ على انفتاح نمط التلقّي، بيد أنّه يجعل من القارئ/ الناقد قارئاً حرّاً في تلقّيه الخطاب السرديّ، فهو قارئ نموذجيّ قادر على القبض على أنساق هذه السرديّات، على الرغم من أن هذه الأنساق مضمرة ومخاتلة، على اعتبار أن حضور المؤلّف في عملية التأويل في النص تمثل صوىً يمكن للقارئ أن يتكئ إليها في قراءة هذه السرديّات، وقمينةٌ الإشارةُ إلى أنّ هذا الاستيلاد المنهجيّ محفوفٌ بمكاره عديدة؛ أما أولاهما محاولة إسقاط حياة المؤلّف على مروياته السردية، دون أي احتراس من مغبات الربط الدائب، والمفترض بينهما، وأما ثانيتهما فهي افتراض القارئ الضمنيّ أن تأويلاته هي التأويلات الصائبة، وذلك لأنها مباركةٌ بتأيد القارئ، الذي عقد اتفاقاً ضمنياً مع القارئ الضمنيّ، على صحة ما يذهب إليه هذا القارئ من تأويلات[12].

3 – 2 – معجب العدواني: القارئ التناصيّ والقراءة الثقافيّة:

تتشكّل هذه المقاربة من نمطين من القرّاء، أما أحدهما فالقارئ الثقافيّ الذي يدرس النصّ بغية استخراج أنساقه الثقافيّة المضمرة كما يتجلى ذلك في المرجعيات الكبرى للنقد الثقافيّ، وأما ثانيهما فالقارئ التناصيّ، الذي يقرأ تفاعلات النصوص من منظورٍ جديد، هو منظور الهيمنة الذي يتأطّر بسياقات التأثر والتأثير[13].

وبناءً على السابق فقد استغلّ العدواني انشغالاته الممتدة ردحاً من الزمن بالنظرية التناصية في سبيل تطوير النقد الثقافيّ، مفيداً من انفتاحه على المناهج الأخرى، وقدرتِه على الاندماج معها في بوتقةٍ منهجيّةٍ واحدة[14].

ويبدو ارتباط التناصيّة بالدراسات الثقافيّة والنقد الثقافيّ وبما يتصل بهما من تيارات نقديّة كالنقد الدنيويّ، والنقد الطّباقي، حافزاً على إمكانية أن تمسي التناصيّة تناصيّة ثقافيّة، ترتبط بأسئلة منهجيّة مختلفةٍ وشائكةٍ في الآن عينه تصدر «من درس العلاقات بين أنواع النصوص المختلفة والسياقات، مثل: سياقات الإمبرياليّة، وعلاقتنا مع الآخر...»[15].

ولعلّه من اللافت للنظر في هذه المقاربة أنّ العدواني سعى إلى إعادة صوغ مفهوم التناصية في إطارٍ منهجيّ جديد، يرفض ما قرّ لدى المتلقّين بشأنها، ويخلّصها من أدران سوء الفهم، الذي بُلِيَتْ به هذه النظريّة، خاصة في تلقّيها العربيّ[16].

وفي سياق ذلك يمكن القول: إنّ مقاربة العدواني تتنازع بين النقد الأدبيّ ممثلاً بالنظرية التناصية، والنقد الثقافيّ أو القراءة الثقافيّة كما يسميها بذلك العدوانيّ؛ إذ تبقى التناصية أو التناص ذات طموح منهجيّ، يتغيا الانفتاح على مختلف المناهج والتخصصات، بما هي مشروع حيويّ، أو بما ركّب فيها من قدرة على مساءلة النصوص، والنفوذ إلى بناها، وعليه فالقراءة التناصيّة الثقافيّة تحاول «الكشف عن أدوار الهيمنة والنفوذ، وتمثيلات الهوية، لتتمكن من خلق علاقات واسعة بين الأدبيّ وغير الأدبيّ، في إطار تيارات ما بعد الاستعمار والنسويّة والنقد الثقافيّ»[17].

3 – المتنَ المنهجيّة والجهاز المفاهيميّ:

1 – 3 – يوسف عليمات ومرجعيات النقد الأدبيّ:

تنقسمُ مقاربة يوسف عليمات حول حكاية أبي القاسم الطنبوري إلى مسارينْ اثنين نظريّ وإجرائيّ؛ أما النظريّ فقد حاول عليمات خلاله أن يؤصّل لمصطلح الفنتازيا والعجائبي عند (تودوروف) و(كاترين بالسي)، ولمصطلح ثقافة الإشهار عند (كاترين هيوم) و(سعيد بنكراد)[18].

أما خلال المسار الإجرائيّ فقد حاول عليمات أن يبحث في العلاقة المُتوتّرة بين الطنبوري ومجتمعه كما يتبدّى ذلك في حكايته هذه، إذ تمثّل هذه الحكاية عند عليمات «الحكاية السرديّة التراثيّة القادرة على إضمار الأنساق الثقافيّة المخاتلة التي تنتج اللامتوقّع والعجائبيّ» [19].

وتنقسمُ دراسة عليمات حول القامة البِشريّة إلى مسارين اثنين نظريّ وإجرائي؛ أما النظريّ فقد حاول عليمات خلاله أن يؤصّل المصطلح لسردية بوصفه المصطلح الرئيس في دراسته هذه، كما نظرية تتبدى في النظريّة النقديّة الحديثة عند (تودوروف) و(كولر) و(جيرار جينيت) [20]، أما خلال المسار الإجرائيّ؛ فقد حاول عليمات أن يبحث في العلاقة المُتوتّرة بين الهمذاني ومجتمعه كما يتبدى ذلك في مقاماته هذه، إذ تمثّل هذه المقامة عند عليمات «بوصفها نصّاً ثقافيّاً يرتبط بسياقاتٍ ثقافيّة وإيديولوجية منتجة» [21].

وفي هذا السياق يؤطّر عليمات مقاربته حول الطنبوريّ من خلال تقسيم هذه الحكاية إلى وحداتٍ حكائيّةٍ أربع هي [22]: (المتوالية السرديّة الأولى: الطّنبوريّ وفلسفة الإشهار)، و(المتوالية السرديّة الثانية: رحلة المَداس الإشهاريّ: القَرين وسُلطة القضاء)، و(المتوالية السرديّة الثالثة: العبور الثقافيّ المداسيّ: بين الهاجس والمقاومة)، و(المتوالية السرديّة الرابعة: ثقافة التبرؤ بوصفها مخاتلة).

وهو يفعل الأمر ذاته في مقاربته حول المقامة الهمذانية: (أولاً: تشكّل الذّات وتجليات الفعل)، و(ثانياً: نسقية الحوار ومخاتلات القصّ الأنثويّ)، و(ثالثاً: جدلية الانفصال والاتصال)، و(رابعاً: نسقية القناع وثقافة التخريف، و(خامساً: ثقافة الهيمنة وبلاغة المقارقة) [23].

وتدلُّ العنوانات المُنتخَبَة من لدن عليمات، في ضَوْء معطياتها السيميائية، على وعيه بوظائف العنوان، ومركزيّة اسم العلم، بوصفه دالاً مركزيّاً، في المقاربة الأولى، إذ يغدو المِداس أو مداس الطنبوريّ، كما ينمذجه عليمات في

عنوان المقاربة، وعنوانات مباحثها، مركزاً بُؤَرِيّاً، وهو ما سيمسي أُسَاً تتكى إليه في محاولتها تبيانَ مركزيّة المداس، مُحَرّكِ الأحداث في هذه الحكاية/ النصّ العجائبي/ـة[24].

وإذا كان المداسُ بؤرةً مركزيّة تتفرعُ منها العنوانات الأخرى، فلا ريب أنّ هذه العناوين تحملُ في أعطافها أبعاداً رمزيّة، كما هو الأمر بالنسبة إلى عنوان المقاربة، ولكنها ذاتُ إحالة مرجعية منفتحة على الصور القارة في المتخيل الشعبي، فضلاً عن مساهمتها في حفز القارئ واستيهامه[25]، وهي تندرج في إطار موضوعة كبرى، هي محنة المداس، قرين أبي القاسم أو ظِلّه.

ولعلّ الإشارة تجدرُ إلى أن السابق لا يعني، بالضرورة، أنّ عليمات يقيم قراءته على منهج تلفيقي؛ يجمع بين مناهج مختلفة، بصورة غير ناظمة، بل نجده يسعى إلى الانطلاق من منهج مركّب، تنتقل خلالها ممارسته المنهجيّة والنقديّة من النقد المُؤْتَلِف إلى المِراس المختلف[26].

وإذا كان عُليمات ينطلق من حقيقة مُؤداها هو التواشج الحتميّ الذي يجب أن يفترضُ بين النصّ وسياقاته المختلفة، فإن النصّ الأدبيّ، يغدو بالنسبة إليه، نصّاً ثقافياً منفتحاً على السياقات المختلفة، مرهوناً بخواصّها، وآثارها الجليّة في تشكّلاته الرؤيويّة والموضوعيّة.

ويتأسّس الجهاز المفاهيميُّ لهاتين الأطروحتين بفِعْل انفتاحهما على مناهج النقد الأدبيّ على ائتلاف مفاهيميّ عريض، يضمُّ مفاهيم تنتمي إلى مناهج وحقول مختلفة، ومنها: (التلقّي)، و(الدهشة)، و(اللامتوقع الإشهار)، و(العجائبيّ)، و(الأنساق الثقافيّة المخاتلة)، و(النسق)، و(الثقافة)، و(جماليات السرد)، و(أفق الانتظار)، و(كسر أفق التوقع)...إلخ، مصطلحات تمثل العَصَبَ المفاهيميّ لهذه المقاربة.

وذلك في صورة توليفية منهجيّة يغدو خلالها الجهاز المنهجيّ لهاتين

الأطروحتين عابراً للمناهج والتخصصات والحقول المعرفيّة المُختلفة، وهي منهجيّة تقوم على تراكب منهجي يجمع بين النقد الثقافيّ والنقد الأدبيّ .

ويبدو أنّ عليمات حاول أن يراوح منهجياً في أطروحتيه هاتين بين النقد الثقافيّ والنقد الأدبيّ، بصورة متوازنة، بحيث إنّه «لا يستسلم لجاذبية جمال النصّ، كما يفترض كذلك عدم انصياعه لأوامر النسق الثقافيّ»[27]، وعليه فإنّ القراءة الثقافيّة تغدو بفعل هذه التقاطعات المعرفيّة مع المعارف الأخرى حقلاً من المعارف والعلوم، وهو ما تجلّيه هذه المقاربة، إذ يبدو عليمات متدثراً بدثار الناقد الأدبيّ، الذي يضيف البحثَ في أنساق النصّ الثقافيّة إلى عمله النقديّ.

2 – 3 – الغرافي ومرجعيات نظرية التلقّي:

تنتظم مقاربة الغرافيّ في مبحثين اثنين يتوزّعان في متن الدراسة وهما: (السرد والمرجعيّة الثقافيّة)، و(السخرية والقصْديّة الإيديولوجية)، ويجلّي الغرافي في (السرد والمرجعيّة الثقافيّة) فكرةً مؤداها أنّ السرد عند ابن قتيبة الدينوريّ في (عُيون الأخبار) محكوم بمرجعيات ثقافيّة، تحكمه، وتضبط مساراته[28] .

أما خلال (السخرية والقصْديّة الإيديولوجية) فيتناول الغرافي عدداً من السرديّات التي تعتمد على ثيمة السخرية، وتضمر نقداً حادّاً للفرق الإسلامية الأخرى[29]، وتبدو العنوانات/ الموضوعات التي تؤطر مسار مقاربة الغرافي مُنمازة بميزتين اثنتين أما أحدهما فهو إيحاؤها، ودلالاتها السيميائية، وأما ثانيهما فهو أيديولوجيتها، أي تعبيرها عن القيم الأيديولوجية التي تناقش هذه المقاربة تجلياتِ حضورها في أخبار ابن قتيبة المنتخبة للدراسة، وتبدو تجليات سلطة الغذّاميّ جليّةً في عنوان مقاربة الغرافي، وذلك في تبنّيه فكرة الأنساق المضمرة التي صاغها الغذّامي ــكما سبقت الإشارة ــ ، فالنسق لا يعمل سوى في حالة الإضمار والمخاتلة.

إن الوظيفة النسقيّة للنسق لا تحدث إلا في وضع مُحدّد، وهذا يكون حينما

يتعارضُ نسقان، أو نظامان من أنظمة الخطاب، أحدهما ظاهر والآخر مضمر، ويكون المضمر ناقضاً، وناسخاً للظّاهر، ويكونُ ذلك في نصٍّ واحدٍ، أو في ما هو في حكم النصّ الواحد[30]، وينطلق الغرافي في مقاربته هذه من فكرة منهجية مؤدّاها أن الموروث السردي لا يزال بحاجة إلى قراءات تسبره من منظور النقد الثقافيّ، إذ «يمكن أن يدرج هذا البحث ضمن المحاولات الرامية إلى قراءة الموروث السردي في ضَوْء الأنساق الثقافيّة والفكريّة التي ارتبطت بها، وانبثقت عنها»[31].

ولا بُدَّ من الإشارة إلى أنّ مصطفى الغرافي في قراءته هذه يتمثل مفاهيم نقديّة كبرى، تعدّ مفاهيم رئيسة في نظرية النقد الثقافيّ ونظريّة التلقّي، وهي: (سلطة التاريخ)، و(سلطة المؤلّف)، و(المؤلّف الضمنيّ)، و(القارئ الضمنيّ)، و(الأنساق المضمرة)، و(السياق الثقافيّ)[32].

ولا ريب أن الجهاز المفاهيمي في هذه المقاربة يبقى مرتبطاً ارتباطاً وثيقاً بنظرية التلقّي التي دشنت حضور المتلقّي المركزي في قراءة العمل الأدبيّ، وفي سياق ذلك يمكن القول: إنّ البحث في تجلّيات النسق والنسقيّة في النصّ الأدبيّ مثّل المروم المركزيّ لهذه المقاربة، وقد بدا أن الغرافي مسكون بسؤالات الأنساق الثقافيّة ــ إن جاز التعبير ــ على اعتبار أنّ الأخبار السرديّة تؤدّي وظيفة ثقافيّة ونسقيّة مخاتلة؛ انسجاماً مع الطُروحات الرئيسة في مدرسيّات النقد الثقافيّ؛ إذ تتموضع الأنساق الثقافيّة ــ على الدوام ــ في الخطابات في المناطق اللا متوقعة من النصوص؛ وهي بذلك ما تفتأ تنسرب إلى بناها العميقة، مستترة خلف جماليات القول.

ويعدُّ مصطلح اندماج الآفاق الذي اقترحه هانز غادمير (Hans Gadamer) توصيفاً ناجعاً لمقاربة فهو يدمج بين أفقيْن اثنين، نمط التلقّي الذي يمثل الأفق الأبويّ وهو الأفق الماضي، والأفق الحاضر الذي يكوّنه أو يشيده الغرافيّ، والذي ينفتح بالنمط على نظرية التلقّي[33].

ولا يختلف مفهوم القراءة الثقافيّة في هذه الأطاريح ذلك أنّها القراءة التي تكشف أنساق النصوص، وتستبطن الشفيرات النصيّة التي تنتظم النصوص، من خلال إعمال البحث في العقد الوثيق بينها وبين السياقات الثقافيّة التي تُحيط بها، وهي لا تختلف كذلك حين تجعل مصطلح النسق مصطلحاً مركزياً لها[34].

3 – 3 –العدواني والنظرية التناصية:

تنشعب مقاربة معجب العدواني إلى فصول ثلاثة، أما أولها فـ(أطوار التناص)، يؤسس خلاله لمنهجية الدراسة، أما ثانيها فهو (الرواية والقراءة التناصية الثقافيّة)، ويقاربُ العدواني فيه نماذج من التناص في الرواية، ورحلة الأجناس تناصيّاً، ورحلة ابن فضلان، ونماذج من الحكاية الشعبية، وضروباً من الصّور الإشهاريّة[35].

أما مقاربته حول رحلة ابن فضلان – موضعِ هذه الدراسة – فتسير في اتجاهيْن كذلك أمّا أحدهما يبحث في أنساق النصّ، وهي أنساق مضمرة، يسمّيها العدوانيّ بالتحيّزات الخفيّة، وأمّا ثانيهما فيدير رحى البحث في علائق التأثر والتأثير بين رحلة ابن فضلان وما تنطوي عليه من تحولاتٍ أصابت المركز والهامش، أو قل: تحولات المركزيّة والهامشية بين العرب والغرب.

وأمّا العنوانات التي تأثّثُ عليها مرتكزاتُ هذه المقاربة فقد اشتملت على الإشارات التالية: (أولاً: التحيّز الخفيّ: الأمّة والسرد)، (ثانياً: التحيّز في المعتقد)، (ثالثاً: التحيّز في تشكيل الجنس الأدبيّ)، و(رابعاً: التحيّز الجُغرافيّ) [36].

وهي عنوانات تكشف عن معالم الاشتغال المنهجيّ لهذه المقاربة، وفي هذا السياق يأتي اجتراح مُعجِب العدواني لمصطلح أو (التناصيّة الثقافيّة) (Cultural Intertextualiy) منهجاً لمقاربته الراهنة، انسجاماً مع الانفتاح المنهجيّ الذي ينماز به النقد الثقافيّ؛ ذلك أن التناصيّة الثقافيّة كما يتجلى في أنظار العدواني

منهجيّة مُركّبة تمتلك فاعليّة نقديّة في الكشف عن الأنساق الثقافيّة الثاوية في بنى النصوص، والكشف عن تمثيلات الهيمنة في النصوص المتناصة بين الثقافات المختلفة.

ويصرّح العدواني بحقيقة هذا الانتماء المنهجيّ، إذ إنّ مقاربته تنتمي إلى «النقد الثقافيّ» (37)، في صورةٍ من صور التحالف المنهجيّ مع النظرية التناصية (Intertextualiy)، بما يمكن أن يطلق عليه (Cultural Intertextualiy) بالقراءة التناصية الثقافيّة.

وهنا فلا بدّ من الإلماع إلى أنّ العدوانيّ جعل من النظرية التناصية في عددٍ من المقاربات والأبحاث والدراسات مرتكزاً منهجيّاً يتكئ إليه، بصورة شكّلت النظريّة التناصية خلالها بالنسبة إليه منهجاً أو حقلاً نقدياً/ معرفيّاً يستوجب الإفادة الدائبة من ممكناته(38).

إنّ القراءة التناصية الثقافيّة لدى مُعجِب العدواني تمثّل انفتاحاً منهجياً على النقد الثقافيّ والدراسات ما بعد الكولونياليّة التي ترعرعتْ في أتون الدراسات الثقافيّة التي صعدت في نهايات القرن المنصرم؛ بوصفها دراساتٍ اهتمّت، بصورة مستفيضة، بمسائل الهامش والمركز من قبيل(39): (الآخرية)، و(أسئلة الهوية والاختلاف)، و(الهيمنة)، و(السلطة).

وبذا يبدو أنّ مقاربة العدواني قد أبانت عن مواطن التشابه أو الالتقاء التي تجمع أفقي القراءة الثقافيّة وأفق القراءة التناصية، في ظلال غفلةٍ من النقاد الذين انشغلوا سنين طِوالاً بالنقد الثقافيّ دونما أن يقيموا أود مقارباتهم على الممكنات التي تضمها هذه المناهج، ولا فكاك من الإشارة إلى أن مفهوم التناص قد طُرِحَ في مدونات النقد الثقافيّ، وإن كان ذلك بصورة مغايرة، إذ تتصادى مقاربة العدوانيّ مع مفهوم الدوائر الثقافيّة الذي اقترحه ليتش (V.Leitch)، ومؤدّاها أنّ أنساق النص مرتبطة بأسئلة السلطة والهيمنة(40)، وتأسيساً على هذا

الطرح السابق فقد مثلت طروحات ليتش – والحال هذه – مهاداً خصيباً أتاح أمام «التاريخانيّة الجديدة والنقد الثقافيّ وغيرهما من نظريّات ما بعد الحداثة وما بعد الكولونياليّة والنسويّة وغيرها، أتاحت الفرصة لتجاوز الحدود التي تفصل بين التاريخ، والأنثروبولوجيا، والفنّ، والسياسة، والأدب، والاقتصاد، وبذلك تَمَّ تقويض مبدأ اللاتداخل»[41].

وعليه فإن التناصية بعبارة الأوائل آخذة من كل منشط منهجيّ بطرف، فهي تتخطى الحدود المنتصبة بين المناهج ابتغاء هدمها، ولا يجد المرء متسعاً من مدافعة حقيقية مؤداها أن التناصية تظلُّ نهباً بين فروع مختلفات، إذ إنّ كلّ فرع يدعي حيازته لسبب من أسباب الاتصال بها.

4 - استراتيجيّات المقاربة النقديّة ومستويات التلقّي:

1 – 4 – يوسف عليمات: الناقد الثقافيّ والأدبيّ وجهان لصورة واحدة:

– تعدُّد الآليات وقوّة التنويع:

تنماز مقاربة عليمات بـ(قوّة التنويع)[42] المتّأتية من تعدد الآليات، ذلك أنّ عليمات يقيم أود مقاربته هذه على تراكبٍ منهجيّ، يفيدُ من مقولات النقد الثقافيّ وأدوات النقد الأدبيّ في سياق منهجيٍّ واحد، يمكن أن يستدرج النص السرديّ العجائبي عند الطّنبوريّ والمقامة البشرية عند الهمذاني[43]، ليفصح عن أنساقه، ومضمراته، إذ يلحظُ في هذه المقاربة أنّ عليمات يفيد من مناهج النقد الأدبيّ على تنوّعها إفادة منهجية واضحة؛ كالسيميائية، ونظرية التلقّي وغيرها، بصورة تغدو خلالها القراءة الثقافيّة عنده قراءةً عابرةً للتخصصات.

ويغدو (التأويل المُضاعف) (Double Interpretation)[44] الاستراتيجيّة التي تَضْبِطُ إيقاع هذا التنوع المنهجيّ، ذلك أنّ عليمات ينطلقُ من فكرةٍ مؤسّسة قِوامها أنّ النصّ الثقافيّ غيرُ بريء، يخاتلُ المتلقّي، ويراوغه؛ فضلاً عن أنّ

حركة الأنساق الثقافيّة فيه تكون لوّابة تتوسّلُ بالجماليّ، والعجائبيّ، كما في حكاية أبي القاسم الطّنبوريّ.

والتأويل المضاعف الذي أقصده هنا ليس سوى «ربط النصّ بالميكانيزمات العامّة للحكي والصُّور والأيديولوجيا»[45]، وقد أشار جوناثان كالر إلى أنّ التأويل المضاعف يشتبكُ مع السيميائيّات، التي يتشابه مسعاها مَعَ هذا المسعى فهي كذلك «تقوم بالضبط على السنن المنتجة للدلالة داخلَ مناطق متعددة من الحياة الاجتماعيّة»[46]، ولا ريب أنّ عليمات شكّل في هذه المقاربة مساراً قرائيّاً نوعيّاً حين انفتح بالنقد الثقافيّ على نظريات النقد الأدبيّ، بيد أنّ هذا الانفتاح الواعيَ، بالطبع، كان بحاجة إلى رؤيةٍ مؤطّرةٍ تُفتتح بها المقاربة، لتشرعن هذا الانفتاح أو التلاقح، وتضبطه، وتبيّن حُدوده، وتجلّي معالمه.

ــ المقامة والحكاية العجائبيّة ومسارات المراوغة:

تغدو الحكاية العجائبية والمقامة في ضَوْء القراءة الثقافيّة الفاحصة، كما يُسمّيها يُوسف عُليمات، حكايات ذوات أبعاد دلاليّةٍ عميقةٍ، ورامزةٍ، ومُوحية، تستطلبُ قراءةً ثقافيّةً واعية بأبعادها السرديّة السيميائيّة /العلاماتية في سبيل الكشف عن تمظهرات النسق الثقافيّ في ثناياها، وعليه فإنّ النصّ العجائبي تمثل من منظور عليمات نصّاً ثقافيّاً، مفارقاً، ومساراً فاعلاً في إضمار المخاتل، والمضمر، والمسكوت عنه في بنية النصّ السرديّ العجائبيّ، ولعلّ حديثه عن ثقافية النصّ، أو نظرته إليه بوصفه حادثة ثقافية[47]، يؤكد أن عليمات يرمي عن ذات القوس التي يرمي عنها عموم المنخرطين في مدارات النقد الثقافيّ[48] .

ولا ريب أنّ هذه الحكاية تمثّل، بمنطق النقد الثقافيّ، حدثاً مراوغاً، ولكن عليمات لا يبين هذه المراوغة، ولعلها تتأتى من خلال الغواية السردية التي تخلقها أنظمة الخطاب السردي العجائبيّ بوصفها مراحاً لإضمار الأنساق، وتمرير الرسائل المبطنة، والقدح، والتضاد، والصدام، في ظلال غطاء يسلب

لبّ المسرود له، ويوقعه في فخاخ هذه الغواية، وإذا كانت هذه المقاربة ترى أن هذه السردية، تنطوي على محمولات إيديولوجية، فإن النقد الأدبيّ ينظر إليها بوصفها حكاية الفكاهة أو الحكاية المرحة (Anecdotes)[49]، في حين أنها في هذه المقاربة نصٌّ ثقافيّ يتجاوزُ في وظيفته الأبعادَ الإمتاعية بما فيها بوصفها محفزة على الإضحاك والإمتاع؛ ليشكّل فضاءاتٍ ناميةً للرّؤيةِ وتشريح المُتواري.

ـ القراءة الثقافيّة والنقد الأدبيّ والتضافر المنهجيّ:

ينطلقُ يوسف عليمات من حقيقة معرفيّة مؤداها تواشج المناهج النقديّة، ولزوب مدّ وشائج الاتّصال وحبائله فيما بينها، ويتجلّى ذلك في إفادته من السيميائية، ونظرية التلقّي، والنظرية السردية، وفي هذا السياق يجعل عليمات حكاية الطنبوري في أربع متواليات سرديّة، في صورة من صور التأثر بفكرة المتواليات السرديّة التي اقترحها الناقد الفرنسيّ رولان بارت[50]، وتمسي شهرة مداس الطنبوريّ كما يرى يُوسف عُليمات، في بادئ الأمر، إشاريّةً، تشي بمركزيته الفاعلة الناجزة، ذلك أنّ المداس يمثل قناعاً للطنبوريّ، وهو ما تعضُدُه الإشاريّات السيميائية الأخرى[51]، كالفعل يُعرف، الذي تُفْتَتَحُ به هذه الحكاية، وكنية أبي القاسم، ولقب الطنبوري، إذ إنها جميعاً تسهم في تخليق مبدأ المركزيّةُ، وعليه فيمسي مبدأ مركزيّة الذات علامةً تميّز الطنبوريّ في مسارات هذه الحكاية[52]، وهنا يبدو الانفتاح المنهجيّ على مقولات النظرية السيميائيّة انفتاحاً بارزاً، يعضد مسارات التأويل، ويفتّق أكمامها.

وتنقدحُ إشاريّات أزمة المداس عند الطنبوريّ في ظِلال حديث السارد عن مداسه، الذي رُقعَ رُقعات كثيرة، حتى غدا ثقيلاً، ينوء به جَهْدُ حامله، يقول السارد: «وله مداس له مدة سنين كلما انقطع منه موضعٌ جعل عليه رقعةً إلى أن صار في غاية الثقل، وصار يُضرب به المثل، فيقال: أثقل من مداس

أبي القاسم الطنبوري»(53)، غير الإصرار على إصلاحه كلّ مرة، هو تدليلٌ على نسقيّة المواجهة، التي يتحلّى بها الطّنبوريّ في مواجهته مع أنساق الزّمن السالب، ويستغل عليمات الإشكاليّات العجائبية التي تحفُّ بالمداس، في نمذجته بوصفه نموذجاً إشهارياً(54)، يحقّق لصاحبه أبي القاسم شهرة تطبّق الآفاق، بوصفه علامة أو ماركة مسجلة، مفيداً من النظريات السيميائية، والإشهاريات الدلالية(55)، ويفيد الباحث من النظريات السرديّة ــ بصورةٍ ضمنيّة ــ في دراسة زمانيات القص/ السرد، أجْلَ الكشف عن أنساق هذه الحكاية، ذلك أن المسافة الزمنية التي لا تكاد تكون بين فِعْلِ الحكْي والدخول في مسارات السرد، تؤكّد عند عليمات أنّ السارد أراد أن يختصر الزمن في تخليق مبدأ المركزيّة الذي أشرتُ إليه آنفاً، ولعلّ هذا الاقتضاب ينطوي كذلك على فكرة الإسراع في الدخول إلى مباهج القص، إذ إنها تفصح عن بدء فعْل القصّ، وانفتاحه على ممكنات المتوقع واللامتوقع والمعقول والعجائبيّ(56)، خاصةً إذا قُرِأتْ هذه الحكاية في ضَوْء مرجعياتها العجائبيّة، إذ يمكن أن تكون العجائبيّة بما تنطوي عليه من مفارقاتٍ وكسرٍ لآفاق المتوقّع، هي السبب الرئيس في هذا الاقتضاب، ولعلّ السارد يغدو في ضَوْء ذلك راغباً في دخول القارئ إلى عوالم القصّ دون توطئة، وفي خلال هذا السياق يمكن الإشارة إلى ما تختزنه الذاكرة الشعبيّة حول محمولات الفعل حُكِيَ، بوصفه فعلاً تكثيفياً ينبني على أسٍ منها السرد العجائبي(57).

ولعلّ مردّ هذا الاقتضاب يرتدُّ كذلك إلى أنّ بنائية الحكاية العجائبية تختلف عن البنائية التي تحكم الأنواع السردية الأخرى، فالحكاية العجائبية غيرُ معنيّةٍ بتحقيق مبدأ المصداقيّة، الذي يضفيه السند المتواتر إلى السرديّات العربيّة، فهي تدخل في باب الإحماض، دون الخضوع لقوانين المنطق، وتشيعُ مصطلحات نظريّة التلقّي في هذه المقاربة؛ ممّا يؤكّد أنّ عليمات يجعل من النقد الأدبيّ شريكاً منهجياً لأدوات النقد الثقافيّ، وتضحى مصطلحات من قبيل: (التوقّع)، (الدهشة)، مصطلحاتٍ مركزيّة هنا.

ولعلّ الذي استجلبها هو العجائبية التي تظلّ تُكَسِّر آفاق المنتظر، دوران العِلّة مع المعلول، وفي ضَوْء ذلك يقول عليمات في مفتتح المقاربة: «حيث يحرص السارد المختلف على التوسّل بمنطق العجائبيّة لكي يفارق هذه التصورات الجمعيّة حول المداس، ويجابه ممارسات الوعي الجمعيّ بالدهشة الشاغلة والمغايرة للتوقعات»[58]، ويؤكد عليمات ذلك في قراءته للحَدَثِ الذي يجمعُ الطَّنبوري مع السماسرة، دون ذكر لأسمائهما، إذ يدلّ ذلك على أنّ السارد الممسك بإيقاعات السرد، كان يريد أن يصنع فرائدية للطنبوري[59]، ولعلّ هذا الحَدَثَ يشير كذلك من منظورٍ مختلفٍ إلى أنساق الحضور والغياب، وهي أنساق تمتدّ على امتداد هذه الحكاية، إذ إنّ أبا القاسم هو الشخصية الوحيدة التي يرسم السارد لها صورة مكتملة، في حين أنّه لا يقدّم غيرها سوى في صورةٍ ضبابيّة.

وإذا كان النقد الثقافيّ كما سبقت الإشارة مشغولاً بالصّراعات الطبقيّة، كما يقول عبدالعزيز حمودة، فإن هذه المقاربة تبدو على وَعْي بتجليات صراعات المجتمع، حين أشارت إلى أن ارتداء الطنبوريّ حذاءَ القاضي، وترك مداسه مكانه، يُسْفِرُ عن معالم النديّة، والصّراع الصريح، التي يعيشه الطنبوري مع السلطة، فهو يتجرّأ عليها دون أدنى خوف من انكشاف أمره[60].

ولعلّ ارتداء هذا المداس، عُقْبَ الاغتسال، الذي يمثّل الحدثَ التطهيريّ، يمكن أن يشي، بمنطق عليمات، بمحاولة التخلص من المداس، واستيلاد حياةٍ جديدة، مُفتتحها ارتداء حذاء القاضي/ المركز من لدن الطنبوري/ الهامش في الحكاية، وهو أوماً إليه عليمات سِراعاً دون أن يتلبّث عنده كثيراً، وإذا كان التأويل بوصفه فعلاً قرائياً، ينفتح على متعدّد القراءات، فيمكن أن يغدو هذا الحدثُ ذا دلالةٍ إشاريّةٍ، تشي بالرغبة في الانتقام من القاضي، الذي ظلّ يقسو على الطنبوريّ في أحكامه على امتداد مُجريات هذه الحكاية.

وتبدو الانكسارات التي يتلقاها الطنبوري في صراعه مع السلطة، والمجتمع، وخسارتها رهاناتها بصورة متنكرة، علامةً على العذابات التي تَلْقَاها الذّات في

سيرورتها الحياتيّة، في سبيل تحقيق ذاتها، على الرغم مما يحيط بها[61].

ويمضي عليمات في تتبع المسارات العجائبيّة التي ينتحيها المداس في عالم السرد، إذ تمثل تلك المسارات صورة من صور كسر آفاق التوقع التي بناها التسريد المتوقع لأحداث هذه الحكاية، ولا ريب أنّ وقوع المداس على امرأة حاملٍ بذكر، هو دليلٌ على إدراك السارد لأنساق الذكورة، والفحولة، التي تتكشف عن نسقيّة موقف الثقافة العربيّة من المرأة، فالفَحْلُ هو من يحظى في المأثور العربيّ بالحُبّ والقَبول، بخلاف الأنثى التي لا تحظى بذلك، وهنا يبدو أنّ أبا القاسم يحقق انتصاراً ضمنياً حين يقدم بدلاً من دية الذّكر دية عبد، على اعتبار أنه سيغدو ذكراً/ فحلاً في مستقبل الأيام[62]، وعليه فإن وعي عليمات بقيمة الفحولة في المخيال العربيّ الجمعيّ، وحضورها المُلغز في النصّ، هو محاولة لربط النص بالسياق الثقافيّ الذي أنتجه، بوصف هذا الربط، مبدأ من مبادئ القراءة الثقافيّة.

وتغدو هذه المقامة في ضَوْءِ القراءة الثقافيّة الفاحصة، كما يُسمّيها يُوسف عُليمات، مقامة ذات أبعاد دلاليّةٍ عميقةٍ، ورامزةٍ، ومُوحية، تستطلبُ قراءةً ثقافيّةً واعية بأبعادها السرديّة السيميائيّة /العلاماتية في سبيل الكشف عن تمظهرات النسق الثقافيّ في ثناياها؛ ذلك أنّ الخطاب السردي في هذه المقامة يمثل خطاباً مخاتلاً، يراوغ المتلقّي، ويشرح الواقع، ويؤسس كذلك لعالم المثال، الذي يتطلع إليه الهمذاني في ظلال علاقته المأزومة بمجتمعه.

ويمسي خُروج الهمذاني عن (النسق السجعيّ)، أو (الإيقاع السجعيّ) كما يسميه يُوسف عُليمات، في بادئ الأمر، رمزاً للتمرد، وعلامة دالة، تعمل على أن تأطر حياة الصعلوك، الذي يمثل قناعاً للهمذانيّ كما أشرت سابقاً، «فقد جاء غياب الإيقاعات السجعية منسجماً، والحال هذه، مع موتيف الصّعلكة الذي تتمحور حوله المقامة»[63].

ويقدح حديث عليمات عن مسألة خرق الهمذاني (النسق السجعيّ) في الذهن

نار التذكار للإلماعة التي قدمها الغذامي في قراءته لهذه المقامة في منتصف التسعينيات من القرن المنصرم[64]، فقد أشار الغذامي إلى أن هذه المقامة تكاد تكون غير مسجوعة، ذلك أن «أول ما نلحظه على هذه المقامة هو تراجع السجع فيها، حتى لكأنَّها غير مسجوعة، لقد طغى السرد فيها على الإيقاع، ولعل هذه المقامة من ضمن المقامات المُرتجلة»[65].

وتشيعُ مصطلحات نظريّة التلقّي في هذه المقاربة ممّا يؤكّد أنّ عليمات يجعل من النقد الأدبيّ شريكاً منهجياً لأدوات النقد الثقافيّ، وتمثل مصطلحات من قبيل التوقع، الدهشة، كسر المتوقع، جماليات القص، السرد، يقول عليمات في مفتتح المقاربة: «وأما التشكيل الداخليّ للمقامة فإنه يخيّب توقعات المتلقّي، ويثير دهشته»[66]، ويقولُ في موضع آخر: «إذن نتوقع من بديع الزمان الهمذاني أن يجعل المقامة البشرية نصّاً للدهشة والمتعة بحيث تتأسس على أحداث غير متوقعة»[67].

ويبدو يُوسف عُليمات في قراءته لمقامة البشرية على وعي بضرورة جلاء الأبعاد السيميائيّة التي تشي بها اختيارتُ الهمذاني في بناء مقامته هذه، عنواناً وشخوصاً وسنداً ومتناً، إذ يؤكد عليمات أن اختيار الهمذاني (المقامة البِشريّة)؛ اسماً لهذه المقامة، يحفلُ بعلامات سيميائيّة رامزة، تشير إلى أنّ «خاصية البِشْر: السعادة تبدو مركزيّة في أحداث المقامة مفتتحاً ومنتهى»[68]، ويتحدّث عليمات عن (الدلالة السيميائية) التي تستدعيها القاصة، التي تمثل في السرد العربيّ القديم، لازمة تكراريّة، تُؤطر (مسارات السرد)، وثم تقوده إلى مباهج القص، ومفاتنه، إذ إنها « تفصح في جوهرها عن تصوّرات وتجلّيات لكينونة الحدث، ومن ثم عجائبيته»[69]، ويشيرُ يُوسف عُليمات إلى أنّ راوي المقامة وبطلها (عيسى بن هشام) الذي اختاره الهمذانيّ، على أنّ عليمات يهملُ الأبعاد السيميائية التي يحفل بها النظام الإخباريّ / السندي، الذي تنماز بها المقامة، إذ يستدعي اسم الراوي عيسى بن هشام اسماً برز في القص السيري في السيرة

النبوية، وهو عيسى بن هشام صاحب السيرة، ولذا فإن هذا النظام السنديّ ينتمي إلى علم الحديث النبوي الشريف، مما يضفي إلى المقامة بعداً دينياً توثيقياً.

– الطنبوريّ وبِشْر والهمذاني وابن حجة وأزمة المثقّف:

لا ريب أنّ العالَم الذي يؤسس له الطنبوري يتأطّر في سياق عالم جديد، أو رؤية مختلفة للكون، يصنعها بواسطة قناعه/ المداس، وذلك من خلال الاستناد إلى ثقافة القوّة والفحولة ومركزيّة الذات، في سبيل إنجاز تحقق فِعْليّ وفاعل للذات، التي تعاني من إشكالية المناصرة والمعاصرة، إذا أسلمنا بقولةِ عليمات بوشائج الاتّصال بين ابن حِجّة الحمويّ، صاحب كتاب ثمرات الأوراق والطنبوري، إذ يغدو توظيف قناع الطنبوري من لدن ابن حجّة الحمويّ تعبيراً عن تجربة الذّات، ومعاناتها في الوجود[70].

وإذا كان النقد الثقافيّ قد أعاد للمؤلف بعضاً من سلطته فإن ذلك تبدى في هذه المقاربة، إذ تبيّن لعليمات بعد بحثه في سيرة ابن حِجّة أنّه كان مرفوضاً في مجتمعه، حيث جعل عليمات ذلك أحد أركان العملية التأويلية لديه.

ولعل دراسة معمقة لسيرة ابن حجة تقف على صحة هذا الرأي، ولعلّ عليمات يرى أنّ الحكايات التي يحتويها كتاب ابن حجّة بوصفه مصنِّفاً لا مؤلّفاً تمثل إرهاصاتٍ للتوجه الفكريّ، وعليه فإنّ التوجه التأويليّ الذي سلكه عليمات يمكن أن يكون متقبّلاً إذا أسلمنا بقولة أبي تمام بأنّ اختيار المرء قطعة من عقله وقلبه، وعليه فيغدو اختيار ابن حِجّة لحكاية الطنبوريّ اختياراً واعياً ومقصوداً، وجماع القول إنّ حكاية الطنبوريّ تغدو في محصِّلَةِ الأمر حكايةً إيديولوجيّة، في أتون صراع مجتمعيّ لاهب.

وفي ضَوْءِ هذا الطرح؛ تعكس المقامة موقف المجتمع من الهمذاني، الذي يشابه موقف القبيلة من الصعلوك، إذ يغدو بِشْر الصعلوك، في ظلال تمرده،

وخروج عن أنساق القبيلة، ذلك أن «بِشْر قناع الهمذانيّ الذي يبدو في رؤية المرأة نسقاً ثورياً فوضوياً، وهامشياً ينذرُ بالخطر والموت»[71].

إن هذا العالم الذي يؤسس له الهمذاني عالم جديد، أو رؤية مختلفة للكون، يصنعها بواسطة قناعه الصعلوك، من خلال الاستناد إلى ثقافة القوة والفحولة ومركزية الذات، في سبيل إنجاز تحقق فِعْليّ وفاعل للذات، التي تعاني من إشكالية المناصرة والمعاصرة، ولعل هذا ما أشارت إليه سرديّات وأخبار كثيرة متواترة عن موقف الهمذاني من مجتمعه، أو موقف مجتمعه منه[72].

ويشير عليمات إلى أنّ (بِشْراً) في هذه المقامة يرنو نحو تشييد عالم إنساني تجسّده قيمة الصَّعلكة، في سبيل تأكيد قوة الذّات، ومنعتها، وقدرتها على الفاعلية والإنجاز، وتأسيس كينونة الذّات المضادة.

ولا ريب أن احتفاء الهمذاني بالخطاب الشعري على لسان (بِشْر)، يشي ضمناً بمركزية هذه الذات، ومحوريتها، في سياق صراعها مع المجتمع من حولها، وهو ما أومأ إليه عليمات، فالخطاب الشعري العربيّ، يتسم بثيمة الخطابية أو الغنائية، ويعبر في أغلبه عن تجربة الذّات، ومعاناتها في الوجود.

ويرى عليمات أنّ هذه المقامة تنقام على تناصيّة، يتناصّ فيها موقف الهمذاني الذي يمثله بشر من مجتمعه، بموقف الشاعر الجاهلي الصعلوك من مجتمعه، وكذلك فإن الغواية السردية التي تستخدمها المرأة التي يتزوجها بشر بعد أن يُغير على ركب قومها، تتصادى مع الغواية الأنثويّة، التي تتكئ إليها في ألف ليلة وليلة[73].

ويتحدّث عليمات عن (مخاتلات القصّ الأنثوي)[74]، التي تتكئ إليها المرأة في هذه المقامة، في محاولة منها للإيقاع بالصعلوك بشر في حبائل الغواية السرديّة، ومن ثم الرمي به إلى حتفه، فالمرأة، تبدو وفقاً لـ عليمات، على وعي بمركزية قانون الاستحواذ الذي يسيطر على بشر، مما يجعلها تفيد من ذلك

في عملية الإيقاع به، إذ تقصُّ عليه خبر ابنة عمه، التي يغدو بشر، كما تومئ زوجته، هو الأحق من غيره بالظفر بها[75].

وتضمرُ هذه الحواريّة الأنثويّة مع بشر أنساقاً مضادّةً تسفرُ عن نسقية موقف المرأة، التي تمثل صوت المجتمع، من زوجها بِشر، الذي يتصف بالغباء، والعماء، والسواد، كما تعبر مضمرات الخطاب في حواريتها معه[76].

ولعل تأويل عليمات لبعض أجزاء هذه الحواريّة التي قامت بين بشر وزوجته، يتسم بما يمكن أن يتسمى بالتأويل المفتوح، إذ ليس شرطاً أن يكون حديث المرأة عن قيمة البياض، التي تنماز بها المرأة التي تصفها زوجة بشر له، في هذا السياق، نوعاً من القَدْحِ في سواد الصعلوك بشر، إنّما ربما أن يقرأ في ضوء تأويلي آخر، هو تعزيز لِخِطاب الإغواء، الذي تغري به المرأة زوجها للذّهاب والزّواج بالمرأة الأخرى، وهو ما وعاه عليمات لكن لم يتلبث عنده كثيراً.

لقد وعى عليمات أن مخاتلات القص أضمرت فعلاً إغوائياً لبشر، وهو ما مثّل مرتعاً خضباً خاض عليمات في تجلية أبعاده، واستثمار بنائية هذه الحوارية، في الكشف عن أساليب بنائية هذا الخطاب الحجاجيّ.

ويغدو قتل الأسد والأفعى لدى عليمات، تجلياً من تجلّيات الذّات الفاعلة، وانتصاراً من لدن الهمذاني لبشر بن عوانة، بطل المقامة الذي يمثل ثقافة الصّعلكة، ومعتقداتها، في قبالة ثقافة القبيلة، التي أرادت الإيقاع به، والتخلص منه، من خلال اشتراطها عليه إن ما رام تزوّج ابنتها[77]، أن يمهرها خمسين ناقة من نوق خزاعة، بغية الدفع به إلى الوقوع في قبضة الأسد والأفعى وهو في طريقه إلى ديار خزاعة، ومن ثم التخلص منه، إذ يمثل الأسد والأفعى وحشين خرافيين وفتاكين في المخيال الجمعيّ العربيّ[78].

وتشير ولادة الفتى الأمرد امتداداً لتجربة الصعلكة، وكسراً لآفاق التوقع[79]، وينتهي عليمات في مختتم دراسته هذه إلى أنّ (المقامة البِشريّة) عند الهمذاني،

هي مقامة إيديولوجية؛ تجلّي صراعات الهيمنة، وتمثيلات الآخر، وإشكالات الهُويّة، في أتون صراع الهمذاني ومجتمعه.

إن بزوغ هذا الفتى الأمرد وظهوره على عالم السرد يمثل صورة أخرى من صور كسر آفاق التوقع التي بناها التسريد المتوقع لأحداث المقامة، وهو ما أومأ إليه عليمات سِراعاً[80]، على أنّ هذا الانبعاث حقق فعلاً انتصاراً حقيقياً في إعادة بناء هذه المقامة ومساراتها السردية.

ولا ريب أنّ ثمّة تقاطعات واضحةً بين المنهجيّة التي تناولها عليمات في قراءة المقامة البِشْرية من منظور النقد الثقافيّ، المنهجيّة التي تحكم تناولها من منظور المدرسيّات النقديّة التقليدية[81]، كالنقد الاجتماعي[82]، والنظرية الحجاجية[83] وغيرها، ذلك أن مقاربة عليمات تتشابه مع هذه المقاربات في نظرها إلى المقامة بوصفها نصاً ثقافياً اجتماعيّاً، يعكس صراعات المجتمع، فضلاً عن تسليمها بأن الخطاب الذي تتضمنه (المقامة البِشريّة (مشحونٌ بالمحمول الحجاجيّ التداولي، الذي يحفز على الحجاج والإقناع).

2 – 4 – مصطفى الغرافي: القراءة الثقافيّة وتمثيلات القارئ الضمنيّ:

– تعرية النسق المضمر والمؤلّف الضمنيّ:

يمثل إحياء المؤلف والكشف عن الأنساق المضمرة استراتيجيّات المقاربة النقديّة اللتين تؤطران فِعْلَ القراءة النقديّة في مقاربة الغرافي، إذ يغدو بناء الجهاز المفاهيميّ للمقاربة على مقولات النقد الثقافيّ وممكنات نظرية التلقّي اختياراً منهجيّاً يسفر عن أهمية الائتلاف المنهجيّ في إنجاز قراءة ناجزة، ولا ريب أنّ مفهوم سلطة المؤلّف يمثّل مفهوماً مركزياً في هذه المقاربة، فالغرافيُّ يسلِّم برسوخ سُلطة ابن قتيبة في بِنية أخباره، ولذا فإنه لا بدّ من قراءة هذه الأخبار قراءةً لا تُغْفِلُ سُلطة صاحبها من منظوره.

ويبدو الطرح السابق عند الغرافيّ مؤيَّداً بمقاربة إبراهيم صحراوي، الذي يرى أن كثيراً من كتب الأخبار، تؤدي وظائف أيديولوجية معيّنة، يرومها المصنِّفُ لهذه المدونات، ذلك «أنها بقدر ما تأتي عفويّة في مؤلفات ما لشرحٍ أو تبريرٍ أو إثبات شاهد، بقدر ما تكون متوخاة لذاتها، أي واردة في الكتاب عمداً، وعن سابق إصرار»[84]، ولعلّه من اللافت للنظر أنّ الغرافي أنجز عدداً من المقاربات التي تتمحور حول البنى السرديّة والثقافيّة في أخبار ابن قتيبة، بصورة شكّلت خلالها هذه الأخبار بالنسبة إليه خطاباً سردياً منمازاً، يسترعي المساءلة في إطار مشروع نقديّ متكامل[85]، وفي هذا السياق يذهب الغرافيّ إلى أنّ ابن قتيبة قد استخدم في سرديّاته في بثّ أنساقه، ذلك أن أخباره التي ضمنها (عيون الأخبار) جاءت محمّلة بالأنساق التي تسعى إلى ترسيخ أنساق السنة قبالة أنساق المذاهب الأخرى[86].

– الغرافيّ وتمثيلات القارئ الضمني:

يفيد الغرافيّ من مفهوم (القارئ الضمنيّ) (Implied reader) كما تنمذجه نظريات التلقّي، ذلك «أن نصوص الخبر مثّلت إطاراً سرديّاً استثمره ابن قتيبة من أجل توصيل رسالته إلى القارئ المفترض على نحو ضمنيّ»[87]، على اعتبار أنه قارئ ضمنيّ يستطيع أن يفهم شِيفرات النصّ ورسائل مؤلفه، من خلال «تسليط الضَوْء على ما لم يقدر المؤلف على قوله أو لم يشأه، والذي يفصح عنه النصّ»[88].

ولذا فإنّ الغرافي يرى أنّ توجيه مسالك البحث ينبغي أن يكون في اتجاه السياق الذي انتُجت هذه الأخبار في سياقه، يقول الغرافي: «لأجل ذلك نعتقد أنّ قراءة أخبار ابن قتيبة، في ضَوْء الموجهات الفكريّة، والمرجعيات الثقافيّة المضمرة التي تحكمت في إنجازها وصياغتها، تسمح باستخلاص أبرز الغايات التي يُراد تحقيقها»[89]، ويحاول الغرافيُّ أن يستخلصَ من بعض الأخبار الواردة

عند ابن قتيبة مضمراتها النسقيّة التي تشي برغبةٍ مقصودةٍ لديه في بثّ أنساق الخطاب السنّي [90]، في مقابل النيل من الأنساق التي تتبناها الفرق الإسلاميّة الأخرى، إذ «مثلت العقيدة السنّية مرجع ابن قتيبة» [91].

وعليه فتغدو هذه الأخبار السرديّة التي ساقها (ابن قتيبة) أخباراً أو سرديّات محملةً بالخطاب بالأيديولوجيّ الذي يشتبكُ فيه الديني بالسياسيّ، بصورة تعكس ضديّة الصراع بينهما، ومركزيّة الذّات في ظلال هامشيّة الآخر عند أصحاب المذاهب الإسلامية الأخرى من مثل: (الخوارج) و(المعتزلة) [92]، ولكنّ الإشكاليّة الكُبرى التي تتمثّل في هذه المقاربة تبرز في تماثل الأنساق المضمرة في جُلِّ الأخبار التي يوردها ابن قتيبة كما يرى الغرافيّ، وهو نسق السنة أو نسق الانتصار للسُنة.

وقد غاب عن الغرافيّ أنّ هذا النسق قد تفرع منه أنساق أخرى، ويعكس خبر المدائني الذي رأى رجلاً يركب بغلته في الصّفا والمروة، وينتهي به الأمر راجلاً في سفره، حيث ينبغي أن يركب، تمثيلاتِ العقاب، التي يُنْزِلُها الله تعالى بمن يخالف أمره [93]، ولا ريب أنّ هذه القراءة قراءةٌ مُتاحة للقارئ ما دامت منضبطة بشروط التأويل، ومسالكه الكبرى، إلّا أن القول بإضماريتها نسق العبادة، الذي يرى الغرافي أنّ هذا الخبر يبثه بطريقة مخاتلة، يمثل رأياً سطحياً، فهذا النسق يمكن أن تكشفه القراءة المباشرة لهذا الخبر، وفي هذا السياق ينتخب الغرافي سروداً أخرى تعكسُ عن موقفٍ مُعادٍ لأبناء الفرق الإسلاميّة الأخرى [94]، وذلك ما تجسّده رواية رجلٍ سأل هشام بن الحكم، هل يعذبنا الله تعالى بما لا نستطيع له صبراً، فيكون ردُّ هشام: «قد والله فعل، ولكننا لا نستطيع أن نتكلم» [95]، إذ يتضمن هذا الخبر أنساقاً وإشارات مخصوصة.

ـ إشكاليّة السند بين الغياب وصناعة النسق:

تنماز أخبار ابن قتيبة بميزة لم ينبه الغرافي إليها، وتتمثل في غياب الراوي،

أو غياب سلسلة الإسناد، مما يعني انفتاح الخبر على عالم الإضافة والتغيير، وهي ثيمةٌ يبدو ابن قتيبة على وعي بها، إذ يغدو غياب الراوي في أغلب أخباره ذريعةً يتخذها الدينوريّ لترسيخ أنساق الجماعة السنية، من خلال ممارسة فعل التعمية على القارئ، وذلك بإيقاعه في إشكالية المؤلف والمصنف التي خلَّفها غياب الراوي، ويتجلى ذلك ابتداءً في هذه الأخبار من خلال اللوازم التكرارية، من مثل: (يروى)، (حكي)، التي تجعل القارئ يتخذ منها موقف المُصدّق المُقرّ، وتبدو الإلمعات التي قدمها محمد القاضي حول إشكاليّة المؤلَّف والمصنَّف على تماس بالأنساق الثقافيّة التي تتضمنها هذه الأخبار من ناحية، وبموجّهات رِوايتها من ناحية أخرى [96].

وحريٌّ الإلماع إلى أنّ إشكاليّة المؤلِّف والمصنِّف تلازمت مَعَ مسألة الرواية أو سلسلة الإسناد في السرديّات العربيّة القديمة بوصفها مسألة معقّدة، تنطوي على أنساق متعددة، ومنها: (الصّدق)، و(الكذب)، و(الترميز)، و(التعمية)، وهي بحاجة إلى فضل بحثٍ ومدارسة، تنضاف إلى الجهود التي قدمها عددٌ من المنشغلين بالسرديّات العربيّة القديمة، ذلك أن غياب الراوي، وإشكاليّة المؤلِّف والمصنِّف، والربط بينهما كان يمكن أن يُفْرِزَ كشوفاً تأويلية غابت عن هذه المقاربة، ويغدو انتخابُ ابن قتيبة لكبراء الفرق الأخرى مثل (هشام بن الحكم) اختياراً واعياً يَهْدِفُ من ورائه للتشنيع عليها، من خلال وَضْعها في مواقفَ محرجة، تكشف عن زيف عِلْمها، وبطلان مذهبها، وذلك «عن طريق وضعها في موقف حرج يبدو أنه فُرِضَ عليها» [97]، غير أنّ هذا الانتخاب بلغة النقد الثقافيّ يضمر كذلك استناداً إلى مخاتلات النسق، نسق الانكسار لنسق السلطة، أو النسق النموذج، وهو الوجه الآخر الذي لم ينبه إليه الغرافي أو لم يتكشّفه.

وعليه فإنّ هذه الشخصيات تكونُ مُجبرةً على الإجابة عن هذه السؤالات، خشية أن تُعيّر بالعي والحُبْسة، التي ترفضُها وتُعيبها (ثقافة الفحولة) في الثقافة العربيّة، مما يمثل فرصةً سانحةً أمام ابن قتيبة لتصوير هذه الشخصيات في مواقفَ ضعيفة، تتكشفُ عن كساد بضاعتها الفكريّة، وضلال منهجها العَقَديّ [98].

- صناعة النسق بين الإضحاك والحجاج:

يلمعُ الغرافيّ إلى أنّ ابن قتيبة قد آثَرَ أن يلبسُ خطابه السرديّ في عيون الأخبار لَبوس الهَزْل، لتمرير أنساقه المضادّة، التي تتضادُ مع أنساق المذاهب الإسلامية الأخرى، ذلك أنّه تعمّد أن يكون الإضحاك ثيمة مركزيّة في كثير من الأخبار التي ساقها؛ بغية الطعن في هذه المذاهب، والنيل منها، ومن أعلامها؛ تبياناً لفسادها، وضلالها، ويرى الغرافيُّ في سياق ذلك أنّ الخبر الذي يورده (ابن قتيبة)، ويروي فيه استقبال الخوارج لابن عرياض اليهوديّ يدخل في حيز ذلك[99].

إنّ ابن قتيبة يسعى من خلال الخبر السرديّ الذي يرتكز على فكرة الإمتاع والإضحاك، على «إثارة سخرية قارئه من الخوارج الذين يفهمون الدين فهماً خاصاً ينطلقون فيه من فهم النص فهماً حرفياً يثير السخرية»[100]، بيد أن الذي لم يتفطّن إليه الغرافيّ أنّ الخوارج ليسوا حرفيين حرفية مطلقة، بل هم أهل تأويل، يعلون من شأنه، ويجعلونه مبدأ من مبادئهم، وعليه فقد تمثل (ابن قتيبة) في اختياره، إذا أسلمنا بأنه مؤلّف هذه السرديّات ثقافة الانتخاب، وهو ما لم يشر إليه الغرافي، التي يمكن أن تقرأ وفقاً للمعطيات التي تطرحها جماليات التحليل الثقافيّ، أو التاريخانية الجديدة (New Historicism)، التي تبحث في الأنساق المضمرة التي يضمرها الخطاب، في ظلال تزيّنه بالبلاغيّ الجماليّ، واستعانته بفتنة السرد أو غوايته.

وتضمر الأخبار التي رواها ابن قتيبة عن سخريّة الجاحظ من المعتزلة أنساق التبكيت، أو أنساق الفاعليّة والقدرة، وهي أنساق تحفل بها هذه الأخبار، فقد بدا أنّ ابن قتيبة كان ذكياً حين روى أخباراً تسخر من المعتزلة عن طريق الجاحظ بوصفه أحد كبرائهم، ذلك أنّ الاستهزاء بهم من خلال مرجعيّة من مرجعياتهم، يكون أوجع، وأفدح، وأكثر إيلاماً[101]، ويبدو أنّه غاب عن الغرافيّ أن هذه الأخبار يمكن ألا تضمر عداءً من لدن الجاحظ تجاه المعتزلة، إذ قد يغدو

ذلك بتراً للنص عن سياقه، ولكنها يمكن أن تقرأ في سياق المنافسة التي كانت على أوجها بين أقطاب المعتزلة فيما بينهم.

وإذا كان النسق الثقافيّ يرسخ نفسه أو يسعى إلى ذلك بالحجاج، فقد أشارت هذه المقاربة إلى المحمولات الحجاجيّة التي تضمرها أخبار (ابن قتيبة) في محاجّة الإنسان الآخر، والتغلّب عليه، حيث «تحوّلت الأخبار عند ابن قتيبة إلى حجج سردية تنطوي على مقصدية صريحة أو ضمنية؛ إنّها وضعيات تواصليّة تتوسّل بالخطاب السرديّ من أجل توصيل رسائل المؤلّف إلى القارئ»[102]، ولا ريب أنّ مقاربة الغرافي هذه لا تتقاطع مع منجز النقد الأدبيّ الذي خصص لقراءة الخطاب السردي في عيون الأخبار لابن قتيبة، فقد ظلت تلك الدراسات تقرأ الخطاب السردي بوصفه تشكيلاً فنياً يتكون من بنى سرديّة[103]، وإن كانت أشارت إلى سُنّيّة الخطاب السرديّ عند ابن قتيبة.

3 – 4 – مُعجِب العدواني: من القراءة الثقافيّة إلى التناصيّة الثقافيّة:

ـ التناصيّة الثقافيّة بوصفها استراتيجيّة قرائية:

تمثل القراءة التناصيّة الثقافيّة والكشف عن الأنساق المضمرة استراتيجيّات المقاربة النقديّة اللتين تؤطّران فِعْلَ القراءة النقديّة في مقاربة العدوانيّ، إذ يغدو بناء الجهاز المفاهيميّ للمقاربة على مقولات النقد الثقافيّ وممكنات نظريّة التناصيّة دالاً وشاهداً على ذلك، ويرى العدواني أنّ القراءة التناصيّة الثقافيّة هي تمثيلٌ من تمثيلات الانفتاح بالتناص على الدراسات الثقافيّة، ودَرْسِ علاقات التأثر والتأثير بين النصوص، وَفْقاً لمعطيات هذه المناهج، التي تهتم بمساءلة خطابات الهيمنة، وآليات التمثيل.

وتسير مقاربة العدواني في اتجاهين اثنين، أما أحدهما فيمارس فعل القراءة الثقافيّة كما تقررت عند أغلب المنشغلين بالنقد الثقافيّ ــ شرقاً ومغرباً ـ، وأما

الآخر فيدرس تمثيلات العربيّ في مرايا الآخر كما تتجلى في رواية (أكلة الموتى) (Eaters of The Dead) لمايكل كرايتون (Michael Crichton)، والفيلم السينمائي (المُحارب الثالث عشر)[104].

وبذا فإنّ العدواني يقترحُ إعادة تشييد مفهوم جديدٍ للتناص، يهدم التصور المنهجيّ الرائج له في النقد العربيّ، إذ يبدو أن التناص نوعٌ من سجالات التأثر والتأثير، ولكن ليس بالمفهوم الذي أسست له جوليا كرستيفا (Julia Kristeva)، وإنما بوصفه مفهوماً يدلُّ على العلاقة الوثيقة بين سياقات الهيمنة، وأسئلة الآخريّة.

ويستشفُّ من مقاربة العدوانيّ أنّ التناص بين النصوص يظلّ تحققه موقوفاً أو مشروطاً بالشمول والقصدية، إذ إنّ التناص يكون في المواقف الأيديولوجيّة، والبنى النصية الكاملة، لا في تشابهٍ بين كلماتٍ أو عباراتٍ بين نصين، وثانياً بأنّ استخدامه يكون استخداماً واعياً، وهو ما يظهر جليّاً في رواية (أكلة الموتى)، والفيلم السينمائي (المحارب الثالث عشر)[105]، ولا ريب أنّ التناصية الثقافيّة بمفهومها العام تتناغم مع مفهوم توظيف التراث في الأدب أو استدعاء التجربّة... إلخ، وكلُّها عناوين رائجة في الأطاريح الجامعيّة، والبحث الأكاديميّ، ولكن اشتراكها الممنهج مع الدراسات الثقافيّة، والنقد الثقافيّ كما يريد العدواني يمثل موطن الجدة والتجديد في مقاربته.

وإذا كان النقد الثقافيّ (Cultural Criticism)، والدراسات النسوية أو النقد النسويّ (Feminist Criticism)[106]، والقراءة الطّباقيّة (Contrapuntal Reading)[107] تنجدلُ بأربطة وثيقة العُرى، فإنّ ذلك لا ينفي أنّ بينها فروقاتٍ بائنات، هي أدعى إلى أن يختار الباحث من بينها الحقل المعرفيّ الذي يتواءم مع مقاربته ومرومها[108].

وتشبه أن تكون دعوة العدواني إلى القراءة التناصيّة الثقافيّة قريبةً إلى

الإنطواء في سياقات الأدب/ النقد المقارِن، إذ يمكن تفعيل هذه المفاهيم في تكوين جهاز منهجيّ يعمل على قراءة طرائق هيمنة الهيمنة الثقافيّة، بين الشعوب والأمم المختلفة، عن طريق النصوص الأدبيّة[109].

ـ تحيُّزات الأنا وسُلطة التمثيل:

تتجلّى في السرد الرحليّ في رسالة ابن فضلان كما يرى العدوانيّ منظومة من أنساق التعالي والتفوّق والفحولة، إذ يبدو العربيّ الناظر إلى الآخر من منظور المركزيّة الإسلامية، كما يعبّر ذلك عبدالله إبراهيم، هو المركز[110]، في حين يغدو الآخر دونياً، وقذراً، وأقلّ قدراً ومنزلة، وهو ما ينعكس في تمثيلات صورة العربيّ في رواية (أكلة الموتى) وفيلم (المحارب الثالث عشر) اللذين يتناصان مع رسالة ابن فضلان.

إنّ رحلة ابن فضلان تغدو بفعل القراءة الفاحصة خطاباً سردياً مُفعماً بالشيفرات النسقيّة والمحمولات الإيديولوجيّة، والمرجعيّات الفكريّة، إذ تتكشفُ هذه الرحلة عن تحيزّات الثقافة العربيّة أو تحيزات الذات العربيّة تُجاه الآخر فقد «بالغ ابن فضلان في إضفاء أوصاف أو تعليقاتٍ مجانبةٍ لما يراه، ليعبّر فيها عن تصوّره لهم...»[111]، وتنقدح شرارة التحيُّز الخفي/ المضمر في الرحلة بدءاً بتصوير الآخر في هذه الرحلة، إذ إنّ ابن فضلان ينظر إلى الآخر من منظور الذات، أو بمعايير الذات، وشرطها التاريخيّ في تلك اللحظة، مما يحدو به إلى التعبير «عن دهشته من عادات تلك الأمم وطقوسهم (...)، إذ كان كثيراً ما يعبر عن دهشته من عادات تلك الأمم، بل يعلن تذمره منها أحياناً»[112]، وذلك في كثيرٍ من المقاطع السرديّة في رحلته، إذ يمثل العدواني لذلك بوصف ابن فضلان للترك بأنهم: «هم كالحمير الضالّة، لأنهم لا يدينون بدين، إذ مرّ بقومٍ من الأتراك يسمون بالغزية، وإذا هم بادية، لهم بيوت شعر، يحلون ويرتحلون...»[113]، وفي قوله: «وكانوا إذا مات أحدهم حفروا له حفرةً كالبيت وجعلوه فيها مع ماله»[114].

وتتجلى أنساق مركزيّة الذّات وتحيُّزاتها من منظور العدوانيّ في الشكل الأدبيّ الذي اختاره ابن فضلان لرحلته، إذ إنّ العدواني يؤكد أنّ ابن فضلان اختار وصف البلاد التي زارها، في قالب سردي تقريريّ، لأنها لا تملك فكراً وثقافة ومعتقداتٍ، تستحقُّ أن تفرّغ في شكل سردي ذي لغة أدبية عالية.

وذلك يكشف كما يرى العدواني عن أنساق الثقافة الفحوليّة المركزيّة، وعليه فإن هذا التحيز يتمظهر باختيار الرسالة لتكون حاضناً أو وعاءً للخطاب السردي «ويتجسد هذا في اعتماد ابن فضلان في ذلك على صيغتين تتكرران كثيراً في رسالته: الأولى صيغة (رأيت) وفيها يعبّر عن مشاهداته الشخصية، أما الثانية فهي رسم، وهي مفردة قديمة تعني صورة، وتتكرر في أشكال نحو ورسم ذلك»[115]، ومن ذلك قول ابن فضلان: «وكذلك الرسم، لا يمد أحد يده إلى الأكل حتى يناوله الملك لقمة»[116]، وكذلك في قوله: «ومن رسم ملك الروس أن يكون معه في قصره أربعمائة رجل من صناديد عصره...»[117]، ولعلّ هذا النسق أو التحيز الذي يشير إليه العدواني يظلّ محلّ نظر ومناقشة، ذلك أنّ هذا التأويل ينطوي على غير قليل من المغالاة، خصوصاً أنّه لا شيء يعضد ذلك في النص الفضلانيّ.

وإذا كانت اللغة التقريريّة هي دافعَ العدواني لهذا القول فإنّ الخطاب الرحليّ في الثقافة العربيّة يكاد يكون ذا سمتٍ بنائي وأسلوبي واحد مطّرد، يتطرد في أغلب هذه الرحلات/ السرديّات، بيد أنه ليس بالضرورة أن يعبر عن تحيّزات أو مضمرات نسقيّة، ولا شية في أن العدواني يصدر في رأيه هذا عن تأثُّر جليّ بقولةٍ لسامي الدهان محقّق هذه الرسالة، الذي رأى أنّ رحلة ابن فضلان هي مثالٌ لكتابة التقارير[118].

ومن الجلي أن العدواني لم يلتفت إلى أن الدهان عاد فعَدَلَ عن تبنيه لهذا الرأي بكلّيته، وذلك بقوله: «والعجبُ أشدُّ العجب في هذه الرسالة، يخطها رجل فقيه، فيجيد في الوصف على أروع ما يجوّد فيه الأدباء (...) فيقرّ بنا من

المشاهد التي رأى تقريب أديب أريب لا فقيه مبشّر، ولولا أنه ذكر مهمّته، وألحّ على بيانها، وأكثر من النصح والنهي والأمر، لسلكناه في الأدباء والقصاصين، لبراعة قلمه، وحُسْنِ بيانه...»⁽¹¹⁹⁾، وإذا المكان على ارتباط وثيقٍ بأهله، فإن العدواني يرى أن أنساق التحيّز في هذه المقاربة تستعلن في الوصف الجغرافي عند ابن فضلان، إذ إنّها «معتمدة على ذكر الأماكن ورسم خطة السير التي تمر بلاد: الأتراك، الصقالبة، الروس، الخزر، وما تبعها من ذكر أسماء للمدن»⁽¹²⁰⁾، ولا ريب في الإشارة إلى أن العدوانيّ لا يكشف في مقاربته هذه عن تجلّيات هذا التحيّز، أو أنساقه.

ــ تحيُّزات الآخر وانقلاب التمثيل:

لا تتوقف المقاربة ـ كما أشرت ـ عند تمثيلات الآخر وأنساق الذات في رحلة ابن فضلان، ذلك أنها تجلي سياقات الاختلاف بين المحمولات الأيديولوجية والتمثيلات النمطيّة بينها وبين رواية (أكلة الموتى) لمايكل كرايتون، والفيلم السينمائي (المحارب الثالث عشر)⁽¹²¹⁾.

وتأسيساً عليه فإنّ العدواني يبحث في تمثيلات العربيّ في هذين العملين⁽¹²²⁾، التي تبدو متسقةً مع الصورة النمطية للغربي في المخيال العربيّ، بل متطابقة مع الاستيهام الغربي تجاه العربيّ، الذي جَلاه إدوارد سعيد في كتابه (الاستشراق)⁽¹²³⁾، الذي بيّن خلاله أن قُصاراه هو تصوير العربيّ جاهلاً متخلّفاً، هائماً بالمرأة والمتع الحسيّة⁽¹²⁴⁾، وتبدو صورة العرب في رواية (أكلة الموتى) صورة متحيزة كذلك، إذ إنّ العرب كما يرد في الرواية: «وحشيون، دائماً يتذمرون، ولا شيءَ مبهجاً في عيونهم»⁽¹²⁵⁾، ويمسي افتتاح فيلم (المحارب الثالث عشر) بالمرأة والشعْر مرتبطاً بمحمولاتٍ مضمرة، تعكس صورة العربيّ في المخيال الغربيّ، إذ إن موتيفَي (المرأة والشعْر) يغدوان علامتين على الأمة العربيّة، بوصفها أمّة مولهة بالنساء، إذ «تَظهر فيه الصورة الاستشراقيّة

الاستهلاكيّة والمتخيّلة عن الثقافة العربيّة: نقاب، فتنة»(126) وأما من ناحية أخرى فإنها تبدو أمة قول لا فعل؛ لأنها أمة شاعرة أو قل: أمة شِعر، تقدّس ثقافة القول، وتفضّلها على ثقافة العمل.

وتتجلى تحيُّزات (التحيز في تشكيل الجنس الأدبيّ) في رواية (أكلة الموتى)، والفيلم السينمائي (المحارِب الثالث عشر) من خلال اختيار الرواية والفيلم بوصفهما نوعين فنيين يملكان حضوراً مركزيّاً في المجتمعات الغربية «فالرواية الجنسُ الأدبيُّ الغربيُّ المعبِّر عن الحضارة الغربيّة بامتياز، وهي الجنس الأقدر على التهام ما سِواه من نصوص سرديّة»(127)، أما الفيلم فإنّه من وجهة نظر العدوانيّ هو «الذي كان أكثر قدرة على ممارسة تلك الهيمنة الرمزيّة من خلال الحضور الإعلاميّ القويّ والجماهيريّة الفاعلة بوصفها منجزاً غربياً صرفاً من جانب، ولكونها مرتهنةً على نمط الحداثة الغربية من جانب آخر»(128)، وعليه فإنّ السرد الرحليّ عند ابن فضلان كان مادةً خصيبة عند المنشغلين بالصناعة الفِلْميّة، لبثِّ أنساق الأنا والآخر بصورة مواربة مما يؤكّد أن النقد الثقافيّ يمكن له أن يجسّر الفجوات التي تفصل بين العلوم والفنون والحقول المختلفة.

- تركيب:

لا ريب أنّ الناظر في مقاربات عليمات حول حكاية الطنبوريّ والمقامة البشرية يُسْلِمُ بأنهما تنمازان بخصيصة مائزة، وهي ما يمكن أن يوسم بالتأويل الجموح، أو المضاعف، الذي يكسر آفاق المعهود، ويجنح في عوالم القراءة والتلقّي والتأويل، حتى يكون التأويل مضاعفاً، وتبدو القراءة الثقافيّة عند عليمات هي القراءة المنتجة، التي تحاول أن تقرأ الخطاب بوصفها حدثاً ثقافياً يتوسّل بجماليات النصوص من أجل صنع التحولات النسقية، وتجلية عناصر الصراع في ثنياته.

وتتمثّل التوليديّة المنهجيّة عند عليمات في انتهاج سُبُل منهجية جديدة، تفضي إلى تعددية المناهج وتشابكها في صلب القراءة/ المقاربة الواحدة، وتفيد مقاربة

عليمات من نظريّات كالتلقّي والسيميائية والنظرية السرديّة، وذلك انسجاماً مع الانفتاح المنهجيّ، الذي ينمازُ به النقد الثقافيّ، ولذلك تغدو مصطلحات هذه المناهج هي المصطلحات التي تمثل العَصَبَ المفاهيميّ لهذه المقاربة.

وانطلاقاً من السابق فإنّ حكاية الطنبوري على وجه الخصوص تمسي في ضَوْء القراءة الفاحصة، كما يُسمّيها يوسف عليمات، سَرْدِيّتين ذاتيتي أبعاد دلاليّةٍ عميقةٍ ورامزةٍ ومُوحية، تستطلبُ قراءةً ثقافيّةً واعية بأبعادهما السرديّة والعلاماتية في سبيل الكشف عن تمظهرات النسق الثقافيّ في ثناياها، وتكشّف في الوقت ذاته عن توترات العلاقة بين المجتمع والطنبوري والهمذاني.

ويشير عليمات إلى أنّ (الطنبوريّ) في هذه الحكاية يرنو نحو تشييد عالم إنسانيّ تجسّده قيمة التفرد، في سبيل تأكيد قوة الذّات، ومَنَعَتِها، وقدرتها على الفاعلية والإنجاز، وتأسيس كينونة الذّات المضادة، من خلال الدفع بالهوامش نحو المركز، أو من خلال جَعْلِ الهامشيّة مصدراً للمركزيّة، وعليه فإن (حكاية أبي القاسم الطنبوري) من منظور عليمات حكايةٌ إيديولوجيّة؛ تجلّي صراعات الهيمنة في أتون صراع ابن حجة/ الطنبوريّ ومجتمعه.

وإذا كان عليمات في المقاربة ينطلق من القراءة الغذامية، فليس للمرء سوى أن يقول، بعد وضعهما في سياق المقارنة والمقايسة، إن مقاربة عليمات تمثل القيمة المضافة، إلى التأويل الأول، أو الفورة الأولى، بصورة تغدو القراءة الثانية، أقصد قراءة عليمات، قراءةً منتجةً، وعليه فإن مفهوم القراءة الثقافيّة هي القراءة التي تحاول أن تقرأ الخطاب حدثاً ثقافياً يتوسل بجماليات النصوص من أجل صنع التحولات النسقية.

يبدو أنّ الغرافي مسكونٌ بسلطة القارئ أو واقع في فتنتها، ذلك أنّه في مقاربته هذه يعيد حبائل الاتصال أو يعقدها أوّل مرة بين نظرية التلقّي، التي أحيت المؤلف، أو ابتعثته من مرقده من جديد، والنقد الثقافيّ الذي يرى أن

179

القراءة الثقافيّة للنص عليها أن تظل محكومة بأفق تاريخي، هو أفق مؤلفها، ولا يمكن أن تغدو القراءة منتجة أو نافعة، إذا عزلت عن سياقاتها تلك.

وبذا يبدو أنَّ مقاربة الغرافي قد أبانت عن مواطن التشابه أو الالتقاء التي تجمع أفقي القراءة الثقافيّة وأفق نظرية التلقّي، في ظلال غَفْلَةٍ من النقّاد الذين انشغلوا سنين طوالاً بالنقد الثقافيّ دونما أن يقيموا تلاقحاً مثمراً أو تزاوجاً خصيباً بين هاتين النظريتين أو بين هذين المنهجيّن، وعليه فيمثل مفهوم القراءة الثقافيّة لدى مصطفى الغرافي ائتلافاً من الأدوات المنهجيّة التي يمكن الاتكاء عليها في الكشف عن سلطة التاريخ أو تجليات القارئ الضمني في النص السردي التراثي عند ابن قتيبة، وفي هذا السياق لا يخرج الغرافي عن نمط التلقّي سوى عند الاشتباك بمفهومات عُمَدٍ في نظرية التلقّي.

لقد أثث الغرافي سبيلاً جامعة بين النقد الثقافيّ ونظرية التلقّي، وحاول أن يقرأ نص ابن قتيبة من خلال منهج يجمع بين أدوات هذين المنهجيّن، أما فيما يتعلق بالآليات التي اعتمدتها هذه المقاربة في القراءة الثقافيّة فهي بعث المؤلّف من مرقده، وتعرية النسق المضمر، بغية الكشف عن مضمرات الخطاب، والصراعات الأيديولوجية الثاوية في أعماقه.

وعليه فإن أخبار ابن قتيبة مثلت عند الغرافي خطاباً إيديولوجيّاً يفيضُ بالأنساق المذهبيّة والاجتماعيّة والسياسيّة، التي تتخذ من هذه الأخبار مرتعاً خصباً لها، إذ تغدو في ضَوْء القراءة الثقافيّة نصوصاً مضطلعة بمهمّة إيديولوجية من خلال خاطبها المُخاتل، وأنساقها المضمرة.

لقد تمرس معجب العدوانيّ بمقولات النظرية النقديّة الحديثة، ومن ثم فإنه انتخب النظرية التناصيّة، ليجعلها محور انشغاله المنهجيّ، فكان ولوجه إلى هذه المنطقة ــ أقصد التناصيّة الثقافيّة ــ ولوجَ العارف الخبير، وقد تأتّى له ذلك من كثرة اشتباكاته معها منذ سنين طوال ماضيات.

ويبدو أنّ العدواني مسكونٌ بالتناصية أو واقع في فتنتها، ذلك أنه في مقاربته هذه يعيد مد حبائل الاتصال أو يعقدها أوّل مرة بين نظرية التناص، التي تباحث والتأثر والتأثير بين النصوص، والنقد الثقافيّ، الذي يرى أنّ قراءة النصّ يجب أن تكون معنيّة بأن تجلّي صراعات الأنساق، وتمثيلات التحيز.

وعليه فإن التناص الثقافيّ أو القراءة التناصيّة الثقافيّة هي مساءلةٌ لمنطق القوّة، وآليات التمثيل، وكشفٌ عن أمارات الاختلاف، والتضاد، لا أسيقةِ التشابه والتلاقح، إذ لا بُدّ أن يدرس النصّ في ظلال أبعاده المعرفيّة والاجتماعيّة والثقافيّة، وليس بوصفه بنيةً مجرّدةً أو تعبيراً عن النص اللاحق، وفي هذا السياق ينفتح العدوانيّ بالنقد الثقافيّ على النظرية التناصيّة التي تمثل عُمْدَةً في مناهج النقد الأدبيّ الحديث، حيث لقي العدوانيّ سبيلاً جامعة بينهما، وحاول أن يقرأ رحلة ابن فضلان والنصوص الموازية لها في الثقافات الأخرى من خلال منهج مركّب يجمع بين أدوات هذين المنهجيّن.

أما فيما يتعلق بالآليّات التي اعتمدها العدوانيّ في هذه المقاربة فتتمثل في انتخاب نص ثقافيّ هو رحلة ابن فضلان، وانتخاب نصوص تتناصُّ معه من الآداب الأخرى، ومن ثمَّ بث تعرية النسق المضمر فيها، والكشف عن مضمرات الخطاب، وما يرتبط بذلك من صراعات الأيديولوجيا، المرتبطة بالأنا والآخر، وعليه فإن رحلة ابن فضلان ليست خطاباً بريئاً وإنما هي خطابٌ مؤدلج، تتوجب قراءته في ظلال أبعاده التاريخيّة، وفي ضَوْء الأيديولوجيات التي تحكمت في مؤلَّفها، لتكشف عن مواقف أيديولوجية مُضمرة من الآخر.

هوامش الفصل الثالث:

1 – سـباتنز، جون، الدراسـات الثقافيّة، ترجمة: لطفي السـيد منصور، مجلة فصول، الهيئة المصرية العامة للكتاب، المجلد (25)، العدد (99)، 2017م، ص239.

2 – عليمات، يوسف، جماليات السرد: قراءة في المقامة البشرية لبديع الزمان الهمذاني، المجلة العربية للعلوم الإنسانية، الكويت، مج27, ع107، 2009م، 149 – 190..

3 – الغرافي، مصطفى، السـرد والمُضمر: دراسـة فـي أخبار ابن قتيبة، مجلة البلاغـة والنقد الأدبيّ، المغرب، العدد (2)، 2015م، ص179 – 193.

4 – العدوانـي، معجب، القراءة التناصية الثقافيّة، ط1، 2019م، المركز الثقافيّ للكتاب، بيروت، الدار البيضاء، لبنان، المغرب. وقد سـبق للعدوانيّ نَشْـرُ هذه المقاربة في مجلّة جامعة الطائف العلميّة: العدواني، معجب، مرايا الآخر: مقاربة ثقافيّة لرسـالة ابن فضلان وانعكاسـاتها في الثّقافة الغربية، مجلة جامعة الطائف للعلوم الإنسـانية، جامعة الطائف، الطائف، المملكة العربيّة السعودية، المجلد (4)، العدد (15)، 2017م، ص93 – 110.

5 – المرجع السابق، ص149.

6 – القفاري، أميرة، النقد الثائر...، (م.س)، ص135.

7 – باتنز، جون، الدراسات الثقافيّة: التاريخ، المادة، المنهج، الأهداف، (م.س)، ص239.

8 – ويليامــز، موكيش، التاريخانية الجديدة والدراسـات الأدبيّة، مجلة فصـول، الهيئة المصرية العامّة للكتاب، القاهرة، مصر، المجلد (3/25)، العدد (99)، 2017م، ص331.

9 – ينظـر: زرفـاوي، عُمر، النقـد الثّقافيّ بين عبدالله الغذاميّ ويوسف عُليمات: معضلـة المنهاجويّة والتّأويـل المغلول، مجلة فصول، الهيئة المصريـة العامّة للكتاب، القاهرة، مصر، المجلد (3/25)، العدد (99)، 2017م، ص144 وما بعدها.

10 – ينظر: المرجع السابق، ص179 – 180.

11 – الغرافي، مصطفى، السرد والمُضمر...، (م.س)، ص180.

12 – ينظر إلى تجليات هذه الإشكاليّة في: سمير، حميد، المؤلف في التراث الأدبيّ: موت أم حياة، مجلة علامات في النقد، النادي الثقافيّ بجُدّة، جُدّة، المملكة العربيّة السـعودية، المجلد (9)، العدد (35)، 2000م، ص125.

13 – ينظـر للاسـتزادة في الدوال الشـواهد مـن مقاربات العدوانـيّ الآتية: العدوانـي، معجب، رحلة

التناصيّـة إلــى النقد العربـيّ القديم، مجلة علامات في النقد، النادي الثقافيّ بجُـدّة، جُدّة، المملكة العربيّـة السعودية، المجلـد (11)، العـدد (44)، 2002م، ص743 – 784. والعدوانـي، معجب، القـراءة التناصيـة الثقافيّة: مدخـل نظري، مجلة البلاغـة والنقد الأدبيّ، المغـرب، العدد الثاني، خريف شتاء 2014 – 2015م، ص167 – 197.

14 – العدواني، معجب، القراءة التناصيّة الثقافيّة، (م.س)، ص7 – 11.

15 – المرجع السابق، ص15 – 40.

16 – ومنهـا: العـدوانـي، معجـب، من موت المؤلف إلى مـوت التناص: القـراءة التناصية في إطارها الجديـد، مؤتمـر الجمعية المصرية للنقد الأدبـيّ (التأويلية والنظرية النقديّـة المعاصرة) القاهرة، مصر، 14 – 18 ديسمبر 2010م.

17 – العدواني، معجب، القراءة التناصية الثقافيّة، (م.س)، ص15 – 40.

18 – ينظر: بنكـراد، سـعيد، سيميانيّات الصّـورة الإشهاريّة: الإشهار والتّمثلات الثقافيّة، ط1، 2006م، أفريقيا الشرق، الدار البيضاء، المغرب، ص57 – 58.

19 – عليمات، يوسف، العجائبيّة وثقافة الإشهار: قراءة ثقافية في حكاية أبي القاسم...، (م.س)، ص81.

20 – عليمات، يوسف، جماليّات السرد: قراءة في المقامة البِشْرية...، (م.س)، ص.

21 – المرجع السابق، ص154.

22 – المرجع السابق، ص88.

23 – عليمات، يوسف، جماليّات السرد: قراءة في المقامة البِشْرية...، (م.س)، ص149 – 190.

24 – بلعابد، عبد الحق، عتبات: جيرار جينيت ...، (م.س)، ص87.

25 – قطّوس، بسّام، سيمياء العنوان، (م.س)، ص147.

26 – للاستزادة حول جدليات النقد الثقافيّ والنقد الأدبيّ ينظر:

Hayden White, Tropics of Discourse: Essays Cultural Criticism, London: The Johns Hopkins University Press, 1985.

27 – ينظر: يوسف، عبدالفتاح أحمد، في استراتيجيات القراءة في النقد الثقافيّ: نحو وعي نقديّ بقراءة ثقافيّـة للنّصّ، مجلة عالم الفكر، منشـورات المجلس الوطني للثقافة، الكويت، المجلد (36)، العدد (1)، 2007م، ص164.

28 – الغرافي، مصطفى، السرد والمُضمر...، (م.س)، ص180 – 186.

29 – المرجع السابق، ص186 – 191.

30 – الغذاميّ، عبدالله، النقد الثّقافيّ: قراءة في الأنساق الثقافيّة العربيّة، (م.س)، ص77.

31 – الغرافي، مصطفى، السرد والمُضمر...، (م.س)، ص179.

32 – المرجع السابق، ص191.

33 – ينظر: غادامير، هانز جورج، الحقيقة والمنهج: الخطوط الأساسية لتأويلية فلسفية، ترجمة: حسن

ناظم وعلي صالح، ط1، 2007م، دار أويا للطباعة والنشــر، طرابلس الجماهيرية العظمى، ليبيا، ص417 – 418.

34 – الغرافي، مصطفى، السرد والمُضمر...، (م.س)، ص179.

35 – العدواني، معجب، القراءة التناصية الثقافيّة، (م.س)، ص7 – 11.

36 – المرجع السابق، الصفحة نفسها.

37 – العدواني، معجب، القراءة التناصية الثقافيّة، (م.س)، ص47.

38 – المرجع السابق، ص48.

39 – المرجع السابق، ص50.

40 – ينظر: كاظم، نادر، الهُويّة والسرد ...، (م.س)، ص49.

41 – المرجع السابق، الصفحة نفسها.

42 – التمارة، عبدالرحمن، نقد النقد: بين التّصوّر المنهجيّ...، (م.س)، ص81.

43 – حُكِيَ أنّه كان ببغدادَ شخص يُعرف بأبي القاسم الطنبوريّ (...) وله مداس له مدّةُ سنين كلما انقطع منه موضعٌ جعل عليه رقعةً إلى أن صار في غاية الثّقل، وصار يُضرب به المثل فيقال: أثقل من مداس أبي القاسـم الطنبوريّ، فاتفق أنّه دخل ســوق الزّجاج فقال له سمسار: يا أبا القاسم قد وصل تاجر من حلب، ومعه زجاج مُذهّب قد كَسَدَ فابتعه منه، وأنا ابيعه لك بعد مدّة بمكسب المثل مِثُلين (...) ولما خَرَجَ من الحمام، ولبس ثيابه وجد إلى جانب مداسـه مداسـاً جديداً، فلبسه، ومضى إلى بيته، وكان القاضي دخل الحمام يغتسل ففقد مداسـه (...)، فوجدوا مداس أبي القاسم فإنه معروفٌ فكبسوا بيته، فوجدوا مداس القاضي عنده، فأخذ منه، وضرب أبو القاسم، وحبس وغرم جملةَ مال حتـى خـرج من الحبس، فأخذ المداس، وألقاه في الدجلة، فغاص في الماء، فرمى بعض الصيادين شـبكة (...) فحملـه إلى بيت أبي القاسم، فلم يجده، فرمـاه من الطّاق إلى بيته فسقط على الرف الذي عليه الزجاج، فتبدّد ماء الورد، وانكسـر الزجاج، فلّما رأى أبو القاسم ذلك لطَمَ على وجهه، وصاح: وافقراه، أفقرني هذا المداس، ثم قام يحفر له في الليل حفرةً فسمع الجيران حسَّ الحفرة، فظنّوا أنّه نقب فشكوه إلى الوالي فأرسل إليه من اعتقله، وقال له: تنقب على الناس حائطهم، (...) فأخذ المداس ورماه في مُستراح الخان، فَسَدَّ قصبة المستراح (...) فحملوه إلى الوالي، وحكوا له مـا وقـع، فقال: غرموه المصروف جملة، فقال: ما بقيت أفارق هذا المداس، وغَسَلَهُ وجعله على الســطح حتى يجفّ، فرآه كلب ظنه رمّة فحمله، وعبر به إلى سـطح آخر، فسقط على امرأة حامل فارتجفت وأسـقطت ولداً ذكـراً (...)، فرفع عليـه غرةً فابتاع لهم غلاماً، (...) فأخذ المداس، وجاء به إلى القاضي، وحكى له جميع ما اتفق له فيه، وقال: أشـتهي أن يكتب مولانا القاضي بيني وبين هذا المداس مباراة بأنه ليس مني ولسـت منه، وإني بريء منه، ومهما فعله يؤاخذ به، ويلزمه فقد أفقرني، فضحك القاضي، ووصله بشـيء، ومضى، وانتهى. الحمويّ، ابن حِجة، تقي الدين أبو بكر بن علي بن عبد الله (ت837هـ)، ثمرات الأوراق في المُحاضرات، شـرحه وضبطه: مفيد محمد قميحة، ط1، 1983م، دار الكتب العلميّة، بيروت، لبنان، ص287.

44 – كالـر، جوناثـان، دفاعاً عن التأويـل المضاعف، مجلة علامات، المغرب، العدد (11)، 1999م، ص47 – 58.

185

45 – المرجع السابق، ص52.

46 – المرجع السابق، ص52.

47 – عليمات، يوسف، العجائبيّة وثقافة الإشهار: قراءة ثقافية في حكاية أبي القاسم... (م.س)، ص87.

48 – وهذا التعبير شائع لدى أغلب المنشغلين بالنقد الثقافيّ. ينظر: الغذاميّ، عبدالله، النقد الثقافيّ... (م.س)، ص78.

49 – ينظر: رمضان، علاء الدين، الحكاية المرحة في التراث الشعبي العربيّ، مجلة الحرس، السعودية، العدد (231)، 2001م.

50 – يقول رولان بارت في هذا السياق: «إنّ المتوالية تتبع منطقي للنوى، وعلاقة التضامن هي التي توحد بينها». بارت، رولان، مدخل إلى التَّحليل البنيويّ للقصص، ترجمة: منذر عيّاشي، ط1، 2014م، دار نينوى للدراسات والنشر والتوزيع، دمشق، سوريا، ص57.

51 – عليمات، يوسف، العجائبيّة وثقافة الإشهار: قراءة ثقافية في حكاية أبي القاسم... ص89 – 90.

52 – جيرو، بيير، السيميائيات: دراسة الأنساق السيميائية غير اللغويّة، ترجمة: منذر عيّاشي، ط1، 2016م، دار نينوى للدراسات والنشر والتوزيع، دمشق، سوريا، ص108.

53 – الحمويّ، ابن حِجة، ثمرات الأوراق في المُحاضرات، (م.س)، ص287.

54 – عليمات، يوسف، العجائبيّة وثقافة الإشهار: قراءة ثقافية في حكاية أبي القاسم... ص89 – 90.

55 – ينظر حول مفاهيم «الصورة الإشهاريّة» في: بنكراد، سعيد، سيميائيات الصورة الإشهاريّة: الإشهار والتمثلات الثقافيّة، ط1، 2006م، الدار البيضاء، المغرب.

56 – عليمات، يوسف، العجائبيّة وثقافة الإشهار: قراءة ثقافية في حكاية أبي القاسم... (م.س)، ص89.

57 – ينظر: الشاهد، نبيل، العجائبيّ في السرد العربيّ القديم: مئة ليلة وليلة والحكايات العجيبّة والأخبار الغريبة نموذجاً، ط1، 2012م، منشورات دار الورّاق، عمّان، الأردن، ص21 – 72.

58 – عليمات، يوسف، العجائبيّة وثقافة الإشهار: قراءة ثقافية في حكاية أبي القاسم... (م.س)، ص88.

59 – المرجع السابق، ص92.

60 – عليمات، يوسف، العجائبيّة وثقافة الإشهار: قراءة ثقافية في حكاية أبي القاسم... (م.س)، ص98.

61 – المرجع السابق، الصفحة نفسها.

62 – عليمات، يوسف، العجائبيّة وثقافة الإشهار: قراءة ثقافية في حكاية أبي القاسم... (م.س)، ص105.

63 – المرجع السابق، ص155.

64 – وفي سياق ذلك فقد قدّم الغذامي في هذه المقاربة قراءةً تأويليةً تمحورت حول البنى السردية التي تكون نصّ المقامة البشرية من منظور ثقافيّ تأويليّ. يُنظر: الغذامي، عبدالله، القمر الأسود أو النصّ القاتل، مجلة فصول، الهيئة المصريّة العامّة للكتاب، القاهرة، مصر، المجلد (13)، العدد (3)، 1994م، ص40 – 58.

65 – الغذامي، عبدالله، القمر الأسود أو النصّ القاتل، (م.س)، ص42.

66 – عليمات، يوسف، جماليّات السرد: قراءة في المقامة البِشْرية... (م.س)، ص155.

67 – المرجع السابق، ص156.

68 – المرجع السابق، ص156.

69 – المرجع السابق، ص149 – 190.

70 – المرجع السابق، ص98.

71 – عليمات، يوسف، جماليّات السرد: قراءة في المقامة البِشْرية...، (م.س)، ص157.

72 – عليمات، يوسف، جماليّات السرد: قراءة في المقامة البِشْرية...، (م.س)، ص157.

73 – المرجع السابق، ص161.

74 – المرجع السابق، ص161 وما بعدها.

75 – عليمات، يوسف، جماليّات السرد: قراءة في المقامة البِشْرية...، (م.س)، ص159.

76 – المرجع السابق، ص161 وما بعدها.

77 – عليمات، يوسف، جماليّات السرد: قراءة في المقامة البِشْرية...، (م.س)، ص165.

78 – المرجع السابق، ص165.

79 – المرجع السابق، ص183.

80 – المرجع السابق، ص184.

81 – ويمكـن في سـياق ذلك الإشـارة إلى الأنظـار التـي تناولت قراءة المقامة في ضَـوْءِ «النقد الأدبيّ الحديث» أو «الدراسات السرديّة الجّديدة» في الدراسات الآتية: الجديع، خالد بن محمد، الدراسات السـرديّة الجّديدة: قراءة المقامة أنموذجاً، مركز بحوث كليّة الآداب، جامعة الملك سعود، المملكة العربيّة السعودية، ط1، 2007م. وكاظم، نادر، المقامات والتلقّي...، (م.س).

82 – يُنظـر: المبـارك، مازن، مجتمع بديع الزمـان الهمذاني من خلال مقاماتـه، دار الفكر المعاصر، دمشـق، سـوريا، ط2، 1981م. وأبانمـي، إبراهيم بن محمد، أحبولة الهمذانـي الإبداعية الكبرى: قراءة في السيرة الثقافيّة المُضمرة في مقاماته، مجلة العلوم العربيّة، جامعة الإمام محمد بن سعود الإسلامية، العدد (36)، 2014م.

83 – يُنظر: بوقرة، نعمان عبدالحميد، المقامة البِشْـريّة لبديع الزمان الهمذاني: قراءة نصيّة تداوليّة في ضَـوْءِ نظرية الحجاج، المجلة العربيّة للعلوم الإنسـانيّة، جامعة الكويـت، الكويت، المجلد (31)، العدد (123)، 2013م، ص138 – 180.

84 – صحـراوي، إبراهيـم، السـرد العربيّ القديم: الأنـواع والوظائف والبنيـات، ط1، 2008م، الدار العربيّـة للعلوم ناشـرون (بيروت/ لبنان)، منشـورات الاختلاف (الجزائر العاصمة/ الجزائر)، ص55.

85 – الغرافـي، مصطفـى، التّأصيل الثّقافيّ وبناء الهُويّة عند ابـن قتيبة، مجلة فصول، الهيئة المصرية العامّة للكتاب، القاهرة، مصر، العدد (87 – 88)، 2010م، ص90 وما بعدها.

86 – الغرافي، مصطفى، السرد والمُضمر...، (م.س)، ص186 وما بعدها.

87 – المرجع السابق، ص179.

88 – يُنظر: إيكو، أمبرتو، القارئ في الحكاية...، (م.س)، ص235.

89 – الغرافي، مصطفى، السرد والمُضمر...، (م.س)، ص180.

90 – ومن طريف ما وقعتُ عليه من الدراسات في هذا الجانب دراسة عبدالله السالم الخلف الموسومة بـ«الفكر السنيّ في أدب ابن قتيبة». يُنظر: الخلف، عبدالله السالم، الفكر السنيّ في أدب ابن قتيبة، رسالة ماجستير (غير منشورة)، 1980م، جامعة الإمام محمد بن سعود الإسلامية، الرياض، المملكة العربيّة السعودية.

91 – الغرافي، مصطفى، السرد والمُضمر...، (م.س)، ص183.

92 – المرجع السابق، ص186 وما بعدها.

93 – «قال المدائنيّ: رأيتُ فلاناً مولى باهلةَ يطوفُ بين الصَّفا والمروة على بغلة، ثم رأيته بعد ذلك راجلاً في سَفَر، فقلتُ لـه: أراجلٌ في هذا الموضع؟ قال: نعم، إني ركبتُ حيث يمشي الناس، فكان حقاً على الله أن يرجّلني حيث يركب الناس». يُنظر: الدينوري، ابن قتيبة عبد الله بن قتيبة (ت276هـ)، عيون الأخبار، تحقيق: داني بن منير الزهوي، (د.ط)، 2003م، المكتبة العصرية، بيروت، لبنان، ج1، ص245. والغرافي، مصطفى، السرد والمُضمر...، (م.س)، ص180.

94 – الغرافي، مصطفى، السرد والمُضمر...، (م.س)، ص187.

95 – «قال رجلٌ لهشام بن الحكم: أتُرى اللهُ عزَّ وجلَّ في فَضْلِهِ وكرمِهِ وعدله كلّفنا ما لا نُطيق ثم يعذِّبنا؟ فقال هشام: قد والله فَعَلَ، ولكننا لا نستطيع أنْ نتكلم». الدينوري، ابن قتيبة، عيون الأخبار، (م.س)، ج1، ص245. وقد ترجم الزركلي في الأعلام له فقال: «هشام بن الحكم الشيباني بالولاء، الكوفيّ، أبو محمد: متكلم مناظر، كان شيخ الإماميّة في وقتـه». الزّركليّ، خير الدين، الإعلام، ط15، 2002م، دار العلم للملايين، بيروت، لبنان، ج8، ص85.

96 – ينظر: القاضي، محمد، الخبر في الأدب العربيّ...، (م.س)، ص223 – 350.

97 – الغرافي، مصطفى، السرد والمُضمر...، (م.س)، ص188.

98 – عشا، علي، الفُحولة فى الوعي الثقافيّ العربيّ...، (م.س)، ص159 – 190. والغرافي، مصطفى، السرد والمُضمر...، (م.س)، ص188.

99 – روى ابن قتيبة: «استقبل الخوارج ابن عرياض اليهودي وهو بحروري فقال هل خرج إليكم في اليهود شيء، فقالوا لا: فامضوا راشدين». الدينوري، ابن قتيبة، عيون الأخبار، (م.س)، ج1، ص180.

100 – الغرافي، مصطفى، السرد والمُضمر...، (م.س)، ص182.

101 – المرجع السابق، الصفحة نفسها.

102 – الغرافي، مصطفى، السرد والمُضمر...، (م.س)، ص190 – 191.

103 – يُنظر: خليفة، علي محمد، بنية السرد في النادرة: نوادر الأعراب في كتاب عيون الأخبار نموذجاً، ط1، 2010م، دار الوفاء لدنيا الطباعة والنشر، الإسكندرية، مصر.

104 – العدواني، معجب، القراءة التناصية الثقافيّة، (م.س)، ص151.

105 – المرجع السابق، الصفحة نفسها.

106 – حــول مفهوم «النقد النسـويّ« ينظــر – مثلاً – : الرويلي والبازعي، ميجان وسـعد، دليل الناقد الأدبيّ...، (م.س)، ص231.

107 – حــول مفهــوم «القراءة الطّباقيّة «ينظر – مثلاً – : سـعيد، إدوارد: الثقافة والإمبرياليّة، نقله إلى العربيّة وقدم له: كمال أبو ديب، ط1، 1997م، دار الآداب، بيروت، لبنان، ص20.

108 – العدواني، معجب، القراءة التناصية الثقافيّة، (م.س)، ص50.

109 – ينظــر – مثــلاً – : العدواني، مُعجِب، المــوروث وصناعة الرواية: مؤثـرات وتمثيلات، ط1، 2013م، الدار العربيّة للعلوم ناشرون (بيروت/ لبنان)، منشورات الاختلاف (الجزائر العاصمة/ الجزائر)، دار الأمان (الرباط/ المغرب).

110 – ينظــر: إبراهيــم، عبدالله، المُطابقة والاختلاف: بحـث في نقـد المركزيّات الثقافيّة، ط2، 2004م، المؤسسة العربيّة للدراسات والنشر، بيروت، لبنان.

111 – العدواني، معجب، القراءة التناصية الثقافيّة، (م.س)، ص156.

112 – العدواني، معجب، القراءة التناصية الثقافيّة، (م.س)، ص156.

113 – ابــن فضــلان، أحمد بـن العباس (ت349هـ)، رسـالة ابن فضلان: في وصـف الرحلة إلى بلاد التـرك والخزر والروس والصقالبة، حققها وعلّق عليها وقدم لها: سـامي الدهان، ط1، 1960م، مطبوعات المجمع العلمي العربي بدمشق، دمشق، سوريا، ص91.

114 – المصدر السابق، ص92.

115 – العدواني، معجب، القراءة التناصية الثقافيّة، (م.س)، ص167.

116 – ابن فضلان، أحمد بن العباس (ت349هـ)، رسالة ابن فضلان...، (م.س)، ص116.

117 – المصدر السابق، ص165.

118 – المصدر السابق، ص28.

119 – المصدر السابق، الصفحة نفسها.

120 – العدواني، معجب، القراءة التناصية الثقافيّة، (م.س)، ص167.

121 – المرجع السابق، ص171.

122 – المرجع السابق، ص172 – 173.

123 – سـعيد، إدوارد، الاستشـراق، ترجمة: محمد عصفور، تقديم: محمد شاهين، ط1، 2022م، دار الآداب، بيروت، لبنان، ص83 وما بعدها.

124 – اصطيف، عبدالنبي، تلقّي الغرب لرسـالة ابن فضلان، مجلة التراث العربي، منشـورات اتحاد الكتاب العرب، دمشق، سوريا، العدد (129)، 2013م، ص67 – 76.

125 – العدواني، معجب، القراءة التناصية الثقافيّة، (م.س)، ص160.

126 – العدواني، معجب، القراءة التناصية الثقافيّة، (م.س)، ص163.

127 – المرجع السابق، ص171.

128 – المرجع السابق، ص172 – 173.

الفصل الرابع:

تفاعلات نمط التلقّي:

النقد الثقافيّ بين تحليل الخطاب وبلاغة الصورة

لا مندوحة من الإشارة في البَدْءِ إلى أنّ النقد الثقافيّ شكّل منعرجاً خطيراً في مسيرة النقد العربيّ المعاصر، بوصفه منهجاً قادراً على الاشتباك مع معظم المناهج النقديّة، والحقول المعرفية المختلفة، بصورة أضحى النقد الثقافيّ خلالها ذا غوايةٍ مثيرةٍ على استثمار مقولاته، وأدواته، بصورة متنامية، تسهم في إنجازِ القراءات المختلفة لمختلف النصوص والظواهر، أجْلَ الكشف عن أنظمتها وبلاغتها، وأنساقها.

وفي هذا الفصل يشتبك النقد الثقافيّ بحقلَيْن جديدَيْن هما تحليل الخطاب والدرس البلاغيّ، وهو ما يتجلى في مقاربات شرف الدين ماجدولين وهيثم سرحان، موضع الدراسة في هذا الفصل، وإذا كان تحليل الخطاب يحاول فكّ أنظمة هذه الإشارات فإنّ النقد الثقافيّ يتداخلُ معه في المهمّة ذاتها، وإن اختلفت المرجعيّات المعرفيّة، والأدوات المنهجيّة، وإذا كان النقد الثقافيّ يعرّي البلاغة من جمالياتها، ويلتفت إلى مقصدية النصّ، فإن الدرس البلاغيّ المعاصر كذلك إنما هو في ضربٍ من ضروبه كشف عن مقصدية النصّ وأسراره، وخفاياه، ورسائله المشفّرة.

وفي هذا السياق تكشف مقاربات شرف الدين ماجدولين (الصورة والنسق والسلطة: قراءة في السرد الشطاريّ العربيّ)، (الآخر ودائرة الألفة قراءة لنسق التفاعل في نص: طوق الحمامة لابن حزم)، و(الهامشي والآخر والسرد الهزلي: قراءة في الموروث الخبري) عن سيمياء الناقد اللذويّ، الذي تتقاسمه مقولات النقد الثقافيّ ودراسات الصورة والنقد الأدبيّ، وفي هذا السياق فإنّ هذه

السرديات من منظور ماجدولين تدورُ في أصلها خارج حدود البلاغة البلاطيّة، ضارباً بينها وبين الأدب الرسميّ بسُورٍ ليس له باب، جاعلاً محورها فتنة المناصفة، ولذّة اللعب، وإغواءات النصب، ونسق الذات، تأسيساً للعالم الجديد المِثال، الذي يمثل الشاطر/ الهامش/ العاشق محوره، وقد مثَّلت هذه السرديات لدى شرف الدين ماجدولين أنواعاً سرديّة مهمّشة وفاتنة يستأهلُ افتراع مسار قرائيّ يوازي هذه الفتنة المهمّشة، ويقرأ هذه اللذة بمنهجية لذويّة يندغم فيها القارئ بالسرد اندغاماً، تسودُهُ محفزات الأُلفة والإعجاب والإدهاش.

وتغدو بلاغة الصورة التي رسمها السارد للشطار والعشاق والهامشيين هي المَحْضَنَ الملائم الذي يمارسُ فيه السارد ضَرْباً من المخاتلة، وترسيم حدود الصورة المضادة، اتّكاءً على ممكنات الصورة الجديدة، التي يجتهد في ترسيمها، إعادةً لتشكيل الذات بما يختلف مع الصورة الذهنيّة التي تأسست على الدوام من الإقصاء والتهميش لهم، والانزواء عنهم.

أما مقاربات هيثم سرحان حول الوصايا السرديّة الموسومة بـ(اللسان والبهتان: شِعريّة الوصية في السرد العربيّ الكلاسيكيّ) والسرديّات الجنسانية الموسومة بـ(خطاب الجنس: مقاربات في الأدب العربيّ القديم) فإنّها تفيءُ منهجيّاً إلى أدوات تحليل الخطاب، وخاصة، الفرع المعرفي الموسوم بـ(التحليل النقديّ للخطاب)، ومقولات النقد الثقافيّ، ذلك أنّ كليهما يهتمّ بتلونات الخطاب، ومُضمراته، وطرائق الهيمنة اللغويّة والثقافيّة، وينماز هذا الفرع المعرفيّ كما النقد الثقافيّ بالانفتاح المنهجيّ وهو معنيٌّ بإبراز أشكال السلطة والهيمنة[1]، وهنا تبرز الوظيفة المركزيّة التي نيطتْ بها مقاربة سرحان، وهي الكشف عن سلطة الأب، وطرائق هيمنته، ومسالك ترسيخ هذه السلطة الأبويّة.

1 – مدخل: النقد الثقافيّ بين الخِطاب والصورة:

تنقام مقاربات شرف الدين ماجدولين (الصورة والنسق والسلطة: قراءة في

السرد الشطاري العربي)[2]، و(الآخر ودائرة الألفة قراءة لنسق التفاعل في نص: طوق الحمامة لابن حزم)[3]، و(الهامشي والآخر والسرد الهزليّ: قراءة في الموروث الخبريّ)[4] بوصف السرد الشطاريّ وسرديّات العشق وسرديّات الهامش سرديّات مخاتلة، تضمر في بنيته العميقة أنساقاً ثقافيّة، تتستر بغوايات اللعب والمناصفة والاحتيال ومركزيّة الذات والسخرية، ببلاغة القول والإنشاء بما تخلّفه من أبعادٍ تشويقية تمسُّ شغاف المتلقّي، بغية تفكيك/ نقض مسلّمات المخيال الشعبيّة حول هذه الفئات، واستيلاد صورة جديدة لها تتكئ إلى بلاغة الخطاب، وترفض سلطة الصورة الذهنية، عبر بناء خطاب يمجد مركزية الذات.

وتنتسبُ مقاربات هيثم سرحان (خطاب الجنس: مقاربات في الأدب العربيّ القديم)[5]، و(اللسان والبهتان: شعريّة الوصية في السرد العربيّ الكلاسيكيّ) [6]، وإلى إطار القراءات الثقافيّة التي تتوسّل بمقولات النقد الثقافيّ وتحليل الخطاب والدرس، في قراءة نماذجَ من خطاب الجنس (Sexual narratives)، والوصايا السرديّة (Narrative Commandments)، والنص الجاحظي (Narrative Commandments)، التي تغدو في ضوء القراءة الفاحصة سُروداً مفعمة بالشيفرات النسقيّة، التي تهدفُ إلى تكريس السلطة الأبويّة، والثورة على مسلّمات المجتمع، وقواعده القارّة، وتمجيد شخصية المكدّي، أو ثيمة الكدية، والتمرد على الثقافة الأبويّة، وجعلها سبيلاً إلى حيازة مركزيّةٍ وامتدادٍ لا ينتهي أبد الدهر.

2 – سيمياء القارئ: من القارئ اللذويّ إلى محلل الخطاب:

1 – 2 – شرف الدين ماجدولين: القارئ اللذويّ والقراءة الثقافيّة:

تجيءُ مقاربات شرف الدين ماجدولين منمازة بفرادة تتأتى من محاولة استثمار مفاهيم الصورة (The Image)، وبلاغة الصورة (Rhetoric Image)، ودراسات الآخريّة (Other studies)، وتوسيع نمط التلقّي من ناحية

النصوص السرديّة التي يشتغل عليها، بوصفها سرديّات مهمَّشة، لم تحظَ بما حظي به الأدب الرسميّ، أو الأدب البلاطيّ من احتفاء ومتابعة وقراءات في النقد الأدبيّ الحديث[7].

ويبدو أنّ شرف الدين ماجدولين يمثّل في هذه المقاربات مساراً قرائيّاً جديداً في إطارات النقد الثقافيّ، إذ يتأسس هذا المسار على مفاهيم مستمدة من مفهوم لذة النصّ (The Pleasure of the Text) عند رولان بارت، ودراسات الصورة دراسات الصورة (Image Studies)، والدراسات البلاغيّة بمفهوماتها الجديدة، التي اتسعت لشتمل حقولاً معرفيّة عديدة[8]، وعليه فيغدو السرد الشطّاريّ وسرديّات العشق والهامش من منظور ماجدولين، خطاباً يستوجب القراءة الثقافيّة اللذويّة، من خلال الانخراط في محاولة قراءة هذه السرديّات المهمشة، والكشف عن أنساقها، وغوايتها، بوصفها أبنية حكائيّة فاتنةً، تنبني في أسّ بنيانها على بلاغة الاستهواء، أو بلاغة الإمتاع بيد أنّها تضمر من منظور مختلف أنساقاً تهدف إلى غاية رئيسة هي مناوأة السلطة، وإعادة إنتاج المتخيّل القارّ عن الشطّار والهامشيين[9]، في حين تمثل سرديّات العشق والهامش خطاباً يمجد سلطة الذات، ويتكئ إلى بلاغة الذات والإنشاء في بث أنساق هذه الذات، وإذا كان فعْل الكتابة وغوايته مرتبطاً ارتباطاً وجوديّاً بفعل القراءة، فإن شرف الدين ماجدولين ينتحي لنفسه مساراً خاصّاً في قراءة هذه السرديّات، وهو مسار استثنائيّ ينبني – والحال هذه – على توجيه المسار القرائيّ لاقتناص لذة النصّ، ذلك أنّه قد قرّ عند بارت فإنه ثمة «فعاليّتان للمتعة، تنطلقُ منها كلُّ عملية إبداعيّة، الأولى: وهي فعالية الكتابة. الثانية: وهي فعاليّة القراءة»[10].

لقد التفت ماجدولين إلى السرد الشطاريّ أو قصص اللصوص والشطّار حسب تعبير سهير قلماوي[11]، وسرديّات العشق كما تتجلى في طوق الحمامة لابن حزم، والسرود الهزلية كذلك، وهو على وَعْي بنسقيتها، وبلاغتها، ومفارقاتها، وبنائها الصُوَرِيّ، أو التعدد الصوري الماثل في أعطافها، التفاتاً يشي بأن النقد

الثقافيّ قادرٌ من منظوره على أن يستولد – في أتون انفتاحه المنهجيّ المائز –
منهجاً قادراً على تفكيك شفرات النصّ، في سياقٍ تأويليّ، يسترفدُ ممكناتِ مناهج
مختلفة، أو حقولاً معرفيّة متباينة، يمكن أن تنتظم في سياقٍ واحد[12].

2 – 2 – هيثم سرحان: القارئ الثقافيّ وتحليل الخطاب:

تجيءُ مقاربات هيثم سرحان منطوية على محاولة عَقْدِ صلات وثقية بين
النقد الثقافيّ والسرديّات ونظريّات تحليل الخطاب «Discourse Analysis»،
بوصفه قارئاً ما فتئ يشتغلُ على قراءة السرديّات العربيّة القديمة وفقاً لمسارٍ
منهجيّ تندغم في أتونه هذه الحقول المعرفيّة بكل ما تنطوي عليه من مقولات
نظريّة، وأدوات منهجيّة[13].

وعليه فإنّ فعْل التلقّي/ القراءة في هذه الأطروحة يصرف اهتمامه إلى البنية
الخطابية وما تضمره من أنساق، وهو اشتغال مشبوبٌ بممكنات تحليل الخطاب،
والحفر المعرفيّ في بِنياته، لا باعتباره بناءً بريئاً، وإنما بوصفه بناءً حاضناً
للمخاتلات والمُضمرات، التي تستطلبُ أن ينهد لها المحلل الخطابي، أو المنشغل
بتحليل الخطاب، ابتغاء قراءتها، والاشباك معها[14].

ولا ريب أنّ الكشف عن النسق الثقافيّ المُضمر وفاقاً للتّأطير السابق هو
المحورَ الركين الذي يكوّن المنهجيّة الناظمة لهذه الأطروحة، بصورة يتموضعُ
خلالها مصطلح النسق الثقافيّ، بوصفه المفهوم الذي يديرُ رحى هذه المقاربة،
ويوجه مساراتها، وهو مصطلح متّسع تعتوره إشكاليّات كثيرة من الناحية
الاصطلاحية المفاهيميّة، بيد أنّ سرحان يبدو في مقارباته هذه آخذاً بالمفهوم
الذي طرحه عبدالفتاح كيليطو للنسق الثقافيّ، وتبناه في مقاربته حول المقامات،
وهو مفهوم عامّ وأشمل من المفهوم الغذّاميّ[15].

إنّ هيثم سرحان في مقارباته هذه جعل الحديث عن تفاعل منهجي بين

اللسانيّات بوصفها مسباراً يقوم على تحليل الخطاب أو التحليل النقديّ للخطاب والنقد الثقافيّ[16]، أمراً ممكناً، إذ يبدو أن كليهما يمكن أن يكملا بعضيهما[17]، ولعلّه من مُسْتَعَادِ القول الإشارة إلى أنّ زمرةً من المنشغلين بالدرس اللسانيّ الحديث العربيّ ما فتئوا يلمعون ويحضّون إلى التماس المتَشرك بين الدرس اللسانيّ والنقد، ونفي القطيعة المعرفيّة بينهما، بل التطرف إلى حدٍ يجعل من الدرس النقديّ الحديث مديناً بمقولاته الكبرى للدرس اللسانيّ، ولا مناص من الإشارة إلى ما اشتُهر على ألسنة بعض اللسانيين في سياق ذلك[18]، ولعل هذا الضرب من الارتباط ارتباطٌ يمكن نشدانه في هذه الأطروحة.

3 – المتن المنهجيّة والجهاز المفاهيميّ:

1 – 3 – شرف الدين ماجدولين والمرجعيّة البلاغية:

تسير مقاربة شرف الدين ماجدولين حول السرد الشطاريّ في ثلاثة مسارات، أما أولاهما (السرد الشطاريّ والبلاغة المقموعة)[19] فيبحث في خصائص السرد الشطاريّ، ويكشف عن تمثيلات نسق الإقصاء، الذي مارسته مدونات الثقافة العالِمة على هذه السرديّات، ولذلك فإنّ هذا النوع السردي لا يكاد يحضر، مستكملاً شروطه الأجناسيّة، إلا في نماذجَ محصورة، أما ثانيتهما (الاستعراض ونسق الغواية)[20] فيعرض لنسق الغواية، الذي يتمركز في السرد الشطاري، ويعمل مغوياً للقارئ/ المتلقّي والشاطر والمشطور، من خلال فعل اللعب أو المناصفة، أو من خلال بلاغة الاستهواء.

وأما ثالثتهما (الشاطر وضَحاياه: فتنة السلطة وفتنة اللعب)[21] فيجلّي أنساق الذات والغيرية في سرديّات الشطار، إذ تتمثل هذه الأنساق من خلال تحيُّز الشاطر لأبناء مجتمعه، ورغبته الدائبة في أن يكون فعْل المناصفة واللعب موجهاً إلى الآخر، الذي يقع خارج حدود المجتمع الشطاريّ.

أما في مقاربته حول سرديّات العشق فإن عناوينه هي: (الألفة والنسق

المجازي) (التفاعل النصي وإبدالات الآخر: استراتيجية التمركز)، و(ثنائية (ذكر/أنثى): التحكم الخطابي أحادي البعد)، وكلها ترتبط بنسق الفكرة التي يتبناها ماجدولين[22]، وفي مقاربته حول السرد الهزليّ فتتمحور عناوينه حول: (الهامشي وماهية السرد) و(الهامشية وتجليات الغيرية) و(الهامشي ومنزع الهزل)[23].

وفي ظلال هذه اللذة التي ينخرط بها القارئ/ الناقد تجيء هذه العنوانات مكونة بنية معبرة عن هذه المعاني، إذ تنسجم في الأطروحتين في اتّساق منتظم، واتّحاد منهجي، يعبّر عن اغتناء النص السردي الشطاري وسرديّات العشق بهذه الغواية والبلاغة، التي يظلّ دولابها يدور في حركة ممتدة، لا متناهية، تتصل بالشاطر، والمشطور، والعاشق والمعشوق، ويمدها القارئ/ الناقد ليوقع قارئ خطابه النقديّ/ قارئ القراءة في حِبالها، وبذلك يكون العنوان محققاً للوظيفة الإغرائية/التحريضية[24]، ولا ريب أنّ هذه العنوانات تنطوي فيما يبدو على كسر لآفاق التلقّي، وضربٍ من المفارقات الحادة، إذ يغدو المقموعون أصحاب بلاغة، ويمسي اللعب فتنة، في حين يمثّل الاستهواء حدثاً بلاغيّاً، ويغدو خطاب العشق والهامشيّة تمثيلاً لنسقية الذات[25].

ويمكن أن تُوسَمَ القراءة الثقافيّة عند ماجدولين بالقراءة الثقافيّة العاشقة لأنساق الخطاب المضمرة، ذلك أن النصّ لديه يمثل تشكيلاً جماليّاً فاتناً، لا يُسلم قِياده إلا لمن ينخرط في هذه الفتنة، ويحاول أن يفكّكها، وأن يلج إلى بناها العميقة، ولا بُدّ من الإشارة إلى أن شرف الدين مجدولين يتمثل في أطروحتيه مفاهيم نقديّة من قبل: (فتنة اللعب)، (الصورة)، (النسق)، (السرد الشطاريّ)، (البلاغة المقموعة)، (الذات)، (الغيرية)، (الهزلية) وهي مفاهيم تراوحُ بين النقد الثقافيّ والدراسات البلاغيّة، ودراسات الصورة، ولعل ما يؤكد ذلك هذا المنزع أن ماجدولين ينظر إلى صورة الشطار والعشاق والهامشيين، وهو مفهوم ينتمي منهجيّاً إلى علم الصورة أو دراسات الصورة، ويوازيه في النقد الثقافيّ مفهوم التمثيل الذي لم يختره الباحث.

ويمكن القول: إنّ هذا الاختيار يحيل إلى حقل الصورولوجية أو الصورولوجيا (Imageology Approach)[26]، الذي راج في أتون ازدهار دراسات الصورة (Image Studies) في الحقول المعرفيّة المختلفة[27].

وإذا كان الدرس البلاغيّ المُعاصر اتّسع ليشملَ الصورة والحجاج والسرد والمتلقّي والجمهور... إلخ[28]، فإنّه في هذه الأطاريح تتسع لتدرس سرديّات العشق والسرد الشطاريّ وسرديّات الهزل من منظور بلاغة الصورة، أو من خلال ائتلاف تنقام ركائزه على الدراسات الصوريّة والبلاغة والنقد الأدبيّ[29]، ولا ريب أن البلاغة التي يقصدها ماجدولين ليست ذاتها البلاغة التقليدية، بل البلاغة السردية (Rhetorical Narrative) التي تحققها فرائدية الصورة، وتمردها كذلك[30]، وعليه فإنّ الصورة التي يرسمها السارد الشاطر والعاشق والهامشي تتسم ببلاغة نوعيّة، تنطوي على فاعليّة حجاجية، تسهم في ترسيم صورة ذهنية جديدة لهذه الفئات.

2 – 3 – هيثم سرحان ومرجعيات تحليل الخطاب:

تنتظم مقاربات هيثم سرحان في عددٍ من المباحث التي تجلّي أنظمة الخطاب، وأنساقه الثقافيّة، ومن العناوين التي انتخبها سرحان في قراءته للسرديّات الجنسانية[31]: (السبي الجنسيّ)، (التمرد الجنسي وقتل الأب)، ومن العناوين في الوصايا السردية: (الأب سارداً)، (ما بعد الوصيّة)، وتضحى مفردات الجهاز المفاهيميّ عند سرحان متمحورة حول: (السرد)، و(الجنسانيّة)، و(قتل الأب)، و(الخطاب)، و(النسقيّة)، و(الوصيّة)، و(الشعريّة)، و(التمرّد)، و(السبيّ)، و(الأبوة)[32].

ووفاقاً لذلك تتأثث المنهجيّة التي يسلكها سرحان في قراءاته على مفاهيمَ منهجيّةٍ مستمدةٍ من تحليل الخطاب، والدراسات الحجاجية، ممثلة بمفاهيم من قبيل: (الخطاب)، و(الشعريّة)، ومقولات النقد الثقافيّ، من قبيل: (النسق)

و(النسقيّة)، و(المضمر)، إذ يبدو أنّ النقد الثقافيّ، عند سرحان، يظلُّ أقربَ إلى كونه نشاطاً منهجيّاً، يهدف إلى تفكيكِ الخطابات، والكشفِ عن أنظمتها[33] .

ولعلّ الناظر في مرجعيّات النقد الثقافيّ وتحليل الخطاب، وخاصّة التحليل النقدي للخطاب عند أعلامه ومؤسسيه، يلحظ أنّ كليهما لا ينظر إلى الخطاب – على اختلاف أنواعه وأجناسه – نظرة بريئة، وعليه فإنّ الخطاب (Discourse) في نظريات تحليل الخطاب كما في النقد الثقافيّ خطابٌ مراوغ، ومخاتلٌ، وغير بريء، ويسعى كلاهما إلى الكشف عن الهيمنة والسلطة وتجلياتهما في الخطابات، وعليه فقد تجانست مرجعيات هذين الحقلَيْن تجانساً حَفَزَ على الإفادة المعرفية من ممكناتهما، ومن ثم فقد بدا أنهما متقاربان تقارباً منهجيّاً واضحاً.

وتبدو التنظيرات التي قدمها الفلاسفة بول ريكور(Pual Ricoeur)[34] وميشيل فوكو (Michel Foucault)[35] حول مفهوم الخطاب، ومخاتلاته على تماسٍّ مباشر وحميم بالنقد الثقافيّ، وقد بدا أنّ انفتاح تحليل الخطاب والنقد الثقافيّ على شتى الحقول المعرفية دلالة على إمكان الإفادة المعرفية المنهجيّة بينهما[36] .

وإذا كان النقد الثقافيّ يبحث في تحايلات الثقافة في الخطاب، من خلال ترك الجماليات النصيّة، فإنّ الشعرية والبلاغة تغدوان هامشاً فسيحاً للمناورة، وإضمار الرسائل المشفرة، من خلال استخدام اللغة في الخطاب استخداماً خاصّاً.

4 – استراتيجيّات المقاربة النقديّة ومستويات التلقّي:

2 – 4 – شرف الدين ماجدولين: بين القراءة الثقافيّة وبلاغة الصورة:

– التحليل الصوريّ أو الصورولوجيّة:

تمثل استراتيجيّة/ التحليل الصوريّ أو الصورولوجيّة (Imageology Approach)[37] أي التحليل الذي يعتمدُ على جَلاء صورة الشاطر في هذا السرد الشطاري، الاستراتيجيّة أو المبدأ الذي يؤطر هذه المقاربة من الناحية المنهجيّة،

ويُقصد بالتحليل الصوريّ البحثُ «في عناصر إنتاج الصّور، ومكوناتها، وآليّاتها، وطُرُق تشكُّلها»[38]، وقد أشار دوبري في هذا السياق كما ينقل عنه ماجدولين إلى «غواية وسائط الاتّصال، ووظائف التمويه، والتكييف، والقَلْب، التي تنطوي عليها التمثيلات في دولة الصور الحديثة»[39].

ـ سرديّات الشطار: بلاغة الصورة ولذة السرد:

وفي هذا السياق يمثل السرد الشطاري من قبيل سيرة (دليلة المحتالة) و(علي الزّيبق)[40] سرديّات مُضادّة، تحتفي بالهامشيين والشطار، على الرغم من كونها تحظى برعاية السلطة، ممثلة بهارون الرشيد، إذ إنها تحتفي بسيرة عدد من هؤلاء الشطار، الذين يعجب بهم الرشيد، ويأمرُ بأن تحفظ تجربتهم التي صاغها علي الزّيبق في خزانة المُلْك، ليكما تغدو تذكاراً هادياً للمنخرطين في دواليب السلطة، على الرغم من أنّ هذه السيرَ كانت مُقصاةً من التاريخ الرسميّ، التي نصّ كُتّابه على أن أبطالها شُطّار[41]، وعليه فلقد حاول السرد الشطاري إعادة ترسيم حدود التخييل المركوز حول الشطار في الذّاكرة الرسمية، بصورة تهشِّم من خلالها أنساق التاريخ الرسميّ، وتعمل على فرض أنساق المتخيل الشعبيّ، إذ تختلف سِيَرُ هؤلاء الأشخاص في السير الشعبية عن سيرهم في السرديّات الرسميّة، بوصفها سرديّات بديلة حاولتْ أن تنتج من خلال هذا السرد البديل صورةً جديدة لهؤلاء الشطّار[42].

وانسجاماً مع هذا الطرح فتجدرُ الإشارة إلى تمثيلات صورة هارون الرشيد في السرد الشطاريّ، إذ تنبني هذه السرديّة على تخليق صورةٍ جديدةٍ للخليفة/ الحاكم، الذي يغدو مفتوناً بألعاب هؤلاء الشطار، وشريكاً حقيقياً وفاعلاً لهم فيها، إذ «تقترن ليالي الرشيد بحالات قلقٍ وتأزم كانت تدفع الرشيد إلى البحث عن أدوات وحلول يدرأ بها ما يعترضه من قلق وتأزم»[43]، وفي هذا السياق فإنّ السرد الشطاري يُبرِزُ صورةً جديدةً لهارون الرشيد، تتأسس على تصويره

غارقاً في اللهو، وهي صورة مباينةٌ للصورة المركوزة في مرايا التاريخ الرسميّ، التي ترسّخ سيرة الحاكم العادل، الذي كان يحجُّ عاماً ويغزو عاماً، وتغدو الصورة أو التشكُّل الصُوَريُّ لصورة الشاطر ذا/ت فاعليّةٍ مركزيّة في خلْقِ هذا التاريخ الجديد، المنسوج بقوة السرد المُضادّ، وعليه، وبلغة أخرى، فإنّ التشكيل الصوري الذي تتمظهر فيه صورة الشاطر، يمثّل، بمنطق النقد الثقافيّ، بناءً نسقيّاً، أو قل: بُنية نصيّة تضمرُ في ثنياتها، رغبةً في تكريس ثقافة الأنا المُتفردة، التي تستطيع ببراعتها، وبالاتكاء على فتنة اللعب، تحقيق مآربها، من خلال تحقيق المنفعة المعنوية والمادية، أو البراغماتية، من خلال الكسب الذي يحظى به الشاطر، بغضّ الطرف عن مشروعيته، بما في ذلك من ارتباط بالتحقق الفعلي للذات، وإعادة تدوين تاريخها، أو طرح نفسها بصورة مغايرة للقار المألوف[44].

إنّ هذه الصور مصوغة بدقةٍ لتبين سُلطة الذات وفاعليتها في تحقيق فاعليّة مرجوّة، على الرغم من إقصائها من المدونات الرسمية، التي مارستْ عليها فعل الإقصاء، وجعلت الشطار ومروياتهم مرتبطةً دوماً بالكذب والاحتيال والتسول[45]، وتبدو أنساق الذات أنساقاً مركزيّاً في هذه السرديّات، إذ إنّ هذه السرديّات تعمل جهدها على رسم سيمياء التفرّد للشاطر، وترسيخ ذلك، وجعله ذا حضور متفردٍ ومغوٍ ومثير، في ظلال إنحيازه لمجتمعه وانتصاره له، إذ يمثّل فِعْلُ الانتخاب من السارد لضحايا الشاطر تواطؤاً ضمنيّاً مع الشاطر، ونيلاً من رموز البلاغة أو السلطة، وإيقاعها على الرغم من مكانتها في فتنته[46].

ويمثل فعل الغواية بُؤرةً يتأسّس على أس منها السرد الشطاري نوعاً من اللذة المفقودة أو المغيبة في السرديّات الرسمية[47]، ولا ريب أنّ فعْل اللذة يتحقّق في هذه السرديّات بفعل المناصفة أو قانون اللعب الذي يمثّل بُؤرة الحدث السرديّ، بصورةٍ متنامية تسلبُ القارئ لبّه، وتحقق لديه لذّة الإدهـاش والإعجاب، وهي بموازاة ذلك تُبهر المشطور، وتجعله واقعاً في سُلطة الشاطر، وحيله،

ومكائده[48]، وتبدو لذّة اللعب لذّة محوريّة في السرد الشطاريّ، إذ تقع السلطة في غواية هذه الحيل، لشعورها قطعاً بلذّة الفعل أو الحدث المترتّب على المناصفة بالمكر والخداع، المثير للإعجاب، أو اللذة كما أسلفت، وعليه فإنّ نسق الغِواية يبتغي غواية الشاطر، والمَشْطور، والقارئ[49]، ففعل الإدهاش أو اللامتوقع، المتربط بمسارات الحِيْلة، هو الفعل المسؤول في هذه السرديّات عن تحقيق اللذة للشاطر بصورة تحمل ضرباً من المُفارقة الحادّة، التي تجعل الموتور/ المشطور منغمساً بهذه المناصف بفعل وسائل الإقناع والاحتيال[50].

وإذا كان هناك لذةٌ متحققة في النصّ، يقوم عليها، ويذكيها الشاطر بفتنته، فإن هذه اللذة ترتبط بلذّةٍ أخرى عند القارئ، الذي يتفحص فعل الغواية، ويحاول أن يفكك أنظمته، وهنا فإن النصّ اللذويّ يتخلق في رحم المجتمع «فاللذة لذّتان: لذّة الكتابة (The Pleasure of Writing)، ولذّة القراءة (The Pleasure of Reading)، ولن تتحقق الأولى ما لم تتحقق الثانية، فالكاتب والقارئ متلازِمان، فكلاهما ملتبسٌ بالآخر أو كيان مـزدوجٌ يمارس لذّة النص»[51]، ولا ريب أنّ ماجدولين قد أشار إلى سطوة هذه اللذة، المحفزة على قراءة هذا السير، والكشف عن صورة الشطار، وأنساقه، إذ تطفح هذه السرديّات بالرغبة «في فتنة الآخرين المعذبين بالفعل، من خلال استهواء: (التاجر/ الحاكم)، ومن ينافس (بقيّة الشطار)، ومن يتابع (المعشوقة)، ومن يتلقّى صور الحكايات (القراء المتنوعون)»[52]، وعليه فإنّ شرف الدين من خلال «هذه اللذة، يستطيع أن يواجه مثل هذا النص، فيتلقاه بكيانه كلّه، بحسّه وعقله، ويقترب إليه ويستأنسه»[53].

ولا بُدّ من الإشارة إلى أنّ الإقبال على هذا النوع السرديّ من لدن ماجدولين يأتي في أتون الخروج عن أطر النظرة الاستعلائيّة التي يحاكم الناقد الأدبيّ بها هذه السرديّات، ذلك أنّها في منظورهم غيرُ قمينة بالاشتغال المنهجيّ، ويرجع ذلك إلى أنّ مدارها كان حول الهامشيين، الذين تَمَّ أقصاوَهم من مدونات الأدب الرسمي، ولعلّ نسق الغواية يرتبط في هذا السياق بأنساقٍ مضمرةٍ أخرى

هي أنساق الدهاء، وكذلك أنساق الذّات التي تتمثل في بلاغة الاستهواء، التي تمثل بلاغة المقموعين كما يعبّر عن ذلك جابر عُصفور [54]، إذ تمثل البلاغةُ المقموعةُ البلاغةَ المهملةَ «في ظل هيمنة البلاغة التي تتوارثها (...) هذه البلاغة المقموعة أنتجتها المجموعات الهامشيّة التي لعبت دور المعارضة» [55]، وذلك من خلال انتصارها وصورتها المميزة «انطلاقاً من ديناميتها في إنجاز الفعل البارع» [56]، وفي هذا السياق يمكن الإشارة إلى أن ماجدولين ليس بدعاً في سلوكه مسالك هذه القراءة، ذلك أنه يشترك مع كيلطيو في ذلك، الذي يمثل النقد لديه ضرباً من الالتذاء بالنصّ [57]، واتساقاً مع ذلك فإن سرد الشطار بحسب ماجدولين لا بدّ من أن يُنْظَرَ إليه بوصفه محفزاً «لبلاغةٍ مميّزة للعب، ولنسقٍ فريدٍ للغواية والاستهواء» [58].

وتبدو استعانة ماجدولين بفلسفة اللعب عند غادامير تأكيداً لهذه النزعة اللذويّة، إذ يغدو فعل اللعب، مطلوباً لذاته، باعتبار اللعب «وظيفة أوّلية جدّاً للحياة الإنسانية، لدرجة أن الحضارة تكون أمراً غير متصوّرٍ تماماً بدون هذا العنصر» [59]، وتبدو تجليات القراءة الثقافيّة اللذويّة في البناء اللغويّ للخطاب النقديّ، الذي يقوم على الاستعارات، ومن أمثلة هذه العبارات التي يطفح بها الخطاب النقدي عند ماجدولين قوله: (في لحظة ضاجة بالتفاصيل)، و(في مرحلة برزخ بين الإضمار والتشخيص) [60].

ولعلّه من اللافت للنظر في السرد الشطاريّ أنّ ثمة حضوراً مركزياً للمرأة، إذ إن دليلة، وابنتها، تمثلان ذروة الدهاء والمكر والاحتيال، ويبدو أنّ ذلك ليس على علاقة بصورة المرأة في الذاكرة الشعبية، التي تصورها بصورة دونية، ذلك أنهما تشتركان بالدهاء والمكر مع الرجل، مما ينفي أن يكون الدهاء هنا سالباً، كما قررت الثقافة الشعبية، بأن المرأة قرين السوء [61]، ويبدو حضور المرأة في هذا السرد الشطاريّ متماساً مع رغبة المرأة في تكريس ثقافة الحضور والدهاء، في ظلال أبوية المجتمعات الإنسانية عامة والعربيّة خاصة، التي تحرّم عليها

مثل هذه الممارسات، ولا ريب أنّ ماجدولين في ظلال انهماكه بفتنة الغواية، كان في غَفْلةٍ عن حضورها المركزي، على الرغم من تمثيله في مقاربته للسرد الشطاري بسرديّات أو حكايات كانت دليلة النصابة بطلتها[62]، ولعلّ ذلك ينبِئ برغبة دليلة في إعادة تكوين الصورة الذهنية لحضور المرأة، التي ترفضُ أو تتمرد على ثقافة المجتمع، وتحاول أن تتفلت من إساره، ومن إسار النظرة الدونية المركوزة في المخيال الجمعيّ.

وفي هذه السرديّات، تظهر المرأة محتميةً بثقافة الدهاء، التي تسهم في حماية كيانها من الثقافة الذكورية، ولعلّ لغة الخطاب السرديّ تنبِئُ كذلك برغبتها في الحفاظ على وجودها، بما يحفظ لها حياتها، وحياة ابنتها زينب، من خلال فتنة المناصفة، التي يمكن من خلالها الحصول على المال، الذي يساعد في التأسيس لحياة كريمة لها ولابنتها، وهنا فلا بُدّ من الإشارة إلى إلماعة (نبيلة إبراهيم) إلى الدور المركزيّ للمرأة في السير الشعبيّة، إذ إنها تزدحم من منظورها «بنماذج من البطولات النسائيّة يفوق الحصر»[63]، وممّا يؤكّد ذلك أن دليلة تستطيع دوماً الإيقاع بالرجل/ النسق المضاد ـ بصورة نامية ـ تنتصر خلالها ثقافة الدهاء النسوي مقابل هزيمة ثقافة الغباء الذكوري، وهو ما تؤكده نهاية الحكاية، إذ تنتهي الحكاية «بالغاية التي تحددها زينب: جامكية الأب، مروراً بالوسائل المثبتة بدقة: الحِيَل، والخداع، والمناصف»[64].

ـ سرديّات العشق: الحب وأنساق الذات:

تركز قراءة شرف الدين ماجدولين لنسق التواصل في طوق الحمامة لابن حزم في إطار ثنائيات الذات والآخر على فكرة مركزية مؤداها أن النص السيري إنما مثّل صورةً لمركزية الذات الساردة/ ابن حزم، وأنساقها، وذكورتها، وفحولتها، التي تعكس بالطبع معرفتها، وخبرتها، وتجاوزها من سبقها في هذا الميدان، وهي كما يذكر ماجدولين سردية كبرى يتفوق خلالها ووفقاً لمنظور الذات

تجربة السارد على التجارب السابقة التي يعد من أبرزها: «الزهرة» لابن داود، و«رسائل إخوان الصفا» و«روضة المحبين» لابن القيم الجوزية، و«الموشى» للوشاء، و«اعتلال القلوب» للخرائطي، و«ديوان الصبابة» للتلمساني [65].

ولعلّ الاحتماء ببلاغة القول وجماليات التعبير إنما يضمر خلف سجفه مركزية الذات، التي تبرز خبرتها الإنسانية في الحبّ، وماهيته، وسيرورته، ذلك أنها أي الذات الساردة تمثل «بما هي مرجع للحكم والتشخيص والاستدلال، أي أننا منذ الوهلة الأولى أمام انحراف في ضوابط التشكيل النوعي» [66].

وإذا كان ابن حزم الظاهري يصرّح في بداية كتابه هذا بأن كتابه يمثل نظراً عميقاً لتجربة العشق، وما يحف بها، فإن هذا الخطاب يؤكد رغبة الذات الساردة في التجاوز، والتخطي، والاستقلال، وتقديم العلمي على الحسيّ، والمعاين على المتصور، ففي هذه السريات التي يرويها ابن حزم، تجاوز لجل ما أنجزته الذات في تسريد العشق، والحب، والغرام، على اختلافها وتعددها، في صورة من صور «السجال النصي والمعارضة والمحاكاة الساخرة» [67]، مع ما أنجزته الذات الإنسانية فيما سلف من الزمان حول هذه الموضوعة من تواليف وتجارب، يقول ابن حزم: «كلَّفتني ــ أعزَّك الله ــ أن أصنّف لك رسالةً في صفة الحب ومعانيه، وأسبابه وأعراضه، وما يقع فيه وله على سبيل الحقيقة لا مُتزيّداً ولا مفنناً، لكنْ مُورداً لما يحضُرني على وجهه وبحسب وقوعه، حيث انتهى حفظي وسَعة باعي فيما أذكره، فبدرتُ إلى مرغوبك. ولولا الإيجاب لك لما تكلَّفته، فهذا من الفقر، والأوْلى بنا مع قِصر أعمارنا ألّا نَصرفها إلا فيما نرجو به رَحْب المُنقلب وحُسن المآب غداً. وإن كان القاضي حمام بن أحمد حدَّثني عن يحيى بن مالك عن عائذ، بإسناد يرفعه إلى أبي الدرداء أنه قال: (أجمُّوا النفوس بشيء من الباطل ليكون عوناً لها على الحق). ومن أقوال الصالحين من السلف المرضيِّ: (مَن لم يحسن يتفنّى لم يحسن يتقوَّى). وفي بعض الأثر: (أريحوا النفوس؛ فإنها تصدأ كما يصدأ الحديد).

والذي كلَّفتني لا بد فيه من ذكر ما شاهدتْه حضرتي، وأدركته عنايتي، وحدَّثني به الثقات من أهل زمانه، فاغتفرْ لي الكناية عن الأسماء؛ فهي إما عورة لا نَستجيز كشفها، وإما نُحافظ في ذلك صديقاً ودوداً، ورجلاً جليلاً.

وبحسبي أن أُسمي من لا ضرر في تسميته، ولا يَلحقنا والمسمَّى عيبٌ في ذكره، إما لاشتهارٍ لا يُغني عنه الطيُّ وتركُ التبيين، وإما لرضًى من المُخبَر عنه بظهور خبره وقلةِ إنكارٍ منه لنقله.

وسأورد في رسالتي هذه أشعاراً قلتُها فيما شاهدته، فلا تنكر أنت ومن رآها عليَّ أني سالكٌ فيها مسلك حاكي الحديث عن نفسه، فهذا مذهب المتحلِّين بقول الشعر، وأكثر من ذلك فإنَّ إخواني يجشِّموني القولَ فيما يَعْرِض لهم على طرائقهم ومذاهبهم. وكفاني أني ذاكر لك ما عَرض لي مما يشاكل ما نحوتُ نحوه وناسبُه إليَّ.

والتزمت في كتابي هذا الوقوفَ عند حدك، والاقتصارَ على ما رأيتُ أو صحَّ عندي بنقل الثقات، ودعني من أخبار الأعراب والمتقدمين؛ فسبيلُهم غير سبيلنا، وقد كثرت الأخبار عنهم، وما مذهبي أن أنضي مطيَّة سواي، ولا أتحلَّى بحلي مستعار. والله المستغفَر والمستعان لا ربَّ غيره»⁽⁶⁸⁾.

إن هذا النص نص تجاوزيّ، وفتّان، يلعب بالخطاب بصورة مضمرة، ويكرس مفهوم التجاوز الذي يجيء على مستويين «بلاغي ومضموني، في آن معاً: على اعتبار ما تمثله آلية النظر التحليلية في الكتاب من نقلة لتمثيلات الحب من دائرة العجائبي والطقوسي والغرائزي إلى مدار دنيوي يثرى بإحالات الواقعي»⁽⁶⁹⁾.

ولعلّ التمثيل على المسائل المتربطة بالعشق بالشعر في ثنايا الحكايات السرديّة عند ابن حزم يمثّل صورة أخرى من صور المركزية، التي يشير إليها ماجدولين، فهي لا تجيء في ثنايا هذه السرود «لإضافة خبرة جديدة، أو تجريد

يعز أداؤه نثراً، وإنما لغرض الاستعراض الشكلي ومراكمة الظلال المعنوية، والتزيد الإنشائي، قرين الفحولة، والتمركز، واللاحوارية»[70]، ولعلّ ذلك يرتبط بثقافة الذات العربيّة، التي تمجّد الشعر، وترفع من قيمته، وتعكس فحولة الذات، ولذا فإن السارد/ ابن حزم، يظلّ يكرر عدداً من العبارات من مثل: وفي ذلك أقول أبياتاً منها..، أو وفي ذلك أقول شعراً منه[71].

وإذا كانت المرأة تمثل في المخيال العربيّ آخراً، وأقلّ منزلة، فإنّ ابن حزم ينخرط في هذه النظرة الإقصائيّة، ذلك أن تمركز صوت الذكر/ الفحل، وتحكمه في مسارات السرد، إنما هو من صورة من صور «تجذر النظرة الاستعلائية للصوت الثقافيّ الذكوري»[72]، فالرجل الذكر هو المركز، والمرأة الأنثى هي الهامش يقول ماجدولين: «أضحت الأنثى مجرد صدى لصوت الذكر، ومحيطاً يؤثث فعالية البؤرة الطاغية لنشاط الرجل وهيمنته»[73].

ولقد أشار ماجدولين إلى فاعلية الذكورة وهامشية الأنوثة في إطار تجربة الحب، فالرجل هو الذي يحبّ ويكون هو الطرف الفاعل في هذه العملية في حين تكون الأنثى معشوقة، يقول ابن حزم: «وقد أحب من الخلفاء المهديين والأئمة الراشدين كثير، منهم بأندلسنا عبد الرحمن بن معاوية لدعجاء، والحكم بن هشام، وعبد الرحمن بن الحكم وشغفه بطروب، ومحمد بن عبد الرحمن وأمره مع غزلان.. وأما كبار رجالهم ودعائم دولتهم فأكثر من أن يحصوا..»[74].

إن حصر تجربة الحب بالذكر وتهميش الأنثى، وجعل الرجل هو المبادر والعاشق والفاعل، في ظلال غياب الأنثى، وتحولها إلى مفعول به، مستقبل، هامش، تعكسُ ثنائية (ذكر/أنثى) التحكم الخطابي أحادي البعد، وهو ما يشير إليه ماجدولين بقوله: «فثمة دوماً رجال في المقدمة، هم موضوع الإخبار ومرجع التحليل وموئل الاستنتاج، سواء كانوا خلفاء أو أمراء أو فقهاء أو من عامة الناس. فبالإحالة عليهم تستجلي علامات الحب، وباستذكار أحوالهم تستبان أعراضه، بينما تحتل النساء مرتبة المحمول المتأخر والمعطوف على ما سبق،

سواء في رتبة الجملة، أو في مدارات الصور والمشاهد والوقائع المروية»[75] .

ولعلّ الرجل يغدو الفحل ومركز التمكّن في كثير من الأخبار التي يرويها ابن حزم، يقول ابن حزم: «ولقد علمت فتى من بعض معارفي قد وحل في الحب وتورط في حبائله، وأضر به الوجد، وأنصبه الدنف، وما كانت نفسه تطيب بالدعاء إلى الله عز وجل في كشف ما به ولا ينطق به لسانه، وما كان دعاؤه إلا بالوصل والتمكن ممن يجب»[76] .

إن سلطة الذكورة والرغبة في التمكّن من المحب، وحيازته، والتمكن منه، تعكس نسق الذات، وسلطتها، ومركزيّتها فالعلاقة «ذي اتجاه واحد، موسوم بالعنف، وهو ما يمكن أن يستشف من لفظ «التمكن» ممن يحب. بذا يمكن تفسير التحكم بالبلاغي الممارسة بقوة في نص الطوق، والذي على أساسه تتشيد سردية مختلفة تكرس الهيمنة واللاتكافؤ الصوري بين بؤرة الفعل المرتبط بالذات (الذكر) وهامش الانفعال والاستيعاب المتصل بالآخر (الأنثى)، والذي سيتخذ إبدالات وأقنعة عديدة في ثنايا التخييل والتحليل وزاوية النظر»[77] .

– سرديّات الهزل والآخر وتجليات الهامش:

يذهب شرف الدين ماجدولين إلى أن سرديّات الهامشي والهامشيين في الثقافة العربيّة ارتباطات بتحقُّقات متباينة، أما أولها فسرود الفئات الضالة من منظور السلطة، وأما ثانيهما فالسرديّات التي يمثلها الشطار والشواذ وغيرهم محورها.

وترتبط آداب الهامشين من منظور شرف الدين ماجدولين بالسرد والسرديّات، ولذا فإنها تجيء غالباً على هيئة سرديّات أو في قوالب سرديّة، وهو ما يفسر النظر الدونيّ إلى السرديّات، آداب الهامشين، بخلاف الشعر والخطابة والفنون الرسمية من أدب/ آداب البلاط، ولذا «فمن هذا المنطلق، يجدر التنويه، على نحو مبدئي، بأن السرد، بخلاف الشعر، مثّل نسقاً خطابياً غير ذي حظوة في تراث

النظر النقدي العربي، بل إن أفعال القص والحكي والرواية ارتبطت بمجال الترويح، وتجاوز منطق العقل، والاختراع، والكذب»[78].

ولعل ما يؤكد هذه النظرة الدونيّة إلى آداب الضحك والهزل ما يسوقه ماجدولين من أقوال وآراء لعدد من المصنّفين، إذ يقول الوشاء في باب النهي عن مفاكهة الأوداء ومماحتهم: «اعلم أن من زي الأدباء، وأهل المعرفة والعقلاء، وذوي المروءة والظرفاء، قلة الكلام في غير أرب، والتجاهل عن المداعبة واللعب، وترك التبذل بالسخافة والصياح بالفكاهة والمزاح، لأن كثرة المزاح يذل المرء، ويضع القدر، ويزيل المروءة، ويفسد الأخوة، ويجرئ على الشريف الحر، أهل الدناءة والشر»[79].

ويقول ابن الجوزيّ مبرراً تأليفه لكتاب أخبار الحمقى والمغفلين إنه يجيء: «الأول: أن العاقل إذا سمع أخبارهم عرف قدر ما وهب له مما حرموه، فحثه ذلك على الشكر. والثاني: أن ذكر المغفلين يحث المتيقظ على اتقاء أسباب الغفلة إذا كان ذلك داخلاً تحت الكسب وعامله فيه الرياضة، وأما إذا كانت الغفلة مجبولةً في الطباع، فإنها لا تكاد تقبل التغيير. والثالث: أن يريح الإنسان قلبه بالنظر في سير هؤلاء المبخوسين حظوظاً يوم القسمة، فإن النفس قد تمل من الدؤوب في الجد، وترتاح إلى بعض المباح من اللهو...»[80].

ويقول في الباب السادس الموسوم بـ: (لا تؤاخ الأحمق) ما مؤداه: «قال عليه السلام: لا تؤاخي الأحمق فإنه يشير عليك ويجهد نفسه فيخطئ وربما يريد أن ينفعك فيضرك وسكوته خير من نطقه وبعده خير من قربه وموته خير من حياته، وقال ابن أبي زياد: قال لي أبي: يا بني الزم أهل العقل وجالسهم واجتنب الحمقى فإني ما جالست أحمق فقمت إلا وجدت النقص في عقلي»[81].

تأكد هذه الأنظار وغيرها بما لا يدع مجالاً للشك أن هذه السرديّات هي سرديّات الهامش، وأن الهزل يتربط بالهامش والسفه والطيش وقلة العقل، وهو ما لا تتطلبه السلطة من الجد والصرامة ومجانفة اللهو واللعب.

إن سرديّات الهزل تمثل نوعاً من سرديّات الهامش كذلك، في إطار جدليات العقل، واللاعقل، والبله، والحمق، فقد تواترت الأخبار على دونيتها، وانطوائها على السخيف، التافه، من القول، فهي وإن كانت تحقق لذة لدى ذوي الرياسات، والأمراء، والخلفاء، فإنها تظل مع ذلك مرذولة، مرذول أصحابها، وأبطال حكايتها.

ولعلّه من الغنيّ القول إن سرديّات التحامق والتجانّ سرديّات مخاتلة تضمر في بنيتها العميقة أنساقاً ثقافيّة مخاتلة؛ فهي سرديّات أو سرودٌ تنطوي على فاعليّة نقديّة مُضادَة، يتأسّس على أسٍّ منها النسق المُضمر، استناداً إلى الفكرة القائلة بنزوع هذه السرود إلى الثقافة الشعبيّة، وبذا عدم ملاحقة رواتها وأبطالها، مما يفسح المراح أمامهم لتوجيه خطاب نقديّ قويّ إلى السلطة تحت أقنعة (Mask) الجنون والعته والخَبَال والضحك والمتعة، بل إن بعض رجال السلطة يذهبون إلى إعادة هذه النكات والسرود الهزلية في صورة مستعادة، على هيئة تكوّن مفارقة حادة.

إنّ هذه السرديّات هي سرديّات حجاجية، وفي هذا السياق يشير (عيسى برهومة) في دراسته الموسومة بـ(البيانُ الحِجَاجيُ في قصص بخلاء الجاحظ: دراسة في خطاب النادرة) إلى أنّ نوادر الجاحظ مشحونة بالأساليب الحجاجيّة الإقناعيّة من مثل؛ القياس المنطقيّ، وضَرْبِ المَثَلِ، والنموذج، والاستشهاد، والتصوير، والحيلة، والتعجيب، والحِجاج المغالط، فهذه السرود في ضوء الدراسات اللسانية سرودٌ حجاجيّة مفعمة بالمحمولاتِ الحجاجيّة، التي تنطوي عليها حواريّات أبطالها مع مَنْ حولهم[82].

وتشيرُ نعيمة بولكعيبات إلى أن تغييب السارد والتوافق مع اللاشعور الجمعيّ في سرديّات الهزل والضحك يؤسّسان فهي تعكس تقبّل الثقافة الشعبية والمخيال الجمعيّ لهذه النوادر من خلال (مؤلّف ضمني) + (متلقٍ ضمني) يتواضعان على قَبول هذه الرسالة، وتحاول هذه السرود كذلك أن تُؤسس لموقف مضادّ أو

نسق بديل يتبناه صاحبها ضدّ العادات والتقاليد القارّة، وضغوطاتها الإكراهية على المجتمع [83].

وينتخب ماجدولين صورة المرأة في سرديّات الضحك والهزل، بوصفها هامشاً في المخيال الجمعيّ العربيّ، تخضع لقانون التملك والشهوة والاستملاك والتحكم، إذ تغدو المرأة في سرديّات الهزل مادة التندر والضحك والإمتاع، ولذا فإنها لا تعكس صورتها الدونيـة في المخيال الشعبي العربيّ فقط، بل تعكس مركزيّة حضـورها في السرديّات الهزليّة، إذ تغدو المرأة مكوناً مركزياً من هذه السرديّات.

ومن هذه الأخبار ما يسوقه كثير من الإخباريين في الثقافة العربيّة، إذ يروى أنّ الحجّاج «كتب إلى أيوب بن القرية: أن أخطب على عبد الملك بن الحجاج امرأة جميلة من بعيد، مليحة من قريب، شريفة في قومها ذليلة في نفسها، مواتية لبعلها. فكتب إليه: قد أصبتها لولا عظم ثدييها. فكتب إليه: لا يكمل حسن المرأة حتى يعظم ثدياها، فتدفئ الضجيع، وتروي الرضيع» [84].

وفي المدونة السردية الهزلية تجلّيات أكثر انتقاصاً من المرأة فقد بدت فيها بلا عقل، إذ تكشفُ كثير منها عن تحيّزات الثقافة العربيّة التي تحتقر المرأة وتهينها؛ إذ تكشف هذه السرود عن أنساق الثقافة الفحوليّة المركزية؛ استناداً إلى الحديث النبويّ الموضوع الذي مؤداه أن المرأة ناقصة عقل ودين، فجحا الذي يمثل صوت المجتمع، يؤكد مقولة من مقولاته المتداولة التي تؤكد أن المرأة أقلُّ عقلاً وقَدْراً من الرجل، ومن ذلك ما روي عن حجا أنه قيل لجحا «إنّ امرأتك قد أضاعت عقلها. ففكّر قليلاً ثم قال: أنا أعلمُ أنّه لا عقل لها، فدعني أتذكّر، يا تُرى ما الذي أضاعه؟» [85].

ولا فكاك من القول إن النقد الأدبيّ ألمع في بعض تطبيقاته المختلفة إلى ما تحفلُ به هذه السرديّات من تمثيلات انتقاصية تؤطر صورة المرأة في المجتمع

العربيّ أو في المخيال الجمعي، أو ما تحفل به كذلك من إشاريات رامزة، تهدف إلى النيل من السلطات السياسية والاجتماعية[86].

ويؤكد ماجدولين أن صورة الآخر حظيت في السرد العربيّ بصورة وهو ما يروى في سرديّات مختلفة «انطلاقاً منه تم تصوير الهامش الجغرافي بمعيار القدرة الحسية المجاوزة لحدود المألوف، ومجافاة النظر العقلاني، ولعل الهدف من هذا التزيد التغريبي، إظهار التفوق الأخلاقي للمركز العربيّ الإسلامي كجزء من جبلة إنسانية تنبتها الطبيعة؛ فالبغدادي نبيل وكريم وحليم؛ لأنه من إقليم شريف، بينما المغربي أسود ولئيم وحقود ... لأنه من إقليم «خسيس»»[87].

وينتخب ماجدولين عدداً من السرديّات لعل أبرزها سردية تروى عن عمر بن الخطاب، وسردية تروى عن أهل الرحلة والسفر، أما السردية الأول فهي: «أن عمر بن الخطاب، رضي الله عنه، سأل كعب الأحبار عن البلاد وأحوالها، فقال يا أمير المؤمنين، لما خلق الله، سبحانه وتعالى، الأشياء ألحق كل شيء بشيء، فقال العقل: أنا لاحق بالعراق، فقال العلم: وأنا معك. فقال المال: أنا لاحق بالشام، فقالت الفتن: وأنا معك، فقال الفقر: أنا لاحق بالحجاز، فقالت القناعة، وأنا معك. فقالت القساوة: أنا لاحقة بالمغرب، فقال سوء الخلق: وأنا معك»[88].

أما السردية الثانية فهي: «قال ابن سعيد والإقليم الثالث هو صاحب سفك الدماء والحسد والحقد والغل وما تبع ذلك ثم قال وأنا أقول إن الإقليم الثالث وإن كثرت فيه الأحكام المريخية على زعمهم فإن للمغرب الأقصى من ذلك الحظ الوافر لا سيما في جهة السوس وجبال الدرن فإن قتل الإنسان عندهم كذبح العصفور قال وكم قتيل قتل عندهم على كلمة وهم بالقتل يفتخرون ثم قال إن الغالب على أهل المغرب الأقصى كثرة التنافس المفرط والمحاققة وقلة التغاضي والتهور المفاتنة»[89].

إنّ الآخر في السرد العربيّ كان يخضع لقانون الهامشية، والتابعية، انطلاقاً

من مركزية الذات، ونظرتها المتعالية نحو ذاتها، بوصفها مركز الإسلام وداره، وقد كان الآخر في بعض الأخبار مثيراً للظّرف، والفكاهة والضحك، فهو آخر علج كافر... إلى غير ذلك من النعوت التي تشي بموقف الذات العربيّة من الآخر.

2 – 4 – هيثم سرحان: القراءة الثقافيّة وآفاق تحليل الخطاب:

– النقد الثقافيّ وتحليل الخطاب والتحليل النقدي للخطاب:

يمثل الكشف عن الأنساق المضمرة وتحليل الخطاب آليّات المقاربة النقديّة الآلتين اللتين تؤطران فِعْلَ القراءة النقديّة في مقاربة سرحان الأولى، إذ يغدو بناء الجهاز المنهجيّ للمقاربة على ائتلافٍ من مقولات النقد الثقافيّ وممكنات التحليل النقدي للخطاب كما تتمذجها اختياراً منهجيّاً يسفر عن وعْيٍ بوظيفة الاختيار المنهجيّ.

ولعلّه من اللافت للنظر أنّ هيثم سرحان مضى في عددٍ من المقاربات يساءلُ البنى السردية والثقافيّة في السرديّا ت العربيّة القديمة، بصورة شكّلت السرديّات العربيّة خلالها بالنسبة إليه خطاباً سردياً يحفز على مداومة القراءة والبحث[90].

– السرديّات الجنسانيّة والأنساق الثقافيّة:

تمثل السرديّات الجناسية عند هيثم سرجان نصّاً ثقافياً مرتبطاً بثقافة المجتمع العربيّ، وأنساقه الثقافيّة المتعددة، من مثل أنساق الحرب، وأنساق الكرم، وأنساق العشق، وأنساق البخل، وغيرها من الأنساق الثقافيّة المختلفة[91].

وتفيض السرديّات العربيّة حول موضوعة الجنس بأنساق ثقافية مخاتلة، ترتبط بالسياق الثقافيّ والاجتماعي والسياسيّ الذي نشأت في أتونه، وإذا أعرض صفحاً عن تمثيلات الجنس في الفقه، والطبابة، والتدوين، والكتابة، والقضاء، فإنّ الأدب العربيّ سرداً وشعراً مثل مدونة جنسانية متنوعة، ومكتملة الأركان،

يمكن للقارئ أن يجوس خلالها في سبيل الكشف عن تجليات الثقافة العربيّة، وأنساقها المختلفة.

وينتخب سرجان صورة المرأة في السرديّات الجناسية العربية محاولاً أن يكشف عن تمثيلات صورتها، وما تضمره هذه الصورة من تمثيلات ثقافية وأنساق مضمرة، فهي على الرغم من أنها تحضر في سرديّات كان الرجل ساردها، فإنها تحضر حسب سرحان في صورتين متباينتين، أما أولاهما فتتماهى مع النسق الثقافيّ العربيّ المقصي للمرأة، وأما ثانيهما، فثائر على قوى التسلط الدينيّ والثقافيّ والاجتماعيّ التي تظلّ تحاول أن تُسكته وأن تُقصيه.

ويحلّل سرحان الخطاب الشعريّ الذي تتضمنه (سرديّات السبي) في قصة سلمى بنت المحلق، والفارعة بنت معاوية، وزوجة الحارث بن عمر، ذاهباً إلى أنه خطابٌ يفعل فعله في أتون سرديّات السبي، ويضمر بعداً ثورياً، وكسراً لآفاق الانتظار، حين تبدي المسبية رغبتها وإعجابها في سابيها، مخالفة القار الثابت من الأنساق الثقافيّة في المجتمعات العربيّة، ومما قالته هؤلاء النساء في تلك ما قالته الفارعة بنت معاوية حين سُبيت[92]:

مِنَّا فَوارِسُ قاتَلُوا عَنْ سَبْيِهِمْ

يَوْمَ النسارِ وَلَيْسَ مِنَّا أَشْطُرُ

وَلَبِئْسَ ما نَصَرُوا الْعَشِيرَةَ ذُو لِحَىً

وَحَفِيفُ نافِجَةٍ بِلَيْلٍ مُسْهِرِ

ضَبُعا هِراشٍ تَعْفِرانِ اسْتَيْهِما

فَرَأَتْهُما أُخْرَى فَقامَتْ تَعْفِرُ

حاشا بَني الْمَجْنُونِ إِنَّ أَباهُمُ

صاتٌ إذا سَطَعَ الْغُبارُ الْأَكْدَرُ

لَـوْلا بُيُـوتُ بَنِـي الْحَريشِ تَقَسَّمَتْ

سَـبْيَ   الْقَبـائِلِ   مـازِنٌ   وَالْعَنْبَـرُ

زَعَمَـتْ بُـزُوخُ بَنِـي كِلابٍ أَنَّهُمْ

هَـزُّوا   الْجَمِيـعَ   وَأَنَّ   كَعْباً   أَدْبَـرُوا

كَـذَبَتْ بُـزُوخُ بَنِـي كِلابٍ إِنَّها

تَـأْتِي   الضِّـرَّاءِ   وَبَظْرُها   يَتَعطَّـرُ

إنّ هذا الخطاب الشعري الذي يُروى عن السبايا لحظة سبيهنّ لا يتواءم مع السنن الثقافيّة العربيّة، والأنساق الثقافيّة القارة، فلا يمكن أن يستساغ أن تجاهر المرأة بكونها سبية «ولذتها بمواصلة سبيها»، ولعلّ ذلك يغدو أكثر وضوحاً، يقول السارد: «غزا ابن هبيرة الغسّاني الحارث بن عمر فلم يصبه في منزله، فأخرج ما وجد له، واستاق امرأته فأصابها في الطّريق، وكانت من الجمال في نهايةٍ، فأعجبت به، فقالت: له انج فوالله لكأنّي به يتبعك كأنّه بعيرٌ أكل مراراً، فبلغ الخبر الحارث فأقبل يتبعه حتّى لحقه فقتله، وأخذ ما كان معه، وأخذ امرأته. فقال له: هل أصابك؟ فقالت: نعم، والله ما اشتملت النساء على مثله قط. فلطمها ثمّ أمر بها فوثّقت بين فرسين ثمّ أحضر هما حتى تقطّعت. ثمّ أنشأ إذ تقول زوجة الحارث بن عمر حين سباها ابن أبي هُبيرة الغسّاني:

إِنَّ مَـنْ غَـرَّهُ النِسَـاءُ بِـشَـيْءٍ

بَـعْـدَ هِـنْـدٍ لَـجَـاهِـلٌ مَـغْـرُورُ

حُـلْـوَةُ الْـعَـيْـنِ وَالْـحَـدِيـثِ وَمُـرُّ

كُـلِّ شَـيْءٍ أَجَـنَّ مِنْهَا الضَّمِيرُ

كُـلُّ أنـثَى – وَأن بَـدَا لَـكَ مِنْهَا

آيَـةُ الْحُـبّ – حُبُّهَا خَيْتَعُورُ ⁽⁹³⁾

وفي هذا السياق يحلّل سرحان بنية الخطاب في هذه السردية، ويتوقف عند المضمرات النصية التي تضمرها، ويتوقف عند دلائل الاستفهام في (هل أصابك؟)، والجواب: (نعم)، والأسلوب التقريري بالقسم (والله ما اشتملت النساء على مثله قط)، والشيفرات النصية التي تنطوي عليها[94].

وإذا كانت هذه السرديّات السالفة وما شاكلها تمثّل خرقاً لأنساق الثقافة العربيّة، التي تؤسس لدونيّة المرأة، وتابعيتها، وتعكس رغبة المرأة في الخروج عن قوانين المجتمع، وسلطاته الدينيّة، والثقافيّة، والاجتماعية، فإنّ المدونة السرديّة العربيّة الجنسانية، تحفل بعدد هائل من السرديّات التي تعكس نسق الفحولة العربيّ.

وينتخب سرحان في هذا السياق حكاية رويت عن أعشى همذان حين أُسر في بلاد الديلم، إذ يروي الأصفهاني في أغانيه ما يأتي: «كان أعشى همدان أبو المصبّح ممن أغزاه الحجّاج بلد الديلم ونواحي دستبي، فأُسر، فلم يزل أسيراً في أيدي الديلم مدّة. ثم إن بنتاً للعلج الذي أسره هويته، و صارت إليه ليلاً فمكّنته من نفسها، فأصبح وقد واقعها ثماني مرّات؛ فقالت له الديلمية: يا معشر المسلمين، أهكذا تفعلون بنسائكم؟ فقال لها: هكذا نفعل كلّنا؛ فقالت له: بهذا العمل نصرتم؛ أفرأيت إن خلّصتك، أتصطفيني لنفسك؟ فقال لها نعم، وعاهدها. فلما كان الليل حلّت قيوده وأخذت به طرقاً تعرفها حتى خلّصته وهربت معه. فقال شاعر من أسرى المسلمين:

فمن كــانَ يفديه مـن الأسـر مـاله

فهمدان تفديها الغداة أيو...ها[95]»

ويرى سرحان أنّ هذه السرديّة تضمرُ أكثر ممّا تفصح، فهي تضمر التدابير الاحترازية لحماية الأسير، وتفاصيل انسلال ابنة العِلْج إلى أعشى همذان/ الأسير، وغياب الأب، ويخلص سرحان إلى أنّ الذات العربيّة أو المتخيّل العربيّ الذكوريّ لم يكن مهتماً سوى بتأكيد فحولته، ومركزيته، وبذا ترسيخ أنساقه/

218

فالأمر الذي تكرسه هذه السردية هو فقط «إبراز القدرة الجنسية الكبيرة التي يتمتع بها أعشى همدان» [96].

وعليه فإنّ هذه السرديّات التي انتخبها سرحان تمثل خطابات نسقية، فهي خطابات تحفل بعدد من الأنساق الثقافيّة، التي تربط بالذات العربيّة، وفحولتها، وموقفها من المرأة، وموقف المرأة منها.

ــ الوصايا السرديّة وهيمنة الأبويّة:

وفي أتون ذلك يحاولُ هيثم سرحان أن يفيد من معرفته أو انشغالاته بتحليل الخطاب، أو التحليل النقدي للخطاب على وجه أدقّ، في الكشف عن الأساليب اللغوية، والمسالك الحجاجية، والتناصات، التي تبيّن هيمنة الأبِ /الموصّي على ابنه الموصّى، ولا ريب أن اشتغالات السرد في الوصايا السردية اشتغالات تكاد أن لا تبين، في ظلال سطوة الخطاب الوصائي، وهو ما مثل في إشكالية أجناسية تنتظم هذه السرود، تستطلب من الناقد العملَ على الإنباه إلى ذلك في مفتتح الدراسة.

ولا ريب أنّ مفهوم (شعريّة الوصيّة)، الذي يقابل (شعريّة السرد) يمثّل مفهوماً مركزيّاً في هذه المقاربة ، ذلك أنّ سرحان ينطلقُ من افتراض رئيس مؤدّاه أنّ شعريّة القصّ، أو شعريّة السرد، هي المحضن الملائم لاحتضان هذه الأنساق، من خلال تكثيف اللغة، والاتكاء على سِحْر العبارة، في إطار توليفة يمكن وسمها بـ(لذة السرد وغوايته)، التي تعينه على بثّ أنساقٍ ثقافيّة مضادة، تعملُ على الطّعن في ثوابت المجتمعات، وكسر قوانينها، وترسيخ سلطة الأبّ المكدّي، ومنحه نَسْغِ البقاء والحضور؛ تعويذةً في وجه الزمن، والموت، والغياب، وتمارسُ شعريّة الوصيّة بحسب منظور سرحان غواية ومخاتلة تضمر أنساق الأبوة والتعالي والقبض على الحكمة، وإن كان ظاهر الخطاب حافلاً بأنساق العطف، والحبّ، والأبوّة [97].

ولا ريب أنّ الشعريّة (Poetics) التي يتحدّث عنها سرحان، هي الشعريّة الخطابيّة، التي تعدّ إحدى أهمّ وظائف اللغة، كما تقرّر لدى رومان جاكوبسون (Roman Jakobson)[98]، والشعريّة اللسانيّة / الخطابيّة هي استعمالُ اللغة بصورةٍ مائزة وخاصة، كما هو استخدامه لمصطلح البلاغة، وفي ذلك توازٍ بين مفهوم الجماليات في النقد الثقافيّ، بحيث إن كلاً من الجماليات والشعرية والبلاغة يقومان بمخاتلة القارئ، وبث رسائل مشفرة.

وتمثل الوصايا السرديّة سلطة المعرفة، والكشف، والحقيقة، التي يمتلكها الموصّي وحده، وذلك بتكريس ثقافة احتكار هذه الحكمة والمعرفة، والسعي سعياً حثيثاً إلى تنمية تجربة الموصّى، من خلال مراس فِعْل الوصاية/ الوصيّة، التي تتجلى فيهـ/ا أنساق الذات، والمعرفة، والتعالي، قُبالة حضور هامشيّ للآخر الموصّى، وفي ضَوْء هذا السابق تسعى الذّات الموصيّة في الخطاب السرديّ في السرديّات المنتخبة «إلى ترسيخ تقاليدها، وتعميق أثرها، وتخليد مفعولها في مستقبل الأبناء، عبر سلطة إبلاغيّة يمتلك الآباء سلطانها، واستجابة إذعانية يتوافرُ عليها الأبناء الذين لا يحرصون على قَتْلِ آبائهم»[99]، ويتجلى نسق الذّات وفحولتها وأنساق محْو الآخر في النماذج الوصاية السرديّة التي ينتخبها سرحان، وهي وصيّة خالد بن يزيد (خالويه المكدّي) التي أوردها الجاحظ في كتـاب البخلاء، والمقامة الوصية التي وردت في مقامات الهمذانيّ، والمقامة الساسانية التـي جاءت في مقامـات الحريريّ[100]، ولا ريب أنّ الموصّي استخدم في بنائه لخطاب الوصية (Discourse Command) عدداً من الاستراتيجيّات الخطابية، التي ألمع إليها سرحان، وهي الاستراتيجيّات: التضامنيّة، والتوجيهيّة، والتلميحيّة، والحجاجيّة[101].

وتغدو شخصيات (خالويه المكدّي)، و(أبي الفتح الإسكندريّ)، و(أبي زيد السروجيّ)، ممثّلة لشخصيّة البطل، أو محتلّة لموقع البطولة في الخطاب السرديّ، وممثلة لمفهوم الأبويّة، التي تسعى إلى إظهار خبرتها، من خلال

عددٍ من الممارسات من مثل: نمذجة الذات، والهُزْءِ بمعارف الابن[102]، ويبدو سرحان على وعْي بإشكاليّة المؤلّف والبطل ووَهْمِ التطابق بينهما، إذ إنّ فصل رُوَاهما عن بعضها، أو جعْل صوت البطل صدىً لصوت المؤلّف لا يمكن أن يُطَمئنّ إليه أبداً، فقد تداخلا تداخلاً لا يمكن أن يفضّ، ولا يمكن أن يُنفى بسبب «فعل المحاكاة الذي يغيّبُ أثر المؤلّف، ويخلق في النصّ بلبلةً صوتيّةً ما تنفكُ تشتت سمع القارئ، وتبعث في النصّ علامات سيميائيّة لا تفتأ تزيغُ بصره»[103]، ويبدو حضور الموت في هذه الوصايا علامةً دالّةً على وعْي الذات بضرورة تكريس ثقافة البعث بعد الموت، لأنها تمتلكُ حضوراً إنسانيّاً مركزيّاً، وقميناً بألا يغيبه الموت، وهو ما يشير إليه سِرحان سِراعاً دونما كثيرِ تلبّث.

وفي هذا السياق يحفلُ الخطاب السرديّ بالوصايا والأنساق الثقافيّة، التي تكرس ثقافة الأبويّة، وقدرة الذّات، وفضل الأول «ذلك أنّ الموصي يوجّه خطابه، وقدرته على لمن يندرج في سياق سلطته الرمزيّة التي تتضمن استعلاءً، وقدرةً على استعمال الإذعان والإرضاخ لا سيما إذا كان الخطاب صادراً من الأب لابنه»، ويمثل الهُزْءُ من الابن، ومن تجربته، ومن خبراته في معاركَةِ للحياة، قطبَ الرحى في محاولة قتل الابن/ الهامش، في سبيل تكريس ثقافة الذات (subjectivity)، وسلطتها، ويتمثّل قتل الابن الرمزيّ في سرديّة الجاحظ بعدم وثوق (خالويه المكّدّي) FI، فهو كما يقول سرحان: «غيرُ واثقٍ بابنه، مرتابٌ منه، قلقٌ من مستقبله»، ولا يتوقّف خالويه عند ذلك بل إنّه يستخف بعقله، وذلك بقوله: «وأنت غلام، لسانُكَ فوق عقلك، وذكاؤك فوق حَزْمِك لم تعجُمْكَ الضّرّاء...»، وتغدو الإلماعةُ الذكيّةُ التي التقطها سرحان في خطاب (خالويه المكّدّي)، وهو رغبته في تجهيل ابنه، إشارة دالّةً، على رغبته في قتل الابن قتلاً نهائيّاً، بتجهيله، وعدم الإفصاح له بالخبرات، التي يمكن له من خلالها أن يعيش كريماً، ولعل في ذلك ضمانة للأب بأنّك لن يسطع نجم ابنه من بعد موته، ليعلن أفول هذا النجم الأبويّ، وهذا الموقف من الابن هو ذاته موقف

أبي الفتح الإسكندري من ابنه، إذ يقول أبو الفتح: «يا بني، إنّي وإن وثقت بمتانة عقلِك، وطهارة أصلِك، فإنّي شفيق، والشفيق يسيءُ الظّنّ...»، وعليه فإنّ هذا الخطاب، لا يمكنُ أن يكون بريئاً، ذلك أنّه قدّم، وهو ما لم يلتفت إليه سرحان، خطاب التحبب بقوله يا بني، وهو ما يشير إلى رغبة الأب في تقديم النصيحة إلا أنه، يستدرك على ذلك، بالتأكيد على أنّ هذا الفتى، لا يمكن أن يُؤْمَنَ على سلطة الشهوة، وسلطانها، ولا ريب أنّ استعمال الموصّي يا بني في الوصايا السردية المنتخبة يتصادى بما لا يدع مجالاً للشك مع الخطاب اللقمانيّ، الذي يقدمه القرآن الكريم، إذ إنّ أسلوب النداء يمثل لازمة تكراريّة يفتتح بها لقمان – عليه السلام – وصاياه لابنه رغبة في استمالته، والتحبب إليه، بمخاطبته بخطاب الأبوّة الحانية، ولا ريب أن النداء في أصله، أو في إحدى وظائفه يؤدي وظيفة تواصليّة، تعمل على أن تعَقُّدِ أواصر الاتصال بين المنادى والمنادي.

ولعلّ الغريبَ في هذه الوصايا السردية أنها تَقْرِنُ الابن وسوءه وجهله بسوء الأم الخبيثة التي أنجبته، فهو نابتٌ من أصل خبيث، ولا ريب أنّ ذلك يرسّخ منظور الثقافة العربيّة من المرأة، قرينة السوء والمكر والخبث، التي كان سبباً في هبوط الرجل من الجنة إلى الأرض، وهو الأمر الذي تشترك فيه هذه الوصايا، بيد أنه لم يمثّل حدثاً، أو إشارة دالة، تستوجب الإسهاب في التحليل الذي قدّمه سرحان، ولعلّ من الواجب الإنباه إلى أنّ هذه النظرة الإقصائيّة إلى المرأة تمثل مشتركاً بين جميع ثقافات الشعوب والأمم؛ إذ لا يعدُّ هذا النسق نسقاً ثقافياً عربياً خالصاً؛ فقد نصّت المجاميع الفكريّة والمدوّنات الثقافيّة على الانتقاص من المرأة، أما المقامة في المقامة الساسانية فإن أبا زيد السروجي، يفتتح خطابه السرديّ/ وصيته، بقوله: «وأنتَ بحمْدِ اللهِ وليُّ عهْدي. وكبْشُ الكتيبةِ الساسانيّة مِنْ بعْدي»، إلا أنه يحاول أن يقتل الابن، حين يجعل تفوقه، ونبوغه، مرتبطاً بالتزامه بالتقاليد الأبوية، يقول أبو زبد: «وإني أوصيكَ بما لمْ يوصِ بهِ شيثٌ الأنباطَ. ولا يعْقوبُ الأسْباطَ، فاحفَظْ وصيّتي، وجانِبْ معْصِيتي»[104]، وعليه

فإنّ هذه التقاليد التي ينمذجها أبو زيد لابنه، تحفظه، بيد أنّ أيّ خَرقٍ لها، تبوّئ هذا الابن العاقّ منازلَ الفشل والخذلان.

ويتحدّث سرحان عن حجاجيّة الخطاب السرديّ في النماذج التي ينتخبها في قراءاته هذه، ذاهباً إلى أنّ السارد في هذه الوصايا قد آثر أن يلبسُ خطابه السرديّ لَبوس الخطاب الحجاجيّ؛ لتمرير أنساقه المضادّة، ويغدو التدرّج في طرح الوصايا وبنائها بناءً منطقياً في وصية (خالويه المكدّي) ملمحاً مائزاً في صناعة النسق، وجَعْلِ تجربةِ الابن تجربةً مستنسخةً من تجربة الأب.

إنّ عَرْضَ هذه التجارب من لدن (خالويه المكدّي) لابنه، هي ضَرْبٌ من الإغواء الذي يمارسه الأب على ابنه، رغبةً في ترسيخ أنساق المكر والخداع والبخل في ذهن الموصى ابنه، والاحتجاج الحاد على سلطة المجتمع، وعاداته المقيتة، التي تحثُّ على الكرم والتبذير، أما في الخطاب السرديّ في الوصية الساسانيّة فإنه يغدو حافلاً بأنساق الرفض، التي تكشف تمرّد الأب، الهازِئ بالموروث، إذ إنه يوصي ابنه من سلطة المجتمع، في صورة رفضٍ للواقع، وأنساقه، ويلحظُ سرحان أنّ السروجي يفيءُ إلى التناصّ الحِجاجيّ مع القرآن في سبيل ترسيخ هذه المعتقدات النسقيّة في ذِهْن ابنه، وجعلها مركوزة في وعيه وكيانه، إذ يتناص قول أبي زيد السروجيّ: «قيّدِ الدرْهَمَ بالربْطِ. وشُبِ البَذْلِ بالضّبْطِ. ولا تَجْعَلْ يدَكَ مغْلولَةً إلى عُنقِكَ ولا تَبسُطْها كلّ البسْطِ»، مع قوله تعالى :« وَلَا تَجْعَلْ يَدَكَ مَغْلُولَةً إِلَىٰ عُنُقِكَ وَلَا تَبْسُطْهَا كُلَّ الْبَسْطِ فَتَقْعُدَ مَلُوماً مَّحْسُوراً»[105] .

ويلمح سرحان إلى أن هذه التناصات تضمر في أعطافها ضرباً من الاستهزاء بالابن، ولا بُدّ من الإشارة إلى أنّ التصور الذي أنتجته قراءة سرحان لهذه المرويات يبدو على تماسٍ مباشر مع ما انتهت إليه أغلب الدراسات الباحثة في السرديّات العربيّة القديمة، وذلك أن أنساق الفحولة وانتقاص المرأة، تكاد تكون خيطاً ناظماً يجمع أجناس السرديّات العربيّة القديمة جلّها، وإذا كان سرحان قد أبان عن إدراكه لإشكالية المؤلف في العمل السرديّ، وأسطورة التطابق

فإنه يرتدُّ على نفسه، محاولاً في نهاية مقاربته هذا الإلماعَ إلى أن بناء هذه السرديّات يمكن أن تكون مرتبطةً بقصدية المؤلف، دون الاحتراس من إشكالات هذا الافتراض.

– تركيب:

لقد تمكنت القراءة الثقافيّة اللذوية عند شرف الدين ماجدولين من اختراق أفق (السرد الشطاريّ) و(سرديّات العشق) و(سرديّات الهامش) ومن الكشف عن أنظمته، وتشكلاته الرؤيويّة، من خلال تشكيل أفق قرائي خاص، تمثّل فيه القراءة ضرباً من التلذّذ بالنصّ، وهو أفق يتماثل مع الأفق الذي أسسه عبدالفتاح كيليطو.

وهنا لا بُدّ من الإشارة إلى أنّ القراءة الثقافيّة اللذويّة هي القراءة التي يشتبك القارئ خلالها بالنص اشتباكاً حميماً، يتأطر في محاولة تكثيف فعل القراءة للارتقاء في مرتقيات الكشف والتأويل، من خلال فكّ النظام الشِفري المعقَّد، الذي يكوّن معمارية السرد الشطاريّ، وبدا الجهاز المفاهيمي عند ماجدولين مبنياً على تصورات خاصة للصّورة والنسق والسرد الشطاري، وما يرتبط بذلك من مفاهيم.

وتكشّفت مقاربة ماجدولين عن استثمار السرد الشطّاريّ لفتنة اللعب، أو المناصفة، وسرديات العشق لنسقية الذات، وسرديات الهامش لنسق الهزلية، في محاولة التأسيس لنوع أدبيّ خاص، يقيم كيانه ووجوده خارج أطر البلاغة المغلقة، أو دوائر الثقافة الرسميّة، من خلال استثمار فتنة السرد في تكوين صورة جديدة، إزاء مسائل عديدة، من مثل: دور المرأة، وإشكاليات الهامش، وصورة السلطة، وفلسفة اللعب.

وعليه فإنّ السارد يعمد إلى توظيف فعل المناصفة وبلاغة الذات أداةً للتعبير عن رُؤيته للواقع والحياة والسلطة من حوله، ورغبته في ترسيم حدود عالمٍ

مضاد يقدّس ثقافة الدهاء والمكر، للانتقال بالذات الهامشية من دوائر الهامشيّة إلى دوائر المركزيّة.

ويحرو القول: إنّ القراءة الثقافيّة اللذوية بالمفهوم البارتي الذي يبدو شرف الدين ماجدولين متبنّياً له في هذه المقاربات قد حاولت أن تشق درباً جديدة ومختلفة نحو السرديّات المهمشة، فاشتبكت معها، وحاورتها، وانساقت خلف فتنتها، لعلها تكشف عن جدلياتها، وأنظمتها.

وتمثّل القراءة الثقافيّة عند هيثم سرحان ائتلافاً من السرديّات وتحليل الخطاب مكونة فضاءً منهجياً منمازاً يمكن الركون إليه في قراءة النص السرديّ، كما يتجلّى لدى هيثم سرحان في مقارباته، لأنّ دراسة النص في ضَوْء ممكنات القراءة الثقافيّة وتحليل الخطاب، يسفر عن عوالم قرائيّة وفتوح تأويليّة قد لا يمكن بلوغها عبر منظورات المناهج النقديّة الأخرى.

ولا ريب أنّ هذه المسلكيّة البحثيّة تمثل ابتداعاً لفجاج جديدٍ في مسارات القراءة الثقافيّة، فقد برهنت في هذه المقاربات، والحالُ هذه، على قدرتها على الإفصاح عن مضمرات النصوص، وإشاريّاتها، وأنظمتها.

وقد أضحى تفاعل تحليل الخطاب مع النقد الثقافيّ وممكنات النظريّة السرديّة بهذه الصورة صورةً لاندغام منهجيّ له أثافٍ ثلاثٍ يستعين سرحان بممكناتها جلّها، في استنطاق مضمرات النص السردي، وأنظمته الخطابية، ويبدو سرحان على وعي بمركزيّة مفهوم النسق ومخاتلاته في مدرات النقد الثقافيّ؛ والوظيفة الشعرية للغة، بوصفها حاضنة لهذه المخاتلات، ولذا فتساوقاً مع ذلك يؤطّر سرحان في مفتتح مقاربته مقترباً مفاهيمياً، ومنهجياً، يؤصل لمفهوم (النسق)، و(الشعرية)، و(البطل، و(السرد).

وبعدُ، فإنّ هذه الوصايا السرديّة والسرديّات الجنسانيّة تمثل في ضَوْء هذه المقاربة نصّاً شِفريّاً، يتزيّا بجماليات اللغة الشعريّة، ومخاتلات الخطاب، في محاولة التأسيس لمفهوم الأبويّة المكدّية، التي تجعل من الهامش/ المكدّي مركزاً.

هوامش الفصل الخامس:

1 – وهـي تقوم على مفاهيم مسـتمدة مـن «البلاغة» و «الفلسـفة» و «التّداوليّة» و «الدراسـات النقديّة واللغويّة» ينظر: فوداك ومايـر، روث وميشـيل، التحليل النقدي للخطاب التاريخ والبرنامج والنظرية والمنهجيـة، ضمن: مناهج التحليل النقدي للخطاب، ترجمة: حسـام أحمد فرج وعزة شـبل محمد، مراجعـة وتقديم: عمـاد عبداللطيف، ط1، 2014م، منشـورات المركز القومـي للترجمة، القاهرة، مصر، ص18.

2 – ماجدولين، شرف الدين، الصّورة والنسـق والسـلطة: قراءة في السـرد الشـطاري العربيّ، مجلة ثقافات، جامعة البحرين، البحرين، العدد (14)، 2005م، ص95 – 101.

3 – ماجدولين، شرف الدين، الآخر ودائرة الألفة قراءة لنسق التفاعل في نص: طوق الحمامة لابن حزم، مجلة فكر ونقد محمد عابد الجابري، العدد (59 – 60)، 2004م، ص121 – 129.

4 – ماجدولين، شـرف الدين، الهامشـي والآخر والسـرد الهزلي: قراءة في المـوروث الخبري، مجلة ثقافات، جامعة البحرين، البحرين، العدد (23)، 2010م، ص95 – 101.

5 – سـرحان، هيثم، خطاب الجنـس: مقاربات في الأدب العربي القديـم، ط1، 2020م، المركز الثّقافيّ العربي، بيروت، لبنان.

6 – سرحان، هيثم، اللسان والبهتان: شِعريّة الوصية في السرد العربيّ الكلاسيكيّ، ضمن كتاب «الذّاكرة والخطاب: مقاربات في النثر العربي الكلاسيكيّ»، ط1، 2020م، منشورات جامعة الكوفة «سلسلة دراسات فكرية»، دار الرافدين، بيروت، لبنان، ص59. وقد سبق لسرحان نشرها. ينظر: سرحان، هيثم، شِـعريّة الوصية في السـرد العربيّ الكلاسـيكيّ، المجلة الأردنية في اللغـة العربيّة وآدابها، جامعة مؤتة، الكرك، الأردن، المجلد (13)، العدد (3)، 2017م، ص81 – 112.

7 – المرجع السابق، ص95.

8 – المرجع السابق، ص96.

9 – ينظر: ماجدولين، شرف الدين، الصّورة والنسق والسلطة...، (م.س)، ص95.

10 – عيّاشي، منذر، الكتابة الثانية وفاتحة المُتعة، ط1، 1998م، المركز الثّقافيّ العربيّ، بيروت، الدار البيضاء، لبنان، ص5.

11 – قلماوي، سهير، ألف ليلة وليلة، دار المعارف، القاهرة، مصر، (د.س)، ص232.

12 ــ عيّاشي، منذر، الكتابة الثانية وفاتحة المُتعة، (م.س)، ص5 ــ 6.

13 ــ ينظر في عددٍ من أطروحاته: سرحان، هيثم، الأنظمة السيميائية...، (م.س)، ص13 ــ 43.

14 ــ سرحان، هيثم، اللسان والبهتان: شِعريّة الوصية ...، (م.س)، ص61.

15 ــ كيليطو، عبدالفتاح، المقامات: السَّرد والأنساق...، (م.س)، ص8.

16 ــ ينظر: عبدالكريم، جمعان، النقد الثقافيّ وتحليل الخطاب، صحيفة المدينة، مؤسسة المدينة للصحافة والنشر، الرياض، المملكة العربية السعودية، 19 ديسمبر 2012م.

17 ــ سرحان، هيثم، اللسان والبهتان: شِعريّة الوصية ...، (م.س)، ص59.

18 ــ وفي هذا السّياق يقول المسّدَي: «إنّ للنقد الأدبيّ مع اللسانيّات ارتباطاً، بل أضرباً من الارتباط تتعدَّد بتعدُّد وجهات النظر». المسدي، عبدالسلام، اللسانيات وإبيستيمية النقد، مجلة منظمة العربية للتربيـة والثقافة والعلوم، منشـورات جامعة الدول العربية، القاهرة، مصـر، المجلد (16)، العدد (32)، 1997م، ص10.

19 ــ ماجدولين، شرف الدين، الصّورة والنسق والسلطة...، (م.س)، ص95.

20 ــ المرجع السابق، ص96.

21 ــ ماجدولين، شرف الدين، الصّورة والنسق والسلطة...، (م.س)، ص98.

22 ــ ماجدولين، شـرف الدين، الآخر ودائرة الألفة قراءة لنسـق التفاعل في نص: طوق الحمامة لابن حزم، ص121 ــ 129.

23 ــ ماجدولين، شـرف الدين، الهامشـي والآخر والسرد الهزلي: قراءة في الموروث الخبري، ص95 ــ 101.

24 ــ قطّوس، بسّام، سيمياء العنوان، (م.س)، ص83.

25 ــ عبد الحق بلعابد، عتبات: جيرار جينيت...، (م.س)، ص88.

26 ــ ذاكـر، عبد الغني، المغرب وأوربا: نظرات متقاطعة، ط2، 2007م، منشـورات كلية الآداب والعلوم الإنسانية بجامعة ابن زهر، أكـادير، المغرب، ص22.

27 ــ أفـرد شرف الدين ماجدولين فصلاً خاصاً في دراسـته «بيان شهرزاد» للحديث عن دراسـات الصورة وبلاغتها في الفلسفة، والأدب، والنقد الأدبيّ، وقد وسـمه بـ«الصّورة وإمكانيات البلاغة الحكائيّة»ـ ينظر: ماجدولين، شـرف الدين، بيان شهرزاد: التشكلات النوعية لصور اللياليّ، ط1، 2001م، المركـز الثقافيّ العربيّ، بيروت، الدار البيضاء، لبنان، المغرب، ص11 ــ 91. وينظر: هوتر، جيرالد، سـلطة الصّورة الذهنيّة: كيف تغير الرؤى العقل والإنسان والعالم؟، ط1، 2014م، ترجمة: عُلا عادل، عين للدراسات والبحوث الإنسانية والاجماعية، الجيزة، مصر.

28 ــ ينظر: أنقار، محمد، صورة الآخر بين العلم والنقد، أعمال ندوة خطاب الغيرية: النظرية والتطبيق، (د.ط)، 1997م، كلية الآداب والعلوم الإنسانية بتطوان، تطوان، المغرب، ص11.

29 ــ مشبّال، محمد، بلاغة النص السردي: مراجعة نقديّة، مجلة فصول، الهيئة المصرية العامّة للكتاب، القاهرة، مصر، المجلد (1/26)، العدد (101)، 2017م، ص537.

30 – ينظـر: مشبـال، محمد، عن بدايات الخطـاب البلاغي العربي الحديث نحو بلاغة موسّـعة، ط1، 2017م، دار كنوز المعرفة للنشر والتوزيع، عمان، الأردن، ص67 – 117.

31 – سرحان، هيثم، اللسان والبهتان: شِعريّة الوصية ...، (م.س)، ص159 – 109.

32 – سرحان، هيثم، اللسان والبهتان: شِعريّة الوصية ...، (م.س)، ص61 – 62.

33 – ينظـر: كيليطـو، عبدالفتـاح، المقامات: السـرد والأنسـاق الثقافيّـة، (م.س)، ص7 – 8. وجبر، عبدالسـتار، كيـف نحلل الحكاية؟ التـراث والتأويل في النقد العربي الحديـث (عبد الفتاح كيليطو أنموذجـاً، ط1، 2020م، منشـورات جامعة الكوفة «سلسـلة دراسـات فكريـة»، دار الرافدين، بيروت، لبنان.

34 – ريكـور، بـول، نظرية التأويل: الخطـاب وفائض المعنى، ترجمة: سـعيد الغانمي، ط1، 2003م، المركز الثقافيّ العربيّ، بيروت، الدار البيضاء، لبنان، المغرب، ص34.

35 – فوكو، ميشـيل، نظام الخطاب، ترجمة: محمد سـبيلا، ط2، 2007م، دار التنوير للطباعة والنشر، بيروت، لبنان، ص6 وما بعدها.

36 – ينظـر: سرحان، هيثم، اللسان والبهتان: شِعريّة الوصية...، ص62 – 63. وروث فوداك، وميشيل مايـر، التحليل النقدي للخطاب التاريخ والبرنامج والنظرية والمنهجية، (م.س)، ص18. وآنغ، إين، النقد الثقافيّ وتداخل الحقول المعرفية...، (م.س)، ص60 – 61.

37 – ذاكر، عبد الغني، المغرب وأوروبا: نظرات متقاطعة، (م.س)، ص22.

38 – سـرحان، هيثـم، صورة هارون الرشـيد بين تمثيل التّاريخ وتخييـل الأدب، مجلة الآداب بجامعة الملك سـعود، جامعة الملك سـعود، الرياض، المملكة العربيّة السعودية، المجلد (26)، العدد (3)، 2014م، ص90.

39 – ماجدولين، شرف الدين، ترويض الحكاية: بصدد قراءة التّراث السرديّ، المركز الثقافيّ العربيّ، ط1، 2007م، بيروت، الدار البيضاء، لبنان، المغرب، ص43.

40 – يُنظر: ماجدولين، شرف الدين، الصّورة والنسق والسلطة...، (م.س)، ص96 – 97. وسيرة علي الزّيبق المصريّ أو مدير الشرطة في عهد الدولة العبّاسيّة، (م.س).

41 – الكعبيّ، ضياء، السرد العربيّ القديم: دراسة في الأنسـاق الثّقافيّة ...، (م.س)، ص246.

42 – ماجدولين، شرف الدين، الصّورة والنسق والسلطة...، (م.س)، ص95.

43 – المرجع السابق، ص113.

44 – ماجدولين، شرف الدين، الصّورة والنسق والسلطة...، (م.س)، ص95.

45 – المرجع السابق، ص95.

46 – المرجع السابق، ص98.

47 – بارت، رولان، لذّة النصّ، ترجمة: منذر عياشـي، ط1، 1992م، مركز الإنماء الحضاري، حلب، سوريا، ص50.

48 – ماجدولين، شرف الدين، الصّورة والنسق والسلطة...، (م.س)، ص98.

49 – المرجع السابق، ص99.

50 – المرجع السابق، ص100.

51 – شقرون، دليلة، لذة التناص لدى رولان بارت، مجلة علامات، المغرب، العدد (46)، 2016م، ص50.

52 – ماجدولين، شرف الدين، الصّورة والنسق والسلطة...، (م.س)، ص97.

53 – العشي، عبدالله، بلاغة النقد...، (م.س)، ص65.

54 – يُنظـر: عصفور، جابر، بلاغة المقموعين، عدد: (المجاز والتمثيل في العصور الوسطى)، ط1، 1992م، مجلة ألِف البلاغة المقارنة، دار إلياس العصرية، القاهرة، مصر.

55 – يُنظر: عصفور، جابر، بلاغة المقموعين، (م.س)، ص6.

56 – ماجدولين، شرف الدين، بيان شهرزاد: التشكلات النوعية لصور الليالي، (م.س)، ص80.

57 – يُنظر: بو علي، عبد الرحمن، القراءة العاشـقة أو اسـتراتيجيّة قراءة النصّ السـرديّ الكلاسـيكيّ: عبدالفتاح كيليطو نموذجاً، الندوة الثانية: قراءة التراث الأدبيّ واللغوي في الدراسات الحديثة، ط1، 2014م، جامعة الملك سعود، السعودية، ص337.

58 – يُنظر: ماجدولين، شرف الدين، الصّورة والنسق والسلطة...، (م.س)، ص95.

59 – غادامير، هانز جورج، تجلّي الجميل، تحرير: روبرت برناسكوني، ترجمة ودراسة وشـروح: سعيد توفيق، ط1، 1997م، منشورات المشروع القومي للترجمة، القاهرة، مصر، ص98.

60 – وهنـاك أمثلـة كثيرة على ذلك. ينظر: ماجدولين، شـرف الدين، الصّورة والنسـق والسـلطة...، (م.س)، ص95 – 99.

61 – عطية، رانيا جمال، مسار التّحوّلات السرديّة بين المحكيّ والمكتوب في سيرة علي الزّيبق، مجلة سرديات، الجمعية المصرية للدراسات السردية، القاهرة، مصر، العدد (25)، 2017م، ص36.

62 – «وكان فـي البلدة عجوز تسـمّى الدليلة المحتالة ولها بنتٌ تسـمّى زينب النصّابة فسمعتا المناداة بذلك، فقالت زينب لأمها الدليلة: انظري، هذا أحمد الدنف جاء من مصر مطروداً، ولعب مناصفَ فـي بغداد إلى أن تقرب عند الخليفة، وبقي مقدَّم الميمنة، وهذا الولد الأقرع حسـن شـومان مقدم الميسـرة» ألف ليلة وليلة، تقديم: محمد فتحي أبو بكر، تصدير: صلاح فضل، ط1، 2018م، الدار المصرية اللبنانية، مصر، ج3، ص301 وما بعدها.

63 – إبراهيـم، نبيلة، مسـار البطولات العربيّـة والذاكرة التّاريخيّـة، ط1، 1995م، المكتبة الأكاديمية، مصر، ص279.

64 – يُنظر: ماجدولين، شرف الدين، الصّورة والنسق والسلطة...، (م.س)، ص98.

65 – ماجدولين، شرف الدين، الآخر ودائرة الألفة قراءة لنسـق التفاعل في نص: طوق الحمامة لابن حزم، (م.س)، ص98.

66 – المرجع السابق، ص98.

67 – المرجع السابق، ص98.

68 – ابن حزم الظاهري الأندلسي، رسائل ابن حزم الأندلسي، جمعها وحققها: إحسان عباس، المؤسسة العربيّة للدراسات والنشر، بيروت، لبنان، 1980، ج1، ص84 – 319.

69 – ماجدولين، شرف الدين، الآخر ودائرة الألفة قراءة لنسق التفاعل في نص: طوق الحمامة لابن حزم، (م.س)، ص98.

70 – المرجع السابق، ص98.

71 – المرجع السابق، ص98.

72 – المرجع السابق، ص98.

73 – ماجدولين، شرف الدين، الآخر ودائرة الألفة قراءة لنسق التفاعل في نص: طوق الحمامة لابن حزم، (م.س)، ص98.

74 – المرجع السابق، ص98.

75 – المرجع السابق، ص98.

76 – المرجع السابق، ص98.

77 – ماجدولين، شرف الدين، الآخر ودائرة الألفة قراءة لنسق التفاعل في نص: طوق الحمامة لابن حزم، (م.س)، ص98.

78 – ماجدولين، شرف الدين، الهامشي والآخر والسرد الهزلي: قراءة في الموروث الخبري، (م.س)، ص95 – 101.

79 – الوشّاء، أبو الطيب محمد بن اسحق بن يحيى (ت325هـ)، الموشّى أو الظرف والظرفاء، تحقيق: كمال مصطفى، مكتبة الخانجي، مصر، ط2 1953م، ص21

80 – المرجع السابق، ص98.

81 – ماجدولين، شرف الدين، الآخر ودائرة الألفة قراءة لنسق التفاعل في نص: طوق الحمامة لابن حزم، (م.س)، ص98.

82 – يُنظر: برهومة، عيسى، البيانُ الحِجَاجيُّ في قصص بخلاء الجاحظ: دراسة في خطاب النادرة، مجلة فيلولوجي، كلية الالسن، جامعة عين شمس، جمهوريّة مصر العربيّة، العدد (60)، 2013م.

83 – بولكعيبات، نعيمة، النسق المضمر في نوادر جُحا، مجلة فصول، الهيئة المصرية العامّة للكتاب، القاهرة، مصر، المجلد (25/3)، العدد (99)، 2017م، ص429 – 445.

84 – الموسوي، محسن جاسم، سرديات العصر العربي الإسلامي الوسيط، ط1، 1997م، المركز الثقافيّ العربي، بيروت/ البيضاء، ص35 – 36.

85 – يُنظر: الجاويش، محمّد إسماعيل، ابتسامات جحا الحكيم الساخر، دار العلم والإيمان للنشر والتوزيع، دمشق، سوريا، ط1، 2008م، ص132.

86 – يُنظـر: خليفـة، علي محمد السـيد، صورة المرأة في النـادرة، دار الوفاء لدنيا الطباعة والنشـر، الإسكندرية، مصر، ط1، 2000م، ص44 وما بعدها.

87 – يُنظر: الجاويش، محمّد إسماعيل، ابتسامات جحا الحكيم الساخر، ص132.

88 – يُنظر: الحموي، ياقوت، معجم البلدان، (د.ت)، دار إحياء التراث العربي، بيروت، ج1، ص 48.

89 – يُنظر: الحموي، ياقوت، معجم البلدان، ج1، ص 48.

90 – المرجع السابق، ص59.

91 – سرحان، هيثم، خطاب الجنس: مقاربات في الأدب العربي القديم، ص16.

92 – المرجع السابق، ص16.

93 – سرحان، هيثم، خطاب الجنس: مقاربات في الأدب العربي القديم، ص16.

94 – المرجع السابق، ص16 – 20.

95 – الأصفهانيّ، علي بن الحسـين (356هـ)، الأغاني، تحقيق: إحسـان عبّـاس وبكر عبّاس وإبراهيم السعافين، ط1، 2002م، دار صادر، ج6، ص27.

96 – سرحان، هيثم، خطاب الجنس: مقاربات في الأدب العربي القديم، ص213.

97 – سرحان، هيثم، اللسان والبهتان: شِعريّة الوصية ...، ص59.

98 – جاكبسـون، رومان، قضايا الشـعريّة، ط1، 1988م، دار توبقال للنشـر، الدار البيضاء، المغرب، ص31 – 32.

99 – المرجع السابق، ص64.

100 – سرحان، هيثم، اللسان والبهتان: شِعريّة الوصية ...، (م.س)، ص84.

101 – الشـهريّ، عبدالهادي بن ظافر، استراتيجيات الخطاب: مقاربة لغوية تداولية، ط1، 2004م، دار الكتاب الجديد المتحدة، بيروت، لبنان، ص256 – 549.

102 – المرجع السابق، ص73 – 85.

103 – المرجع السابق، ص84.

104 – المصدر السابق، ص434.

105 – سورة الإسراء، الآية (29).

خاتمة

أمحضتْ هذه الدراسةُ الراهنةُ الوَسْعَ في دراسة مستويات التلقّي ومساراتِ التأويل التي انتظمت مقاربات النقد الثقافيّ التي تَصَدّت لقراءة السرديّات العربيّة القديمة، وعليه فيمكن القول:

1 ـ أضاءت هذه المقاربات مواطنَ مُعتمة في هذه السرديّات، لم تكن مضاءةً من ذي قبلُ، فكان أن اختطت لنفسها سبيلاً غيرَ مطروقةٍ، من خلال الاتكاء على أدوات النقد الثقافيّ، التي اهتدى بها النقاد خلال دراستهم السرديّات العربيّة القديمة، بُغية استبار أسرارها، والكشف عن أنساقها.

2 ـ راوحت المقاربات التي قدمها عبدالله الغذامي حول (السرديّات الحكائية)، وعلي فرحان حول (المقامات)، ومحمد المحفليّ حول (السرديّات السلطانية) بين سُلطة النموذج ومحاولات خرق هذا النموذج، والخروج عن تعاليمه القارّة، ووفاقاً للسّابق:

ـ مثّلت مقاربة الغذاميّ التلقّي المعياري حين دشنت عمليّة التحول من النقد الأدبيّ إلى النقد الثقافيّ، ومثلت مقاربة علي فرحان المتنبي الذي استطاع بكفاءة مُثلى تطوير مقولات الناقد الأول، وأصيبُ نمط التلقّي ببعض الخروفات، التي تبنّاها المحفليّ، حين أكّد أنّ الأنساق الثقافيّة التي تضمرها النصوص تبدو غيرَ

مراوغةٍ في حالاتها جميعاً، كما دأب النقاد الثقافيّون على تكرار ذلك، ذلك أنّ تحقُّقَ نسقيته ليس موقوفاً على أن يتلفّع بالإضمار والمراوغة.

3 – حاولت المقاربات التي قدمها نادر كاظم حول (السود في السير الشعبيّة)، وضياء الكعبيّ حول (سرديّات المجانين والسير الشعبية)، إخصابَ نمط التلقّي من خلال ربط النقد الثقافيّ بمرجعياته في الدراسات ما بعد الكولونياليّة، وبناءً عليه:

– أبرزت مقاربة كاظم سيمياء الناقد المثقّف، الذي أبحر عَبْرَ متوسطات ممكنات ما بعد الكولونيالية، وجَرَّبَ فِعْل الإخصاب، إذ تشكلت مقاربته على مبادئ عديدة، أطّرت فِعْل القراءة لديه.

– كثفت ضياء الكعبيّ في تلقّيها عن ضرورات العمل على تجنيس سرديّات الجنون والسير الشعبية، ودَوْرِ ذلك في الكشف عن التمثيلات المضادة، التي يؤطرها المتجانُّ أو البطل الشعبيّ في قوالبَ تنطوي على خواصّ أجناسية، تعكس أصداء مقولة متداولة في الدراسات ما بعد الكولونياليّة هي (الردّ بالسرد).

4 – تجيء مقاربات يوسف عليمات حول (الحكايات العجائبيّة والمقامات)، ومصطفى الغرافي حول (الأخبار)، ومعجب العدوانيّ حول (السرديّات الرحليّة)، منمازة بفرادة تتأتّى من محاولتها الانفتاح بنمط التلقّي على النقد الأدبيّ، وتأسيساً على ذلك:

– أعلن يوسف عُليمات عن إقامة ائتلافٍ منهجيّ بين النقد الثقافيّ والنقد الأدبيّ من خلال تأثيث منهجيّة مركّبة، كان النقد الأدبيّ دائرتها والنقد الثقافيّ نقطة توسّطها، وقد بدا أن هذا التحالف المنهجيّ تحالفٌ منهجيٌّ واعٍ.

– نفث مصطفى الغرافيّ في رَوْع المؤلّف من جديد، وأقام تحالفاً بين النقد الثقافيّ ونظريّة التلقّي، فقرأ الأنساق التي تتضمنها أخبار ابن قتيبة بوصفها غير معزولةٍ عن سياقاتها المختلفة.

– حاول مُعجِب العُدوانيّ أن يفيد من الانفتاح الذي يميّز النقد الثقافيّ، وذلك

بإقامة وشيجةٍ تربطه بالنظرية التناصيّة، في ظلال مفاهيم التأثّر والتأثير، وسلطة الأنا، وتمثيلات الآخر.

5 – تتجلّى في مقاربات شرف الدين مجدولين حول (السرد الشطاريّ وسرديات العشق وسرديات الهامش)، وهيثم سرحان حول (الوصايا السرديّة والسرديّات الجنسانية)، التفاعلاتُ التي يمكن أن تنتظم مسارات القراءة الثقافيّة مع الحقول المعرفية الأخرى، وعليه فقد:

– تجلّت في مقاربات شرف الدين ماجدولين سيمياء القراءة الثقافيّة اللذويّة، التي تجعل من النصّ خطاباً جماليّاً من جهة، ونسقياً وثقافيّاً من جهة أخرى، وذلك في الآن عينه، مما يعيّن على قارئه أن يشتبك بلذّاته في سياق اشتغالاته عليه.

– أقامت مقاربات هيثم سرحان أوَدَها على تفاعل منهجيّ بين النفد الثقافيّ ومقولات تحليل الخطاب، استناداً إلى أنهما يشتركان في مقصديّة بحثية، تروم الكشف عن مواضع المخاتلة والمكر في الخطاب، في ظلال زئبقيته، وانفلات عُقُل دلالاته، وتحولاتها الدائمة.

6 – تبيّنَ برجع النظر في المقاربات المدروسة أن آليات المقاربة النقديّة التي انتهجها المنشغلون بقراءة السرديّات العربيّة القديمة يمكن أن تتأطّر في عددٍ من الآليّات التي تأتلف فيما بينها، ولكنها تأخذ مسميات مختلفة، ومنها: (تعرية الأنساق الثقافيّة المُضمرة)، و(البحث في النسقين الظاهر والمضمر)، و(تفكيك التمثيلات الثقافيّة) و(الكشف عن التمثيلات المُضادةّ).

7 – امتلكت المقاربات المدروسة في كلّ نمطٍ من أنماط التلقّي جهازاً مفاهيميّاً خاصّاً، شاعت مصطلحاته الخاصة بين ثنايا المقاربات المنتمية إليه:

– مثّلت مفاهيم (النسق المضمر)، و(النسق المعلن) (المخاتلة)، و(الأنساق الثقافيّة)، المصطلحات المفاتيح للمقاربات التي انتمتَ إلى الأفق الذي أسس له الغذّاميّ.

- كوّنت مفاهيم (الأنــا)، و(الآخـــر)، و(التمثيل)، و(آليات التمثيل)، و(الهامش)، و(المركز)، مفردات الجهاز المفاهيميّ لمقاربات النمط المنفتح على ممكنات ما بعد الكولونياليّة.

- برزت مفاهيم (البنية السرديّة)، (السيميائية)، (التوقع)، (كسر الانتظار)، (الدهشة)، (المؤلف)، في الجهاز المفاهيمي للمقاربات التي اشتبكت بمقولات النقد الأدبيّ.

- مثّلت مفاهيم (البلاغة)، (اللذة)، (اللعب)، (الصورة) (الشعرية)، (بلاغة الصمت)، العصب المفاهيمي للمقاربات التي راوحتْ بين النقد الثقافيّ وتحليل الخطاب ودراسات الصورة.

8 - ظهرت الموضوعات/ العنوانات التي انتخبها النقاد الثقافيّون بوصفها عتبات نصية وبحثيّة ومنهجيّة، ذات أماراتٍ علاماتية وسيميائيّة تتشابك، والحالُ هذه، مَعَ الطرح المنهجيّ لكل ناقد، فضلاً عن اتّصافها في الغالب بالغواية التي تفتن القارئ، وتمارس عليه فعل الاستدراج.

9 - انتظمت هذه المقاربات في إشكاليّاتٍ عديدة، وهي تستأهل النهوض بدراساتٍ تفيدُ من أدوات نقد النقد للبحث في آليات تلقّي النقد الثقافيّ في آفاق النقد العربيّ، ومنها:

- ممارسة جلُّ المقاربات المدروسة فِعْلَ تبئير القراءة، على تمثيلات النسق الثقافيّ الذي يتضمنه النصّ، واطّرحاهت غير ذلك، مهملة جماليات النصوص، وأبنيتها السردية،... إلخ، مما جعلها أُحادية النظرة، غيرَ قادرةٍ على تقديم قراءة متكاملة للنصوص.

- بعثت كثيرٌ من المقاربات المدروسة بالمؤلّف من مرقده، وجعلت حضوره حضوراً مركزيّاً في تلقّي هذه السرديّات، وتأويلها، ممارِسةً ضرباً من

الاعتساف، والإكراه، الذي لم يحترسْ من إشكاليّة المؤلّف والمصنّف، والفروق البائناتِ بينهما.

– أنّ النقد الثقافيّ الذي قرأ السرديّات العربيّة القديمة انفتح على المناهج الأخرى، وتفاعل مع الحقول المعرفيّة المختلفة، بصورة لا يحكمها قانونٌ ضابط، وذلك في الغالب الأعم، إذ لم يكن هذا الانفتاح محكوماً بمقولاتٍ نظريّة تكشف عن معالمه، وتؤطّر حدوده.

– مركزيّة النموذج الغذاميّ في بعض من المقاربات المدروسة، ولعلّ في ذلك نكوصاً على الأعقاب، لا يتواءم مع السنن الجارية على النظريات النقديّة، التي تظل دوماً نزّاعة إلى التطور والتقدّم.

وأخيراً فيشبه أن يكون لازباً على المشتبك بمراجعة هذه المقاربات أن يعلن صُراحاً أن هذه المقاربات/ القراءات، استطاعت، والنظرية النقديّة العربيّة تعيش إشكالات كبرى، أن تخلقَ هامشاً بحثياً جديداً، يفسحَ المراح للانشغال بموضوعاتٍ بحثيّة جديدة، ولا ينفي ذلك أنّ على النقد العربيّ أن يقدّم مقاربات تستقرئ هذه السرديّات، مقيمةً أودها على ائتلاف يجمع بين النقد الثقافيّ والنقد الأدبيّ، تحكمه رؤىً منهجيّة مؤطّرة، تبين حدود هذا الائتلاف، وشروطه، دون إغفال خصوصية النقد العربيّ الحديث.

ولعل المرء لا يكون طوباويّاً أو شاعراً حين يقول: إنّ هذه السرديّات ظلّت مزنّرة بسحرٍ خاص، وهي لا تزال مُشْرِعةً أبوابها أمام النظريّات النقديّة في سبيل تلمُّس سرّها المكنون، أو اكتشاف كُنهها، ذلك أنّ بعضاً من أسرارها ظلّ عصيّاً على الكشف، غامضاً أمام كل هذه القراءات المتعاقبة، وعليه، ومع إلقاء عصا الترحال المعرفيّ فإنّ كلَّ مشروعٍ جديدٍ لقراءة السرديّات العربيّة القديمة يظلُّ مُحتاجاً، بالضّرورة أو بالقوّة والفِعْل كما يقولُ الفلاسفة، إلى أن نستثمر مقولاته، ومفاهيمه، وأدواته بما يأتلفُ مَعَ خواصّ ثقافتنا العربيّة، وبما تنماز به من غيرها.

ثبت المصادر والمراجع

ــ المصادر:

ــ الأصفهانيّ، علي بن الحسين (356هـ)، الأغاني، تحقيق: إحسان عبّاس وبكر عبّاس وإبراهيم السعافين، ط1، 2002م، دار صادر، ج9.

ــ ألف ليلة وليلة، تقديم: محمد فتحي أبو بكر، تصدير: صلاح فضل، ط1، 2018م، الدار المصرية اللبنانية، مصر، ج3.

ــ ألف ليلة وليلة، منشورات دار مكتبة الحياة، بيروت، لبنان، (د.س).

ــ الجاحظ، عمر بن بحر (ت150هـ)، البيان والتبيين، تحقيق: عبدالسلام هارون، ط7، 1998م، مطبعة الخانجي ومطبعة المدني، القاهرة وجدة، مصر والسعوديّة.

ــ ___________ ، الحَيَوان، تحقيق وشرح: عبدالسلام هارون، مطبعة مصطفى البابي الحلبي، ط2، 1965م، القاهرة، مصر، ج1.

ــ ابن حزم الظاهري الأندلسي، رسائل ابن حزم الأندلسي، جمعها وحققها: إحسان عباس، المؤسسة العربيّة للدراسات والنشر، بيروت، لبنان، 1980، ج1.

ــ حكاية أبي القاسم البغداديّ، تحقيق: آدم متز، ط1، (د.س)، مطبعة المثنى، بغداد، العراق.

ــ الحمويّ، ابن حِجّة، تقي الدين أبو بكر بن علي بن عبد الله (ت837هـ)، ثمِرات الأوراق في المُحاضرات، شرحه وضبطه: مفيد محمد قميحة، ط1، 1983م، دار الكتب العلميّة، بيروت، لبنان.

ــ الدينوري، ابن قتيبة عبد الله بن قتيبة (ت276هـ)، عيون الأخبار، تحقيق: داني بن منير الزهوي، (د.ط)، 2003م، المكتبة العصرية، بيروت، لبنان، ج1.

ــ سيرة الأميرة ذات الهِمّة وولدها عبدالوهاب،(د.ط)، 1980م، المكتبة الثقافيّة، بيروت، لبنان.

ــ رسائل ابن حزم الأندلسي (ت456هـ)، تحقيق: إحسان عباس، المؤسسة العربيّة للدراسات والنشر، بيروت، ط1، 1980 ــ 1983.

ــ السيرة الشعبيّة للحلّاج أو سيرة حسين الحلّاج، تحقيق: رضوان السح، دار صادر، بيروت، لبنان، ط1، 1998م.

ــ سيرة الملك الظّاهر بيبرس، مكتبة التربية للطباعة والنشر والتوزيع، بيروت، لبنان، ط1، 1983م.

ــ سيرة الملك سيف بن ذي يزن فارس اليمن، المكتبة الثقافيّة، بيروت، لبنان، ط2، 1986م.

– سيرة بني هلال، ط1، 1981م دار الكتب الشعبيّة، بيروت، لبنان.

– سيرة علي الزيبق المصريّ أو مدير الشرطة في عهد الدولة العبّاسيّة، دار عمر أبو النصر وشركاؤه، بيروت، لبنان، ط1، 1971م.

– سـيرة عنترة بن شدّاد، نسَّقها وهذّبها: عمر أبو النضر، (د.ط)، 1993م، المكتبة الشعبيّة، منشورات مكتبة المعارف، بيروت، لبنان.

– الشريشـي، أبـو العباس، كمـال الدين أبو العباس أحمـد بن عبد المؤمن (ت619هـ)، شـرح مقامات الحريري، 2004م، تحقيق: محمد أبو الفضل إبراهيم، المكتبة العصرية، بيروت، لبنان، ج1.

– ابن أبي شـيبة، أبو بكر عبدالله بن محمد (ت235هـ)، المصنف لابن أبي شـيبة، حقّقه وقوّم نصوصه وخـرّج أحاديثـه: محمـد عوّامة، ط1، 2006م، شـركة دار القِبلة ومؤسسـة علوم القـرآن، الرياض ودمشق، السعودية وسوريا، ج10.

– أبـو عبيـدة، معمـر بن المثنى (ت209هـ)، شـرح نقائض جريـر والفرزدق، تحقيـق: محمد إبراهيم حور ووليد محمود خالص، ط2، 1998م، منشـورات هيئـة أبوظبي للثّقافة والتراث، إمارة أبوظبي، الإمارات، ج2.

– ابـن فضـلان، أحمد بن العباس (ت349هـ)، رسـالة ابن فضلان: في وصـف الرحلة إلى بلاد الترك والخـزر والروس والصقالبة، حققها وعلّق عليها وقدم لها: سـامي الدهان، ط1، 1960م، مطبوعات المجمع العلمي العربيّ بدمشق، دمشق، سوريا.

– القلقشـنديّ، أحمد بن علي (ت821هـ)، صبح الأعشـى في صناعة الإنشـا، شرحه وعلّق عليه وقابل نصوصه: محمد حسين شمس الدين، ط1، 2012م، دار الكتب العلمية، بيروت، لبنان، ج14، ص125.

– ابن المقفّع، أبو مُحمّد عبد الله (ت142هـ)، كليلة ودمنة، دار الهلال، القاهرة، مصر، 1999م.

– ابن منظور، جمال الدين بن مكرم (ت711هـ)، لسان العرب، (د.ط)، 1978م، الدار المصريّة، مصر.

– الميدانيّ، أبو الفضل النيسـابوريّ، مجمع الأمثال، (د.ط)، 1995م، دار مكتبة الحياة للطباعة والنشـر والتوزيع، بيروت، لبنان.

– النفـراويّ، أبو عبدالله عمر بـن محمد، الروض العاطر في نزهة الخاطر، تحقيق: جمال جمعة، ط2، 1993م دار رياض الريس، لندن، بريطانيا.

– النيسـابوريّ، ابن حبيب (406)، عُقلاء المجانين، تحقيق: عمر الأسـعد، ط1، 1987م، دار النفائس، بيروت، لبنان، ص292.

– الوشّـاء، أبو الطيب محمد بن اسـحق بن يحيى (ت325هـ)، الموشّـى أو الظرف والظرفاء، تحقيق: كمال مصطفى، مكتبة الخانجي، مصر، ط2 1953م.

– ياقوت الحمويّ، معجم البلدان، (د.ت)، دار إحياء التراث العربي، بيروت، ج1.

– المراجع العربيّة:

– إبراهيـم، عبدالله، التلقّي والسياقات الثّقافيّة: بحث في تأويل الظاهرة الأدبيّة، العدد (93)، 2001م،

منشورات سلسلة كتاب الرياض، مؤسسة اليمامة الصحفية، الرياض، المملكة العربيّة السعودية.

– إبراهيم، عبدالله، الثقافة العربيّة والمرجعيّات المُستعارة، ط1، 2010م، الدار العربيّة للعلوم ناشـرون (بيروت/ لبنان)، منشورات الاختلاف (الجزائر العاصمة/ الجزائر).

– _______، السـردية العربيّة: بحثٌ في البنية السـردية للمورث الحكائي العربي، ط2، 2000م، المؤسسة العربيّة للدراسات والنشر، بيروت، لبنان.

– _______، المُطابقـة والاختـلاف: بحـث في نقـد المركزيّات الثقافيّة، ط2، 2004م، المؤسسة العربيّة للدراسات والنشر، بيروت، لبنان.

– _______، النثـر العربـيّ القديم: بحث في السـرديّة العربيّة، ط1، 2002م، منشـورات المجلس الوطني للثقافة والفنون والتراث، الكويت.

– إبراهيم، نبيلة، مسار البطولات العربيّة والذاكرة التّاريخيّة، ط1، 1995م، المكتبة الأكاديمية، مصر.

– أبو شهاب، رامي، الرسيس والمخاتلة: خطاب ما بعد الكولونيالية في النقد العربيّ المعاصر: النظريّة والتطبيق، ط1، 2013م، المؤسسة العربية للدراسات والنشر، بيروت، لبنان.

– آل مريع، أحمد، خطاب الجنون: الحضور الفيزيائيّ والغياب الثقافيّ (الاستبعاد والنفيّ)، ط1، 2014م مكتبة العبيكان، الرياض، المملكة العربيّة السعوديّة.

– أنقـار، محمد، صورة الآخر بين العلم والنقد، أعمال ندوة خطاب الغيرية: النظرية والتطبيق، (د.ط)، 1997م، كلية الآداب والعلوم الإنسانية بتطوان، تطوان، المغرب.

– البازعيّ، سـعد، استقبال الآخر: الغرب في النقد العربيّ الحديث، المركـز الثقافيّ العربيّ، بيروت، الدار البيضاء، لبنان، المغرب، ط1، 2004م.

– بلعابـد، عبد الحق، عتبـات: جيرار جينيت من النص إلى المناص، ط1، 2008م، الدار العربيّة للعلوم ناشرون (بيروت/ لبنان)، منشورات الاختلاف (الجزائر العاصمة/ الجزائر).

– بنكـراد، سـعيد، سـيميائيّات الصورة الإشهاريّة: الإشـهار والتّمثلات الثقافيّة، ط1، 2006م، أفريقيا الشرق، الدار البيضاء، المغرب.

– البهلـول، عبدالله، في بلاغة الخطاب الأدبيّ: بحث في سياسـة القـول في نصوص من الأدب العربيّ القديم، ط1، 2007م، التسفير الفني، تونس.

– التمـارة، عبدالرحمـن، نقد النقد: بين التّصـوّر المنهجيّ والإنجاز النصـيّ، ط1، 2017م، دار كنوز المعرفة للنشر والتوزيع، عمان،ـ الأردن.

– ثامـر، فاضـل، اللغة الثانية: في إشـكاليّة المنهج والنظريّـة والمُصطلح في الخِطـاب النقديّ العربيّ الحديث، ط1، 1994م، المركز الثقافيّ العربيّ، بيروت، الدار البيضاء، لبنان، المغرب.

– الجاويش، محمّد إسماعيل، ابتسامات جحا الحكيم الساخر، دار العلم والإيمان للنشر والتوزيع، دمشق، سوريا، ط1، 2008م، ص132.

– جبر، عبدالسـتار، كيف نحلل الحكاية؟ التراث والتأويل فـي النقد العربيّ الحديث (عبد الفتاح كيليطو أنموذجاً)، ط1، 2020م، منشورات جامعة الكوفة، دار الرافدين، بيروت، لبنان.

- جواد، علي، المُفصّل في تاريخ العرب قبل الإسلام، ط2، 1993م، جامعة بغداد، العراق، ج2.

- الحجاجي، أحمد شـمس الدين، مولد البطل في السـيرة الشـعبيّة، ط1، 1990م، مؤسسـة دار الهلال، القاهرة، مصر.

- الحجيلان، صالح، الشخصية في قصص الأمثال: دراسة في الأنساق الثقافيّة للشخصيّة العربيّة، ط1، 2009م، المركز الثقافيّ العربي، بيروت، الدار البيضاء، لبنان، المغرب.

- حمّودة، عبد العزيز، الخُروج من التيه: دراسة في سُلطة النصّ، العدد (298)، نوفمبر 2003م، سلسلة عالم المعرفة، المجلس الوطنيّ للثقافة والفنون والأدب، الكويت.

- حمَـودة، عبد العزيز، المرايا المُحَدّبة: من البنيويّة إلى التَّفكيك، العدد (232)، إبريل 1998م، سلسـلة عالم المعرفة، المجلس الوطنيّ للثقافة والفنون والأدب، الكويت.

- الخفاجـي، عبدالمنعـم، أبو الفتح الإسـكندريّ: بطل مقامات بديع الزمان وشـخصيته المجهولة، ط1، 1996م، مكتبة الإنجلو المصرية، القاهرة، مصر.

- خليفة، علي محمد السـيد، صورة المرأة في النادرة، دار الوفاء لدنيا الطباعة والنشـر، الإسـكندرية، مصر، ط1، 2000م.

- خليفـة، علي محمد، بنية السـرد فـي النادرة: نوادر الأعراب في كتاب عيـون الأخبار نموذجاً، ط1، 2010م، دار الوفاء لدنيا الطباعة والنشر، الإسكندرية، مصر.

- خورشيد، فاروق، أضواء على السيرة الشعبية، (د.ط)، (د.س) منشورات اقرأ، بيروت، لبنان.

- الدغمومـي، محمـد، نقد النقد وتنظير النقـد العربيّ المُعاصر، ط1، 1999م، منشـورات كلية الآداب والعلوم الإنسانية بالرباط، الرباط، المغرب.

- ذاكـر، عبد الغني، المغـرب وأوروبـا: نظرات متقاطعة، ط2، 2007م، منشـورات كلية الآداب والعلوم الإنسانية بجامعة ابن زهر، أكـادير، المغرب.

- ذيـاب، صفاء، السـيرة الشـعبية فـي النقـد المُعاصـر، ط1، 2020م، دار الرافدين للطباعة والنشـر والتوزيع، بيروت، لبنان.

- الرباعي، عبدالقادر، جماليات الخطاب في النقد الثقافيّ، ط1، 2015م، دار جرير، عمّان، الأردن.

- رومية، وهب، شـعرنا القديم والنقد الجديد، سلسـلة عالم المعرفة، منشـورات المجلس الوطني للثقافة والفنون والآداب، الكويت، العدد (207)، مارس 1996م.

- الرويليّ والباز عيّ، ميجان وسعد، دليل الناقد الأدبيّ: إضاءة لأكثرَ من سبعين تياراً ومصطلحاً نقدياً معاصراً، ط3، 2002م، المركز الثقافيّ العربي، بيروت، الدار البيضاء، لبنان، المغرب.

- الزَّركليّ، خير الدين، الإعلام، ط15، 2002م، دار العلم للملايين، بيروت، لبنان، ج8.

- زغلـول، هشـام، الناقد الثقافيّ وأفق التلقّي: من التيار الغذاميّ.. إلـى التيار الربّاعيّ، ضمن: (نَمارقُ مَصْفوفةٌ دراسـات ـ مقالات ـ شهادات تكريماً للأستاذ الدكتور عبدالقادر الرباعيّ بمناسبة نيله لقب «أسـتاذ شـرف» من جامعة اليرموك)، إشراف وتحرير: عمر الفجاوي وعامر أبو محارب، ط1، 2024م، دار المؤسسة العربيّة للدراسات والنشر، بيروت، لبنان.

– زِيّاد، صالح، القارئ القياسـيّ: سلطة القصد والمصطلح والنموذج: مقاربات في التراث النقديّ، ط1، 2009م دار الفارابي، بيروت، لبنان.

– سـرحان، هيثم، الأنظمة السيميائيّة دراسـة في السرد العربيّ القديم، ط1، 2008م، دار الكتاب الجديد المتحدة، بيروت، لبنان.

– سـرحان، هيثـم، خطاب الجنـس: مقاربات في الأدب العربـيّ القديـم، ط1، 2020م، المركز الثّقافيّ العربيّ، بيروت، لبنان.

– الشـاهد، نبيل، العجائبيّ في السـرد العربيّ القديم: مئة ليلة وليلة والحكايات العجيّة والأخبار الغريبة نموذجاً، ط1، 2012م، منشورات دار الورّاق، عمّان، الأردن.

– الشهريّ، عبدالهادي بن ظافر، استراتيجيّات الخطاب: مقاربة لغويّة تداوليّة، ط1، 2004م، دار الكتاب الجديد المتحدة، بيروت، لبنان.

– صحراوي، إبراهيم، السرد العربيّ القديم: الأنـواع والوظائف والبنيات، ط1، 2008م، الدار العربيّة للعلوم ناشرون (بيروت/ لبنان)، منشورات الاختلاف (الجزائر العاصمة/ الجزائر) .

– الطائي، معن، السرديّات المضادة: بحث في طبيعة التّحولات الثّقافيّة، ط1، 2014م، المؤسسة العربيّة للدراسات والنشر، بيروت، لبنان.

– عبدالحميد بن يحيى الكاتب وما تبقّى من رسـائله ورسـائل سـالم أبي العلاء، دراسـة وإعداد: إحسان عباس، ط1، 1988م، دار الشروق، عمان، الأردن.

– العدواني، مُعجِب، الموروث وصناعة الرواية: مؤثرات وتمثيلات، ط1، 2013م، الدار العربيّة للعلوم ناشـرون (بيروت/ لبنان)، منشـورات الاختلاف (الجزائر العاصمة/ الجزائر)، دار الأمان (الرباط/ المغرب).

– العشـيري، محمود، الشـعر سَـرْداً: دراسـة في نصّ المُفَضَّليّات، ط1، 2014م، المؤسسـة العربيّة للدراسات والنشر، بيروت، لبنان، ص33.

– عصفور، جابر، نظريّات معاصرة، دار المدى للثّقافة والنشر، دمشق، سوريا، ط1، 1998م.

– عليمات، يوسـف، النسق الثّقافيّ: قراءة ثقافية في أنساق الشعر العربيّ القديم، ط1، 2009م، دار عالم الكتب الحديث، إربد، الأردن.

– عيّاشـي، منـذر، الكتابة الثانية وفاتحـة المُتعة، ط1، 1998م، المركز الثّقافـيّ العربيّ، بيروت، الدار البيضاء، لبنان.

– الغانميّ، سـعيد، الكنز والتّأويل: قراءات في الحكايـة العربيّـة، المركز الثّقافيّ العربيّ، ط1، 1994م، بيروت، الدار البيضاء، لبنان، المغرب.

– الغذّامـي، عبدالله، الخطيئة والتكفير من البنيوية إلى التشـريحية: نظرية وتطبيق، ط4، 1998م الهيئة المصريّة العامة للكتاب، القاهرة، مصر.

– الغذّامـي، عبدالله، واصطيـف، عبدالنبي، نقد أدبي أم نقـد ثقافيّ، ط1، 2004م، دار الفكر، دمشـق، سوريا.

– فرحان، علي، مقامات الحريريّ حجاجية السـرد والنسـق الثقافيّ دراسـة في البنية والخطاب، ط1، 2017م، منشورات الجامعة الأهلية، المنامة، البحرين.

– القاضي، محمد وزملاؤه، معجم السـرديّات، ط1، 2010م، دار الفارابي ومؤسسـة الانتشار العربي، بيروت، لبنان .

– قطّوس، بسّام، سيمياء العنوان، ط1، 2001م، منشورات وزارة الثقافة الأردنية، عمان، الأردن.

– القفـاري، أميرة، النقـد الثائر: قراءة النقد الثقافيّ للتّراث الأدبيّ، ط1، 2019م دار الانتشـار العربيّ، بيروت، لبنان.

– قلماوي، سهير، ألف ليلة وليلة، دار المعارف، القاهرة، مصر، (د.س).

– كاظـم، نـادر، المقامات والتلقّي: بحث فـي أنماط التلقّي لمقامات الهمذاني فـي النقد العربيّ الحديث، المؤسسة العربيّة للدراسات والنشر، بيروت، لبنان، ط1، 2004م.

– ــــــــــ، تمثيـلات الآخر: صورة السـود في المتخيّل العربيّ الوسـيط، ط1، 2004م، المؤسسـة العربيّة للدراسات والنشر، بيروت، لبنان .

– ــــــــــ، الهُويّة والسرد: دراسات في النظريّة والنقد الثقافيّ، دار الفراشة، الكويت، ط2، 2016م.

– الكعبيّ، ضياء والعدواني، معجب، السـرديّات الشـعبيّة العربيّة؛ دراسـة في التمثيلات الثقافيّة، دار الانتشار العربي، بيروت، لبنان، ط1، 2014م.

– الكعبيّ، ضياء، السـرد العربيّ القديم: دراسـة في الأنسـاق الثقافيّة وإشكاليّات التأويل، ط1، 2005م، المؤسسة العربيّة للدراسات والنشر، بيروت، لبنان.

– كيليطو، عبدالفتاح، المقامات: السـرد والأنساق الثقافيّة، ط2، 2001م، ترجمة: عبدالكبير الشرقاوي، دار توبقال للنشر، الدار البيضاء، المغرب.

– ــــــــــ، بحبر خفي، ط1، 2018م، دار توبقال للنشر، الدار البيضاء، المغرب.

– ماجدولين، شـرف الدين، بيان شـهرزاد: التشـكلات النوعية لصور الليالـيّ، ط1، 2001م، المركز الثقافيّ العربيّ، بيروت، الدار البيضاء، لبنان، المغرب،

– ــــــــــ، ترويض الحكاية: بصدد قراءة التّراث السـرديّ، المركز الثقافيّ العربيّ، ط1، 2007م، بيروت، الدار البيضاء، لبنان، المغرب.

– المبارك، مازن، مجتمع بديع الزمان الهمذانيّ من خلال مقاماته، دار الفكر المعاصر، دمشق، سوريا، ط2، 1981م.

– المبخوت، شـكري، جماليّـة الألفة: النصّ ومنقبّله في التراث النقـديّ، (د.ط)، 1993م، بيت الحكمة، منشورات وزارة الثقافة، تونس.

– مشـبال، محمد، عن بدايات الخطاب البلاغي العربيّ الحديث نحو بلاغة موسّـعة، ط1، 2017م، دار كنوز المعرفة للنشر والتوزيع، عمان، الأردن.

– الموسـوي، محسـن جاسم، النظرية والنقد الثقافيّ، ط1، 2005م، المؤسسة العربيّة للدراسات والنشر، بيروت، لبنان.

– الموسـوي، محسن جاسم، سـرديّات العصر العربيّ الإسلامي الوسيط، ط1، 1997م، المركز الثقافيّ العربي، بيروت/ البيضاء.

– ناصف، مصطفى، محاورات مع النثر العربيّ، العدد (218)، 1997م، سلسلة عالم المعرفة، منشورات المجلس الوطني للثقافة والفنون والآداب، الكويت.

– يقطين، سـعيد، الكلام والخبر: مقدمة للسّـرد العربيّ، ط1، 1997م،المركز الثقافيّ العربيّ، بيروت، الدار البيضاء، لبنان، المغرب.

– يقطيـن، سـعيد، قراءة التراث الأدبيّ: التراث السـرديّ أنموذجاً، الندوة الدوليـة الثانية قراءة التراث الأدبيّ واللغوي في الدراسـات الحديثة، جامعة الملك سـعود، الرياض، المملكة العربيّة السـعوديّة، 2014م.

– يوسف، أحمد، القراءة النسقيّة: سلطة البنية ووَهْم المحايثة، ط1، 2007، الدار العربيّة للعلوم ناشرون (بيروت/ لبنان)، منشورات الاختلاف (الجزائر العاصمة/ الجزائر).

– المقالات المحكّمة:

– أبانمي، إبراهيم بن محمد، أحبولة الهمذانيّ الإبداعيّة الكبرى: قراءة في السـيرة الثقافيّة المُضمرة في مقاماته، مجلة العلوم العربيّة، جامعة الإمام محمد بن سعود الإسلامية، العدد (36)، 2014م.

– ابن تميم، علي، النقاد ونجيب محفوظ: الرواية؛ من النوع السـرديّ القاتل إلى جماليّات العالم الثالث، ط1، 2008م، هيئة أبوظبي للثقافة والتراث، إمارة أبوظبي، الإمارات.

– اصطيف، عبدالنبي، تلقّي الغرب لرسـالة ابن فضلان، مجلة التراث العربي، منشورات اتحاد الكتاب العرب، دمشق، سوريا، العدد (129)، 2013م.

– اصطيف، عبدالنبي، نحو تجديد لمفهوم النقد الأدبيّ، مجلة مواقف، لبنان، العدد(47)، 1983م.

– آنـغ، إيـن، النقـد الثقافيّ وتداخل الحقول المعرفيّـة الآن، ترجمة: عطارد حيـدر، مجلة اتحاد الكتاب العرب، دمشق، سوريا، السنة (34)، العدد (138)، 2009م.

– البازعي، سعد، الدراسات البينية وتحديات الابتكار، مجلة كلية الآداب، جامعة الملك سعود، الرياض، المملكة العربيّة السعودية، المجلد (25)، العدد (2)، 2013م.

– باعشـن، لميـاء نظريّـات قـراءة النصّ، مجلة علامات فـي النقد، النادي الثقافيّ بجُـدّة، جُدّة، المملكة العربيّة السعوديّة، المجلد (10)، الجزء (39)، 2001م.

– برهومـة، عيسـى، البيـانُ الجِجَاجيُّ فـي قصص بخلاء الجاحظ: دراسـة في خطـاب النـادرة، مجلة فيلولوجي، كلية الألسن، جامعة عين شمس، جمهوريّة مصر العربيّة، العدد (60)، 2013م.

– بريمـي، عبدالله، الكون السـيميائيّ والكـون الثقافيّ (يوري لوتمان)، مجلة فصـول، الهيئة المصرية العامّة للكتاب، القاهرة، مصر، المجلد (3/25)، العدد (99)، 2017م.

– بنحدو، رشيد، قراءة في القراءة، مجلة الفكر العربيّ المعاصر، مركز الإنماء القومي، بيروت، لبنان، العددان (48 – 49) 1988م.

- بوقـرة، نعمــان عبدالحميد، المقامة البِشـريّة لبديع الزمــان الهمذاني: قراءة نصيّـة تداوليّة في ضَوْءِ نظرية الحجاج، المجلة العربيّة للعلوم الإنسانيّة، جامعة الكويت، الكويت، المجلد (31)، العدد (123)، 2013م.

- بوعلي، عبد الرحمن، القراءة العاشـقة أو اسـتراتيجيّة قراءة النصّ السـرديّ الكلاسـيكيّ: عبدالفتاح كيليطو نموذجاً، عبدالفتاح كيليطو نموذجاً، الندوة الثانية: قراءة التراث الأدبيّ واللغوي في الدراسات الحديثة، ط1، 2014م، جامعة الملك سعود، السعوديّة.

- بولكعيبـات، نعيمة، النسـق المضمر في نـودار جُحا، مجلة فصول، الهيئـة المصرية العامّة للكتاب، القاهرة، مصر، المجلد (3/25)، العدد (99)، 2017م.

- الجديع، خالد بن محمد، الدراسـات السـرديّة الجديدة: قراءة المقامة أنموذجاً، ط1، 2007م، مركز بحوث كليّة الآداب بجامعة الملك سعود، الرياض، المملكة العربيّة السعودية.

- ______، الدراسات السـرديّة الجديدة: قراءة المقامة أنموذجاً، مركز بحوث كليّة الآداب، جامعة الملك سعود، المملكة العربيّة السعوديّة، ط1، 2007م.

- الجرطـي، أحمد، النصّ الأدبيّ في ضَوْء إبدالات النظريّة الأدبيّة المعاصرة: اسـتراتيجيات التّأويل ورهانات الدراسات الثّقافيّة، مجلة تبيُّن للدراسات الفكريّة والثّقافيّة، المركز العربيّ للأبحاث ودراسة السياسات، بيروت، لبنان، المجلد (6)، العدد (23)، 2018م.

- حامد، عبدالله، النقد الثّقافيّ للغذاميّ: سؤال المرجع وإشكالات النسق، السجل العلميّ للدورة الثانية من ملتقى النقد الأدبيّ: الخطاب النقدي المعاصر في المملكة العربيّة السعودية، النادي الأدبيّ بالرياض، الرياض، السعوديّة، 2008م.

- الخضـراويّ، إدريس، المتخيّل والتمثيل الثّقافيّ للآخر: قـراءة فى كتاب تمثيلات الآخر لنادر كاظم، مجلة العلوم الإنسانيّة، البحرين، 2006م.

- الداهـي، محمد، السـلطة العمياء في كليلة ودمنة، مجلة الكوفة، مجلـة علمية محكمة تصدر بدعم من جامعة الكوفة، العراق، العدد (10)، 2016م.

- رمضـان، علاء الدين، الحكاية المرحة في التراث الشـعبيّ العربيّ، مجلة الحرس، السـعودية، العدد (231)، 2001م.

- زرفـاوي، عمـر، النقد الثّقافيّ بين عبدالله الغذاميّ ويوسف عُليمات: معضلـة المنهاجويّة والتّأويل المغلول، مجلة فصول، الهيئة المصرية العامّة للكتاب، القاهرة، مصر، المجلد (3/25)، العدد (99)، 2017م.

- ______، نقـد النقد: مقاربة إبسـتيمولوجيّة، مجلة كليّـة الآداب بجامعة الملك سـعود، الرياض، المملكة العربيّة السعودبة، المجلد (28)، العدد (2)، 2016م.

- سباتنز، جون، الدراسات الثّقافيّة، ترجمة: لطفي السيد منصور، مجلة فصول، الهيئة المصرية العامة للكتاب، المجلد (25)، العدد (99)، 2017م.

- سرحان، هيثم، اللسان والبهتان: شِعريّة الوصية في السرد العربيّ الكلاسيكيّ، ضمن كتاب «الذّاكرة

والخطــاب: مقاربـات في النثر العربيّ الكلاسـيكيّ»، ط1، 2020م، منشــورات جامعــة الكوفة، دار الرافدين، بيروت، لبنان.

ـــــــــــ ، شِعريّة الوصية في السرد العربيّ الكلاسيكيّ، المجلة الأردنية في اللغة العربيّة وآدابها، جامعة مؤتة، الكرك، الأردن، المجلد (13)، العدد (3)، 2017م.

ـــــــــــ ، صـورة هارون الرشـيد بيــن تمثيل التّاريخ وتخييل الأدب، مجلــة الآداب بجامعة الملك سعود، جامعة الملك سعود، الرياض، المملكة العربيّة السعودية، المجلد (26)، العدد (3)، 2014م.

السـعوديّ، نـزار، الملامح التّفكيكيّة للنّقـد الثقافيّ، المجلة العربيّة للعلوم الإنسـانيّة، جامعة الكويت، الكويت، المجلد (37)، العدد (147)، 2019م.

ـــــــــــ ، تفاعل النقد الثقافيّ مع المناهج النقديّة والمعارف المتعددة: قراءة لأهم المفاهيم الرئيسة، مجلة جامعة الشــارقة للعلوم الإنسـانية والاجتماعية، الإمارات العربيّة المتحدة، المجلد (14)، العدد (2)، 2017م.

سـلدن، رامــان، بروكس، بيتر، النظريّــات الموجّهة إلى القارئ، ترجمة: محمـد نور النعيمي، مجلة الآداب العالمية، منشورات اتحاد الكتاب العرب، دمشق، سوريا، المجلد (26)، العدد (106 – 107)، حزيران 2001م.

سمير، حميد، المؤلف في التراث الأدبيّ: موت أم حياة، مجلة علامات في النقد، النادي الثقافيّ بجُدّة، جُدّة، المملكة العربيّة السعوديّة، المجلد (9)، العدد (35)، 2000م.

شــاكرإباري، دييبيش: دراسـات التابع والتأريخ ما بعد الكولونيالي، ترجمة: ثائر ديب، مجلة سطور، المركز العربيّ للأبحاث ودراسة السياسات، الدوحة، قطر، العدد (3)، كانون الثاني 2016م.

شبانة، ناصر يوسف، أنماط السرد في تراثنا العربيّ، مجلة جامعة النجاح للأبحاث/ العلوم الإنسانية، جامعة النجاح الوطنية، رام الله، فلسطين، المجلد (21)، العدد (2)، 2007م.

شقرون، دليلة، لذة التناص لدى رولان بارت، مجلة علامات، المغرب، العدد (46)، 2016م.

صالــح، فخـري، أزمة النقد العربيّ في الوقـت الراهن وفواتنا الحضاريّ، مجلــة علامات في النقد، النادي الأدبيّ الثقافيّ بجُدّة، جُدّة، المملكة العربيّة السعوديّة، الجزء (76)، 2013م، ص20.

طاهر، حامد، نوادر جُحا: تراث شعبيّ ونقد اجتماعيّ، مجلة دراسات عربية وإسلامية، مركز اللغات الأجنبية والترجمة، جامعة القاهرة، القاهرة، مصر، الجزء (74)، 2015م.

عبابنة، سامي محمد، التفكيكيّة وقراءة الأدب العربيّ القديم: عبد الفتاح كيليطو نموذجاً، مجلة دراسات للعلوم الاجتماعية والإنسانية، الجامعة الأردنية، عمان، الأردن، المجلد (42)، الملحق (1)، 2015م.

عبيد الله، محمّد، السرد العربيّ القديم: من الهامش الى المركز، المجلة العربيّة للعلوم الإنسانيّة، جامعة الكويت، الكويت، المجلد (25)، العدد (98)، 2007م.

العدوانـي، معجب، القراءة التناصيـة الثقافيّة: مدخل نظري، مجلة البلاغـة والنقد الأدبيّ، المغرب، العدد الثاني، خريف شتاء 2014 – 2015م.

ـــــــــــ ، مرايا الآخر: مقاربة ثقافيّة لرسـالة ابن فضلان وانعكاسـاتها فـي الثقافة الغربية، مجلة

جامعــة الطائف للعلوم الإنســانية، جامعة الطائف، الطائف، المملكة العربيّة السـعودية، المجلد (4)، العدد (15)، 2017م.

ــ ــــــــــــــ، رحلــة التناصيّــة إلى النقد العربيّ القديم، مجلة علامات في النقـد، النادي الثّقافيّ بجُدَة، جُدَة، المملكة العربيّة السعوديّة، المجلد (11)، العدد (44)، 2002م.

ــ ــــــــــــــ، من موت المؤلف إلى موت التناص: القراءة التناصية في إطارها الجديد، مؤتمر الجمعية المصريـة للنقـد الأدبيّ (التأويليــة والنظرية النقديّــة المعاصرة) القاهرة، مصر، 14 ــ 18 ديسـمبر 2010م.

ــ عشّــا، علي مصطفى، الفُحولة فى الوعي الثّقافيّ العربيّ: كتاب المرأة واللغة نموذجاً، المجلة العربيّة للعلوم الإنسانية، جامعة الكويت، الكويت، المجلد (37)، العدد (147)، 2019م.

ــ العشـي، عبـدالله، بلاغة النقد: النصّ النقديّ خـارج خطابه، مجلة أنسـاق، تصدر عـن كلية العلوم والآداب، جامعة قطر، الدوحة، قطر، المجلد (1)، العدد التجريبي، 2017م.

ــ عصفـور، جابر، بلاغة المقموعيـن، عدد: (المجاز والتمثيل في العصور الوسـطى)، ط1، 1992م، مجلة ألِف البلاغة المقارنة، دار إلياس العصرية، القاهرة، مصر.

ــ عطية، رانيا جمال، مسـار التّحوّلات السـرديّة بين المحكيّ والمكتوب في سـيرة علي الزَّيبق، مجلة سرديات، الجمعية المصرية للدراسات السردية، القاهرة، مصر، العدد (25)، 2017م.

ــ عليمات، يوسف، العجائبيّة وثّقافة الإشهار: قراءة ثّقافيّة في حكاية أبي القاسم الطّنبوريّ، مجلة جامعة الشارقة للعلوم الإنسانية والاجتماعية، جامعة الشارقة، الإمارات العربيّة المتحدة، المجلد (16)، العدد (2)، 2019م.

ــ ــــــــــــــ، أنساق الخطاب الحكائي.

ــ ــــــــــــــ، عليمات، يوسـف، جماليات السـرد: قراءة في المقامة البشـرية لبديـع الزمان الهمذاني، المجلة العربيّة للعلوم الإنسانية، الكويت، مج27, ع107، 2009م.

ــ الغذامي، عبدالله، القمر الأسود أو النصّ القاتل، مجلة فصول، الهيئة المصرية العامّة للكتاب، القاهرة، مصر، المجلد (13)، العدد (3)، 1994م.

ــ الغرافي، مصطفى، التّأصيل الثّقافيّ وبناء الهُويّة عند ابن قتيبة، مجلة فصول، الهيئة المصرية العامة للكتاب، القاهرة، مصر، العدد (87 ــ 88)، 2010م.

ــ ــــــــــــــ، السـرد والمُضمر: دراسـة فـي أخبار ابن قتيبة، مجلة البلاغـة والنقد الأدبيّ، المغرب، العدد (2)، 2015م.

ــ غرينبلات، ستيفن، الثّقافة والشـعرية الثّقافيّة، ترجمة: معتز سـلامة، مجلة فصول، الهيئة المصرية العامّة للكتاب، القاهرة، مصر، المجلد (3/25)، العدد (99)، 2017م، ص303 وما بعدها.

ــ فوداك وماير، روث وميشيل، التحليل النقدي للخطاب التاريخ والبرنامج والنظرية والمنهجيّة، ضمن: مناهج التحليل النقدي للخطاب، ترجمة: حسـام أحمد فرج وعزة شـبل محمد، مراجعة وتقديم: عماد عبداللطيف، ط1، 2014م، منشورات المركز القومي للترجمة، القاهرة، مصر.

- فيدوح، عبدالقادر، ألفة النصّ ومستويات التلقّي، مجلة علامات في النقد، النادي الأدبيّ الثقافيّ بجُدّة، جُدّة، المملكة العربيّة السعوديّة، المجلد (10)، المجلد (34)، 1999م

- القسطنطيني، نجوى، في الوعي بمصطلح نقد النقد وعوامل ظهوره، مجلة عالم الفكر، منشورات المجلس الوطني للثقافة والفنون والآداب، الكويت، المجلد (38)، العدد (1)، 2009م.

- كالر، جوناثان، دفاعاً عن التأويل المضاعف، مجلة علامات، المغرب، العدد (11)، 1999م.

- الكعبي، ضياء، الذات والآخر في السير الشعبية العربيّة: دراسة في التمثيلات الثقافيّة، بحث مقدم إلى المؤتمر الدولي السادس، كلية دار العلوم، جامعة القاهرة، مصر، 2009م.

- الكعبــيّ، ضياء، منهجية النقد الثقافيّ وتطبيقاته: السـرد العربيّ القديم أنموذجاً: تصوُّر مقتَرح، بحث محكَّم في الندوة العلميّة: قضايـا المنهج في اللغة والأدب، النظريّة والتطبيق، جامعة الملك سـعود، السعوديّة، 2010م.

- ماجدولين، شرف الدين، الآخر ودائرة الألفة قراءة لنسق التفاعل في نص: طوق الحمامة لابن حزم، مجلة فكر ونقد محمد عابد الجابري، العدد (59 – 60)، 2004م.

- ــــــــ، الصورة والنسـق والسـلطة: قراءة في السـرد الشـطاريّ العربيّ، مجلة ثقافات، جامعة البحرين، البحرين، العدد (14)، 2005م.

- ــــــــ، الهامشـيّ والآخر والسـرد الهزليّ: قراءة في الموروث الخبريّ، مجلة ثقافات، جامعة البحرين، البحرين، العدد (23)، 2010م.

- خمري، حسين، نظريّات القراءة وتلقّي النصّ الأدبيّ، مجلة العلوم الإنسانية، جامعة منتوري قسنطينة، الجزائر، العدد (12)، 1999م.

- المحفليّ، محمّد، الأنسـاقُ الثقافيّةُ في كِليلة ودمنة، مجلة سِـمات، جامعـة البحرين، البحرين، المجلد (4)، العدد (1)، 2014م.

- محمد، باقر جاسم، نقد النقد أم الميتا نقد؟، مجلة عالم الفكر، منشورات المجلس الوطني للثقافة والفنون والآداب، الكويت، المجلد (37)، العدد (3)، 2009م.

- مشـبال، محمد، بلاغة النص السـردي: مراجعة نقديّة، مجلة فصول، الهيئة المصرية العامّة للكتاب، القاهرة، مصر، المجلد (1/26)، العدد (101)، 2017م.

- مقابلة، جمال، وعي النقد ونقد الوعي في المقامة الموصليّة: قراءة تداوليّة ثَقافيّة، المجلة الأردنية في اللغة العربيّة وآدابها، جامعة مؤتة، الكرك، الأردن، المجلد (2)، العدد (2)، 2006م.

- المناصـرة، عـزّ الدين، إشـكالات التجنيس الأدبيّ، مجلـة البصائر، جامعة البتـرا الخاصة، عمان، الأردن، المجلد (9)، العدد (2)، 2005م.

- موسـى، عبدالله، في المنهـج الأركيولوجيّ: الحفريّ: قداسـة النصّ وجدوى المنهـج، مجلة الجمعية الفلسفية العربيّة، القاهرة، مصر، المجلد (25)، العدد (25)، 2016م.

- النعمي، حسـن، غواية السـرد: قراءة في المقامة البغداديّة للحريريّ، المجلة العربيّة للعلوم الإنسانيّة، جامعة الكويت، الكويت، المجلد (19)، العدد (73)، 2001م.

- ويليامـز، موكيـش، التاريخانية الجديدة والدراسـات الأدبيّـة، مجلة فصول، الهيئـة المصرية العامّة للكتاب، القاهرة، مصر، المجلد (3/25)، العدد (99)، 2017م.

- يوسف، عبدالفتاح أحمد، في استراتيجيات القراءة في النقد الثقافيّ: نحو وعي نقديّ بقراءة ثقافيّة للنّصّ، مجلة عالم الفكر، منشورات المجلس الوطني للثقافة، الكويت، المجلد (36)، العدد (1)، 2007م.

- المراجع المترجمة:

- اشـكروفيت وجريفيـث وتيفيـن، بيـل وجاريـث وهليـن، الردُّ بالكتابـة: النظرية والتطبيـق في آداب المستعمرات القديمة، ترجمة: شهرت العالم، ط1، مارس 2006م، المنظمة العربيّة للترجمة، بيروت، لبنان.

- أندرسن، بندكت، الجماعات المتخيّلة: تأملات في أصل القومية وانتشارها، ترجمة: ثائر ديب، تقديم: عزمي بشارة، ط1، 2009م، شركة قدمس للنشر والتوزيع، دمشق، سوريا.

- آيزابرجـر، أرثـر، النقد الثقافيّ: تمهيـد مبدئي للمفاهيم الرئيسية، ترجمة: وفـاء إبراهيم ورمضان بسطاويسي، المشروع القومي للترجمة، القاهرة، مصر، ط1، 2002م.

- بـارت، رولان، لـذّة النصّ، ترجمة: منذر عياشـي، ط1، 1992م، مركز الإنمـاء الحضاري، حلب، سوريا.

- ـــــــــ ، مدخـل إلى التّحليل البنيويّ للقصص، ترجمة: منذر عيّاشـي، ط1، 2014م، دار نينوى للدراسات والنشر والتوزيع، دمشق، سوريا.

- بابـا، هومـي، موقـع الثّقافة، ترجمـة: ثائر ديب، ط1، 2004م، منشـورات المجلـس الأعلى للثّقافة، القاهرة، مصر.

- برنـس، جيرالـد، المصطلح السردي: معجم مصطلحـات، ترجمة: عابد خزنـدار، مراجعة: محمد بريري، ط1، 2003م، منشورات المشروع القومي للترجمة، القاهرة، مصر.

- بلـوم، هارولـد، خريطة للقراءة الضّالة، ترجمـة: عابد إسـماعيل، ط1، 2000م، دار الكنوز الأدبيّة، بيروت، لبنان.

- تودوروف، تزيفيتان، الشعريّة، ترجمة: شكري المبخوت ورجاء بن سلامة، ط2، 1990م، دار توبقال للنشر، الدار البيضاء، المغرب.

- ـــــــــ ، نظريّة الأجناس الأدبيّة: دراسة في التّناص والكتابة والنقد، ترجمة: عبدالرحمن بوعلي، ط1، 2016م، دار نينوى للدراسات والنشر والتوزيع، دمشق، سوريا.

- تودوروف، تزيفيتان، نقد النقد، ترجمة: سـامي سـويدان وليليان سويدان، ط2، 1996م، دار الشؤون الثقافيّة العامة، بغداد، العراق، ص16.

- تومبكنز، جين، نقد استجابة القارئ من الشكلانيّة إلى ما بعد البنيويّة، ترجمة: حسن ناظم وعلي حاكم، مراجعة وتقديم: محمد جواد محسـن الموسـويّ، ط1، 1999م، المشـروع القوميّ للترجمة، القاهرة، مصر.

– جيرو، بيير، السيميائيات: دراسة الأنساق السيميائية غير اللغويّة، ترجمة: منذر عيّاشي، ط1، 2016م، دار نينوى للدراسات والنشر والتوزيع، دمشق، سوريا.

– دريدا ودي مان، جاك وبول، وآخرون، مداخل إلى التفكيك (البلاغة المعاصرة)، تحرير وترجمة: حسام نايل، تصدير: محمد بدوي، ط1، 2013م، الهيئة المصرية العامة للكتاب، القاهرة، مصر.

– ديورنغ، سايمون، الدراسات الثقافيّة: مقدمة نظرية، ترجمة: ممدوح يوسف عمران، العدد (425)، يونيو2015م، سلسلة عالم المعرفة، المجلس الوطني للثقافة والفنون والأدب، الكويت.

– ريكور، بول، نظرية التأويل: الخطاب وفائض المعنى، ترجمة: سعيد الغانمي، ط1، 2003م، المركز الثقافيّ العربيّ، بيروت، الدار البيضاء، لبنان، المغرب.

– سعيد، إدوارد، الثقافة والإمبرياليّة، نقله إلى العربيّة وقدّم له: كمال أبو ديب، ط1، 1997م، دار الآداب، بيروت، لبنان.

– ________، الاستشراق، ترجمة: محمد عصفور، تقديم: محمد شاهين، ط1، 2022م، دار الآداب، بيروت، لبنان.

– ________، العالِم والنصّ والناقد، ترجمة: عبد الكريم محفوض، منشورات اتحاد الكتاب العرب، دمشق، سوريا، ط1، 2000م.

– سوسير، فريدناند، علم اللغة العام، ترجمة: يوئيل يوسف عزيز، ط1، 1985م، دار آفاق، العراق.

– غادامير، هانز جورج، تجلّي الجميل، تحرير: روبرت برناسكوني، ترجمة ودراسة وشروح: سعيد توفيق، ط1، 1997م، منشورات المشروع القومي للترجمة، القاهرة، مصر.

– ________، الحقيقة والمنهج: الخطوط الأساسية لتأويلية فلسفية، ترجمة: حسن ناظم وعلي صالح، ط1، 2007م، دار أويا للطباعة والنشر، طرابلس الجماهيرية العظمى، ليبيا.

– غريماس، جوليان، سيميائيّات السرد، ترجمة: عبدالمجيد نوسي، ط1، 2018م، المركز الثقافيّ العربيّ، بيروت، الدار البيضاء، لبنان، المغرب.

– فوج، أجنر، الانتخاب الثقافيّ، ترجمة: شوقي جلال، ط1، 2005م منشورات المشروع القومي للترجمة، القاهرة، مصر.

– فوكو، ميشيل، نظام الخطاب، ترجمة: محمد سبيلا، ط2، 2007م، دار التنوير للطباعة والنشر، بيروت، لبنان.

– فيتش، ستانلي، هل يوجد نصّ في هذا الفصل؟ سلطة الجماعات المفسّرة، ترجمة: أحمد الشيمي، ط1، 2004م، منشورات المشروع القومي للترجمة، القاهرة، مصر.

– كون، توماس، بُنية الثورات العلميّة، العدد (168)، 1992م، سلسلة عالم المعرفة، المجلس الوطني للثقافة والفنون والأدب، الكويت.

– لومان، نيكلاس، مدخل إلى نظريّة الأنساق، ترجمة: يوسف فهمي حجازي، ط1، 2010م، منشورات الجمل، بغداد، كولونيا، العراق، ألمانيا.

– لومبا، آنيا، نظريّة الاستعمار وما بعد الاستعمار الأدبيّة، ترجمة: محمد عبد الغني غنّوم، ط1، 2017م، دار الحوار، اللاذقيّة، سوريا.

– ليتش، فنسـنت، النقد الأدبيّ الأمريكيّ من الثلاثينيات إلى الثمانينيات، ترجمة: محمد يحيى، مراجعة وتقديم: ماهر شفيق فريد، ط1، 2000م، منشورات المشروع القومي للترجمة، القاهرة، مصر.

– ميشـيل فوكـو وآخـرون، التحليل الثقافيّ، تحريـر: إيدث كريزويل، ترجمة: فـاروق أحمد مصطفى وآخرون، ط1، 2008م منشورات المركز القومي للترجمة، القاهرة، مصر.

– هوتـر، جيرالد، سـلطة الصورة الذهنيّـة: كيف تغير الرؤى العقل والإنسـان والعالم؟، ط1، 2014م، ترجمة: عُلا عادل، عين للدراسات والبحوث الإنسانية والاجتماعية، الجيزة، مصر.

– هولب، روبرت، نظرية التلقّي: مقدّمة نقديّة، ترجمة: عز الدين إسماعيل، المكتبة الأكاديمية، القاهرة، مصر، ط1، 2000م.

– جاكبسون، رومان، قضايا الشعريّة، ط1، 1988م، دار توبقال للنشر، الدار البيضاء، المغرب.

– ياوس، هانس، جماليّة التلقّي: من أجل تأويل جديد للنّصّ الأدبيّ، تقديم وترجمة: رشـيد بنحدو، ط1، 2016م، الدار العربيّة للعلوم ناشـرون (بيروت/ لبنان)، منشـورات الاختـلاف (الجزائر العاصمة/ الجزائر)، دار الأمان (الرباط/ المغرب).

– ينظر: ماكدونالد، رونان، موت الناقد، ترجمة وتقديم: فخري صالح، ط1، 2014م، منشورات المركز القومي للترجمة، القاهرة، مصر.

– الرسائل العلميّة:

– الخلف، عبدالله السـالم، الفكر السـنيّ في أدب ابن قتيبة، رسـالة ماجسـتير (غير منشورة)، 1980م، جامعة الإمام محمد بن سعود الإسلامية، الرياض، المملكة العربيّة السعوديّة.

– مسالتي، محمد عبدالبشير، الجاحظ في قراءات الدارسين المحدثين، رسالة ماجستير (غير منشورة)، 2014م، جامعة سطيف (2)، الجزائر.

– المراجع باللغة الإنجليزيّة:

– Arthur Asa Berge, Cultural Criticism: A Primer of Key Concepts, California: Sage Publications, 1995.

– Hayden White, Tropics of Discourse: Essays Cultural Criticism, London: The Johns Hopkins University Press, 1985.

– John Storey, Cultural Studies: An Introduction; in What is Cultural Studies: A Reader, edited by: John Storey, New York: Arnold, 1997.

– Vincent B. Leitch, Cultural Criticism, Literary Theory, Post Structuraslim, New York: Columbian University Press, 1992.

ثبتُ الأعْلَام

(الحاء)

- ابن حجّة الحمويّ، علي بن عبد الله (ت837هـ)
- أبو حيان التوحيديّ، علي بن محمد (ت414هـ)
- الحاجب بن زُرارة

(الخاء)

- ابن خلدون، عبد الرحمن بن محمد(ت809هـ)
- خالد بن يزيد المكدّي

(الدال)

- أبو داود المتكلّم
- دليلة النصّابة
- دي سوسير

(الراء)

- رايموند ويليامز
- رجيس دوبري
- رولان بارت
- رونان ماكدونالد

(الزاء)

- زينب ابنة دليلة النصّابة

(السين)

- سامي الدهان
- ستانلي فيتش
- ستيفن غرينبلات
- سهير قلماوي

(الشين)

- شرف الدين ماجدولين

(العين)

- ابن عرياض اليهوديّ

(الميم)

– ابن المقفّع، عبد الله بن المقفع (ت142هـ): مايكل كرايتون

– محمد البنكيّ

– محمد الدغموميّ

– محمد القاضي

– محمد المحفليّ

– محمد بن المبارك: محمد رجب النَّجار

– مُحمّد عبيد الله

– مخارق المغنّي (ت240هـ)

– المدائني، علي بن محمد (ت255هـ)

– مصطفى الغرافيّ

– مصطفى ناصف

– معجب العدواني

– ميشيل فوكو

(النون)

– نادر كاظم

– نوح – عليه السلام –

– نورثروب فراي

– النيسابوري، محمد بن حبيب (ت406هـ)

– نيكلاس لومان

(الهاء)

– هارون الرشيد، هارون بن محمد (ت193هـ)

– هشام بن الحكم (ت190هـ)

– هيثم سرحان

(الواو)

– وهب روميّة

(الياء)

– يوري لوتمان

– يوسف عليمات

256

ثبتُ المُصْطَلَحاتِ

(الألف)

– الآخر

– الإبستمولوجيا/ـة (المعرفيّ)

– الأبويّة

– أفق التّوقع

– الأنساق الثقافيّة

– السرديّات العربيّة القديمة

(الباء)

– بلاغة السرد

– بلاغة الصمت

– بلاغة الصورة

– بلاغة النصّ: البنيويّة

(التاء)

– التابع

– التاريخانيّة الجديدة

– التأويل المُضاعف

– تحليل الخطاب

– تفكيك النقد

– التفكيكيّة

– التقويض: التلقّي المعياريّ

– التلقّي النقديّ

– التناصيّة

258

الفهرس